WARTIME LETTERS

ALSO BY GEOFFREY ROBERTS

The Unholy Alliance: Stalin's Pact with Hitler
The Soviet Union and the Origins of the Second World War
The Soviet Union in World Politics, 1945–1991
Ireland and the Second World War (co-edited with Brian Girvin)
The History and Narrative Reader (editor)
Victory at Stalingrad: The Battle That Changed History
Stalin – His Times and Ours (editor)
Stalin's Wars: From World War to Cold War, 1939–1953
Molotov: Stalin's Cold Warrior
Stalin's General: The Life of Georgy Zhukov
Churchill and Stalin: Comrades-in-Arms during the Second World War (with Martin Folly and Oleg Rzheshevsky)
Stalin's Library: A Dictator and His Books

WARTIME LETTERS

KATHLEEN HARRIMAN

EDITED BY
GEOFFREY ROBERTS

YALE UNIVERSITY PRESS
NEW HAVEN AND LONDON

Copyright © 2026 Geoffrey Roberts

All rights reserved. This book may not be reproduced in whole or in part, in any form (beyond that copying permitted by Sections 107 and 108 of the U.S. Copyright Law and except by reviewers for the public press) without written permission from the publishers.

All reasonable efforts have been made to provide accurate sources for all images that appear in this book. Any discrepancies or omissions will be rectified in future editions.

For information about this and other Yale University Press publications, please contact:
U.S. Office: sales.press@yale.edu   yalebooks.com
Europe Office: sales@yaleup.co.uk   yalebooks.co.uk

Set in Minion Pro by IDSUK (DataConnection) Ltd

Printed and bound in the UK using 100% renewable electricity at CPI Group (UK) Ltd

Library of Congress Control Number: 2025947245
A catalogue record for this book is available from the British Library.
Authorized Representative in the EU: Easy Access System Europe, Mustamäe tee 50, 10621 Tallinn, Estonia, gpsr.requests@easproject.com

ISBN 978-0-300-27854-5

10 9 8 7 6 5 4 3 2 1

CONTENTS

ABBREVIATIONS

ABDA	American, British, Dutch and Australian (Command in Southeast Asia)
AEF	American Expeditionary Force
AP	Associated Press
ARC	American Red Cross
ARP	Air Raid Precautions
ATA	Air Transport Auxiliary
ATC	Air Transport Command
ATS	Auxiliary Territorial Service
AVG	American Volunteer Group
CD	Corps Diplomatique
CFM	Council of Foreign Ministers
CIGS	Chief of the Imperial General Staff
DSO	Distinguished Service Order
FO	Foreign Office
INS	International News Service
IRC	International Red Cross
LST	Landing Ship Tank
MAAF	Mediterranean Allied Air Forces
MAP	Minister of Aircraft Production
MOI	Ministry of Information
MP	Military Police
NEA	Newspaper Enterprise Association

NKVD	Narodnyi Komissariat Vnutrennikh Del (People's Commissariat of Internal Affairs)
OCTU	Officer Cadet Training Unit
OGPU	Obedinennoe Gosudarstvennoe Politicheskoe Upravlenie (United State Political Directorate)
OSS	Office of Strategic Services
OWI	Office of War Information
PRO	Public Relations Officer
RAF	Royal Air Force
RN	Royal Navy
SHAEF	Supreme Headquarters Allied Expeditionary Force
UJ	Uncle Joe (Stalin)
UP	United Press
USAAC	United States Army Air Corps
USAF	United States Air Force
USN	United States Navy
VJ	Victory over Japan (Day)
WAAC	Women's Army Auxiliary Corps
WAAF	Women's Auxiliary Air Force
WAC	Women's Army Corps
WRNS	Women's Royal Naval Service
WVS	Women's Voluntary Service

EDITOR'S NOTE

This book contains the texts of nearly all Kathleen Harriman's wartime letters, although the total word count has been reduced by about 10 per cent through the deletion of repetitive, extraneous or inconsequential material. I have also taken the liberty of correcting Kathy's spelling, polishing her punctuation and curbing her enthusiasm for the use of ampersands. All the words in the reproduced letters are Kathleen's, except for the editorial interpolations in square brackets, including additions to a few letters that were unsigned or lacking a salutation. The titles of all books, newspapers and magazines have been editorially italicised.

Most of the letters were dated by Kathy at the time she wrote them (not always accurately). Many years later she added some dates. The dating in this book reflects a combination of her and my efforts.

Kathy wrote or typed her letters on the headed paper of a variety of residences. Such addresses have been retained where it is clear that this was where she actually wrote the letter in question. In other instances, such as when she used scraps of paper with no heading at all, a generic 'London' is given as the address. While in Moscow, Kathy used the US embassy's headed paper, but these letters were mostly written at home, at the ambassador's residence, Spaso House. In these cases, the given address is 'Moscow'.

I have tried to identify and provide basic biographical information about the people that populate the pages of Kathy's letters but not everyone is identified. In some instances the person is sufficiently well known or identified by Kathy herself. In a small number of cases, identification has proved impossible. But I was delighted when History Consultant, Michelle O'Mahony, was able to track down the biographical data for 'Mouche' – Kathleen's childhood English governess, who was one of her most important wartime correspondents. Mouche (Elsie Marshall) was a policeman's daughter, born in 1893 in the village of Margaretting, not far from the Essex county town of Chelmsford. A nursery maid, who emigrated to the United States after the First World War, she ended up working for Kathy's mother, Kitty. Mouche naturalised as an American citizen in 1943 but made regular trips home, and died in London in 1974. She was held in great affection by the Harrimans and lived and worked for many years in the family's ancestral home in Arden, Orange County, New York. Indeed, Mouche's body was shipped back to the United States and buried in the cemetery of the local church at Arden.

It was Mouche who retyped Kathy's letters when they reached the United States, often collating extracts for circulation among family and friends. Mouche, like Kathleen's sister Mary and her stepmother Marie, wrote many letters to Kathleen, but they are nowhere to be found. Among Kathleen's regular correspondents, the one surviving batch of incoming letters are those that Pamela Churchill sent to her in Moscow. Pamela, who had an affair with Kathleen's father Averell Harriman, was Kathy's best friend during the war. Following Marie's death in 1970, Averell and Pamela resumed their romance and got married. Pam's letters to Kathy, which were invariably simultaneously addressed to Averell, may be found in the Pamela Harriman Papers, which, like those of Averell and Kathy herself, are housed in the Manuscript Division of the Library of Congress.

The Further Reading section mostly consists of works by authors cited in the running editorial commentary. The index lists first names and nicknames as well as family names.

CHRONOLOGY OF KATHLEEN HARRIMAN'S INTERNATIONAL TRAVELS, 1941–6

8–16 May 1941	New York to London via Bermuda, the Azores, Lisbon and Bristol
5–9 August 1943	Gourock (Scotland) to Halifax (Canada) on the RMS *Queen Mary* Late August: return to Britain on the *Queen Mary*
13–18 October 1943	London to Moscow via Algiers, Cairo and Tehran
26 April–5 May 1944	Moscow to New York via Cairo, Tripoli, Naples, Algiers, Casablanca, Newquay, London, Prestwick (Scotland) and Stevensville (Newfoundland)
23 May–1 June 1944	Washington to Moscow via Stevensville, Prestwick, London, Casablanca, Naples and Tehran
27 July–1 August 1944	Moscow to Naples via Tehran, Cairo, Tripoli and Casablanca (visits to Rome and Capri)
17–20 August 1944	Naples to Moscow via Cairo, Tehran and Baku
19–21 October 1944	Moscow to Washington via Poltava (Ukraine), Cairo, Tripoli and Casablanca

10 November–5 December 1944	Washington to Moscow via Stevensville, Prestwick, London, Paris, Naples, Cairo and Tehran
22–24 January 1945	Moscow to Yalta (Crimea) via Orel, Kharkov, Pavlograd, Zaporozhe and Simferopol (by train)
12 February 1945	Yalta to Moscow (by plane)
17–18 April 1945	Moscow to Washington via Bari, Casablanca, the Azores and Stevensville
21–25 May 1945	Washington to Moscow via Stevensville, London, Paris and Torun (Poland)
12–18 July 1945	Moscow to Stockholm via Leningrad, Helsinki and Turku (by train and ship) Early August: return from Stockholm to Moscow (by plane)
12–17 September 1945	Moscow to London via Frankfurt and Nice
4–9 October 1945	London to Moscow via Frankfurt, Berlin and Vienna (visit to Budapest)
31 December 1945	Moscow to Bucharest Early January: return to Moscow via Paris and London
24 January–14 February 1946	Moscow to Washington via New Delhi, Shanghai, Seoul, Tokyo, Guam, Honolulu and San Francisco

INTRODUCTION

Was it before or after the 9/11 terrorist attacks that I discovered Kathleen Harriman's wartime letters? I can't remember exactly. I was in the Library of Congress as the 9/11 tragedies unfolded, examining the voluminous private papers of Kathleen's father, Averell Harriman, searching for information about Stalin and the Grand Alliance of the Second World War. Interspersed among the hundreds of files were copies of Kathy's letters.

I started to read them. The letter that hooked me was written soon after she arrived in Moscow in October 1943, in the company of Averell, the newly appointed US ambassador to the Soviet Union. Her mocking commentary on State Department diplomatic dispatches characterised them as 'lengthy and usually [managing] to say nothing at all of importance. (If you don't say anything you don't get blamed for creating an impression which at some future date will be proven false.)' Eagerly I searched for more Kathy letters, and found a treasure trove of correspondence. As a Soviet history specialist, I was intrigued by her offbeat portrayal of the Kremlin elite and amused by her experiences of the vagaries of the communist system. I was impressed by her determination to avoid what she called the 'Moscow rut'. She learned Russian and tried as much as she could to interact with the world beyond the Moscow diplomatic ghetto, visiting Soviet schools, hospitals, churches and military bases. She also pursued her own interests, such as horse riding, and skied against top-class Soviet competitors on the slopes of Moscow's Lenin Hills. But it was her irreverent attitudes that attracted me most. At the end of that mocking letter, Kathy added a PS, telling her sister Mary, 'On re-reading, I've discovered I'm in a very blasphemous mood. So please for God's sake read this letter and tear it up and don't show it to anyone.'

Kathy became something of a celebrity in Russia during the war. As the *New York Herald Tribune* reported, she was the best-known American woman in the Soviet Union, with the possible exceptions of Eleanor Roosevelt and the Hollywood musical star Deanna Durbin. The renowned Soviet film director Sergei Eisenstein imagined Kathy as a 'dollar princess' and drew caricatures of her.[1]

Kathy's wartime letter writing began in May 1941 when, aged twenty-three, she crossed the Atlantic by seaplane to join her father in London, where he was serving as expeditor of President Roosevelt's growing programme of American aid to Britain. Averell's wife Marie (Kathy's stepmother) couldn't make the journey for medical reasons, while Kathy's slightly older sister, Mary, had recently been married. So it fell to Kathy to keep her father company in war-torn Britain. 'I felt that Kathleen's presence', recalled Averell, 'would be looked upon as a mark of American confidence.' While being a journalist was her day job in London, she also spent a lot of time acting as Averell's hostess. 'Ave', as Kathy called him, provided her with an entrée to the British military-political elite, while her role as a reporter for the US-based International News Service (INS) meant that she saw and experienced those early war years from many different angles.

As Kathy herself said, the letters were a substitute for the diary she didn't feel capable of keeping, and that she feared would become too intimate and revealing if she tried. While her letters were often highly political, they were always deeply personal; importantly, they were rarely just about herself. Her depictions of high society in Britain and Russia were frank reportage, not boasts about who and what she knew as a consequence of her privileged life. She wrote about the

1 The caricatures and the fragments of Eisenstein's memoirs may be found in Naum Kleiman, *Eisenstein on Paper*, Thames & Hudson, London, 2017.

people she met, the circles she moved in and the events she witnessed, and above all sought to convey to others her unique wartime experiences. While the letters were intended for circulation among family and friends, Kathy often wrote on the hoof – between assignments or social engagements – which gave her writing a spontaneous, visceral quality that kept it fresh. But she also wrote with an eye to posterity, composing a record she could later look back at, and which might come in handy if and when Ave got round to authoring a book about his wartime missions.

By and large, Kathy's correspondence escaped wartime censorship, though she was circumspect about the information she shared. Most of the letters were addressed to Mary. She also wrote regularly, though less frequently, to Marie and to her childhood English governess, Elsie Marshall ('Mouche'). Anglo-American tourism ground to a halt upon the outbreak of the Second World War but journalists, diplomats, military personnel and business people crossed the Atlantic in ever-greater numbers, providing a steady stream of 'couriers' who posted Kathy's letters when they got to the United States. There were fewer such opportunities when Kathy moved to Moscow but Ave's position as ambassador gave her access to the American diplomatic bag, although this meant that her father could also read the letters.

That Kathy's letters existed was not a secret. Indeed, they had been on historians' radar since the 1975 publication of Averell Harriman's war memoir, *Special Envoy to Churchill and Stalin, 1941–1946*, co-authored with Eli Abel. Most of Harriman's memoir was based on extensive interviews conducted by Abel, which Eli then redrafted as chapters. Curiously, he chose not to interview Kathy, Ave's constant wartime companion, although he did ask for copies of her letters, which he then quoted – extensively and memorably. Instead of handing over untouched copies of her letters, however, Kathy selected, retyped and edited them. (It was these edited versions that ended up in the chronological files of the Averell Harriman Papers, housed in the Manuscript Division of the Library of Congress.) Abel was very pleased, writing to Kathy that 'your vivid descriptions and reactions have been enormously helpful in recreating the mood and feel of those years in London and Moscow'. Kathy was not so sure, rather feeling that Abel had failed to also convey the emotions and pressures of the war.

Abel's quotations from Kathy's letters were read avidly, and quickly became part of the evidential narrative of Soviet–Western wartime relations. Of particular interest was Kathy's inadvertent role in the Soviet cover-up of the Katyn massacre of thousands of Polish POWs. Invited to the murder site in January 1944, Kathy and a group of Western journalists by and large accepted Moscow's version of events – that the Germans had killed the Poles when they occupied the Katyn area. In contrast, on a lighter note, there was Kathy's account of Winston Churchill's dinner with Joseph Stalin at the Bolshoi Ballet in October 1944, where the Soviet dictator joked that if the 'Big Three' were the Holy Trinity, then Churchill must be the Holy Ghost since 'he flies around so much'. Whether he considered himself or Roosevelt to be God, Stalin did not say.

I wasn't the first historian to be enchanted by Kathy's letters. Colleagues who had worked on the Harriman Papers before me had reported the same reaction, but I did have what I thought was a novel idea: that they should be published as an independent source and record of her experiences, not merely serve as an adjunct to her father's wartime exploits. To me, Kathy's story seemed as interesting as her father's. Not until I got back home to Ireland at the end of September 2001, however, did it occur to me that Kathy – born in 1917 – might still be alive. And indeed she was! So having tracked down her eldest son, David Mortimer, who gave me her address in New York City, I wrote to her, making my pitch for an interview:

> At first I read [the letters] for light relief, and with no little amusement. I often found myself laughing aloud at your descriptions of incidents and personalities. Then I became captivated by your picture of diplomatic life in Moscow during the war. It finally dawned on me that your observations on the times and its politics offered unique insights and evidence that ought to be available to a wider public. The letters are an invaluable source of information on your father's missions to London and Moscow. They illuminate

> the character and personality of wartime politicians and diplomats. The letters are astutely observed, well-written, lively, graphic, personable, very human . . . what more can I say?

'I am quite flabbergasted by your letter,' replied Kathy. 'I haven't read my letters in years but feel you exaggerate their historic worth. I haven't really changed my mind about publishing them. As peace returned many underlings of the war leaders sprang into print. I felt they abused their wartime privilege (& luck) of being on hand as history was made & swore I'd not do likewise. However, I'd be delighted to meet you!'

We met in her New York apartment in March 2002. It was by no means Kathy's first rodeo. She had testified to a Congressional Committee about her trip to Katyn and appeared as a witness in television documentaries about the Second World War and the Cold War. In the 1980s she had given a long interview to her father's biographer, Rudy Abramson. But our conversation was different – it focused on her and the letters, not on her father or the famous people she had met and the great events she had witnessed.

I envisaged an open-ended conversation rather than a formal interview. I gave her the heads-up on what I wanted to talk about; she sent me a short memoir about life in Moscow during the war that had been written at the request of Rebecca Matlock, the wife of Jack Matlock, US ambassador to the USSR from 1987 to 1991. She also prepared for our meeting by rereading her letters. From my point of view that was not such a good idea. I was seeking additional information, not what I could read in the letters myself. As I liked to tell my college students, it was a classic example of the perils of doing oral history: you think you are getting access to the person's memory, when in fact you are the beneficiary of their research! But during the course of several hours of conversation – most of which I recorded – I found out quite a lot from Kathy, and I left New York well satisfied.

In fact, I was on my way back to the Library of Congress, which had recently received the Pamela Harriman Papers. Although they were not yet available to scholars, I had special permission from Pamela's son Winston (known as 'Baby Butch' in Kathy's correspondence) to make copies of letters Kathy had written to her during the war. At that time, Pamela was Mrs Churchill, married to Winston Churchill's son Randolph. Kathy and Pam were about the same age and the best of friends. Famously, Pamela had an affair with Kathy's father during the war, a romance they rekindled in the 1970s, when she became Mrs Harriman. In New York, Kathy had made a point of telling me she'd got on very well with Pam – until the rupture caused by a rancorous family dispute about the handling of Averell's estate following his death in 1986. In the Library of Congress I found a tranche of letters Kathy had written to Pam from Moscow. Some of these overlapped in content with letters she had written to Mary, but there was plenty that was unique to the correspondence with Pamela. These letters circulated widely, too. A big fan was Winston Churchill's wife Clementine, who told Kathy that her letters were 'delightful' and would 'make a wonderful book one day – not, however, to be published just now!'

My most important find among Pamela's papers was letters Kathy wrote from Yalta in February 1945, where the 'Big Three' – Churchill, Roosevelt and Stalin – had convened a conference to discuss their vision of the new world order that would emerge from the ashes of Hitler's defeat. She made the trip because Roosevelt's daughter, Anna Boettiger, was to be there and needed someone to keep her company. Also present was Churchill's daughter Sarah Oliver (whom Kathy knew very well from London). Humorously dubbed the 'little three', the daughters got on well and spent a lot of time together. Sarah recalled that both Anna and Kathleen were 'charming and highly intelligent companions'. Anna's feelings towards Kathy were not quite so warm. 'I like Kathleen,' she wrote to her husband, 'but not as much as Sarah. The former is so damn self-assured, and to me, she lacks warmth of personality.' These three daughters of Yalta were by no means the only women at the conference. Churchill's top female administrator Joan Bright was on hand, while Royal Navy Wren Joan Evans worked in the cypher office. There were no high-status Soviet women present at Yalta but, needless to say, there were plenty of unsung females working as security or support staff. Kathy travelled from Moscow to the Crimea ahead of the conference – a three-day train journey through the devastated landscape of southern Russia and Ukraine. Her travelogue, and the witty and insightful reportage of the comings and goings at the Big Three summit, are among the highlights of her correspondence.

As promised, I provided Kathy with a copy of her letters to Pam. She was delighted to see them after nearly sixty years: 'What a fat bunch of letters! Thank you so much. Many anecdotes are unremembered, people mentioned faceless.' But while the Pamela letters were an exciting discovery, my main mission was stymied, since Kathy continued to veto publication, notwithstanding my efforts to persuade her of the difference between publishing letters – warts and all – and self-serving memoirs. Nor was she at all impressed by my suggestion that publication of the letters would make her a twenty-first-century feminist icon! She was happy to let the copies she had made reside in the Library of Congress and to leave it at that. 'You are absolutely correct my interest in publishing my letters still nil,' she wrote to me in 2003. But she added an enigmatic coda: 'You're welcome!' A year or so later, Kathy had a stroke, and although she recovered, our communications petered out. But after her death in 2011, at the age of ninety-three, David Mortimer gave me access to her private papers, where I discovered that the story of her wartime correspondence was not as simple as it had seemed.

The first surprise was the sheer number of letters – nearly three times as many as those deposited in the Library of Congress – among them a whole tranche written to Miss Marshall, or Mouche, as she was called. Mouche remained a Harriman family retainer and it was to her that Kathy directed requests for personal items from the United States – clothes, cosmetics, cigarette lighters, chewing gum, medicines, magazines, books, bobby pins and, above all, stockings – for friends as well as herself. But Kathy shared plenty of feelings and observations with Mouche as well. To Mouche she confided her sadness when an RAF pilot friend went missing over France in 1941. In June 1945 she wrote Mouche a memorable letter about the great Victory Parade in Red Square, where she had seen two hundred Nazi banners captured by the Red Army on its march to Berlin being piled not at Stalin's feet but at those of his Deputy Supreme Commander, Marshal Georgy Zhukov – a spectacle that portended the latter's banishment to the provinces by a suspicious Stalin.

The second surprise was the large number of additional letters from London, many of which chronicled her activities as a war correspondent, initially as a reporter for INS and then as a writer for *Newsweek* magazine. These left no doubt that Kathy was a professional journalist, worthy of a place in the pantheon of top female correspondents at work during the war. Also to be found were many colourful vignettes of elite life in wartime London. The two years Kathy spent in London, I now realised, were an important, formative experience that prepared her for the personal and political challenges of life in Moscow.

The third surprise concerned Kathy's editing of the letters deposited in her father's Library of Congress papers. These were replete with ellipses, indicating a lot of omissions. When I asked her what she had left out she told me it was personal stuff and family business, not material of public interest. Her answer had satisfied me. It was, after all, her private correspondence, and what she had decided to make public was revealing enough. But comparison of the Library of Congress letters with the unexpurgated originals in Kathy's archive revealed that her self-censorship had been quite far-reaching. Most of the omissions were, as she had said, of a private nature, the effect being to make the letters seem more political and less personal than they actually were. Also redacted were some lovely descriptions and reported experiences of the places – North Africa, Italy, France, Romania, Austria, Hungary – she had visited during the war. She was also inclined to cut out catty remarks about people who were private citizens as opposed to public figures. (This was the 1970s, remember, when those concerned may well have been still alive.) Kathy could also be quite kind to those she felt had been hard done by. In May 1941 she wrote to Mary about meeting Sir Hugh Dowding, head of Fighter Command during the Battle of Britain:

> The American conception of the London conservative club is without exaggeration. I walked into the library and at least 20 chairs were filled with readers of the *London Times*. Not one looked up. Sir Hugh is about to retire. They haven't any place for him in even the administrative end of the RAF. They don't either

> need or want him. I feel rather sorry for him because he wants to work, to help just as every other Englishman does, but they don't want him.

This passage was omitted from the version of the letter provided to Abel, as was her report home in July 1943 that Dowding had 'turned spiritualistic . . . He's perfectly sane mentally, but honestly believes in inter-communication between the dead & the living!'

Kathy was a woman of her times and not immune to prejudice or prevailing racist and sexist stereotypes. Significantly, such language was excised from the letters she gave Abel (and has mostly been omitted from this book). But, in all the hundreds of letters and the tens of thousands of words she wrote, there were barely a handful of such instances.

The fourth surprise was a hint that at some point Kathy may herself have contemplated publication of the letters, prompted, perhaps, by the enormous amount of work entailed in preparing the selection for Abel. The evidence of intent includes a retyped and full version of all the letters she wrote to Mary from Moscow. But it seems she thought better of the idea. Quite possibly, the task was simply too daunting, especially if the plan was to include the London letters, which were in a much more dilapidated state than those she had sent from Moscow. As I know all too well, the letters Kathy retrieved from Mary and Mouche after the war were a motley bunch that required a lot of work to make them presentable. Most were typed but many were handwritten and sometimes barely legible. Not all the letters were dated and some were misdated; quite a few were unsigned and seemingly incomplete. There was mispagination and scraps and fragments of text that fitted nowhere. They were populated by obscure as well as famous people, personages hidden from history, faded from memory and hard to track down, even with the aid of online sources.

While the letters were the core of Kathy's archive, she had also retained some wartime appointment diaries and a miscellany of other artefacts. Most important were two large photo albums, into which she had carefully pasted captioned photographs, cuttings of articles by or about her, various press passes and the telephone directory of the British Military Mission in Moscow during the war – an invaluable resource when it came to identifying people mentioned in her letters.

Kathy had rarely talked about the war and the family were shocked to discover the letters, the albums and all the other memorabilia. Why, David Mortimer wondered, had his mother kept all these letters but left them so disorganised and casually stuffed into boxes? What unrealised project did she have in mind? His guess was that 'Pam becoming her mother-in-law sealed the project and those boxes for ever'. Another possibility, though, is that she kept them for posterity and a place alongside Averell's and Pamela's papers in the Library of Congress, which is where Kathy's archive eventually landed. Or perhaps she had an inkling that someday someone would want to retrieve and publish the letters on account of their unique information and fascinating insights about life in wartime London and Moscow.

When Kathy died in February 2011, the obituaries emphasised the great wealth and privilege that had underpinned and shaped her wartime adventures, and understandably so. She was, after all, the daughter of an extremely rich businessman, who had inherited a fortune from his railroad-owning father and used it to build his own finance and business empire. Kathy's maternal family was rich, too. Her mother, Kitty Lanier Lawrance, was an outdoor type who also played a good hand of bridge – interests that Kathy shared. Kitty had two children with Averell – Mary, born in January 1917, and, in December of the same year, Kathy. Averell and Kitty divorced in 1929. The daughters remained with their mother, but went to live with Averell in 1936 when, aged forty-two, Kitty died of cancer. Miss Marshall, their governess, was with them.

Kathy and Mary were educated at Foxcroft, an elite Virginia girls' boarding school whose motto was *mens sana in corpore sano* (a healthy mind in a healthy body). Foxcroft was famous for its outdoor pursuits, at which Kathy excelled. She was a top-class horsewoman and a keen tennis player, and she skied well enough to be considered for the US Olympic team. But it was Bennington, the Vermont women's liberal arts college, where she honed her intellect, broadened her horizons and developed her writing voice. As Europe stumbled towards war in the late 1930s, Kathy studied international affairs, writing essays and reviews about world politics, Hitler and the Nazis, German–Czechoslovak relations, the 1938 Munich crisis, Franklin Roosevelt's New Deal, American neutrality, contemporary France and the US entry into the First World War. Organised, well written and crystal clear, Kathy's high-quality work earned praise from Averell as well as her academic advisers. During vacations Kathy helped out with the hosting and publicity for Sun Valley, the Idaho ski resort founded by her father in 1936. Graduating from Bennington in 1940, she joined a PR company, where she specialised in newspaper work.

While Kathy proved to be a talented journalist and a highly effective writer, it was Ave who pulled the strings that got her a job at INS and secured the diplomatic passport she needed to travel to Britain, where she was welcomed with open arms by the Anglo-American elite, including Prime Minister Winston Churchill, son of the New York-born heiress Jeanette Jerome. For my part, being someone from an utterly different background, what always struck me about Kathy – in person as well as in her letters – was how, in extraordinary circumstances, she had managed to transcend the potential confines of her upbringing to reach across class and cultural barriers. This was the ability that made her such an acute and imaginative observer of both the people she met and the historic events she witnessed.

After she returned to the United States in early 1946, Kathy stepped back from public life. For a while she worked for *Newsweek*, reporting on international affairs and the discussions of the newly created United Nations. She also advised *Voice of America* on the launch of its Russian-language radio broadcasts. She took part in her father's political campaigns for the governorship of New York in the 1950s, and there was a brief flurry of publicity when she testified to Congress about the Katyn affair, but never again did she seek or experience the limelight of the war years. As Kathy herself said to me, she was not the kind of person who liked to re-live past lives. Life moved on, and so did she. Her life changed fundamentally in October 1947 when she married Stanley Mortimer, and from this point on she was always known as Kathleen H. Mortimer, or Mrs Stanley G. Mortimer. An advertising executive and the son of a New York stockbroker, Stan (who died in 1999) had served as a naval officer in the Pacific theatre and had two young children (Stanley and Amanda) from a previous marriage. Kathy and Stan's first child – David – was born in 1948, followed by Jay (1950) and Averell (1956).

Kathy made quite a few foreign trips during the postwar years but did not return to the Soviet Union until 1974, when she accompanied her father and his new wife, the former Pamela Churchill, on a trip to Moscow and Leningrad. In tow were also Pam's son Winston (Churchill's grandson) and his wife Minnie. As I had discovered, Kathy always did her homework and she prepared for the trip by revising her Russian. When she returned home, the detailed notes she had made during the course of the visit were written up into quite a long travelogue. While noting a few comparisons with wartime Moscow and Leningrad, she was more interested in contemporary people and life in the Soviet Union than in her own memories. Averell read Kathy's report and compiled a detailed list of corrections and suggestions, including making it more of a war memoir, but she seems to have taken no notice and, in any event, her account of the trip remained unpublished. Stan didn't make the journey and Kathy missed him terribly, but was still glad to have gone, especially to Leningrad, which, she told him, was as 'magnificent' as she remembered it from 1945. 'We really are having a very interesting time,' she wrote to Stan in her very last letter from Moscow, dated 29 May 1974.

PART ONE
LONDON LETTERS (1941–3)

CHAPTER 1

'THE P.M. IS MUCH SMALLER THAN I EXPECTED AND A LOT LESS FAT – LOOKS RATHER LIKE A KINDLY BLUE TEDDY BEAR'

Kathy's first trip across the Atlantic to wartime Britain was by far the safest, and the most luxurious. She took the same route as her father – Pan Am's 'Clipper' service from New York to Lisbon via Bermuda and the Azores. As Averell Harriman recalled of his trip, 'Transatlantic passengers enjoyed many of the comforts of sea travel. They could move freely about the Clipper, read or play cards in the lounges, sit down to a table for their meals, and when flying overnight, they were assigned roomy bunks.'

During the journey, Kathy reflected on her motives for going, hinting that London was a place that she wanted, as well as expected, to challenge her self-assurance. She also wondered if she'd 'outgrown being depressed. Surely by now I should have had at least one minor attack, yet I haven't felt badly since college & I've certainly been alone a good deal of the time.'

The seaplane's scheduled flight time was twenty-seven hours but Kathy's journey was delayed by bad weather. After a few days in neutral Portugal she took a KLM flight to Bristol, arriving on 16 May 1941. Her impending arrival in Britain was flagged by London's *Evening Standard*. 'Girl from the U.S.A.' was the paper's headline, the article reporting that 'Miss Harriman, slender with brown hair and blue eyes, will write dispatches from the woman's point of view for the International News Service'.

America was still neutral and would remain so until December 1941, when Japan attacked Pearl Harbor and Hitler declared war on the United States. By mid-1941, however, the Americans were already Britain's de facto ally. America was the self-declared 'arsenal of democracy' and it was US-protected supplies from across the Atlantic that kept Britain fighting. Hopes were high that President Franklin D. Roosevelt would soon lead his country into the war on Britain's side, as his First World War predecessor, Woodrow Wilson, had done in 1917.

Averell had arrived in Britain a couple of months before Kathy. His role was to troubleshoot the delivery of US aid to Britain under the Lend-Lease Act of March 1941. Under Lend-Lease, the Americans supplied – free of charge – billions of dollars' worth of supplies. Supported by a small team of military and civilian experts, Ave worked to expedite the flow of aid. His so-called 'Mission' was based in the US embassy but was independent of the State Department or any other government agency. Such ad hoc arrangements were Roosevelt's preferred way of working: it empowered the White House and created a network of loyal special envoys who had direct and personal access to the president.

American aid was vital to Britain's ability to fend off a German invasion now that Hitler controlled continental Europe, and therefore to its long-term survival as an independent state. Unsurprisingly, Averell was popular and feted, and it was his connections that provided Kathy's entrée to elite social, political and military circles. Of particular import were his friendships with Prime Minister Winston Churchill and the charismatic Minister of Supply Lord Beaverbrook, the influential proprietor of the *Daily Express*, Britain's highest-selling newspaper. One marker of Churchill's esteem for Averell was that after Crete fell to the Germans at the end of May 1941, he asked him to undertake a fact-finding mission to northern Africa and the Middle East – a trip that lasted thirty-seven days. Averell and Kathy were frequent visitors to Lord Beaverbrook's mansion, Cherkley Court, as well as the PM's official country residence, Chequers, both located conveniently close to London. Kathy wrote many letters about her interactions with the Churchills, but her 'engagement' books show that these encounters were just the tip of an iceberg of lunches, dinners and parties at No. 10 Downing Street and Chequers.

Upon arrival in London, Kathy lived with Ave in the swanky Dorchester Hotel, which was just around the corner from the American embassy in Grosvenor Square. By the time she moved in her father was already having an affair with Pamela Churchill, the wife of Randolph Churchill, Winston's only son. Kathy's letters contain many clues to her complicity in Averell and Pamela's wartime affair, but more than anything they reveal that the two young women quickly forged their own enduring relationship. Within days of meeting they decided to rent a weekend house – Petersfield Farm near Dorking in Surrey – as a refuge from the London Blitz. Retrospective depictions of Pam as the dominant partner in their friendship are way off the mark. It was an equal and mutually beneficial relationship.

Kathy didn't keep a diary during the war but from time to time she wrote daily notes on her thoughts, feelings and activities that she then recycled in her correspondence, though not everything made it into the letters. The most extensive set of these notes relates to her first three months in Britain. There may be found Kathy's first impressions of Pamela: 'Pam Churchill is charming – has deep-founded common sense – a born leader in a quiet, effective way. The Foxcroft type!' A few days later, when they discussed getting a house together, she wrote, 'Pam is almost a bitch – very clinging – lousy temper, impressionistic. I like her and think we'll get on OK.' Less charitable was a barb of a couple of weeks later: 'Have decided Pam has a narcissus complex – not quite – but she sure does fancy herself – all her pictures around the room – has [Cecil] Beaton do new ones every week.' Another confidence Kathy didn't share with the folks back home was Pam telling her she had slept with Randolph before they got married. 'Actually, such things seem rather unimportant these days,' was Kathy's comment to herself.

Belmont Manor and Golf Club, Bermuda
May 9, 1941

Dear Mary,[1]

After raising our hopes last night that we'd go right on they decided to wait until this afternoon. Weather is warm & humid – no sun.

This hotel is horribly noisy. When I got up this morning I found all the fellow companions in a dejected group in the lobby. I decided exercise was in order and so I inspected the golf course. Just glad I don't have to play it!

The woman with the red dyed hair turned out to be English. The only other gal is young – perhaps American but she doesn't look it. Uses an English passport & has a German name. She's very nice.

The rest of the crew are an assortment of English, Americans, Japanese + one Negro.

For some reason or other the customs office was tense. We all talked in whispers & most people looked terrified as their names were called up. Having a diplomatic passport makes things easy – no inspection at all.

I've just heard we move on at 3:30 this afternoon – will be at Horta at dawn & Lisbon early tomorrow afternoon.

Kathleen

Estoril Palacio Hotel, Costa do Sol, Portugal
May 13, 1941

Dear Mary,

The trip over was very uneventful – we got held over in Bermuda the first night after much discussion & changing of minds & didn't get to Horta until Saturday morning.

Three of us went for a ten-minute drive in an antiquated vehicle of sorts to see the sights. Our escort was the "big business man" of Horta – the Vacuum Oil representative & he tore through the narrow streets – a three-noted horn blowing continually. We didn't kill anyone or anything – God knows why not. Every inch of the

1 Mary Averell Harriman Fisk (1917–96), Kathy's sister.

Azores are cultivated & the natives do a lot of whaling. It ought to be prosperous but the houses look dirty and the people old and wrinkled. Thank goodness we weren't held over there.

The fellow passengers were very nice. A Mr Charles Hargraves – a big English industrialist – who apparently hires and fires 100,000 men a year. He may have something to do with shipping too as he talks a lot about the Far East. You can only get a rather sketchy picture of people here and many are afraid to talk at all about themselves. Then there was a Commander (Navy) Townsend who had a diplomatic pouch. He leaves for London tomorrow. A man called Robinson – an engineer of Wright Aeronautical – was the first of our passengers to get off. I can't quite figure out why.

We played a certain amount of bridge – so the time passed quickly.

Arrived at Lisbon in the late afternoon – the bay is lovely – filled with large one-sailed fishing boats & motored out here to Estoril. The man from the embassy tried to get me to stay in Lisbon – but thank goodness I didn't as it will be a while before I can get moved out. Each Clipper brings more important diplomats, army and navy people who have higher priority over me.

On Sunday three of us went out to Sintra – an old palace of the King of Portugal that's now a museum. Parts of it were nice – particularly the old Moorish tiles. The outside was lovely but inside the furniture was a mixture of 14th to 18th C.

After that we took a walk through the village and up the mountainside to an old ruined fortress. That was really the pleasantest part of all. The roads are all cobbled with mosaic designs on the sidewalks.

Yesterday I trained into Lisbon – a tiny electric affair that takes forever – but everyone seems to use it and had lunch with a Mr Higget of the U.S. embassy.

Everyone you meet has an interesting story to tell. Lisbon seems to be the meeting place of all the main countries of Europe. It's a sort of worryless vacation for all. The only news we get comes from trying to decipher the Portuguese newspapers.

I spent this afternoon on the beach and then took a walk & unless I stay here too long I won't mind it at all.

A block away from the hotel is the "Casino" – it has a three-piece negro orchestra and innumerable tables of roulette, chemin de fer & a dice game. Last night I won 400 escudos! Translated into American money it doesn't amount to much.

I have a very nice room with veranda that overlooks a square and the bay – without bath – but that isn't bad as no one else seems to want to bathe when I do – for only $5 a day including meals.

Gather that Averell is having the time of his life in London. Churchill has taken a great liking to him – hence all is going well.

For the moment that's all the news.

My love to you all,

Kathleen

Leeds Castle, Maidstone, Kent
May 17, 1941

Dear Marie,[2]

This is Ave's first non-Prime Minister weekend. Our host, Lady Baillie[3] is abed with a cold.

I only arrived last evening – but already I'm beginning to feel what Ave is. He seems to stand for something secure that people can hang on to and believe in and they all have great faith in him.

Just in this short time he literally knows everyone of note – everyone who has a constructive part in the workings of the war, and they all love him. It's nice to see.

Last night was my coming-out party: the newspaper world – our foreign correspondents, English reporters as well, with a general or two thrown in to give the party a uniformed & medalled touch. Over 50 people – all unfamiliar & you know my knack for forgetting names. Ave's made a great hit with the press as he's helping them in the fight against censorship.

That was Saturday night. It's now Tuesday.

---

2 Marie Norton Harriman (1903–70), art gallery owner, Averell Harriman's second wife.

3 Lady Olive Baillie (1899–1974), Anglo-American heiress who owned and renovated Leeds Castle, where in the 1930s she hosted gatherings of politicians, royalty and showbiz stars.

I see very little of Ave, as he's terribly busy – breakfasting abed around 9:00 with the papers etc. I see him then until an inevitable businessman or gov't official turns up to talk shop. He gets to the office at 11 a.m. and works until 8 in the evening and unless he has a business dinner, he sees Quent[4] or someone like that. He's very anti-social but there really isn't time for things like that.

Although he's working hard, very hard, he loves it and looks wonderfully. Thanks to various friends he has plenty of milk, butter and the like; besides, living in hotels is very different from the home life with ration cards.

Apparently, some weeks ago he had a slight reoccurrence of ulcer trouble but caught it quickly and is now all cured. He's in the best of spirits – it's hard not to be when you're in his position. He knows everyone and they all think the world of him, and not just because he's Roosevelt's personal representative.

I got out of Lisbon in [three] days. Averell could have gotten me priority for the very next day, but he thought it would be good for me to stay. Actually, it was. I had a nice rest, the weather was beautiful, bathing and swimming, anything you wanted. The people there were a mixed group talking every possible language. It gave me a rather odd feeling eating at dinner with an American expert waiting to go to London, while at the next table were leading members of the German Gestapo in Portugal. Everyone there was waiting to go somewhere – so there was a continual spirit of vacation – parties far into the night, gambling etc. Each person I met had an interesting story to tell. For [three] days it was fun.

André Poniatowski[5] of all people turned up on his way to America on some minor Vichy business.

On purpose I didn't speculate much as to what I expected to find here, so I have had no disappointments or bad shocks. No blitz as yet,

---

4 Quentin Reynolds (1902–65), American journalist who worked for *Collier's Magazine* during the war.

5 André Poniatowski (1864–1954), Paris-born Polish noble who was married to Kathy's aunt Frances Lawrance, the sister of her mother Kitty. An industrialist and tank designer, André remained in France when Marshal Pétain's collaborationist Vichy regime took over following France's surrender to Germany in June 1940.

but the memory of past raids is inescapable. Hardly a block has gone unscathed and today I went down to the East End by the docks. I've read about the flattened houses but it's something quite different to actually see it.

For the moment I am a guest reporter on the *Daily Express*, one of the Beaverbrook papers. The editor is a great friend of Quent's and London's best girl reporter is on the staff.[6] She's showing me around. Actually, I don't see how my stories will make good copy for the English. Somehow I seem to be the only person worrying about that. This way my stuff is also usable for the I.N.S. [International News Service]. As far as I'm concerned, it's an ideal setup.

Life is rather hectic – there's so much to be done before starting, getting press passes etc., and everyone wants to see or entertain me and it's hard to refuse without seeming rude, but going around seeing things all day, dining far into the night, doesn't give much chance to write.

Walt Disney could make a wonderful *Fantasia* movie based on London at night, because things here aren't very realistic. The buildings become a ghostly white and the roving cabs – two dim sidelights without form.

Being American carries with it a peculiar charm, they talk a lot about the Americans these days. Yesterday I met some soldier in a pub off Fleet Street and his one comment was "just wait till I get back and tell them I've met an American."

This letter has been written in odd minutes throughout the day. Averell just blew in for a moment, he's off to Beaverbrook's for the night and I am about to dine with Pam Churchill.[7] She's the nicest, sanest girl I've met so far. She's doing a great job here too. Perhaps someday I'll do a piece on her.

---

6 Hilde Marchant (1916–70), German-born British journalist who reported on the Spanish Civil War, the Soviet–Finnish War and the German Blitz on Britain. She later worked for the *Daily Mirror* and *Picture Post*. 'She's scathing, cynical, a disapproving socialist. I'll learn a lot from her,' noted Kathy about Marchant.
7 Pamela Churchill (1920–97), married to Winston Churchill's son Randolph (1911–68).

I.N.S. head thinks it would be a good start to do a story on Quent in London. He's terrific and the idol of all the newspaper world here. He's being terribly nice to me, which helps no end.

The [invaluable] Bob[8] just phoned to say that some official is leaving for the U.S. tonight.

My love to everyone.

Kath

London
late May 1941

Dear Mary,

I wrote Marie all about Ave. I tried to sound unbiased, but that's rather hard to. He's really terrific. More people, big people and little people, have come up to me and said thank God for your father. It's kind of nice, being here and seeing it all go on!

As I think I told Marie, at the moment I am working for the *Daily Express* as well as I.N.S. Spent last week travelling around with Hilde Marchant, a sob sister reporter – the best in England. She's tiny, terribly efficient and terribly cold blooded, which helps keep me balanced. Went down to the East End of London, the part by the docks where the poorer working class live. It's far more horrible, for some reason, seeing tiny identical houses razed low, half bombed or burned, than the large concrete buildings you find around here. At the moment I'm not used to it.

The people you meet – the 18-year-old girl. She's been bombed out twice, the second time her mother and father killed – now she's all alone and can't hold down a steady job at the brewery because, as she put it, "I keep spitting up blood." I met her at a temporary home for bombed-out people. They can stay there free until they find new lodging. School houses, recreation halls, have all been turned over to nuns and WVS [Women's Voluntary Service] women, who provide food and bedding for the homeless. Imagine sleeping on the floor of an old gymnasium with hundreds of others, cold, dreary and dark,

8 Robert Pickens Meiklejohn (1908–97), Averell's long-time private secretary.

smelling strongly of disinfectant. It's not very pleasant. I wonder if the fighting side of war is any worse.

There hasn't been a raid since my arrival so I haven't seen any of that side yet. I'm glad because this way I'm being broken in slowly.

I started one story with "it's so easy to forget that there's a war going on in England." Believe me it's true, the country is so beautiful and green, wildflowers everywhere, cows and sheep in the fields. Except for the continual stream of tanks and lorries filled with soldiers that pass you on the road, this might be the same England we saw in '36.

Went to a munitions factory, where they employ as many women as possible. Apparently the average semi-skilled woman is four times faster and more efficient than an equally skilled man.

The New Deal was filled with three-initialed words, well England is twice as bad, because here they try to pronounce them. The other day I went down to Aldershot to see some A.T.S. [Auxiliary Territorial Service] work. They are the women attached to the army. Uniforms are all hideous – tight skirts, long-belted jackets and ear-covering hats. They make even a pretty girl look like a battleaxe. I've met plenty of the latter too, most are left over from the last war.

Every possible job, including setting the dials of the anti-aircraft guns, is now being done by women and girls. As yet it's all voluntary work, but women conscription is coming.

I've just returned from seeing my *Daily Express* boss, a man called Christiansen, great friend of Quent's, so I'll probably have to cut this short and get down to work.

None of the American reporters have been the least help to me on my stories, even though they are wonderful help in every other way. I took three stories to Karl Reeves, head of I.N.S. His comment was fine, fine, so I tried Quent. He's all set to see me start on a writing career, but still no constructive criticism. This weekend we again went down to Beaverbrook's where Ave collared Frank Owen,[9] the most brilliant editor over here, and at last I got somewhere. Today I go to

9 Frank Owen (1905–79), editor of the *London Evening Standard*.

my boss, Chris,[10] and he tells me the exact opposite from Frank. I almost laughed in his face. Both men run Beaverbrook papers, which are supposedly run on the same idea – rather Hearst-like. You see it's not very easy to turn overnight into a reporter!

Now that I'm over here I'm desperately trying to think of all the things I most wanted to know back home. Things of course that will pass the censor and the censor is a big and terrible organization right now.

Living in a hotel you get a rather poor idea of the food shortages. I have a ration card and the story about one chop a week is true, but there are communal feeding centers where many people eat for five or ten cents. That way they can pay for their food and save their food coupons for the food they cook at home. The great difficulty is re-educating the lower classes. They prefer to go without rather than change their feeding habits. On Wednesday I'm going down with Pam Churchill, Mrs Randolph – the one on the front-page cover of *Life* some time ago – to see the feeding center she set up and talk to some of the people. She's a wonderful girl, my age but one of the wisest young girls I've ever met – knows everything about everything political and otherwise.

She also was down at Lord Beaverbrook's this weekend. Her baby lives there. Our host looks like a cartoon out of *Punch*. Small, baldish, big stomach and from there he tapers down to two very shiny yellow shoes. His idea of sport is to surround himself with intelligent men, then egg them on to argue and fight among themselves. Sitting at dinner while all this is going on makes N.Y.C. seem very remote. Even his best friends are half scared of him because he's got a fearful temper and no one seems to know when it will break. On top of all this he's kind, very kind, and is wonderful with children and for some reason he doesn't seem to scare them.

Dinner is promptly at 9:00 and after that everyone is expected to retire to his private movie room. I guess seeing American movies is the one form of relaxation he gets. He and Averell get on beautifully.

Everyone is busy these days. I don't know what we'd do without the two hours of daylight-saving time!

---

10 Arthur Christiansen (1904–63), editor of the *Daily Express*.

Thanks to the publicity I got I'm being hounded from all sides with cranks and would-be geniuses. People over here seem to get a great vicarious pleasure out of writing to unknown "friends."

Geoffrey Patterson[11] is hot on my trail again. As luck would have it he's in London on leave.

I lunched today with Hugh Dowding[12] at his club, and he took me around into the parts usually unscathed by female eyes. The American conception of the London conservative club is without exaggeration. I walked into the library and at least 20 chairs were filled with readers of the *London Times*. Not one looked up. Sir Hugh is about to retire. They haven't any place for him in even the administrative end of the R.A.F. They don't either need or want him. I feel rather sorry for him because he wants to work, to help just as every other Englishman does, but they don't want him.

[Kathleen]

London
May 30, 1941

Dear Mary,

It's May 30, the most exciting day I've had in London so far, and as my letter to you is still unmailed I thought I'd go on where I left off.

I did my first spot news story for America today – press conference with Lord Woolton[13] – he's a making an appeal to the women of America. Plus the excitement that I met the queen.[14] She's perfectly

---

11 Geoffrey Thomas Denton Patterson, graduate of Heidelberg University and Jesus College Cambridge, a German-speaker and member of wartime Britain's Intelligence Corps. Kathy knew about his intelligence background but never wrote about it in her letters.

12 Hugh Dowding (1882–1970) was head of RAF Fighter Command during the Battle of Britain. He was relieved of that post in November 1940 and retired from the Air Force in July 1942. Kathy went to the theatre and had dinner with him on 6 June 1941, commenting in her private daily notes that 'he handles me like a piece of breakable china – a very lonely man'.

13 Frederick James Marquis, 1st Earl of Woolton (1883–1964), British Minister of Food.

14 Queen Elizabeth (1900–2002), wife of George VI, better known as the Queen Mother of the future Queen Elizabeth II. Kathy later wrote a story about the sixteen-year-old Princess Elizabeth, pointing out to her young female readers that 'the heiress to Britain's throne uses no make-up'.

beautiful – too bad she hasn't the photogenic type of looks – and she's got more poise than anyone I've met yet. Us American reporters stood around like a bunch of apes and she was wonderful, kept up her end of the conversation, asked questions and seemed interested in the answers. You might have thought she was doing the interviewing.

Hilde Marchant complained the other day that the queen ought to be seen more, that she should wear a uniform or anyway suits and brown grippers. After today I'll fight anyone who says that 'cause it ain't so. She's not the type of person who ever ought to be other than well dressed. Among other things it would lower her to our standards and the English people wouldn't like that.

It's late, I'm exhausted. Tomorrow I go with Ave to see the first Lend-Lease ship with food come in and after that we go to the Churchills for the weekend. You see life here is pretty exciting – my only regret is that I didn't get out of college a year sooner and learn the ropes about reporting. Thanks to Red Mueller[15] I'm learning but it's hard starting from such a rock bottom.

Goodbye now and my love to all and please tell me how people are reacting now that the President has spoken. Wasn't that exciting about the *Bismarck*?[16] Everyone went crazy here.

Love again,
Puff[17]

London
June 4, 1941

Dear Mary,

I'm so tired of my typewriter that I could spit – you'll have to bear my writing. Incidentally, this is Shirley's[18] pen. I love it.

---

15 Merrill Mueller (1916–80), American journalist and broadcaster.
16 The hunting down and sinking of the German battleship *Bismarck* in May 1941.
17 'Puff' was Kathy's family nickname – supposedly on account of the way her breath sounded when she skied at high altitude.
18 Shirley C. Fisk (1910–79), Mary's husband, a doctor who served in the US Army Medical Corps during World War II.

This morning at breakfast Ave got word that he could go to the Red Sea. I don't think I've ever seen him so excited about anything. Yesterday he was terribly discouraged, afraid that F.D.R. wouldn't want his representative to go down there. It's really thrilling. The P.M. wants him to go and feels that he'd be able to help a lot. He's taking two experts & Bob along so they'll probably be gone about six weeks.

Pam Churchill and I are going to take a house together – near London – a place for weekends or bad blitzes. Her child will live there, quite near Beaverbrook's place – so we'll be safe if anything serious happens all of a sudden. The house belongs to Dorothy Beatty[19] & is nicely furnished etc. I haven't seen it yet but I'm visiting her this weekend. Soon I'll be able to write first-hand reports on housekeeping within the ration card!

Last weekend we went to Chequers. It's rather a shock meeting someone you've seen so many times. The P.M. is much smaller than I expected and a lot less fat. He wears an R.A.F-blue, one-piece siren suit (the only way to keep warm in that house) and looks rather like a kindly blue teddy bear. He expresses himself wonderfully – continually comes out with delightful statements. I'd expected an overpowering, rather terrifying man. He's quite the opposite. Very gracious, has a wonderful smile and isn't at all hard to talk to. He's got the kind of eyes that look right through you.

Various members of the R.A.F. were also there – the men who decide what is to be done nightly. Getting their reaction is like entering a new world. The war, the bombing is so completely objective to them – at least they try to make it so.

Word about the fall of Crete came while we were there. I don't think I'll ever forget the look on the P.M.'s face when he came in and told us. Words can't describe it.

Sunday morning & the news of the clothes rationing broke. It may sound funny to you in the U.S. but I'm desperate. I luckily brought one warm suit, but my three blouses and one sweater aren't actually enough. I would like it if you could send me some blouses – there are several in my closet.

---

19 Dorothy Beatty (née Power, 1902–66), American wife of David Beatty, 1st Earl Beatty.

To continue with the C. family. Mother[20] is a very sweet lady. She's given up her whole life to her husband & takes a back seat very graciously. Everyone in the family looks upon the P.M. as God. She's rather left out and when anyone pays attention to her she's overjoyed. Averell played croquet with her & she was so grateful. It seems as though she seldom has any fun. She's got a mind of her own, only she's a big enough person not to use it unless he wants her to.

18-year-old Mary[21] was also there. She's full of enthusiasm; childish in some ways and terribly grown up in others. She cornered me the moment I got to Chequers and asked all about public opinion in the U.S., and questioned me about all sorts of things.

Last night Ave and I gave a dinner in her honor. She's working out near Chequers, running a hospital library and doesn't have much social fun. She was really wonderful and would make a good jitter bug if she ever learned to dance!

Thanks to a long talk with the present I.N.S. boss – a man everyone in the office seems to dislike – at last know where I stand. Apparently my first two articles have reached America and they're OK. I get paid $40 a week and write if and when I have anything to say. No ties and for the moment no spot news. Please get a clipping service so that I can see how much they rewrite my articles. Chris is wonderful, though unconstructive, he uses them as they are. It's rather fun opening the morning papers and seeing a byline story – and actually the kind of stuff they seem to like is rather easy to write. All one needs is an angle and a lot of little instances to prove it.

Heard a wonderful story the other day. Someone asked a little boy what he wanted to be when he grew up – a fireman, pilot or what. The little boy answered: "alive."

The sirens were going – a woman climbed out of bed and woke her husband. They started going to their shelter when he stopped and turned back, "forgot my teeth" he said. "Blimey – what do you think he's dropping – sandwiches!" was her reply. I could go on for pages – there are loads of stories like that going around.

---

20 Clementine Churchill (1885–1977), wife of Winston Churchill.
21 Mary Churchill (1922–2014), daughter of Winston and Clementine Churchill.

Write and tell me what you most want to know. It's hard to tell because the people I know will be just names & after writing a story on the East End I can't get very enthusiastic about writing it all over again in letter form.

Tonight I go to Plymouth and will probably return Friday early – depending on what Ave's immediate plans are. Lady Astor[22] is the big bug of Plymouth & I'm going to stay with her. Next week Liverpool is on the schedule – occasion: the christening of a submarine. Pam & I are going together.

I'm only beginning to appreciate what a wonderful picture I'm getting. Thanks to my job I see one side of England. Ave and his friends show me the other.

The "powers that be" want bombers to come over England – so that they can get at them and down them. The bombed people have a different idea. They don't want the bombers. Seeing both sides is fascinating.

From day to day I guess my life is very normal. London is a gay place – nervously gay. There's not much time for sleep. There are lots of nice nightclubs and places to dine and plenty of people to go out with, American and otherwise. Age over here makes very little difference – that also is something new to me.

Goodbye now,
Puff

Dorchester Hotel, London
early June 1941

Dear Mouche,[23]

I saw your sister shortly after I arrived & gave her the stockings. These days I think you could bribe anyone with just one pair of American nylon stockings!

I'm having a horrible time over here – no Angela or Victoria to pick up my things & I never can find where the hotel maid puts them.

22 Nancy Witcher Astor (1879–1964), American-born wife of Waldorf Astor who succeeded her husband as MP for Plymouth and became the first woman to take her seat in the House of Commons.
23 Elsie Marshall (1893–1974), Kathy's childhood English governess.

Another big problem in my life is letter writing. I've just counted up. I have 10 bread & butter letters to write.

At the moment I'm struggling with Mrs Churchill. Ave's final instructions were not to say just plain "thank you." That's not the way to make a hit with that particular family apparently & they're a good family to be good with if "something" should happen.

It's terrible Ave has picked up so many friends in such a short time. They send him away, so now they all feel they should be nice to daughter Harriman.

Perhaps this letter makes no sense. I'm in a wonderful mood – first time since I returned from Plymouth. Seeing that place did rather get me down. I'm glad I went early in the game because now I think I'll be able to be unemotional about less bad places. I don't think I'll find any worse ones, ever. A dead city filled with such alive, brave people. Seeing it all made me feel very small, smug & horribly depressed.

Life here is very gay – lots of nice people. It broadens the field of play considerably when age doesn't count. It doesn't you know over here.

Incidentally, Pam (Mrs Randolph C.) doesn't look one bit like her *Life* cover picture. She's nearer to American than anything I've found so far. That's meant as a compliment to her. She's just as stubborn as I – so we ought to have some wonderful battles owning a house together.

It's morning now & rumor has it I'm off to Scotland on Monday & then they want me to go to Ireland after that. You see, life is pretty exciting. Seeing England from every possible angle doesn't get dropped at everyone's doorstep. I'm more than lucky.

Love to all,

Kath

London
June 8, 1941

Dear Marie,

The excitement of the moment – Pam Churchill & I have rented a house. It's absolutely divine – 5 bedrooms & 2 baths + servant quarters & a summerhouse. Large kitchen garden, chickens and a goat that helps the food situation.

The house itself is about 400 yr. old – lovely old beams – surrounded on one side with a rose garden, a rock garden with a pool & goldfish, and on the other with a croquet lawn. (Ave particularly likes that.)

Pam is having 2 ponies sent from her father's place. The surrounding countryside is lovely – all that for the price Mary pays for her apartment! Less in fact because we get 2 servants thrown in. We move in in a fortnight. I can't wait, because working in London is rather distracting – the phone continually rings and there's always lunch, tea, cocktails & a million other interruptions.

I went down to Plymouth for 2 days the middle of last week & haven't recovered yet. Stayed with Lady Astor & saw the works thanks to her. It's so depressing and horrible that I don't know how people can stay there. No house is untouched and block after block is absolutely laid low. The people are unbelievable. The Plymouth widows take their losses as a matter of course. They stay on living in half-roof-less houses & evacuate their children to the country (thank God!).

Lady Astor has done a remarkable job down there. Literally everyone knows her & stops and chats on the street. She'd have been a much-admired woman if she'd only stayed out of politics.

Spent last night at Beaverbrook's. I'm getting used to that place and the people in it (a very odd collection) and like it a lot. At first I felt horribly out of place & small. He's so damned kind & lovable that it does not take long to feel at home.

I'm sorry to be so short & inexplicit about Plymouth, but after writing 3 stories on the place it's hard to start all over again. Besides, I'm trying to forget it. Seeing so much destruction & so many heroic people all in one fell swoop got me down.

Tomorrow I go to Liverpool.

My love to you all.

Kath

London
June 9, 1941

Dear Mary,

I saw Averell off at Poole – horrible cold dreary day – haven't heard from him since, so I guess all's well. His trip was all done in the utmost secrecy. No one was supposed to know, and I've been lying like a rug right and left. I just returned from Liverpool, when Quent phoned to ask if I had any news of Ave. All Fleet St. knows but they won't release it until the embassy gives the word. Thank goodness.

No one really knows how long he'll be gone. He thinks about six weeks. Beaverbrook says it will be nearer three. It's very exciting having him asked to go. It shows what he's thought of here, how much he's trusted.

I'm glad to have seen Liverpool – the docks are in ruins – at least the warehouses back of them are – for blocks and blocks.

I was going to ask myself down to Sudbury for the weekend,[24] as this will be the last before we move into our cottage. Then I got invited to Chequers. So there I will go. In case anyone thinks it's "poor little Kathleen" alone in England, you can assure them it isn't so.

[Kathleen]

Kathy made some notes during her weekend at Chequers:

<u>Sat. [June] 14</u> Sat next to P.M. at dinner – he was in wonderful mood – was excited to find he's good at shooting the English brand of Tommy gun – likes it better than the American one.

Saw *That Hamilton Woman*[25] – with Sea Lord there, the P.M. & everyone else. Being in England & so close to the war made the movie mean so much more. All the Churchills cried – that impressed me terribly.

Big battle at Damascus tomorrow. The atmosphere when the P.M. reads out the latest developments is something I hope I'll never forget. Makes the war seem like card games.

The Polish sailors before the battle [with the] *Bismarck* were sharpening their knives – hoping to board her.

---

24 Sudbury Hall, Derbyshire, ancestral home of the aristocratic Vernon family, to whom Kathy was distantly related via her mother.
25 Film directed by Alexander Korda (1941) about Horatio Nelson's mistress, set during the Napoleonic Wars.

Sunday [June] 15 The P.M. was depressed at dinner tonight. Turkey is giving in, Russia won't hold out more than six weeks, he said. All Europe is swaying towards a Hitler victory. We need a victory in the battle started today. America won't come in until we are almost thru.

"I'd like to be a cat – with no worries."

"England will be beaten without America."

At times he talks conversationally. Then when he's interested he lapses into oratory. Always expressive [verbally].

Another Thin Man[26] – movie tonight. I was the only one who enjoyed it.

26 Film directed by W.S. Van Dyke (1939) based on a detective story by Dashiell Hammett.

CHAPTER 2

'WHEN YOU STOP TO THINK ABOUT IT, THIS REALLY IS A GAY WAR'

The social whirl into which Kathy plunged upon arrival in the UK was unending. On her very first night in London, Ave threw a party for her at the Savoy – Noël Coward dropped by to say hello – and the next day it was off to Leeds Castle in Kent for another coming-out party. But the war was never far from her thoughts. The big news that summer was Germany's invasion of the Soviet Union on 22 June. Churchill immediately declared solidarity with the Soviet people and allied himself with Stalin against Hitler. Kathy liked Churchill's speech but thought him overly optimistic about the chances of Soviet survival. The United States remained neutral but Roosevelt signalled that Lend-Lease material aid would be extended to the USSR and sent his very special envoy, Harry Hopkins, to Moscow to meet Stalin. Averell was in the Middle East when Hitler launched Operation Barbarossa, and not long after his return to London in mid-July he was recalled to Washington for consultations. Kathy could have joined him but feared the State Department would not permit her to return to Britain. So she stayed put and sent Mouche the first of many requests for personal supplies – 'loot' – that Averell was to be cajoled into bringing back with him.

Among the people Kathy met was the Conservative politician Henry 'Chips' Channon, who noted in his diary that she was 'a typical American debutante'. Chips changed his mind about her, however, later describing her as 'a shrewd observer, a typical American girl of the more intelligent type; and whilst much in the Churchill clique is by no means blinded to its imperfections'.

The closest village to Petersfield Farm – the seventeenth-century house rented by Kathy and Pam – was Beare Green, near Dorking in Surrey. Just thirty miles from London, the area's road and rail connections, together with the picturesque countryside of rolling chalk hills, made it a favourite destination for escapees from the Blitz, though by the time the Harrimans arrived in Britain the most intense phase of the German bombing of London had ended.

London
mid-June 1941

Mouche dear, you may have lived in England many years but your memory of cold damp English weather has been softened by the New York heat. Until I could collect enough money from Bob Meiklejohn I froze to death, literally, now I have a suit, the last of my size in Fortnum's and a pair of country shoes not exactly my size, but likewise the last. This typewriter literally broke me and I guarantee it is the very last portable in the whole city of London.

I guess it's hard for you to realize how desperate things are over here. The odd thing is that the Ministry of Information won't let anything that says how bad it really is out of the country.

I'm glad to have been in Liverpool – the docks are in ruins. Pamela Churchill did a good job of breaking a champagne bottle on the submarine's hull or whatever you call it. There were thousands of dockers cheering it as it slid off and hit the water, quite thrilling. After that there was a big lunch [that] broke all food regulations and we had both fish and meat.

Spent last night with Lord Derby at his largest house.[1] The house is terrific, miles of pink granite. The oldest part is Tudor, inside is equally hideous. The gardens are lovely, rhododendrons every possible color, pink, orange, yellow, deep red, blue. I was shown the works by Lady Derby this morning. She is old and deaf and not half as charming as her husband. He is delightful, drinks too much port. They

---

1 Knowsley Hall, near Liverpool, stately home of Edward George Villiers Stanley (1865–1948), 17th Earl of Derby.

feel they should economize, at least Lord Derby does, and live simply. At dinner a lackey in livery stands behind your chair, pushes you in and leaves. You serve yourself, then he reappears after coffee and ushers you out. Three lackeys for four of us. It was all very pompous.

Pamela has moved into my suite as Averell did not like the idea of my being alone in a blitz. There are so many people here, looking after me, that I feel rather like a prize cow.

Have you guessed that I'm having the time of my life over here? Actually, had I known quite what I was in for I'd have been scared pink, particularly about the work.

Please tell me something instructive about my copy – what U.S. thinks of it. Any information is gratefully received, because all I hear from this side is that they are OK and that someday I will be a journalist.

[Kathleen]

London
June 18, 1941

Dear Mary,

I just received Mouche's letter saying that you'd almost had a miscarriage – I was horrified because of course I'd had no word. I hope to hell you are alright now. If only I'd known, I'd have cabled earlier. I do feel rather helplessly far away over here – even if I had heard, I'd not have been able to do anything about it.

The Derby was today, so Quent, Pam, and I borrowed Smith [Ave's chauffeur] and Ave's car for the day. God what a day. This year all the races are squashed into one week at Newmarket – that's 80 miles from here.[2] The road was hopelessly jammed 10 miles out of the town and we were giving up hope of ever seeing the Derby when Smith decided to cut out cross country – so we turned off the road and went through 3 planted fields. Why no farmer saw us is beyond me. I had visions of being arrested, accused of using petrol illegally etc., but all turned out well. We saw the Derby – such as one can. The track is one straight, rather hilly so you can't see the horses much of

2 In 1941 the 'Epsom Derby' was run at Newmarket.

the time. They look like a growing furry caterpillar coming at you broadside, and you don't figure out who's ahead until almost the finish. Actually, I didn't care. The funny thing is that no one else did either. Have just finished a story on the subject. Came in at about 11:30 having dined with some of the younger embassy blood, worked until 12:30, then Pam came in with Bill Taylor, Eagle Squadron Leader.[3] He's divine – probably rather cynical, anyway sophisticated.

The funny thing about England is that age makes no difference. Tonight Pam's dining alone with a guy Ave's age. I'm going out with Quent. He's one of the youngest around, with the exception of Michael Tree (he's the son of Ronny Tree – the man under Duff Cooper[4] in the Ministry of Information) and a scattering of others.

Incidentally, Duff came to cocktails yesterday and I think he's a pompous old rooster. Some people seem to like him.

I went to Chequers again last weekend. Ave must have asked the P.M. to "look after" me because I'm being well cared for by about 10 different people. It was a memorable weekend. Last night with that embassy group I found that I know twice as much about what's going on. That all makes it rather hard. I don't dare open my mouth.

Life is unbelievably social. God only knows why. Every night next week is booked up already and the weekend hasn't started. The only thing people seem scared about here is being lonely, so they date up way ahead of time to ensure against an evening alone. At least that's the way I figure it.

Please don't think I'm bragging. I'm just telling one aspect of the life over here.

Who do I go around with? People I've met through Pam, mostly older men. Now I've got some naval observer friends, who are young by comparison. Bill Batt,[5] one of Ave's commission people – who is refreshingly American. He's got so much ambition that it's rather

---

3 William 'Bill' Taylor (1905–91), a former US naval aviator. The Eagle Squadrons were RAF fighter squadrons staffed by volunteer pilots from the United States.
4 Alfred Duff Cooper (1890–1954), Minister of Information.
5 William L. Batt (1916–2004), economist, a member of the team that resourced President Truman's 1948 election campaign. Batt teased Kathy that in her heart of hearts she really wanted to be a politician's wife.

exhausting. He's pleasant though. The other night I dined with him in Soho and walked through Hyde Park afterwards for hours, listening to all the soapbox speeches. One man was talking about why women shouldn't smoke or drink while pregnant. Others spoke on Ireland, politics and religion. I found them rather unenlightening after the various ministerial people I meet. You can't imagine how interesting life over here is.

[Kathleen]

Petersfield Farm, Surrey
June 27, 1941

Dear Mary,

For the first time since I've gotten here, I'm really away from the war. Pam's gone back to London for dinner and I'm sitting on our porch enjoying the birds and the cold summer evening.

We drove down here this morning. Now that it really belongs to us, the house is lovelier than ever. All morning we stored away pictures, silver cups and china animals. This afternoon we went into Dorking and bought food – ration food – such as a joint for Sunday lunch, butter, and a sliver of cheese. Being Mrs Churchill, Pam gets more than we otherwise would – 6 extra eggs and things like that. Without any pull it would have been impossible to have gotten what we need with guests coming tomorrow.

It's after 9:30 but the extra 2 hours makes it still light. In fact these days it seldom gets really dark at all.

Last night I walked home at about midnight – blackout and all – no moon and I still could see easily.

I went to my [first] show – an English Intimate Revue.[6] It left me rather cold. Geoffrey Lloyd[7] was our host. Olive Baillie was the other woman besides Pam and me. She's a bitch of the first degree. Owns lovely old Leeds Castle, where Ave and I went my first weekend. Lady

---

6 An 'Intimate Revue' was a generic term for an upmarket cabaret and stage show.
7 Geoffrey Lloyd (1902–84), Conservative politician who served as a minister in charge of petroleum issues during the war, later described by Kathy as one of her 'beaux'.

Baillie in Chamberlain's time held the important house parties. Now she's forgotten, not wanted – the Trees & Ditchley have usurped her position and she can't stand it.[8] She's mad because Averell didn't pay due attention to her and to get even has been taking it out on Pam & indirectly me. She's the only person I've met so far that I intensely dislike.[9]

My week's work wasn't too productive. I went around with A.T.S. and W.R.N.S. [Women's Royal Naval Service] (army & navy women), collected a lot of boring information and data but no stories.

Red phoned me tonight and apparently I've gotten into trouble with my story on the Derby.[10] The censor thinks I'm trying to give away military secrets! Or at least, I mentioned unmentionable things. All it really means is that I'll have to do some rewriting – something I hate.

Tomorrow I'm going to take pictures of the house. I can rave until Doomsday about the old crooked beams & bricks, but you still won't get an adequate picture.

It's really well nigh impossible to get servants these days. All 23-year-old girls and under have been called up to the services, either the A.T.S., the W.A.A.F. [Women's Auxiliary Air Force] or the Wrens (they are pronounced) and the older women work in munition and other factories. So I guess we'll have to hang on to our one-eyed Mrs Campbell & surly Mary. We are scared stiff the latter will want to leave. She hates waiting on table and so far we haven't heard of a parlor maid. The agencies in London are literally empty. Between us, Pam and I have called them all.

This past week I spent most of my evenings being entertained by the younger generation. I've had enough to last me quite a while.

---

8 Ditchley Park, country house in Oxfordshire owned by Ronald Tree, a Conservative MP. In the early years of the war, Churchill sometimes used it as a weekend retreat, as it was considered safer from German bombers than Chequers or his own house, Chartwell.

9 Kathy's hostility towards Lady Baillie was fuelled by the latter's accusation that Pam was using Kathy to get close to Averell.

10 Kathy's story was published under the headline 'English Turf Followers Have Lost the Carefree Gaiety So Prevalent in Prewar Days'.

They all remind me of the proverbial Southern country gentlemen of the pre-Civil War days – very dashing, good looking in their regiment evening uniforms, but not very intelligent – in fact, intensely boring after 10 minutes. Horse racing used to be their major interest – now it's how to get their work done in a minimum amount of time. Perhaps I'm being a little cruel. When the time comes, they'll probably all be very brave and die fighting – but actually for dinner I'd rather have an interesting older man to talk to. I hope that doesn't sound too strange.

I'm not being very good about keeping a diary – so my letters to you will have to take its place in case I ever want to use them.

Only personal word from Averell was one cable ... "OK love Harriman." Via other sources I gather he's getting all his necessary information and is well looked after.

I've been arguing myself blue in the face what I think is happening to U.S. public opinion now that Russia has joined forces. Has it confused the issue on America's part? Do they think of it in terms of aiding communism or of aiding Britain and Russia against Hitler?

I would very much like it if you can have *Newsweek*, *Life* and *New Yorker* sent to me, air mail if possible, each week, otherwise by boat. I can understand now why Ave asked me to bring over magazines and newspapers! Better late than never.

Thanks to Ave being a friend of Oliver Lyttelton,[11] Pres. of the Board of Trade, I've been allowed extra coupons to buy some tennis & country clothes, two suits and two evening dresses. So I'm not as desperate as I was and can return all the clothes that I borrowed from Dorothy Beatty. However, if anyone is coming over who can bring a few light articles, they'd be much appreciated.

Quent went to Scotland & bought me some lovely country tweed, which I'm having made-up. Soon we won't be able to buy good material, coupons or no coupons. Shoes are the hardest to get. My 5½ oz Belman jobs have almost fallen apart!

It's getting dark now so I'm going in.

Best of love to you all,

Puff

---

11 Oliver Lyttelton (1893–1972), President of the Board of Trade 1940–1.

Sunday, June 29

Our weekend is now over. My it's nice having a place of one's own. Weekend visiting as a continuous dose has its disadvantages.

This evening 7 of us sat in the garden (drinking champagne and Fortnum's best peaches) and watched the planes come back from France. If it hadn't been that 3 of the boys were in uniform, it might have been Long Island on a summer evening with transport planes flying overhead. Only they do sound different here. (I'm beginning to be able to tell one from another now – such things as Spitfires and Hurricanes are easy, but a bomber is still only a bomber to me yet.)

When you stop to think about it, this really is a gay war. Particularly this weekend, isolated by our 4 fields and 12 chickens, I felt it. Everyone seems to be trying to keep up his prewar life wherever possible. On Wednesday I'm going to the opening of Noël Coward's new show – think I'll use it as a means for a story on the gay side of the war.

Quent came down today, but has to go back to London. He made the "postscript" after the 9 o'clock news, which is a great honor.[12] His speech was excellent – part of it the script for a movie he's going to do. The theme: a letter to Dr Goebbels – telling him how England isn't taking it any longer, she's fighting back. He did a damn good job.

I wish to hell I didn't have to go to London [but] at least now I'll have the urge to get my story material early, so the rest of the time I can come here and write it!

Did I tell you I bought a car – a 1939 Ford. It's handy to have now and might come in useful sometime if we ever have to get out quickly. I have a driver's license and everything. Cars like that are almost impossible to get. I paid £125.00 and have since then been offered £140! The one trouble with England today is the way money disappears. £10 goes as fast as $10. Pretty soon, if Averell continues to want to live at the Dorchester, I'll be broke!

It's late now, goodnight,

Puff

---

12 *Postscript* was a BBC radio programme broadcast after the nine o'clock news on Sunday evenings.

PS I'm back in London now – I've just been to see Mr W[inant][13] who had letters and instructions from Averell. My God – what a person – he sat me down and practically gave me a soul talk. He's very intense and stares at you all the time while talking.

Dorchester Hotel, London
July 2, 1941

Mouche dear,

Tomorrow Pam & I are going out to the country. I can't tell you how nice it is having a place of one's own – between us we can collect quite a genial group of people.

I'm amused at you thinking me safe with Pam – she's not in the least tough. We get on beautifully – thank God – because I see her a hellova lot. Now that Ave's gone she's moved down to our apartment as I didn't want to be in it alone. It's too big for one & I didn't want to give it up. The hotels are all crowded. People can't keep houses going – it's too hard to get food & keep servants.

Money goes literally like water these days – God only knows where, because I never pay for a meal except 4/6 for breakfast.

Tonight Noël Coward's new show opened.[14] An amazing conglomeration of people – some in evening clothes (women), others in uniform. The show was absolutely first rate – a sure 2 hr guarantee of forgetting the war. I hope it opens in N.Y. – the plot is unbelievably original – a light, fantastic comedy.

After it was over, Noël Coward made a speech. He had trouble getting thru it – the gallery kept shouting rude remarks. They don't like him over here – I suppose partly because of the flop he made of things in the U.S.[15]

Saw 2 musicals. Parts of both were good but it's hard to get in the mood for a show at 6.30 in the afternoon.

---

13 John G. Winant (1889–1947), former governor of New Hampshire who served as US ambassador to Britain during the war. Married to Constance (1899–1983).
14 *Blythe Spirit.*
15 When Coward visited the United States in summer 1940 he was criticised for having the privilege of being able to leave Britain at such a dangerous time. Reportedly, Coward went to the US on a government mission.

Spent yesterday & today down in West Ham with the A.R.P. [Air Raid Precautions]. It's amazing how being an American gets you anywhere. I spent most of my time being questioned. I hardly could get a word in edgewise & then when people found out I was a friend of Quentin Reynolds, they wouldn't let me leave. He took the country by storm in the Sunday evening B.B.C. Postscript – his speech was directed to Dr Goebbels – called him "dear Dr" & talked about "slap-happy Hermann" & his boys. I'm going to send on a copy – it's well worth reading. When Quent talks in his super-sarcastic voice, it's supreme.

When I stop to think what an abnormal life I anticipated living, it makes me laugh. War or no war, England hasn't changed – daily life hasn't changed. West Ham is the entrance to London by air. I saw a square mile of complete destruction & yet all the people register only contempt for the bombing. It changes, disorders their life momentarily only. Those who were evacuated to the country are coming back now in droves. The housing problem is terrific but they aren't happy in the country. They feel as though they are missing something.

It's amazing how few people the blitzes killed. Statistics in one borough show that out of 5 demolished houses one person gets killed. It will take more than bombing to [beat] England.

I met an R.A.F. wing commander the other day – one of the older boys. He's now working in the Ministry. Last week he got bored with work, took the day off and went on one of the sweeps over France. His attitude was like that of any American playing a game – quite casual. Max Aitken,[16] the Beaver's son – does the same thing periodically. He said last week he was a little out of practice – got careless & found an ME109 on his tail who almost did him in.[17] The thought of death doesn't bother them in the least. It's things like that that make me realize how far away U.S. is from the war.

Bestest love to all,
Kathleen

16 Max Aitken (1910–85), Lord Beaverbrook's son, who served in the RAF during the war.
17 The ME109 was a German fighter plane.

London
July 7, 1941

Dear Mary,

Another wonderful weekend at our farm has come and gone. I really don't know when I've enjoyed the country more, or having a place to go, where the rose garden is in full bloom, and the arbor and summerhouse are covered with pink rambler roses. It's quite divine.

Baby Winston moved in last week. He's the happiest baby I've yet to come across – loves people and does less than no crying, which is a godsend as the walls might as well be transparent.

I was lucky last week and was able to get enough material for stories by Wednesday night, so Pam and I drove down to Dorking. I'm getting very good at remembering to stay on the wrong side of the road! Can you imagine anything more wonderful than relaxing on the lawn in the sun and working at the same time? It's too good to be true.

Rather unfortunately, between Pam and me we have quite a few fighter pilot friends. The big sport at the moment seems to be touring around the country on off-duty moments and "beating up" friends. Frankly, the first time we were beaten up, I was scared stiff. I was working quietly on the lawn, when all of a sudden a Spitfire appeared from nowhere and passed twenty feet over our precious roof. Going at terrific speed, the noise is something unbelievable. My first reaction was that it was a training pilot in trouble but no, it came around again, this time really dangerously close and passed between two large trees at the foot of the garden. Pam's nanny, as a precautionary measure, had put Winston under the bed. "Are they practicing dive bombing?" she asked!

On Saturday night Geoffrey Patterson came down from Bristol, a rather godforsaken hole these days. He works a seven-day schedule and gets a weekend every six weeks. This was his first moment of relaxation since he's been here and it did my heart good to see how much he enjoyed it.

That evening we had a wonderful dinner at [the] local pub. Quent and the Bernsteins[18] came over after dinner and we sat around with the pilots. At 10:30 four of them got up and left. This was their night on duty. Seeing them leave and wondering if they'd all come back gave me a funny feeling.

One boy,[19] with a very badly burned face, was the second man to get a D.F.S. [sic] in the war. He flew all through Dunkerque, got shot down and went in search for a pub for a glass of beer. After a beer he decided to try and get home. Minus both tail fins he wasn't able to get up very high, so he flew under fire just over the waves and finally landed with 400 bullet holes in his plane and two in himself. His one and only thought was to get back to his aerodrome in time for a dinner date with a W.A.A.F.!

Another boy[20] we met that night was celebrating his 20th-month anniversary in the air force. He was particularly sad because he is being transferred to another squadron – he's one of two of the original men of the squadron left. He's about 28 and [probably] hasn't much longer to live.

He gets depressed at times. I guess they all do, and he showed me something he carries to cheer him up when he feels he can't go on any longer – Churchill's bit about the R.A.F.: "never in the history of the world has so much been owed by so many to so few." I like that story, don't you?

Yesterday Mary Churchill – the young girl – came down with one of the many eligible guards. She's a very intelligent girl, but so naive that it hurts. She says such frank things, then people laugh at her, make fun of her, and being super-sensitive she takes it to heart. Down at Chequers, when she's surrounded by old generals and politicians, she's OK, but she has no idea how to conduct herself with young people.

Yesterday I was sent down by I.N.S. to the Free French women's headquarters. Simonne Mathieu, the ex-tennis star, runs the place.

---

18 Sidney Bernstein (1899–1993), British media magnate, who at this time was married to Zoe Farmer, a *Daily Express* columnist.

19 Alan Deere (1917–95), New Zealand-born fighter pilot.

20 Named as Jerry Welsh in Kathy's private notes.

She's the first really human top woman in uniform I've met so far. I liked her a lot.

Incidentally I got the shock of my life yesterday. Brendan Bracken,[21] the P.M.'s parliamentary secretary, phoned asking me to lunch today. My one reaction was: what's happened to Averell, because that's obviously what he wanted to see me about. I was in a complete stew until Bill Batt of the embassy phoned to say that Ave's on his way home and should arrive sometime between Friday and Tuesday. Can't wait to see him. I can hardly remember what London's like with him here!

While in the process of writing this page, two good stories have materialized – tomorrow night I'm going to dinner with the WRNS (the women of the Navy). I've been angling around trying to get such an invitation for weeks and now that it's come through I'm thrilled. Dinner with girl Wrens without any battleaxe standing by to scare her – it ought to make good copy. Then Friday morning I'm going down to Wales with Quent – he's going to see about some factories – mostly women workers – for a movie, and has asked me to come along. Now I'm all set for stories for the next few days.

Last night I went on a party with Americans like the kind I know at home. Gee it was fun. It's the first time I've done that since I got here. After dinner I met most of the top U.S. plane people and had a wonderfully interesting time. It's evenings like last night that help round out the picture of what's really happening over here.

More time has elapsed. I'm in a wonderful mood – a member of the Churchill family died suddenly, an aunt, and Pam's gone out to Chequers for the funeral tomorrow. That doesn't mean I'm glad the dear woman died but we were going to a party this evening with Sarah Oliver[22] (she's the actress member of the P.M.'s family) and it's postponed, so I can pay bills, write a story and generally get caught

21 Brendan Bracken (1901–58), Irish-born businessman, politician, editor and proprieter of the *Financial Times* and other newspapers.
22 Sarah Oliver (1914–82), the Churchills' second daughter, married to the comedian and musician Vic Oliver, whom she divorced in 1945. During the war she had an affair with US ambassador John Winant.

up on sleeping. Even in the country I seldom turn my light out before 2 or 3.

Sarah is a terribly nice girl, but I don't think much of her husband Vic. He's Austrian and she's his third wife. They eloped a while back. Sarah seems desperately unhappy but she's got guts enough to stick with Vic on account of her father. Going on the stage is the one way she can keep from going mad.

They've got a divine little house in Bucks. Seeing it made me terribly envious. It's just what I'd like Petersfield Farm to look like.

I'm not complaining about our house, now that we've taken down two [cupboards] full of bric-a-brac, china, brass and blue plate it looks quite nice. But with a little money and time it could be a dream.

If and when and how I ever get married (I haven't had a serious proposal yet!) I think I'll make a very good housewife because I'm learning under stressed conditions. For one thing our servants think I'm crazy. When I say I don't want afternoon tea or that I want it with ice in it, they're completely dismayed and if I didn't have Pam to back me up, I don't think they'd stay. Our one-eyed cook is a marvel. Last weekend our house guests said the food was like prewar days!

Pam and her kid and nanny are registered in Dorking, and Ave and I at Jacksons here in town, where we have a standing weekly order for 2 duck and 2 chicken. Thanks to every maid in the Dorchester and both doormen on the watch out for a house parlor maid, the servant situation is well in hand.

My love to you all,
Kathleen

London
July 16, 1941

Dear Mary,

I can't bear to type. The noise literally hurts my ears. I filed 4 stories today – the record so far.

Ave got back last night [but] I didn't see him until late. I hadn't realized how worried I was about Ave's process of coming home until the P.M.'s private secretary phoned that he was at last arriving. Since Saturday I've been in suspense. Each day I'd phone my various sources of information and got conflicting reports. These days no names or places are mentioned over the telephone. One talks in circles about my "friend," "that port town you visited," etc. I'm beginning to wonder what it's like to be able to say what you think about people and things. Knowing "off the record stuff" makes me scared to open my mouth, particularly as I go around with so many different circles.

Yesterday I illegally horned in on a visit with those torpedoed American Red Cross nurses to 10 Downing St.[23] I was the only foreign press there. Unfortunately, the P.M. recognized me. I don't yet know if he realized I was there in my working capacity.

It was wonderful seeing those nurses. I picked out one in the bunch who looked young and bright. She turned out to be just my age. She, too, was thrilled to meet a young American. I had her and two friends back to lunch. They stayed until 5:00 p.m. It did my heart good watching them enjoy themselves. I got a terrific story and have them for life friends.

Even if my job isn't a success I'll be glad I came, just to be able to help girls like those nurses. Can you understand? They were lonely. I gave them a good lunch and sat around and chinned. I wonder which of us got the most out of it!

I'll be interested to see if I.N.S. uses my story. They, the nurses, are all very pro [US] escorting [British] ships. I got some swell quotes from them, and a rather bloody story of the torpedoing. It depressed me being with them, but I enjoy being made to feel small by Americans!

Pam was ill & as luck would have it, John Hallet was giving, at our suggestion, a dinner party for Little Mary Churchill. I had to go – English debs are very strictly chaperoned. An older girl even has to see them home.

I didn't want to go to the party but once we were at dinner I got into the happiest mood I've been for years. Last night I loved everyone in the world – except Jerry.[24] Perhaps it was the relief of knowing Ave was safe. Anyway, it was a wonderful feeling.

23 En route to do duty in Britain, the nurses were aboard the Dutch steamer *Maasdam*, which was sunk by a German U-boat in the mid-Atlantic in June 1941.
24 Slang term for Germans.

Mary had the time of her life – just she & four men. She goes out seldom, poor girl. It's nice to get her away from generals, ministers etc. for an evening.

Last week Dorothy Beatty took me down to the Wrens for dinner. I wrote a story about Vicky and Moffett – two Wren ratings we dined with. Meeting them filled me with humility. They were such wonderful girls, so poor and yet so happy. I gave them 2 American lipsticks. In return they've since sent me two bars of chocolate. Chocolate is the greatest luxury they have. When they have money to spare they buy it. This week they sent theirs to me. Sure, I was nice to them. I guess they loved meeting me as much as I loved meeting them. But I'm an American – that means a great deal over here these days. For that reason alone I'm God to those Wrens, to the American Red Cross nurses too. Do you wonder I wish we'd come into the war?

Down in the East End of London they likewise received me with open arms. It bothers me. I'm not used to being treated that way. Someday maybe I'll be able to write copy about just what it means in England today to be American.

I went down to Wales with Quent. His Dear Dr radio speech made him famous overnight. We arrived at the factory during lunch hour. They were having entertainment. He was asked to speak. He is the hero of every man in England. In that famous speech he told the English things about themselves that they want to hear but only a foreigner can tell them. 5,000 people wrote him in thanks. Among them was the P.M.

In that extemporaneous speech in the Wales balloon factory, Quent made those Welsh feel good. He's done a lot of good over here.

• • •

[Next section of the letter was typed:]
I wrote that late last night, I got your letter dated sometime in early July this morning. Thank God you told me none of my stories are coming out. I phoned Earl immediately and read him what you said. He's going to find out just what the situation is, because I'll be damned if I will stay with I.N.S. if they won't use my stuff. There's plenty else I

can do over here and much as I like the I.N.S. group, I think they'd understand if I packed up and left their office.

It makes me damned sore, so sore that I haven't done a lick of work since I read your letter, and I ain't going to. They've gotten somewhere between 20 and 30 stories in the past two months. I'm hoping to be able to dine with Ave tonight and I'll tell him. He went off at the crack of dawn this morning to meet Harry Hopkins.[25]

Please, this letter is strictly confidential but perhaps you would like to know what I think our New England diplomat[26] is like. I sat next to him at dinner last night. We discussed St. Paul's school, Bennington [College] and Foxcroft [school]. He's one of those people who stares at you all the time he's talking, his bushy eyebrows half cover his eyes.

I was particularly intrigued watching his hands. They're clenched almost all the time as though he's going through a critical mental crisis. His ideas remind me of a boy scout. He's worked in prisons. The type who sees no evil, hears no evil, speaks no evil. What a man! He's God to all who come into contact with him. Why? Because he's got a powerful attraction. You never know what's going on in his mind, he scares you and you respect him with a kind of reverence. Please don't misinterpret me. I didn't join his fold. He's built to be a saint. He's so intense that his mind moves slowly. I have seldom met someone so unspontaneous. Do you get the picture? He's a big mystery man. People like to worship mystery men.

As I said, I dined with them last night and Ave's just received word that I made a hit, which incidentally is most important, terribly important. That's why you mustn't repeat the above.

Quent and I pulled a boner yesterday. Ave was horrified, personally I thought it was funny. He, Quent and I were at a cocktail party – lots of celebrities, admirals and Wren officers who must be called ma'am. Our hostess grabbed me by the arm and took me over to an extremely beautiful lady who was talking to Quent. I was introduced, but her name never was introduced. She talked about my work, a

25 Harry Hopkins (1890–1946), confidant and personal representative of President Roosevelt.
26 Ambassador Winant.

rather monotonous subject, and the Wrens. I found her a little dreary so I got up and left Quent to tackle her. God damned if it wasn't the Duchess of Kent.

I'm off now to the country.

Love to all,

Puff

Chequers, Aylesbury, Bucks
July 19, 1941

Dear Mary,

Each time I come here I realize more and more how lucky I am. Outside of Pam, who's one of the family and therefore doesn't count as a guest, I'm the only woman who gets down here on weekends. Call it thanks to Ave and a great deal of luck.

We came down on Friday. Harry H[opkins] is here. He's in the best of spirits. Full of fun. He's the only man I've seen so far with the P.M. who can say anything he wants to and get away with it. Quite a different Harry, I gather, from the one in the White House! Everyone loves him over here. He's quite in his element.

A weekend here is very different from anywhere else. Never for a moment is the war forgotten. Conferences all the time – secretaries running around – notes being passed around. Important people coming and going. Women are rather in the way. They leave right after dinner, and then aren't expected to stay for too long when the men come out of the dining room, which sometimes isn't until way after midnight.

On Friday the excitement of the moment was Brendan Bracken's acceptance of the Ministry of Information. Duff Cooper's being kicked out. Brendan was the P.M.'s Parliamentary Private Secretary. He likes to think himself the glamour boy of the West End, though so far no one's consented to marry him. Very pompous, wonderful dry sense of humor, has a head of hair like Harpo Marx, only Brendan's is real. I like him, he's a lot of fun, but the American press don't. He's too pompous for them, won't treat them as equals. I don't envy him in his new job. No one these days wants anything to do with the MOI (they handle censorship).

General Ismay[27] was also down here. He's the P.M.'s military adviser, a good polo player in his day. He's absolute heaven. Nicknamed Pug. That's what he looks like. I used to like Brendan the better of the two, but Ismay can't be beat.

Then there's the Prof – Professor Lindemann, recently made Lord Cherwell. He's a scientist who's invented most of the "gadgets" now used by the R.A.F. Personally I find him a bore. He's got no personality at all and hides his genius behind a rather inane smile. He's the kind of man who would make a pass at you if he ever got the opportunity.

These three are the regulars at Chequers.

Tonight my favorite R.A.F. man was here – Peirse – the C-in-C bomber command. I was hoping Sholto Douglas, the corresponding man in fighter command would be here too, but he didn't arrive. I want to legally get into the operations room of a night fighter station, so I can do a story. Douglas, who looks like Goering, is very much of a woman chaser. All I wanted was to sit next to him one night at dinner! There are many advantages, you see, in being a girl reporter! Seldom these days do I go out with anyone I can't get something out of. Perhaps that sounds a little mercenary, but you have to be, a little.

Clemmie is an ardent croquet player, so I've been doing a lot of that this weekend, and oddly enough the P.M. loves the single-jumping game of Chinese Checkers. He was in a very jovial mood, Friday night, and took me on for one game. I beat him, which made me go up no end in his estimation. Today I sat next to him at lunch, which was nice because usually admirals and whatnots get the place of honor.

Tonight we had *Citizen Kane* for a movie. It was a violent flop.[28]

Back in London now [Monday, July 21]. I stayed down in Chequers last night so I could horn in on a bomber show this morning for Harry.

---

27 General Hastings Lionel Ismay (1887–1965), Churchill's chief military adviser and NATO's first secretary general. He wrote a number of letters to Kathy during the war but did not mention her in his memoirs.

28 John Colville, Churchill's private secretary, recorded in his diary, 'after dinner we had a deplorable American film, *Citizen Kane*. The P.M. was so bored he walked out before the end. Kathleen Harriman thought it was wonderful and said all Americans did. The fact that we did not, revealed to her much about English people. I replied that the fact Americans did, revealed to me nothing about Americans.'

I missed a party for the American correspondents which I should have gone to on principle, but compared to what I saw instead [it] was rather insignificant.

Five of the biggest bombers all lined up for inspection. I went in all of them and crawled around. It was quite thrilling. Then they showed off. Flying by us just a few feet off the ground. It reminded me of a horse show. On looks alone the Flying Fortress has the rest beat.[29] It's the thoroughbred horse of the lot. The best all-around bomber, English, looks like the Hackney stallion.

I found one of my American test pilot friends there and he told me all the ins and outs. Then I asked the same questions to one of the pilots. Oddly enough they agreed on most scores. Unfortunately, I can't write about any of it, partly because it's secret but mostly because the P.M. asked me along as Ave's daughter, not as a journalist.

I arrived back here and found 3 letters from home – three at a time is pretty exciting!

Another letter disclosed the fact that I'm being given a black poodle puppy called Alabam. I fell in love with it some weeks ago and I guess his master took a fancy to me. The master is off to Russia within the next week so I get the dog!

With Ave back life is more hectic than ever. Tonight is his one free evening so we're going to Petersfield Farm. I can't wait for him to see it!

Lots of love to all,

Kathleen

PS How big are you?

PSS Harry Hopkins came over here with some story about me & Bill Batt being engaged. Unfortunately, you don't know Bill – so you can't appreciate how funny it is!

Dorchester Hotel, London
July 22, 1941

Dear Mouche,

Pam and I took Averell out to the cottage last night. We didn't get there until about 9:30 but it was still light enough to have a short ride

---

29 Boeing's B-17 bomber, so called because it was heavily armed.

before dinner. It makes all the difference in the world having a home to go to over here. Ave loved the place as much as I do, which is nice. He's refused an invitation to Chequers this weekend so's he can go down there again.

The days go so rapidly, it's hard to know what I've done when. On Friday I'm training to Gloucester to see an R.A.F. training center, as they are much the most interesting service. I'm going to try to see all sides of it. Unfortunately it's also the hardest to get to – the operations headquarters are very hush-hush. Whereas friends can get me anywhere, it's another thing to be able to write them up. Tomorrow I have to interview someone long distance to Dublin, special request from Albany. I'm quite terrified.

Red Mueller has unofficially become my editor, so I'm at last beginning to learn this racket. I send him my stories, he edits them and sends them back, then finally they get to C.A. Smith, I.N.S. bureau chief[30] – a rather unimaginative soul, who everyone else in the office dislikes. So far we've hit it off alright.

This morning I took my beautiful black son Alabam around the place – introduced him to the chickens, the goats and the horses.

I can't remember when I started this letter, sometime last week I guess – Averell leaves tomorrow [July 30]. If possible I'm going to fly up to Scotland to see him off, because I've seen hardly anything of him at all.

I'm going to enclose a series of light wants for Averell to bring back with him. I don't think I'll be home in the near future. When I leave I leave for good, and as I have no intention of doing that I guess I stay put.

I would like my brown fur coat & hat. Please can you insure it and send it over with my light blue flannel tea gown as soon as possible.

I may write some more news later on but I now have to work.

Best love,

Kathleen

• • •

I've lost my list of light wants for Averell to bring back – so here goes on a new one:

---

30 Charles A. Smith (1902–71).

Nail Polish Revlon

1 bottle shell

1 bottle Lancer

2 bottles mahogany

1 bottle Resinol (for baby Winston)

4 dressing table combs – the ordinary black ones

My navy, black & brown suede gloves

6 fine % & 10 cent store hair nets

Soothing cream for the face

Bobby pins – you can't buy them anywhere

Couple of packages light hair pins (for red hair)

Small jar of Arjay perfume

2 silk night gowns – no lace – 2 sets of slips & pants (for Pam)

1 dozen 9½ nylon stockings

2 white silk long-sleeved sports blouses – size 14

3 thin mesh girdles

1 size 34 for Pam

2 size 36 for me – maybe that's the wrong size but I like mine at least one size larger than they say I should have

6 lipsticks – same color as the enclosed one – any make will do

2 big bottles (jars?) of Barbisol 9 in 1 (not for me, for the Beaver)

6 pair size 10½ fine silk stockings – Mrs Eden

You can't do business with Hitler & any other new good book that isn't published over here.

Some hairnets that I can wear in bed

Stockings & lipsticks are always wanted. They make the best gifts & neither are buyable over here. My own supply is sufficient at the moment.

• • •

I wish I could be coming home with Averell but that is impossible even for him to work.

Bestest love,

Kathleen

PS I'd love some chewing gum – guess Dentyne takes up least room.

CHAPTER 3

'IMAGINE WALKING UP TO A GUY AND SHAKING HANDS WITH A FINGERLESS STUMP'

Averell's trip home turned out to be more interesting than he could possibly have imagined. In August 1941, Churchill steamed into Placentia Bay, Newfoundland, aboard the battleship *Prince of Wales*, where he met Roosevelt for their first wartime summit. Averell had not been invited to the meeting but the unexpected presence of a senior British civil servant prompted Roosevelt to bring him along, too. During the talks, Averell played his usual role of liaising and mediating between Churchill and Roosevelt but this time it was up close and personal. The upshot was a communiqué that became known as the Atlantic Charter, which pledged Britain and the United States to work for a world free of want and fear, for disarmament and the right to self-determination for all people as well as free trade and freedom of the seas.

'The P.M. has been in his best form,' Averell wrote to Pam and Kathy. 'The President is intrigued and likes him enormously.' Promising to give them all the details upon his return, he concluded, 'I miss London & you both tremendously. I hope life won't be quite as hectic when I get back and I long to be with you at the cottage again. It was great fun. With much love to you both. Affectionately, Averell.'

After what Kathy called the 'Atlantic picnic,' Averell was deputed, together with Lord Beaverbrook, to go to Moscow to discuss supplies issues with Soviet dictator Joseph Stalin. This conference (29 September –1 October 1941), which agreed a schedule of Western aid for the embattled Soviets, was the first of several high-level Anglo-Soviet-American wartime summits that Averell attended.

London
July 29, 1941

Dear Mary,

I had a rather hectic weekend in the country. I motored out on Friday late – Averell, Pam, Harry and Brendan Bracken (the new Minister of Information) were there, arguing about propaganda in the States. Brendan has offered me a job in the ministry, which I'm not going to take – I like what I'm doing too much and it may be more valuable.

I should be working now – writing a story about the burned pilots. I went down to their plastic surgery hospital in East Grinstead on Saturday and spent the day with them. I expected to be horror-struck and depressed. God knows I was.

Imagine walking up to a guy and shaking hands with a fingerless stump. Badly burned fingers curl under and then grow together. After a while they can be operated on and separated. If the operation is successful, they go back into the air force. I know one guy who has already – his hands are OK – his face isn't. He still has to have a new set of false eyelids grafted on.

It's not easy talking to an earless, eyelidless boy of about 21, who also had very little nose structure left. You can't let him realize what you feel. While I was at the hospital I was alright, but I still haven't completely recovered.

On Sunday I was hoping to have a day of rest. We did have time to have a short ride. Ave showed Pam & me how to school one of the ponies, which was fun, but then he got called over to Chequers so I went with him.

We had hoped to get home for dinner but we stayed there to take Harry to the train (he went to Russia). Dorothy Thompson[1]

1 Dorothy Thompson (1893–1961), famous American journalist and broadcaster.

came down for dinner. She tried hard to outtalk the P.M. Thank God she got beat!

What a conceited ass! You might think she was God interpreting the will of the people. Perhaps you gather I wasn't sold on her.

We are desperate – our maid is joining the W.A.A.F.s!

I can't remember if I told you about Alabam or not. He's my poodle puppy – black – given me by a disreputable friend of Pam's who is an intelligence officer in the nearby night fighter station. He's gone to Russia and has given me the dog. Alabam is divine. Has more guts than any puppy I've come across yet. He almost drowned the other day – dove in after the goldfish, Pam's nanny got him out just in time.

Poor Pam is in a state – because Ave teased her about introducing me to such a suspicious character – John Hallett[2] by name – married twice – couldn't be more fun to be with – but I must say I wouldn't trust him around the corner. He's one of those people with a fatal charm as far as women are concerned & Pam's convinced I'm going to fall for him – which makes me laugh. My main interest is his story value. So far I've gotten 2 from him – one on the plastic surgery, another on radio location W.A.A.F.s.

Before I forget, I wrote a story about mobile canteens. They stand up under everything but a direct hit. The more sent over the better. Everything [quadruple underline] that comes over is appreciated more than you can possibly imagine. I certainly ought to know. I get thanked right & left for everything from mobile canteens to babies' layettes!

Goodbye now,

Kathy

PS I can't remember what it sounds like to be called Puff!

---

2 Wing Commander John Prescott Hallett, a well-connected London businessman and socialite before the war, described by Kathy in her private notes as a 'famous crook' and an 'amazing guy'. He later served in India, where he was caught selling land in Japanese-occupied Burma that didn't belong to him. Arrested, court-martialled and sentenced to twelve years in prison, he reportedly commented, 'I'm just sorry that I didn't have more time to spend the money.'

Petersfield Farm, Surrey
August 8, 1941

Dear Mary,

Combine the war & journalism and you'll never have a moment of boredom. This week by way of work I went to a settlement house, interviewed an American W.A.A.F., visited Bebe Daniels, Ben Lyon[3] and Vic Oliver while they were filming a movie, interviewed the man who started the V campaign & got myself 20 gallons [of] supplementary petrol.[4] Life is always varied. Pam and I are down here at Petersfield Farm alone tonight. It's nice to have quiet now and then. We went for a long walk this afternoon. It was raining as usual and now I should be working. As usual I'm putting that off until tomorrow – when Red and Quent arrive. Frankly I don't know what I'd do without Red. He's the only guy in the I.N.S. office who takes the trouble to really edit my work and show me the tricks.

Last week, believe it or not, I wrote a story all the office seemed to like – on the plastic surgery hospital. Actually, it's the best job I've done but I had a good subject.

I loved your last letter about America coming into the war to save the English. When will they understand that it's their own skins, not the English ones that they'll have to save?

Last Monday I filled the car up with paraffin instead of petrol and it refused to run until all sorts of important people had thoroughly dirtied themselves up for at least an hour. Even then it ran badly.

Tony Biddle[5] got me my interview with the V campaign man. He was very nice – a Belgian called Laveleye[6] – middle-aged and very kind looking. We had a nice chat, me trying to act efficient & like a reporter. I wished the hell I'd learned shorthand!

---

3 Bebe Daniels and Ben Lyon were husband-and-wife American film stars. During the war, both worked for the BBC, starring in the radio show *Hi Gang* alongside Vic Oliver, Sarah Churchill's husband.

4 'V for Victory' was a pro-allied propaganda campaign promoted by the BBC.

5 Anthony Joseph Drexel Biddle (1897–1961), American diplomat who was US ambassador to exiled governments in London during the war.

6 Victor Laveleye (1894–1945), liberal politician who called upon Belgians to use 'V for Victory' as a sign of resistance to German occupation.

Just arrived from the country and found a nice new letter from Mouche. Hearing from Helen and her FFF [Fight for Freedom] spurs me on to write, so please show her this.

Number one, the people of England are not fighting this war for any high-sounding ideal. By the people I mean the little man in the services, the little W.A.A.F. or Wren, not Winston Churchill. They are fighting for their country and that's all the Americans will ever fight for – their culture, their flag or whatever you want call it.

The main reason behind my going to the various camps, recruiting offices etc., is to find out why the women join up when as yet it isn't compulsory. It's always for some simple personal reason – a husband, a lover is in the air force so the girl joins the W.A.A.F.s. She'll be helping him. Perhaps she hates her job. She joins up. It's her means of escape. The glamour of the services, being with the men with the chance of getting married. That's why the English girl goes to war. She's not interested in any high-sounding principle or theory of democracy.

Our surly house parlor maid is another example. She joined up because of local opinion down at the local pub.

Last Thursday I went down to the Eagle Squadron. I asked a couple of the Americans why they came over. No one had a profound reason for wanting to fight in the R.A.F. They came without thinking much about it, just as I did.

I've told you about the night fighter boys I've met and how they take the war as a game. They don't think about killing the Germans, few even bother to try and hate them as individuals. They don't think at all – they just go up and fly. If they are lucky they shoot a few huns down and get a decoration. That means they'll be more popular with the girls.

I wonder if I'm getting my point across – going to war is a very simple personal affair. Those who do the less thinking about it, and of their chances of survival, make the best fighters. I'm damned sure no one thinks about ideals. The government declared war – the English people had confidence in their government so they followed them into battle.

It rained all weekend and today too. I stayed over to write my interview with Colonel Britton[7] and the story of the movie business in wartime and then came right to town. I was hoping to be able to ride but it was raining too damned hard.

Red and Quent came down Saturday, both in a towering rage. Quent got illegally scooped by Dorothy Thompson. He was all set to leave England and I gather went so far as to resign from *Collier's*. Red is about to quit I.N.S., that is if he doesn't get fired before he has a chance to resign. They both acted like two righteous little schoolboys with hurt feelings. They left on Sunday afternoon.

I'd like it if you could find out who told W. Winchell the lemon story – those were my own lemons – the ones I brought with me from Lisbon. God damn people for misinterpreting it – everyone over here thought it was funny – my keeping two of them to rinse my hair.[8]

Please send me a picture of you getting fat.

My love to you all,

Kathleen

Petersfield Farm, Surrey
August 15, 1941

Dear Mary,

I hope you meet Lord Beaverbrook while he's in the States. He's a fascinating old gentleman who at first I found exceedingly terrifying. I wonder how Marie will get on with him.

Another week has flown – saw a preview of Quent's Russian picture. It's called *A Day in Soviet Russia*. He does the commentary. I thought it excellent – even he seems pleased.

One thing C.A. (my boss) had to say was I'm going to be put on spot news occasionally, which is just what I want. At the moment I'm working on a series of features on American-born women, what

---

7 Colonel Britton was the pseudonym of Douglas Ritchie (1905–67), a BBC news editor who broadcast to Nazi-occupied Europe.

8 A reference to US newspaper reports that Kathy had brought with her half a dozen lemons – scarce in wartime Britain – and had used them to rinse her hair.

they're doing in this war. Rather boring, I call it. I just finished one on Lady Astor.

Geoffrey Patterson came to town on leave last night, so I was out until all hours. Like most people, he's about dying with boredom with his war job. At the moment he's stationed at Bristol. He ranted on for hours on the horrors of provincial England, so I guess it must be pretty bad.

We met Bebe Daniels and Ben Lyon and now I have some fresh fish for the weekend. A group of fishermen down at Blackpool send the Lyons a "bass" of fish each week – in appreciation for their broadcast. I'm being given some of it this week, which is nice.

On Wednesday I had my first non-restaurant meal since I arrived. The Strathallans[9] still keep their house going, at least a small part of it, and I dined there. It was very pleasant. He works in the Min. of Supply and at the moment on supplies to Russia. He says their efficiency is unbelievable. They get ships docked, unloaded, and refueled in a minimum of time – much less than the English dockers take.

This weekend we have an assorted group – the editor of the *Express* for the whole weekend. Quent maybe, Bill Batt maybe, a wonderful trade union man called Bill Brown and Pam's sister-in-law and husband. He's some kind of minister or something. It will probably continue to rain as it has been the last week. I'm getting sick of being perpetually damp!

[Kathleen]

London
August 23, 1941

Dear Mary,

We've moved from our horrible dirty tan Italian-furnitured suite. I'm in bed now surveying my beautiful blue and glass bedroom. It's almost lovely. I hope Averell won't mind but I got so's I thought I'd go crazy if I spent another day writing in those dreary surroundings. We

9 Averell Harriman's cousin Nancy Seymour Finke was married to the Scottish peer Viscount Strathallan. Nancy was very active in support of the British war effort.

now have a fireplace and a really comfortable sofa. The first floor overlooking the park. That means a possibility of some light for breakfast rather than electric lights!

Between Averell and Harry we collected a goodly amount of loot from the Atlantic picnic. The oranges were the best. My God it's wonderful having oranges for breakfast again!

Went on a trip the middle of last week to see the A.T.S. and the army girls learn the ins and outs of anti-aircraft gunnery. The girls handle the three instruments and the men the guns. As usual I got depressed seeing how easily the women took to camp life, barracks, saluting etc., but I came home and wrote a story by my usual formula. The best part of the excursion was staying with the commanding officer and family. I'd anticipated a dreary evening. He met me at the station and took me out to his own home. He's got an invalided wife and sailor boy and three refugees and no electricity. They were very nice to me and I fed them with American talk and Camel cigarettes. I think they quite liked it!

Almost resigned from I.N.S. again last week. They cabled a story on Lady Astor when I should have had it returned to me first for her approval. Unfortunately, I couldn't blame anyone.

I got initiated into a new form of English life this weekend. We got ditched by Bob Montgomery[10] who was at sea and we had 2 cavalry majors and a Coldstream Guardsman instead. Army-army-army – that's all I heard about. My God they're certainly rabid about their profession. I learned a lot too. One of the majors was an ex-beau of Pam's – married and without doubt the best-looking man I've ever seen. Unfortunately, God forgot about giving him much brains.

Tonight we had dinner with General Ismay and family and Randolph's boss in the Middle East and some other people whose names as usual I've quickly forgotten. I sat between the general and the colonel. The former was delightful, started in conversation by telling me a dirty story. The colonel talked about food we were eating and the food we couldn't eat. I found him deathly boring!

---

10 Hollywood actor, serving in the naval attaché's office in the US embassy.

Incidentally, I've picked up some new friends, or at least they've picked me up. American Army Air Corps boys. I dined with 2 one night last week and then had another 2 at lunch the next day. It's wonderful meeting unadulterated unsophistication these days! One I think can be cultivated by Churchill–Harriman Inc!

My love to you all,
Kathleen

Dorchester Hotel, London
August 27, 1941

Mouche dear,

I can hardly believe that September's already here – or nearly so. When Tex McCrary[11] told me that I'd still be here in September, I didn't believe him. Now I can't picture myself coming home.

Spent a delightful evening. We had about 10 or so people in for cocktails at 6 this afternoon and they didn't leave until 9. After that Pam & I had a quiet dinner together and sat talking.

You all must get rather sick with [my writing] about how much I'm enjoying life over here, but I really can't think when the "pure joy of living" feeling has lasted so long. Pam has it too. I guess that's one reason we get on so well – but so far neither of us have produced a friend that the other hasn't liked.

I don't think I've met so many people or gone out with so many types. It makes me rather annoyed but I can't get up any enthusiasm about any of them.

Tonight the head of the A.T.S. – Mrs Jean Knox – who's the equivalent of a major general – came in to cocktails. She's got more personality, charm, and understanding of her fellow women than anyone I expect I'll ever meet. She's head of 60,000 A.T.S.'s & still retains all womanly qualities. She kept all our guests absolutely spellbound.

Pam & I have cultivated a new friend – one Bob Riskin – Hollywood scenario writer of *Mr Deeds Goes to Washington*, *Mr Smith to Washington*, *Meet John Doe* etc. He's come over & offered his services

11 Tex McCrary (1910–2003), American journalist and PR consultant who served in the US Air Force during the war.

gratis to the Min. of Information for U.S. propaganda purposes. I think he's swell.

I hear periodically from Marie-André.[12] He first wrote he hated it up at the camp, so I found out from Tony Biddle that with a little wangling he could transfer to the Free French Forces. I told André that but he's decided that he'll stick it. I'm hoping that he'll be down on leave soon.

I got sleepy last night in the middle of your letter and now that it's morning I figure that typing is easier.

This morning was the usual routine in my reporting education – diplomatic and military conferences at the Ministry of Information and as usual nothing much was said.

This afternoon I have to cover a French press conf. alone. I'm quite terrified, usually I have a stooge to tell me what's important. With luck Pam and I are going to the country tonight. I want to do a series of stories on food distribution in country villages and I figure the country around us is as good as any. It will be nice to get out to the country alone – that is, minus house guests.

One of the men who went to the Middle East with Ave and a delightful Air Corps col. are coming down on Saturday. They complained to me the other day that they didn't like English week-ends, so Pam and I decided to change their point of view!

I never did get round to finishing this letter. I'm in the country now and about to write a story about the one egg per week ration.

[Kathleen]

Petersfield Farm, Surrey
August 29, 1941

[Dear Mouche,]

The war hit us today – the first time it's hit since I arrived.

It started out as such a nice day too – a nice quiet Friday. The sun was shining for the first time in almost weeks. We took the horses down to be shod, went for a walk and then saw an amusing movie in

12 Marie-André Poniatowski, the son of André Poniatowski, who was married to Kathy's aunt Frances Lawrance.

Dorking. We were in the best of spirits – even the planes coming back from France seemed remote and unwarlike.

We got home and found a message – "Wing Co. Gillan is missing."[13] He was shot down over France this morning and none of his squadron knew if he landed or not. Somehow I can't quite picture him being a prisoner, wondering about escape, and I'm sure he never thought of the possibility. Perhaps because he was older and more experienced than most pilots, he seemed more confident and a great deal more arrogant. He was the one who talked about the "impudence" of the Germans shooting at him.

It seems hard to believe he won't be coming over here anymore. It's all rather depressing – five instead of six for lunch on Sunday – I suppose that's one way of looking at it.

My love to you all,
Kathleen

---

13 John Woodburn Gillan (1907–41). In her engagements book Kathy wrote, "Gillo missing – Pam & I both depressed."

CHAPTER 4

'MY GOD, THE BRITISH PRESS ARE SKUNKS'

As Ave's host and companion, Kathy was a huge political and social asset, but first and foremost she was a war correspondent. Unlike her better-known female contemporaries, such as Lee Miller, Helen Kirkpatrick and Martha Gellhorn, she never worked in combat zones, but as an INS journalist she witnessed air raids, visited bombed cities and munitions factories, toured military bases, interviewed allied leaders and wrote stories about daily life on Britain's home front.

Kathy's first big reporting assignment was a wounded prisoners' exchange between Britain and Germany in October 1941. 'During the past four days I've learned more about reporting than my four months in London taught me,' she wrote to Mary. Unfortunately for the POWs, the deal fell through when the Germans reneged on previously agreed terms of the exchange. Kathy wrote several stories about this episode, the headline above her closing report being 'War Prisoner Swap Plan Is Scuttled'.

Petersfield Farm, Surrey
September 4, 1941

Dear Mary,

Pam's down making speeches in her husband's constituency and gets back tomorrow.

On Monday I got good story material on the women's section of the A.T.A. [Air Transport Auxiliary] – ferry pilots, and also ran into

Wendy Sale-Barker.[1] She's one of the original 8 ferry port pilots and we had a nice talk about skiing etc., sitting in the sunshine on the airfield terrace. I spent the morning writing the story and have just sent it off to the censors.

Elliott[2] Roosevelt has left London, much to all American joy. He behaved disgracefully, got drunk with Piccadilly tarts every night and got his picture on the front page of the papers for one escapade. He's supposedly over here on a secret diplomatic mission and even though he wasn't he should have behaved better, being in uniform. Sometime I'd like to write a story about some of the fools that get sent over here. They all need a good talking to.

[Kathleen]

London
September 15, 1941

Dear Marie,

This has been an exciting day!

Averell got in this afternoon [from a trip to the United States] and I went down to meet him. He got quite a reception at the airport. He and Harry are considered England's best friends and the English aren't very backward in showing their appreciation!

The letters Averell brought depressed me rather. Living over here, closer to the war, it's hard to understand how intelligent thinking people believe that we can do business with Hitler. It must be hell for you.

As usually, Averell rushed off to a conf. the moment he arrived and I was left here to undo all my wonderful [parcels] and to cope with the press. For the most part, they're a terrible species of humanity.

Averell had a dinner date at No. 10 and with his typical thoughtfulness, the P.M. invited me too. He realized I'd like to see Averell his first night back. It was a wonderful dinner – just the four of us.

---

1 Audrey Florice Durell "Wendy" Drummond Sale-Barker (1903–94), British skiing champion.
2 FDR's son Elliott (1910–90) served in the US Army Air Forces and flew more than three hundred combat missions.

I'm beginning to be able to treat the P.M. as a human being – he's so human that it's hard not to.

Sorry, I got waylaid & had to do a story. It's Tuesday now and I have a few minutes before I embark on my first radio broadcast. It's a B.B.C. propaganda program to the continent – in English – I'm talking informally: my impressions of England – what impresses me most – what I expected to find as compared to what I found etc. I imagine it will take about 5 or so minutes. When the time comes I'll probably be terrified – for the moment I haven't started to worry. On Friday morning I'm speaking for the Min. of Food on their kitchen front program.

It's hard refusing these requests, particularly as the Food people have taken lots of trouble in getting me story background data. It all comes under the heading of experience anyway.

My love to you all,

Kathy

London
September 16, 1941

Dear Mary,

That's the most divine nightie I've ever owned – really it is. Pam thinks it's respectable enough for an evening dress!

Tonight we dined with the Beaver and Captain Margesson (Secretary of State for War) and I got so's I thought I'd scream if I heard the words tanks or Russia mentioned again.

I enjoyed watching Ave and Max fight. David Margesson acted as referee and he did it admirably. As a sidelight I'm learning a lot about the relative values of M3s and Mark 3s. Not that I think it will ever do me any good!

Lord Beaverbrook doesn't like being contradicted and he's inclined to be set in his ways and views about people. It's fun watching him at work.

Dinner tonight was a rather sharp contrast with last night – with the P.M. – one's a gentleman and the other is a ruffian. Ave luckily can talk both languages.

In the way of my own affairs, I was guest speaker on B.B.C.'s "London to the Continent" program this evening. For some reason I thought speaking over the radio would be terrifying. Without having time to think much about it, I anticipated being exceedingly nervous when the actual moment to go on air arrived. I even tried to be – but couldn't. It couldn't be easier. I'm doing it again on Friday for the Ministry of Food.

It's Thursday now and I got a minute which I hope'll be enough to finish this. I don't know why, but life always seems more hectic when Averell's around – not that it's got anything to do with him, but I seem to have been running around in circles all week.

This morning I interviewed one of Averell's mission people – the head of the Red Cross man, filed the story and then went out and had my pictures taken in the streets, talking to demolition men etc., for I.N.S. That put me in a thoroughly lousy humor as I spend my time avoiding reporters and photographers, but I.N.S. was adamant that I have this series done. Then I came home and finished tomorrow's broadcast. It's mostly blah blah, patting the English housewife on the back. I think extremely boring but it's what the ministry wants and being a foreigner, I can say it better than an English person.

That accomplished I lunched with Zoe Bernstein. We're doing a profile for the *New Yorker* on Mrs Jean Knox – the head of the A.T.S. (that's not to be repeated because I don't think I.N.S. would approve if they knew!), and now I'm back home waiting for my script to be passed so as I can take it down to the B.B.C. to see if it's the right length. After that I come home and try to write up some of my back stuff – mostly boring: Lady Halifax[3] and what she thinks about Amer. Women, war relief and flying across the N. Atlantic in a bomber; Mrs Churchill opening a British restaurant; Food Advice Centers. The two latter left over from last week! So you see I'm rather behind times.

I.N.S. wants me to write weekly column – London letter or something – however I don't think I'll do it. Not for the present anyway. My salary finances are all fixed up, which pleases me no end – because now I can have fun deciding what I can do with it.

---

3 Lady Halifax (1885–1976) was the wife of Lord Halifax, the British ambassador to the United States.

I have to go now. Please send that picture of yourself & I'll see about the knitting book.

Best love to you,

Puff

Petersfield Farm, Surrey
September 24, 1941

Mouche dear,

The coat in its case is a godsend now that I have to carry my reporting equipment + everything else.

The clothes & the stockings & FUR COAT are wonderful. The underwear all fits & Pam thanks you very much for her share & the lipsticks. It must have been hell trying to get so many stockings in one fell swoop – we both needed them badly. I was much too generous when I first came over here!

It depresses me rather to think of Arden being closed up but I approve of the move.[4] It's about the best way the family has of showing what they think of the war.

The letters Averell brought me were also terribly depressing. I can hardly believe that Eugene[5] is the only anti-isolationist in the Pool family. Thank God I'm not home now – to be frustrated & discouraged as Helen appears to be.

I started this over the weekend – but as usual something happened to keep it from getting finished. Everything is quieting down again and the Moscow mission got off to the maximum of noise about secrecy and the minimum results.[6]

It makes me laugh. They were very particular about making very loud lies about where they'd be for the next few days, but somehow 14 Americans checking out of the Dorchester Hotel all in one day gives away anything they might want to cover up!

---

4 The Harriman family estate, located fifty miles north-west of New York City.
5 Eugene Pool (1874–1949), second husband of Kathy's late mother Kitty.
6 The Beaverbrook–Harriman mission to Moscow to discuss supplies issues with Stalin.

The weekend consisted of motoring back and forth from town. We had two nights down there though, which was an almost inconceivable stroke of luck. Capt. Margesson, the War Minister, came down Saturday, so he and Averell talked more about tanks and production. Then finally after dinner they stopped and Ave got going on the subject of Max in Washington (Lord Beaverbrook) which is one of the funniest stories I've ever heard.

No one seems too encouraging on the subject of my ever being [able] to come home – that is, I can come home but then I wouldn't be able to get back over here. The State Department still takes a very dim view of my getting here in the first place.

The blackout gets longer and longer – starts while dressing for dinner and it's almost impossible to get a cab late in the evening, except at the bottle clubs (the ones that keep going after midnight), but I'm getting rather used to walking in the black!

Last night I was out with our navy and a member of your navy. We went to Quaglino's and danced Viennese waltzes![7] I must say the Navy, which included Bob Montgomery (Lt. Commander) produces the best dancers in London at the moment but that's actually about all I can say in their favor!

Repercussions of my talk on the Kitchen Front program last Friday are still coming in. Perry Brownlow[8] said I made him feel maternal of all things. Some stranger from Oxford suggests that I should practice next month on the Yale football team: "I think yours was the subtlest & most effective pep talk I have ever heard!" The Dorchester lift man got the biggest kick of all – he hopes I'll have to get up at 7:30 again!

Sorry, I again got waylaid – this time to have a suit fitted. It's a divine grosgrain black suit with a matching light blue blouse and hat. My one winter extravagance. As a matter of fact it wasn't very expensive – a hundred dollars plus, I guess, a large purchase tax.

Do you all appreciate what a hellova job [Ave's] doing? I've finally decided that he ought to be triplets, one for Washington, one for

7 Dinner-dance restaurant frequented by British aristocrats and royalty.
8 Peregrine Francis Adelbert Cust, 6th Baron Brownlow (1899–1978), British aristocrat who was Beaverbrook's parliamentary secretary 1940–1.

London, a third for Moscow. That of course leaves out the Middle East – "Averell's war" as it's known in Washington, but we'll chance it and hope that [it] can take care of itself (which it can't!).

I don't know where Averell learned to become such a good diplomat, but he's the best I've come across and he's got everyone over here under his little finger. (They don't know it. That's where he's clever.)

This letter has been lying around for ages – so I think now I'll send it off.

My best love to you all,
Kathleen

London
September 30, 1941

Dear Mary,

I ain't heard from nobody for the last few weeks, but I guess that means you're alright.

Averell took Quent along with him to do some work for him, propaganda on religion and religious freedom in Russia. I gather the U.S. has to be sold on that score. I don't know if that little bit of information is for circulation or not. Quent was rather indiscreet about his leaving and so far I haven't dared ask any of the press if they know what he's going to do. Every outfit is trying to get a man to Moscow and so far no one's succeeded. I imagine Quent will stay there after Ave's through with him.

Today I wrote two not too good stories trying to sell [the] U.S. on helping British prisoners of war in Germany. I feel now that if I see one more letter from an Oflag or a Stalag, I'll scream. They're all much alike and rather depressing. The gal who runs the outfit is prehistoric in her dress, and ideas as well. She's a mild saint and I guess she's doing a good job.

Today I lunched at the Biddles[9] – in honor of Lady Limerick, head of the Brit. Red Cross. She's about to leave for [the] U.S. and some of

9 Ambassador Biddle's wife Margaret (née Thompson, 1897–1956) was very active in relation to women's organisations during the war.

the boys were giving her an idea of what was in store for her. One guy would fire a question and another would answer as she should – an amusing version of "how to cope with the American press."

This afternoon I covered Malcolm MacDonald's[10] press conf. He's High Commissioner of Canada, Ramsay's son and a hellova pompous ass. Rather too young to be pompous, too.

Next time you see dear Dr Knox please tell him that a certain Mr Leatherman's much impressed by his work. One doesn't call London dentists Dr.

Talked to Mr Allen the head of the Amer. Red Cross today and he seems to think that I might do some work for them, other than writing. I'm going to look into it, because one can never be too busy. I'm not really happy unless I have much too much to do. Feature writing is rather spasmodic, whole days can go by without any pouncable prospects, and I feel strongly about being over here and not at least trying to be productive pretty nearly every minute of daylight time. My one hard and fast rule is no social lunches. Don't laugh but it could be very easy to get into a Quent-like rut and lunch from one 'til four just because one didn't have anything really pressing to do.

Incidentally, through my work, I've developed some very nice lady friends. Mary Welsh[11] of *Life* I love, she's much the most human American girl over here. Helen Kirkpatrick[12] I never see other than in the evening. She's more of a man's, particularly a reporter's, type of woman anyway. God knows why: she certainly has no secret sex appeal! I find her a little too sarcastic, but fun in small doses.

The latest additions are Mrs Dunderdale of BWR (British War Relief) and one Lady Chesham, a fortyish American woman. I interviewed her one day and have been seeing her off and on ever since. The debutant type aren't so hot, at least I haven't met one that [I'd] like to make a friend of yet. I only see them anyway when I go out with Guardies and that of course is seldom.

---

10 Malcolm MacDonald (1901–81), son of former Labour prime minister Ramsay MacDonald.

11 Mary Welsh (1908–86), American journalist who later married Ernest Hemingway.

12 Helen Kirkpatrick (1909–97), war correspondent of the *Chicago Daily News*.

Janet Murrow, Ed Murrow's[13] wife, is another nice one.

I picked up some miscellaneous bits about fighting in the air over the weekend from my dream man – Group Captain Payne (he is fat and forty, a professional soldier and has infinite unsophisticated charm). The two Eagle squadrons come under him and he says that since they've lost some men they've at last realized that flying over enemy territory means business and not just excitement.

He says that no matter how good a pilot might be, it takes him a while to catch on to the tricks and avoid "being led down the garden path," which all means that our Air Corps, if and when they come in, will have a hard time at first. Payne saw some of the Russian fighter pilots who came over and he said they were terrific. They knew everything there was to know about instruments and were amazingly good at flying unfamiliar aircraft.

Got to stop now. News just came in that I'm to cover the arrival of the first prisoners of war ship this weekend. My first big assignment!

Love,

Puff

Peacehaven, Sussex
October 3, 1941

Dear Mary,

Well this is my first big assignment. I've certainly learned a lot. At 10:00 a.m. this morning (Friday) I had to put off all weekend house guests and then rush down to the office to get final instructions, passes etc.

The invaluable Smith was borrowed from Mr Biggers for an hour and he led the way out of London, me and my [car] struggling to keep up. It was a beautiful day. The road's good and a thoroughly delightful drive. About 3 hours (counting lunch). I arrived at Newhaven. The docks were still closed to reporters so I set out to find me a telephone. The one "must" my boss had given me. By following the telephone wires, I got to a gasworks – open all night –

13 Edward R. Murrow (1908–65) was an American journalist and broadcaster who was famous for his reporting of the London Blitz.

and the blackened stoker said sure I could use the phone when I wanted to. As the hotels in the town were crammed with photographers & reporters, I figured there'd be no hope up there.

Promptly at 4:00 p.m., I drove down to the dock entrance once more. The opposition (A.P. & U.P. [Associated Press and United Press]), two tough southerners, seemed overjoyed to find I was the only I.N.S. representative. For all their chewing gum and big talk they couldn't have been nicer to me.

From four until seven we waited – about fifty of us. It grew cold. The A.P. & U.P. both wanted to have a quick one, but they didn't dare leave me on the scene of action, so the three of us drove off together. It's amazing the cooperative action that goes on.

While the prisoners came on board the ship, we stood together and checked all figures, numbers etc. By that time I was almost too cold to care. 8:15 I saw my first Jerry. They all passed about 10 feet away from us, only 5 stretcher cases – the rest were legless, armless + one man was blind. I couldn't work up any feeling of animosity, only pity. They looked so forlorn. Only two ventured to speak or give a Nazi salute.

The boats were lighted up like pleasure craft – the red cross standing out plainly. The whole scene seemed rather weird. It was a beautiful moonlit night and the searchlight made it seem very unwarlike.

After the 2nd stretcher case came by, A.P. & U.P. left. I waited for one more (the one completely legless man) and then made my hurried exit. The phone worked alright. The one difficulty – no lights in the shed. With the help of a tiny torch (thank God I had one) I stammered through my notes into the office dictaphone. I must have made very little sense. I pity the poor boy who had to decipher it.

The office then wanted an embarkation story. I rushed out here to Peacehaven (2 miles away) hotel and grabbed a bite to eat with the *Life* photographer & got back to the docks just in time to hear that the boats weren't to sail.

Saturday, October 4

Today's been chiefly inactive. I keep hoping the office will let me leave but they won't. I filed some blah blah about nothing this morning early and then drove down to Brighton with the *Life* man. It's an unbelievable monstrosity of a town. Huge hotels for miles along the waterfront, occasional piers with Moorish domes, architecture Victorian or ultra-modern – lots of iron lace railings. I was glad to get out.

I'm back in the hotel now. I have Shirer's diary to read.[14] The rest of the press are drinking and squabbling down in the village at the horrible Railroad Hotel.

Monday, October 6

I'm still in Peacehaven – heard guns in the distance all morning. During the past four days I've learned more about reporting than my four months in London taught me. There are 4 Americans still here – *Herald Tribune* and the 3 syndicates. Gather anyway this story is getting poor play back home – World Series competing.

The faking that's been going on is unbelievable. My God the Brit press are skunks – no wonder the port officials hate us. Stories of prisoners walking on deck, goose-stepping etc., have appeared in various papers. It's very illuminating. I hope to someday see what A.P. & U.P. have been filing – bet that too is baloney – only hope my office hasn't been adding to my reports.

My *Life* photog. friend has turned out to be the [Zamzam] boy – a nice young smart Jew boy – Dartmouth.[15]

Yesterday we waited around all day with no news, so I phoned Pam at Chequers to find out what the P.M. knew about the Berlin–London prisoner negotiations. Got wire early this morning saying "stick with it" which I interpreted correctly as meaning differences were at last settled. The ships go out at 1:00 a.m. tomorrow morning after which I scoot back to London for a day – the earliest the ships can return is Wednesday and I don't relish the idea of another fruitless day in Newhaven, Brighton or Peacehaven.

Spent most of the morning waiting on docks for developments. My wire from Pam wasn't confirmed until noon. Was back again this

---

14 William L. Shirer, *Berlin Diary: The Journal of a Foreign Correspondent, 1934–1941* (1941).

15 David Scherman (1916–97), famous for his photos of Nazi concentration camps.

afternoon. This time really alongside the ships. Through the portholes I saw some prisoners, all young boys. They smiled and grinned good naturedly at me. They seemed damned nice types. The suspense for them and the British prisoners at Dieppe must be terrific. Poor kids. They're useless for the rest of their life and I doubt Germany will treat them well.

Food lousy – ran out of clean clothes ages ago – my hair needs washing – oh yes and I'm now in bed with the hot water bottle and William [Shirer] – brought no pills with me – a rather drastic slip – hope I won't faint at tonight's seance. The troubles of journalism! What a hellova lot of crummy people too – small, narrow-minded cheats. Hilde Marchant I've discovered is one of the worst!

I see by the papers that Ave is plugging religious freedom in Russia. Hope to have some letters when I get back to London. They are the joy of my existence.

[X] still wonders when I'm coming home. She makes me laugh – so settled in the boredom of mediocracy & marriage – she seems to forget the war. Thank God I'm not home. I'd lose my temper, I fear, too often. I did yesterday too – not visibly though – when one of the Gaumont British men started panning Churchill and Margesson.

Shirer's book's a godsend!

Bestest of love,

Puff

London
October 8, 1941

Dear Mary,

Home again – thank God! As you probably know, the prisoners were all returned to their hospitals yesterday afternoon. I covered their unemotional disembarkation and then drove like hell up to London and got here dirty, tired and a little fed up.

Vic Oliver had a birthday party for Sarah last night which I attended. The other Churchill daughter[16] was there – the unattractive one who is married to Duncan Sandys (Under-sec. of State for War).

---

16 Diana Churchill (1909–63), Churchill's eldest daughter.

Duncan has been handling the official side of the Newhaven fiasco and I was most interested in getting his side of the story during dinner.

Miss Knowles, head of the prisoners of war parcels, phoned me last night in tears. Had I written anything to America? She's been in touch with the families on this side and now it looks as though there'll be no exchange for some time to come.

It's awfully nice to be back in civilization again – away from that smelly dock, the cold and the dampness and those lousy English press. As an alternative from talking to them, I used to go down to the local gasworks and talk to the superintendent – an ardent communist, intelligent in a slow sort of way.

I must stop now and get to work and do some of my back stories.

Goodbye now and love to all,

[Kathleen]

CHAPTER 5

'I GET SO SICK OF BEING POLITE ABOUT OUR AMBASSADOR I FEEL LIKE BLOWING OFF STEAM'

Averell Harriman's mission in London was to expedite the delivery of American military supplies to the British armed forces. His mission staff were a small group of technical experts, who worked from a suite of offices in the US embassy on Grosvenor Square. Within his own sphere of work he communicated and liaised directly with Roosevelt and the White House. Of particular importance was Averell's role as personal go-between for Churchill and Roosevelt. The two leaders shared their private correspondence with him and asked for advice on the composition of their messages to each other.

Averell's role and activities quickly eclipsed those of the US ambassador to London John G. Winant, who had arrived in Britain with great fanfare only a short time before Averell. Winant's memoirs, published immediately after the war, betrayed no hint of any rift with Averell. On the contrary, he wrote in relation to Roosevelt's choice of him as his Lend-Lease expeditor that 'it would have been hard to make a happier choice'.

Averell's recollection of their relationship was a little different – 'both delicate and difficult', not least because, formally speaking, the ambassador was the senior official. According to Kathy, Winant 'did resent Averell. A lot of people did.' Winant, she told an interviewer, 'was a very introverted man. I got to know him quite well and I was not surprised when I saw that he'd committed suicide [in 1947].' Yet, as Kathy admitted in her waspish letters about him, Winant was a highly popular figure in wartime Britain.

As historian David Mayers has suggested, the roles of Winant and Averell were more complementary than conflictual. Winant's highly visible presence and quite charismatic personality provided a considerable psychological boost to British morale, whereas Averell was the charming but practical man of action.

In mid-October Averell returned to the United States to report on his recent trip to Russia with Beaverbrook. Once again Kathy remained in Britain, somewhat consoled by the thought that Ave would be able to bring back some more 'loot'.

London
October 14, 1941

Dear Mary,

I think you're a hellova louse not to have written me for weeks. I've had two letters from you in the last three months. Letters from home are my only means of keeping up, you can't appreciate how much they mean. (Get the hint I'd like to hear from you more often!)

Averell and I had a long discussion at lunch today about my work. He was full of accusations of my lack of initiative etc. I tried hard to hold my own and explain why I couldn't force the office to spend more time educating me. He seems to think that my working for the Red Cross is a bad idea – or intimated as much. I guess there is a certain [advantage] in not doing too many things at once. But it drives me crazy sitting around waiting for I.N.S. to give me an assignment.

Oddly enough, this afternoon I got assigned three good cable stories, including an Ernest Bevin interview. I rather imagine no other I.N.S. correspondent can get one – that's why I landed it.

Went to see Noël Coward's new show again tonight – a party for Averell. Mr and Mrs Eden[1] gave the theater end of it and Beaverbrook the dinner afterwards. Winant was also there – more silent and Lincolnesque than ever. I think he did say "yes" once during dinner!

---

1 Anthony Eden (1897–1977) and Beatrice Helen Beckett (1905–57). Helen left Eden in 1946 and divorced him in 1950.

I'd love to be able to say why in hell or where in the hell he gets his so-called greatness. Too much of an introvert for my liking. Someday I think he's going to break my arm. It's torture to shake hands with him. If only he could find some cause to be a martyr for, I think he might be happier. It annoys me that because people, little people, can't understand him, are scared of him, they consider him a great man. Please be discreet in your parcelling out of my indiscretions, but I get so sick of being polite about our ambassador at times I feel like blowing off steam. Needless to say, he is well liked by the English public.

Averell was unbelievably rude at dinner tonight. He went to sleep after the last course and practically snored once we moved from the table. Anthony Eden is charming. His high staccato laugh during the play irked me, but that is just in passing. His wife seems rather a socialite. I doubt if she takes this war too seriously. She's very pleasant and a lot less horse-like than most of the wives I've met!

The love of my life, Major General Sir Hastings Ismay (you must admit that's a wonderful name) was the cause of much sarcasm at dinner. His lordship hates his guts and refers to him as Puggy. From my point of view, he's a thoroughly charming man, and after all one can't be blessed with all the graces. The spark of genius is his weak point. (He was the military man on the British mission at Moscow.)

Please I want a picture of you and I really mean that.

My love to you and Shirley,

Kathleen

London
October 14, 1941

Dear Marie,

Half an hour ago my long-lost-and-believed-sunk suitcase arrived. What a lovely half hour I've just had! Now I'll have six instead of three blouses to choose from when I dress in the morning! The joy of not having to wear my black evening dress next time I dress for dinner (which is usually a couple of times a week) will be terrific. Another dozen silk stockings! Skirts to wear in the country and riding clothes – you've no idea how exciting the arrival has been.

Averell talks over CBS tonight. I think it will be a success. We went over it at lunchtime and personally I think he says a lot more than Beaverbrook did last night in his 20-minute talk.

Averell and Beaverbrook have started a mutual admiration society. They spend their time patting each other on the back at press conferences. It reminds me of two children. Mr Batt has nicknamed them Alphonse and Gaston![2]

I wished like the devil I could come home with Averell on Wednesday, but Averell says they dislike me more in Washington than they do here and that there'd be no conceivable chance of my getting over here again. If I came home now, I think probably after a month or so I'd regret it, because I'm just about beginning to get the swing of my job. Besides, I think I'd go mad arguing with all my various friends – from their letters I gather they tend to isolationism, or towards non-interest, which is even worse.

Best love,
Kathy

Dorchester Hotel, London
October 14, 1941

Dear Mouche,

My list of wants for Averell to bring back are rather miscellaneous – a Hammacher Schlemmer[3] like mine marked PSC (a bet I lost to Pam!), several cards of bobby pins, an eyelash curler (mine got swiped), my Leica camera, another bottle of liquid rouge (the maid spilled the one you sent almost empty). A20518, lip grease – date 5-6-41. Pair of brown shoes like the black ones you bought me and perhaps blue pair too, mine are getting sad looking. My red silk short dress.

Bob Meiklejohn said he'd bring over my typewriter. This one stinks. Please equip it with some spare ribbons. They are unobtainable over here. Diamond clip too please. A pair of Abercrombie red moccasins would also be very well received – size 5D.

---

2 A reference to an American comic strip that featured a bumbling pair of Frenchmen with a penchant for politeness.

3 A brand of cigarette lighter.

I lost my gold spray clip, which is very sad, God only knows how it came off. I dined quietly at Claridge's with Bob Montgomery & came home in someone's private car.

I personally haven't given up complete hope – however, you should notify the insurance people. I will of course want a copy rather than the money. Please let me know what they say.

Must stop now.

Love,

Kathleen

Dorchester Hotel, London
October 17, 1941

Mouche dear,

Loved your last letter, received this morning. Can't imagine why you haven't been hearing from me. I think I write regularly.

I've sent you a rather garbled letter & gift via Averell, who left this morning.

Unless something now unforeseen happens – like Ave not coming back or being recalled or something – I'll probably be over here for the duration.

I'd have given my eye teeth to have come home with Averell. It would have been wonderful seeing you all. With all the excitement of new faces etc., I haven't forgotten you!

Don't worry, I haven't changed much – at least I don't think I have.

But to get back to the point of this letter – about the 2nd suitcase of clothes I'd like you to send. It's winter things I'd like you to send – like my fur coat. Address everything c/o Ave at the embassy – I'll get it somehow.

You know I've almost forgotten what it's like to be able to walk into a store & buy some crackers – or even a blouse or a pair of socks!

Always I need stockings. It's so nice to be able to give them away. Unfortunately for my own good, I've given too damned many away. I'm on my last dozen now.

I hope you get a chance to see Averell. If his life at home is anything like what it is over here – you won't.

Love to all and use my car if you want to go on a trip.

Kathleen

London
October 23, 1941

Dear Mary,

What a week! I'm so far behind in my writing that I'm almost ready to give up. Two friends arrived in London on leave on Monday which meant I had to stay up all night every night. I've had an out-of-town story each day with interviews between them. I'm exhausted.

Added to all that, Pam in a fit of enthusiasm on Saturday night at Beaverbrook's told someone she wanted to join the ATA – the women ferry pilots force. Hell broke loose between us from then on – amicably – but for a while it looked as though I was going to lose out.

On Wednesday night I brought a bomber pilot friend of mine around and he gave a prepared speech on the horrors of joining the ATA and almost won her around. Did in fact until the pilot friend of hers phoned by chance and got her all enthusiastic again. Today thank God the whole thing collapsed. Much as I like Pam she's not the right type, quite aside from that she knows no math, drives very badly, and is nervous. Now everything is happy here once more.

I had to give up on the typewriter – it's lousy and keeps sticking.

Tell Mouche that one afternoon I drove out to a town near Chelmsford with Mrs Biddle. She was opening an orphan home supported by Mrs FDR and American money and I was covering it. Anyway, I met the Bishop of Chelmsford & wife. They were both charming. She thought I was Mrs Biddle's lady-in-waiting and was amazed when Mrs B informed her that ambassadors' wives don't have such things even in peacetime. I got an interesting point of view out of the Bishop. He thinks that if America declared war tomorrow, Germany would realize she was beat and would quit fighting. It's amazing how much people over here anticipate a terrific change the moment we get in.

Much as I don't really like Mrs B, we had great fun talking together on the trip. Now that Mrs Winant's left, all launchings are thrust on her, everything plus all the goings-on to do with her Poles, Dutch, Belgians, Norwegians and what have you. She wants me to take over some of it, but I flatly refused.

Just as we were getting on so beautifully, something most unfortunate happened. She'd taken great trouble over this particular orphan asylum. Wore her Red Cross uniform with trimmings. There were photogs, newsreels and the B.B.C. The following day the newspapers carried a shot of me playing with some of the kids, instead of her posed beauties. Quite aside from the fact that I hate public participation when I'm reporting, it was rather embarrassing as it was her show.

October 24

There's a terrific wave of frustration over here now. People feel that because there's no bombing, no invasion (second front), the government isn't doing enough. They're all uneasy, itching to do something other than listen to radio reports of how Russia's faring.

Had a fascinating time yesterday. I went to tea with some Belgians who've just got out of Belgium and are now recuperating, waiting until they can pass the services' medical exam. One boy I met took seven months to get to England. Chauffeur by profession, his route was via Belgium, Finland, Russia, Iraq, India, China, South America, U.S., Canada and finally here. 2 others bought a boat and hid it along the coast, swiped an outboard motor and petrol from the Germans. When the time came to start, the engine failed, so they rowed the whole damn way across the Channel. In sight of the English coast, a sub came out to investigate them – a British one. A 19-year-old boy was the worst. He was caught in Spain, beaten and thrown in [a] concentration camp. He escaped, was re-caught and re-beaten. He said it wasn't a question of there being bad food in the camps, there was no food at all. The doctor told him it would take at least a month before he could join the air force. Actually, he looks like absolute death. They think he may have T.B. but he's raring to go. In general, reports were that Belgium's cities are almost foodless (for the Belgians). The country is better. France is better and Spain is unbelievable – no food anywhere. "Un miracle" was what they all felt about being in England.

Other incidental information now on hand is that Anglo-American relations between the little guys is going from bad to worse. Result, our boys go home mad at the English. The fault lies on both sides. Neither knows how to handle the other.

Tomorrow night I'm going to a farewell party given by the Sinclairs – he's air minister – for their son Robin, who leaves shortly for the U.S. to learn to become a pilot. He's a very sweet kid. I should say about 18 yrs. Please be nice to him – have him to dinner if he gets any time in N.Y.

I lunched today with the Greek P.M.'s daughter – about my age – a Cretan by birth – damned intelligent, now working as her father's secretary. Someday I hope to get around to writing up her story.

Must stop now and get to work.

Love,

Kathleen

Please write me

London
October 28, 1941

Dear Mary,

Lunched today at the home for escaped Belgians – the same place I visited with Mrs Biddle last week. They gave a party in my honor. I was quite embarrassed.

Thank God though I didn't have to make a speech. Somehow my French isn't up to it!

It does something to you though to meet those boys who have gone through absolute hell just to get to England where they can once more fight. Some new ones arrived since I was last there – one a kid of 18 and another whose father has stayed behind to try and help. He comes from one of the best-known Belgian political families.

Two toasts were drunk – one before lunch to the king – another before coffee to Liberty. It was quite impressive.

Pam is sick and at last has retired to the country. She's not very strong and refuses to take care of herself when she starts getting one of her monthly colds. Now she has flu. Someday perhaps I'll be able to make her sensible!

I'm as busy as hell this week – work and extracurricular activities as well. I've just heard that the extemporaneous broadcast I did last week is going to America tonight – shortwave though, so you won't have a chance to hear it and there's no chance of a cable getting there in time. I'm sorry.

I think I forgot to tell you, but I looked in every big store for your Vogue pattern book. They all know it and say "we haven't had it for months." Perhaps someday they'll have a new issue – but with a paper shortage probably not.

My love to you,

Puff

I got home late last night and was just putting the light out when Lord Beaverbrook phoned. He'd talked to Averell and reported that everything was OK. Thank God. I was scared stiff that he'd get himself into trouble.

London

November 6, 1941

Dear Mary,

Elsie, my two and six an hour maid, has just told me that I shouldn't work – that I'm much too sick (which isn't true). In fact she suggested I go to a cinema. I'd feel too guilty doing that – as a compromise I'm writing to you. Your wonderful three-page newsy letter put me in a perfect mood this morning. Can't imagine why it should have taken so long getting here though. The censor hadn't opened it. I love the pictures. You're looking very well. How much weight have you gained? Your letter didn't have much of that kind of news. Are your maternity clothes pretty? I hope you're wearing some of my nice dressy winter hats. I'd hate to think they're going to waste, sitting in the closet. Please do, and anything else that you find fitable.

I had one of my super cramp attacks yesterday – the first one in six months. Unfortunately, I was up with Alex (Woollcott)[4] getting a lecture lesson on journalism. It hit very suddenly and I almost fainted sitting in the chair. Poor guy, he was scared stiff. When I got to my room, the hotel nurse came rushing in on his orders, took my pulse

4 Alexander Woollcott (1887–1943), American drama critic and commentator who visited Britain in mid-1941.

and was a general nuisance when all I really wanted was to be left alone. I'm OK today, only a little weak in the knees. Thank goodness I can stay in.

Pam's in the country, house hunting and trying to get over the flu. She wants to buy a house if she can find one and then we could move into it and have all her nice furniture, instead of living in a rented job.

Had a party last week – to eat Averell's caviar and repay all the people who we owe meals and things. It was a success I guess, no one left until midnight. It's the first party I've given since I've been here, which is really rather disgraceful, considering I get entertained [so often].

For the first time in ages I had a whole weekend in the country. Pam's trustee, a man called Lord Melchett,[5] a Jew and the head of International Chemical something, came down on Friday. He's absolute heaven. He's recently had a fight with the Ministry of Supply (Beaverbrook) about whether or not his business of making anti-tank guns will come into the ministry. He won. Beaverbrook had to back down.

An interesting sidelight: the Beaver phoned on Friday with news of Averell and asked Pam and me to dinner at Cherkley. I said yes if we could bring Lord Melchett. He stalled and later had someone phone to say no. I always knew he disliked people who oppose him, but it's damn small not to have them in your house, when they used to be your friends.

My feeling of guilt returned so I got back to work and finished a feature job on the maternity hospital that has the lowest death rate in the Brit. empire. Oddly enough it's one of the poorest hospitals in London. Midwives do all the work. Newspaper is used instead of incubators for the premature children. I was allowed in that room. It makes me laugh when I think of all the trouble hospitals back home take over even the healthy kids. This place had no modern equipment at all, no running hot water [or] sterilizers and still it has the second-best record of the world. One mother told me, coming to the

5 Henry Ludwig Mond, 2nd Baron Melchett (1898–1949), Conservative politician and a director of Imperial Chemical Industries.

hospital to have a baby was the first vacation she'd had in years. She's going to have another baby next year so she can have another two weeks' vacation in the hospital! Most of the mothers I saw are the ones who have lost their homes. They come to the hospital now, because it's a trifle inconvenient having babies in shelters, they say.

Today I did a piece on Mrs Biddle, hard as hell to do, then went on a wild goose chase. Mrs Churchill and some Red Cross ambulances for Russia. No story. A complete waste of time.

Just now returned from a seance with the dentist. X-rays showed I was about to get a nerve infected. He's a good dentist thank goodness, at least he's the one everyone goes to. He's nice too and isn't sadistical like Dr Knox.

I can't think what the news is – stories that I've been on and written up are boring to put down on paper again. I hope you see them. What do you think of them? I'd like to know.

Give my love to everyone.

Bestest love,

Puff

PS I get the magazines regularly and read the [*New Yorker*] from cover to cover, it's the joy of my existence!

• • •

Nov. 10. Much annoyed, took this letter up to Alec at lunchtime today and he said he couldn't take it as it hadn't been censored. Sorry.

Marie-André came down for the weekend. I was scared stiff anticipating his arrival, as all the various relations have been standing around waiting for weeks for the moment when we two would meet.

Coining a phrase from Pam, he turned out to be absolute heaven. As far as looks go he's a blonde edition of his father, but with a much stronger chin and much taller. He couldn't stand up straight in our living room which must make him about 6ft 2.

He's got a good sense of humor, is quiet rather than shy, intelligent but rather reserved about giving his opinion.

I asked him if he was lonely at his camp (he's just an ordinary private, with no friends of his own age – the rest of the men are what he terms "Polish peasants") and his answer was "I try not to think about it."

Perhaps the real reason I got such infinite pleasure out of him is that he's tender, sincere and unspoiled. Maybe he's the idealist who'll float through life getting kicked, but I doubt it – he's got a lot of stuffing. I like him a lot. I hope I'll see more of him. His future after the war is to go back to Poland and reestablish his family there.

I'm getting desperately sleepy.

So going to bed.

Bestest love to all,

Puff

Petersfield Farm, Surrey
November 13, 1941

Mouche dear,

After not having heard a word from any of you for weeks and months, have received three from you and two Mary plus incidental others – all in the last 10 days. It's most exciting getting mail!

Today was my first whole day at the office. It was great fun. I've been wanting for some time to sit on the desk, but the guys down there aren't too receptive to having me around. However, my standby, Red, is heading for Cairo next week and at the present moment is head I.N.S. reporter in Europe, so he was able to make the London boss let me come in and work under him for one day.

Hence most of the I.N.S. items in the Nov. 13 papers were by me. I attended the military conf. and covered it alone. For once they released some decent stuff – something that could be cabled out!

I'm still thinking in the terms of cable release – garbled words and no punctuation. So this letter could be a trifle odd.

Our cook and maid fight like bloody hell every moment of the day. Because it's so hard to get servants I don't dare fire either. The last time he was down, Smith, Averell's chauffeur gave them a talking to, but even that didn't work.

Alex Woollcott's left. He was so damned nice all the time over here that I have to take back all the nasty things I said about him.

Last weekend Marie-André and I went for a much-longer-than-we-expected ride.

I hope I see a lot more of him. I disapprove of the way the other relations treat him. He's about the most attractive kid of 20 I think I've ever met. Unfortunately, he's got the martyr kind of guts.

N.Y. office cabled for series on housewives in war jobs – six. I did one on Parsley Vian watering her tomato plants with the dead morning bath water from second-storey window with aid of stirrup pump. (There was shortage of water this summer.)

Another, which I'll refrain from doing, was on the worn tart who is now a bus conductress. She's a tired-looking redhead cockney but she's on top of the world. Her bus job gets her £4 a week and through it she meets many new evening customers.

I spent an afternoon with the conductresses, 50 percent were tarts, the rest housewives. I wrote my story on the latter.

Next week I do night shift factory working women – tanks and bombers.

All of a sudden I've discovered that I'm very tired, which is understandable as I put in ten hours in the office today so think I'll stop and rest a bit before dinner, and brush up on what one should say to the navy.

The world is certainly full of stupid people isn't it! No dear I'm not getting an attack of intolerance but it just amuses me to think that stupid or not I have fun with them. I wonder if most people get so much unadulterated fun out of life as I do?

Bestest love,

Kathleen

London

November 21, 1941

Dear Mary and the rest of the family,

Averell has been very horrid. He hasn't let me open any of my birthday presents, however the rest of the presents are wonderful. Now I can use as much Kleenex as I like. I have enough bobby pins to keep some in the country – silk stockings galore and three "new dresses," new moccasins and shoes. Life is pleasant!

We expected Ave to arrive on Monday – until about noon I was getting reports at regular intervals of his progress from Portugal. Then suddenly they phoned and said he'd never left Lisbon at all. He finally arrived on Tuesday – I was in Birmingham as luck would have it – story getting – and only saw him for a minute that day. He's taking life fairly easy. At the moment he's concentrating most energy on writing the Sunday night postscript [for the B.B.C.] – which as you may not know is the most listened to program of the week.

My Birmingham trip was a success from the story point of view. I went up there expecting to be met by some little Ministry of Supply man. Instead practically the whole town turned out. A lunch was given in my honor, one other girl and the rest the heads of various Birmingham governmental organizations. Speeches, press, photographers. God I hated it. They want me to work in one of the munition factories sometime in the near future for a week or so. I'm seriously toying with the idea.

I spent most of my time at a light cruiser tank factory – one of the 1,063 factories in Birmingham – it was quite interesting. Over a third of the workers are girls. I met them, talked to them, got the usual answers to my questions and walked my feet off. After lunch I went to a gun and instrument plant where the majority are girls. In some of the quieter rooms music is played and the girls sing while they work. I liked that. When I walked through, they sang American songs.

I got back to London with half an hour to spare before I went out with Min. of Aircraft Production to an airplane parts factory outside London – to do the night shift. It was a small factory and from the outside looked rather like a farmyard. Actually the factory was an ex-film studio – transformed about 18 months ago.

Of the 300 night shift workers about a hundred were girls. The works manager thought it was bad for morale if I just talked to some of the girls, so I was made to chat to practically every damn one of them. This went on until about 2:30. I picked up a lot of miscellaneous information and had a nice chat with the shop steward (the union organizer) [who] complained that conditions were bad. They looked pretty good to me. "Lunch" was served in the canteen at one – that meal looked plenty adequate and hot. The factory runs its own buses. Frankly I see little reason for the union to beef.

All the night shift workers liked their hours. Prefer it to daytime work. It gives them more time to do their shopping, keep house etc. I was amazed to find that several were women with money – "who looks after your children?" – "oh, my nanny" would be the answer. "My cook does all the shopping." "I don't keep house myself." One was the wife of an admiral.

The arguments towards conscripting women or not conscripting them are still raging. It will come eventually – it will have to – so far there haven't been enough volunteers. One of the main difficulties is educating the women to doing the less "dainty" work. I met one wonderful creature who drove the crane in a tank factory. She's the only woman who they can get to [do] that kind of work.

The funny thing is that no matter what a girl is doing, whether it's boring a hole, sorting tiny parts, she thinks her job is interesting. Many of the girls were domestic servants. This is their chance to get out of that much-hated profession. They get better money and like the feeling of being on their own. The general morale is terrific. I heard few complaints and I certainly was not shown the pick of the crop.

The five republican isolationist congressmen arrived yesterday. I covered their press conference. One is Dick Gale, you know, the S.V. [Sun Valley] skier from Minneapolis. They're all tough, unadulterated Americans. It was nice meeting such unsophistication!

Last night Ronnie Tree gave a Thanksgiving dance for the American press and lots of other people. Averell was horrified to hear that the congressmen were there in full force. It's the first party of its kind since I've been here and I guess they'll go home with the idea it happens every night. Unfortunately, too, they met all the worthless West End women. However, the damage is done.

I enjoyed myself thoroughly. I'd quite forgotten what fun dances are. Incidentally while I was there the editor of the *Evening Standard* cornered me and wanted a confirmation on a New York report of my engagement to Red. It took me about ten minutes to convince him it wasn't true. That annoyed me no end. Red, of course, takes the other side of the situation. That annoys me even more.

Unfortunately, I got myself involved in two horrible official lunches this week – Thanksgiving Day that Averell made me go to and one for the Eagle Squadron. Winant spoke equally badly at both. He's not a good speaker or writer, but despite that everyone over here is still convinced he's a great man. Anthony Eden spoke of him yesterday as being "one of the men who can influence the tide of world affairs." God help world affairs! Poor guy, he misses his family terribly.

I read yours and Helen's letters at 5:00 a.m. I was dead tired but [they] made me see such red that I wanted to sit right down and write. Please ask them to write me with their reasons for wanting the Nazis to win. That's about what it amounts to. What's wrong with them anyway – they must read the papers, what possible ground do they stand on? It must be absolute hell living in New York now. It hurts to think of [X] sitting calmly in the country doing nothing. What the hell's gone wrong with her. [And Y] thinks that the most important thing in life today is washing her baby's diapers.[6]

[Kathleen]

Petersfield Farm, Surrey
December 5, 1941

Dear Mouche-Mary,

I'm sorry you didn't get word about Averell's speech until too late. It was a terrific success over here – he told the British just what they wanted to hear. I doubt if it went over at home. There were lots of things I'd rather have heard him say, but he wanted to give them blah blah propaganda and of course that's what they needed. Anyway, it's all over now.

He's been taking things quite easy and is looking better and seems more relaxed. He's been a great help with my work, we argue most of the time as I can't help but get a certain am't [amount] of the reporter viewpoint. It's fun.

---

6 'X' and 'Y', who are actually named in the letter, were acquaintances of Kathy's.

Almost had a big fight with my boss on Wednesday. Ave wanted me to – thank God I didn't because things have since been ironed out by instructions from N.Y. C.A. Smith doesn't want me to get started on spot news and won't let me interview cabinet ministers. Or at least only will, after he's been refused admittance. That makes Averell mad, but frankly I think it's understandable. Anyway, things I hope are fine now.

The news of late centers around having a second front [in North Africa]. People are happy about that, though for a while things looked bad – the P.M. and the communiqués gave the campaign such a terrific build-up that everyone expected it to be over in a few days. Stories about half the enemy tanks being destroyed were inclined to be misleading, though they have since been proved true. It was nice though to hear that the American light cruiser models did well.

I interviewed Beaverbrook on Tuesday when the story about the conscription of women broke and I'm going to follow it up with some others after the Commons debate starts. Probably by then though the Jap situation will have come to a head and conscription will have no cable space.

The thought of being over here for Christmas – with Ave at Sun Valley or Arden – about kills me, but I guess that can't be helped. I must say when I heard about my friends via you and Helen I felt like packing right up and coming home to do a little sensible talking. Instead I wrote 4 carbon letters, which Averell read and made loop-hole proof, I hope. Let me know the state of my unpopularity when they arrive.

I've got me a new boyfriend – two in fact – but one is about to leave having been here only a week. Gunther's[7] one – he's been named by Averell the "crashing bore" which essentially he is, but at times he's most interesting. At least he has a fresh point of view. The other is Dick Scott. He's a Sun Valleyite full of interesting tales about the continent. In France they hate de Gaulle because they think politically he's for the Front Populaire – and they're more scared of the FP than Hitler. Food conditions of course you know about. Spain is

7 Presumably the American journalist John Gunther (1901–70).

starving. The people he met fresh out of Germany say that what Shirer wrote was a lot of hooey – the Germans are fighting for their lives and their hearts are in it. In this connection a man called Hank Taylor breakfasted with us two days ago. He's been to Finland and came back via Berlin. He says there is a tremendous apathy. No results have been shown for all the victories and the Germans are fed up – that is, the civilians. So you see you can never tell who is right. But it's interesting meeting all these people.

Congressmen leave tomorrow. I've been to all their conferences – they are a pleasant not too brainy lot. Dick Gale is heaven as usual. One and all they were amazed to find a will to fight to the end among the British. They seem to think that if Hitler offered a good enough peace the British could accept it.

Things like the determination of the British to see this thing out, their unity and cooperative spirit, I of course always did take for granted. It's interesting to find some people at home don't.

First night in London Congressman Hill, the cowboy from Colorado, woke up and discovered that he had to answer one of nature's calls. He wandered up and down the hall looking for the men's loo and finally went into a door marked W.C. – which he thought stood for woman's comforts!

We gave a party for Mary Churchill during the week. She was home on leave, and full of enthusiasm for the A.T.S. Being with a bunch of girls hasn't had the best influence on toning her down but I guess that can't be helped. She's got no savoir faire at all and bubbles along in conversation saying the most naive things in a completely childish way. She can get away with it when she's with older people, but kids our own age rather resent the way she talks about "Papa."

Averell and I got down to the country in time for late dinner tonight and now he's gone to bed. The peace and quiet of the country is far too pleasant to spoil by sleeping so me and Alabam are sitting downstairs, making conversation to you all.

Next week is going to be pretty busy. I'm interviewing all the heads of the various women services for a series and in between times will be at [the] Commons hearing the Lady Astors shoot their mouths off on the subject of women being conscripted. It's fun being busy though. It's fun going on stories too. The part I hate is having to write them up. I've just finished a series on the British housewife, which doubtless you will never see. Six stories on one of life's most boring subjects – that was almost more than I could stand.

I'm getting sleepy now.

So goodbye, best love, I wish I could be home to watch all the Peanut preparations! If it's a girl we'll have to make a match between it and my godchild!

Puff

PS God damn the stupid old State Department anyway.

CHAPTER 6

'I ALWAYS HOPED TO BE IN LONDON THE NIGHT WE GOT INTO THE WAR. SOMEHOW IT'S MORE EXCITING'

Kathy was at Chequers celebrating her twenty-fourth birthday the weekend Japan went to war against the United States. There was a cake. Churchill gave her a copy of his book about the British military campaign in 1890s Sudan, while Clementine wrote a birthday note. When news of the Pearl Harbor attack came through, Kathy made some notes on a scrap of paper which she then recomposed into a letter to Mary – a document that constitutes a unique contemporaneous account of Churchill's reaction to Japan's bombing of the American fleet on 7 December 1941.

Kathy's letter to Mary was handwritten on headed Chequers paper, but was unfinished, unsigned and unsent, as it must have dawned on her that Churchill's evident enthusiasm for US entry into the war in the given circumstances would not have been a good look had its contents leaked out.

Simultaneously with Pearl Harbor, the Japanese launched attacks on British colonial possessions in Southeast Asia. Britain declared war on Japan on 8 December. A couple of days later Hitler declared war on the United States in support of his Japanese ally. The Americans were now directly involved in the European war. Churchill immediately sailed for the United States, taking Averell with him, and Roosevelt quickly agreed to prioritise the defeat of Nazi Germany rather than the Pacific War against Japan.

The Americans were now finally and fully in the war together with the Brits, and Kathy couldn't have been happier.

Chequers, Bucks
December 8, 1941

Dear Mary,

I always hoped to be in London the night we got into the war. Somehow it's been more exciting.

We heard the news of the bombing of Pearl Harbor just like everyone else – over the 9 o'clock news. It took a while to sink in – the words had a new association. Then there was a clamor. "What was that? Pearl Harbor – where's that?" Martin[1] left to get a confirmation. Ave and Winant wondered – a rumor no doubt – it couldn't be true – but it was.

I don't remember much else of dinner. The P.M. had cheered up – he kept leaving to phone. Winant kept leaving. Then finally me & the coffee-pot were left alone in the dining room. I left, and the men came back to finish & talk.

I was standing by the fireplace when Winant came in – "it's come at last – it's exciting." Winant spoke of his son – "he'll be in it." Why in hell did he have to get personal at this moment?

Plans were made. Parliament called for tomorrow. Washington called. Winston was nervous – he smoked down an all-night cigar in a short hour – "I'm glad we're together."

"The light that flickered. The light that gleamed. The light that shone." Perhaps he'll use that in tomorrow's speech.[2]

"We must see our cinema." For an hour, perhaps, we did. Came down for the midnight news.

"Japan declared war on U.S. & Brit. Emp." P.M. pacing in dragon wrapper[3] – Ave standing by fireplace – Winant in overcoat turned

1 John Martin, British civil servant and Churchill's principal private secretary during the war.
2 Churchill did indeed use that phraseology, both in his speech to Parliament on 8 December and in his radio broadcast the same day.
3 A type of housecoat.

up – standing at different places – puffing a new cigar – God save the King.

"The 1st day of war is always exciting."

[Kathleen]

London
December 16, 1941

Dear Mary,

I was down in the office when Shirley's cable arrived and I let out such a whoop that C.A. thought at least I must have produced!

I'm sitting here now in a dither waiting to hear all the details. What color hair has he got? Did you have a hard time? How are you now? There are so many things I want to know.

It's nice having a boy isn't it? Pam's a little sorry though. She was kind of hoping for a girl who could someday be Mrs Butch Churchill!

News from here seems rather trivial and unimportant compared to yours. I'm working as usual – interviewed Morrison – the Home Sec. yesterday on civil defense.

I hear Inez Robb[4] did a piece on Nancy Astor yesterday. I'd love to see some of her stuff if Averell can bring it back. Unfortunately people keep ringing me up and asking what she's like. Should they see her etc.

After having received her day's army pay, Pam realized she couldn't go through with her plan to join the A.T.S. so she's still with me, now looking around for a munitions job near the house in the country. Perhaps Averell told you, we are leaving Petersfield Farm for a much smaller, more modern and cozy cottage.[5] Tiny with no property, but on a big estate. It costs one third of the price too, which is a distinct asset. We move in as soon as the necessary repairs and bathroom can be installed. The other house is terribly dreary for winter use and quite expensive to run.

We're also looking for a flat. Six months in the Dorchester is about enough. We spent the morning looking at hideous furnished flats but

4 Inez Robb (1900–79), a well-known and highly paid American journalist who arrived in Britain just before the Pearl Harbor attack.

5 Ruckman Cottage, Okewood Hill, near Dorking, not far from Petersfield Farm.

we're quite hopeful. The estate agents are such snobs that I'm sure they are bound to produce something within the next few days.

I made another of my lovely social errors last night. Coming into the Dorchester at about ten o'clock Pam and I met a friend with an obvious foreigner. They were both being very funny and I thought perhaps they were drunk. I was introduced to the foreigner and as you know I never listen to names. I said "how do you do" and left it at that. Pam curtsied and made a hellova fuss. It turned out to be the King of Greece! Later we went and had a drink with them so I was able to mend my ways! I was most polite and called him Sir and all the rest.

I can hardly wait to hear from home now about what everyone thinks about the war. What are they going to do, or are doing. It must be pretty exciting.

I went to a ball on Friday night after seeing Averell off and it was quite terrific. Full evening dress, white ties when uniforms were not worn – about 1,000 people. I went with our navy [*sic*] – who wasn't half as impressed at the turnout as I was. The girls were all in their best prewar dresses. They looked rather dowdy and unsmart I thought and it horrified me the way they were left sitting alone by the side of the dance floor. Wallflower has its real significance over here! Thank the good Lord I came out in America.

I must end now and get back to blackout hints to housewives, my latest.

Love,
Puff

London
December 16, 1941

Dear Marie,

The news of Mary's baby is quite thrilling. Did it come early, or was I wrong in expecting it at Christmas or just after? I'm dying to hear all the particulars.

Averell will probably tell you all the news. The happenings since he left all center around housekeeping, arranging with solicitors about moving, which I find most boring.

The news gets daily more discouraging, but as Averell is always most snooty about my source of information, perhaps I'm really being misinformed, & things are alright. It is a little discouraging though. I hate to hear that the British and Americans in the Far East are retreating "according to plan." Somehow that news doesn't quite offset the more optimistic Middle Eastern and Russian communiqués.

I must be off now.

Love,

Kathy

London
December 18, 1941

Dear Mary,

One valuable asset [of] the present Far Eastern war is that our geography is being rapidly improved. Until last week, Timor was a completely unknown island as far as I was concerned. Now today it's the center of diplomatic attention. My biggest trouble at the moment is being able to pronounce the Middle East towns. This afternoon I had to deal with Tmimi-Mekili over the phone. I had great difficulty!

Yesterday Brendan Bracken had a conf. with the American press. We were given a big pat on the back and a lot of blah, which Brendan does very well. He confirmed "certain rumors" that have been circulating Fleet Street this last week as to the whereabouts of certain gov't officials. I was most grateful. Now people will stop pestering me. "Where is your father?" "Who'd your father go home with?" "How's he getting home?" etc. People must think I'm an awful dumb dodo because I never know anything!!

I'm still looking around desperately for a flat. Saw a beautiful one yesterday. Small, nicely furnished at 3 Grosvenor Square. The tenant suddenly decided that she didn't want to [leave] god damn her hide. So I'm back on the streets again.

Marie-André unexpectedly turned up in town two days ago full of information (misinformation) about Vichy being pro-allied and about to leave Hitler. Undoubtedly what he says is true of the French Military Staff but he also insists on including in this pro-British group

Pétain and Darlan.[6] We argued most of last evening on the latter score. M.A. can't seem to understand why we all hate Vichy so. Poor boy, it must be rather hard for him living in England and being pro a Vichy that no one here thinks exists.

There's a complete lack of Christmas spirit here, which I guess is understandable. To all the shop girls and the like, it means a day of rest – little else. My plans are still in the making. I rather want to go [to] an American party, but that depends a little on where Pam will be.

It's now the 20th & I'm again down at the Ministry.

My lunch date arrived at that point, so the letter once more was returned and forgotten at the bottom of my purse. It's now near Christmas time – the Dorchester sports two trees and had four wedding receptions this afternoon. "Eight suckers" was my friend the elevator man's comment!

Quent's back – arrived the end of last week and threw himself a coming-home party, which was quite something – eight of us and it lasted until about 5. Come Saturday morning at noon, I found it difficult to concentrate on the words of wisdom told us by the military spokesman and consequently got hell from Charlie. I've been spending a certain am't of time down at the MoI and starting next week Charlie is going to take my education in hand as far as the office goes. He gets spurts of interest in me and I guess this is one of them! Obviously I'm going to have to take advantage of it.

Quent's tendencies towards communism have left him forever after his Russian visit. He says he's cured for life!

Our weekend was rather hectic. We had four house guests – Pam's little brother, the new Bill Batt, Marie-André and Geoffrey Lloyd, who arrived at the last minute, self-invited. He brought his "man" with him who did everything from cleaning all my shoes that haven't been cleaned for ages to washing up dishes and bringing around the "morning tea." It's most convenient having friends who travel with valets when one has only a cook!

---

6 Admiral François Darlan (1881–1942), Commander-in-Chief of the Vichy French armed forces.

The saddest thing happened on Monday morning. Eddie (Pam's brother), Win Brown and Marie-André and I trained up to London. Marie-André, being the politest, offered to buy all our tickets. We were wandering around the platform when the train suddenly started to pull out. Marie-André was the only one who didn't make it. He was left sitting in the station with the four tickets. A sad story, but awfully funny.

Last night I had a Polish evening, the Polish ambassador (one to England) and wife, a man called Poklewski-Koziell, Sikorski's[7] aide and Mrs Eden and me. It was quite fun, only Mrs Eden is too much of a night owl. Four of us went on to a nightclub and finally at 4 o'clock I suggested we call it a day. She was still going strong. Perhaps hubby doesn't treat her right; while he's away she makes up for lost time! The result of the evening: I learned a lot about Poland.

Latest news: Churchill to have his Christmas dinner in the White House, or perhaps you've already heard!

Something happened then had to do something. I got three hours' sleep last night, and probably this will make little sense, but the "Pétain resigned" rumor came through and I had to hike down to the Free French headquarters to get a statement from them early this morning. The whole thing's collapsed now and with it rumors of massing troops on the Iberian Peninsula border. However, people are still taking bets as to whether Spain gets invaded tomorrow (Christmas). The Foreign Office spokesman says it won't. Some people say Luzon will be lost any day now. I wonder if it does go if it would be as serious as they think.

Incidentally, a lot of criticism – silently so far – about the P.M. boating across the Atlantic and using so many "protecting" ships. The feeling is that since those ships are so badly needed for convoy purposes, he should have flown. That criticism comes from British sources only.

Quent leaves tomorrow, which makes me very sad. You must see him when he gets home – really he's a unique guy and about the best

7 General Władysław Sikorski (1881–1943) was the prime minister of the London-based Polish government-in-exile.

friend I have over here. He's swell about helping me in various ways. Angel Gabriel would be a better name for him than Mother Superior!

Goodbye & of course I'm dying to hear from you.

Best love,

Kathy

London
January 1, 1942

Dear Mary,

The mail situation is so desperate that there hardly seems any point in writing, but maybe I'll get through this and then hold it over until someone motors over.

In many respects the last week of the year has been most successful, personally I mean. I wondered all day if the Japs would have the Philippines as a New Year's present. We (at the military conference daily) are very blasé about the Russian news. Unless at least six cities are retaken the story isn't worth filing. Today they took a big railway junction, a main road, and a river – no soap.

When Averell left I was in the depth of depression about my job. Now I'm on the crest of the wave. Since Red cleared out to Cairo and Inez Robb arrived, boss C.A. has taken an increased interest in me. Why? Perhaps because I'm the better of the two evils as far as I.N.S. women go. Dear Inez – she's sub-tabled me whenever we have the misfortune to meet and then goes around saying I high-hat her. Me the girl who thought: how nice, perhaps she'll teach me a few tricks. I'm being horribly catty (it is fun!) but so far she's followed me around on the interviewing schedule – Nancy Astor, Bevin, Morrison and so forth – none of her mailers[8] have yet reached N.Y. Am I happy – of course that means none of mine have either but that doesn't matter.

Yesterday I was taken to lunch by Tommy Watson I.N.S. diplomatic correspondent – a hellova nice English guy, and Helen Kirkpatrick. The moment I've been waiting for has come. Helen's taking me under her wing. Tommy has too, he's the one guy who's solved the problem of how

8 A feature story posted to the United States, as opposed to a news report that has been cabled.

to get on with the bureau chief. As opposed to Red's not too satisfactory political approach, Tommy just ignores C.A. After a certain am't of snooping in office files, he decided that my position, too, was sufficiently strong, to march into 72–78 Fleet Street and start demanding. Helen backed him up and promised to teach me anything C.A. won't. After that little seance I wandered innocently into the office, whereupon C.A. started in telling me what I ought to do (of his own free will) so now I have both sides backing me and I'm [the] most happy I have been for untold days, despite lack of sleep, a coming-on cold and cook worries.

Today a certain Mr Peznick (he's worse than his name) phoned and said he had a flat for us in 3 Grosvenor Square. Two bedrooms, two baths, a living room and a dining room. The latter can be converted into a bedroom when Pam comes to town when Averell's here. In case that isn't self-explanatory, Pam's going to spend most of her time in the countryside with Butch and just come up during the day for her work. It's all so good that it will probably fall through before long. If you knew the trouble to get a serviced flat near the embassy to suit his majesty when he's here, a strong building to suit his conscience when he leaves his poor little daughter alone in England near improbable German bombers. SERVICE on the House is my one requirement. It's a full-time job getting food, hassling with rations and servants. I didn't come to England to become an efficient housewife.

Got a cable from Red tonight saying your letter was on its way via Randolph, which also means that I'll be seeing [him] sometime in the near future.

Christmas at the Biddles was most pleasant.[9] I was terribly tired at the time so I found it very restful. The food down there is absolutely terrific. Too good really – it shouldn't be allowed. Quent left on Xmas day for home so he ought to arrive shortly after this letter.

Jan. 6

This is in haste to get taken with Bob Low who leaves tonight. Randolph arrived in town an hour ago and ever since has had Pam

9 The Biddles' house, Saint Hill Manor, was in Sussex. It later became the British headquarters of the Church of Scientology.

and me in stitches about the trials and tribulations of having [an] ex-dressmaker for a boss. He (Randolph) is ever so much nicer than I expected. By that I mean when nice he is nicer than I expected. I haven't had time to see the other side. From the look of things life will be hectic until he leaves, telephone ringing, people calling. With a little coaching from Pam (what not to say!) I expect we'll get on fine.

A major crisis occurred in my life today. Inez Robb called up and called me every name imaginable – from typical deb snob to a tunneller. She was almost hysterical, told me she'd written Barry Ferris and the Foreign Editor about me and torn up some letters she was given to deliver to me. The reason for the sudden outbreak was that she'd heard I'd phoned W.V.S. headquarters after a story and I happened to ask the girl in charge, who I know very well, what kind of story Mrs Robb was writing about the W.V.S. The whole affair has upset me rather. The one thing I wanted to stay clear of was office politics. She also informed me that last night she contemplated cabling I.N.S. either she or I must leave. This is the woman who I have met twice in my life, who each time has tried to make me feel like a complete fool. Have just completed a letter to her, which Pam and I both agree is a masterpiece. In case there are any repercussions in N.Y. please tell Averell about this. As far as I know C.A. is still with me.

If you're up and around when this arrives, see Bob Low. He's full of fascinating stories about Libya and everywhere else. I'll tell him to give you a ring, anyway. He's my latest educator and I'm damned sore he's leaving, because he's full of ideas as to what I should do.

I must stop now, my best love to you all.

Puff

PS My latest is a Polish count. He produced 6 orchids New Year's Eve when I said I couldn't celebrate with him. I'm not sure if that might be called a compliment.

Dorchester Hotel, London
January 5, 1942

Mouche dear,

I got a letter from you dated Dec. 7th. It seems odd to me – you were depressed. I wonder if any event has ever made me happier?

I hope this letter arrives in time, as here's our list of wants:

1) [Small] radio, extra batteries
2) Some "bras"
3) 2 dark & 2 medium lipsticks, non-perfume
4) 2 girdles – one my size, one size smaller
5) A navy snood – the other 2 you sent Pam loves
6) 3 sets of slips & undies (one white), your first batch were swell
7) Tube of mascara
8) Pair dark brown shoes – the Bonwit Teller model
9) A little cake frosting sugar
10) A couple of romper suits (Viyella) – 1½ yr. child (Winston), he's big for his age
11) My cold cream – if possible Nivea cream

News of interest: finally found a flat in No. 3 Grosvenor Sq. – serviced. Also, we've given up Petersfield Farm for a ⅓ cost nicer (smaller) cottage 10 minutes from the older one. I was down there yesterday. Things are messy now as tubs & loos are being installed but it will be nice – modern – no beams or nooked fireplaces. The other cottage got us down it's so dark and dreary.

Can't think of any more immediate news – my work has suddenly taken a turn for the better – with a little more fighting I may get there – but the worst is over.

I'm sorry this letter is so boring but I have only a moment. *Sun Valley Serenade* has come to town.[10] Hope to see it. Also the ski-joring short you spoke about. Nothing like sneaking off to see yourself in the movies!

Best love,

Kathleen

PS A couple of Hammacher Schlemmer lighters would be appreciated by friends, & of course stockings.

---

10 A Hollywood musical set in the Sun Valley, Idaho ski resort created by Averell Harriman in the 1930s. 'Ski-joring' involves the skier being pulled along by an animal or vehicle.

CHAPTER 7

'I'M TRYING TO BRUSH UP ON PAST EUROPEAN HISTORY – I STILL CAN'T TELL A RUMANIAN FROM A CROAT OR A SERB'

Early 1942 was a time of setbacks for the allied war effort. The Japanese were advancing in Asia and the Pacific. The Soviet counter-offensive that had pushed the Germans back from the outskirts of Moscow was faltering. German submarines were devastating British and US merchant shipping in the Atlantic – likewise in the Arctic, where many ships laden with desperately needed supplies for Russia were being sunk.

In February 1942 Beaverbrook was appointed Minister of War Production but resigned after twelve days as a result of a clash with the Minister of Labour, the trade union leader Ernest Bevin. Thereafter Beaverbrook devoted himself to campaigning for an immediate invasion of northern France to draw German forces away from the Eastern Front war in Russia. Like Churchill and her father, Kathy doubted the feasibility of opening a second front in France, at least in the short term.

On the professional front, Kathy was given the job of reporting on the exiled leaders of Belgium, Czechoslovakia, Greece, Luxembourg, the Netherlands, Norway, Poland and Yugoslavia, whose governments had fled Nazi occupation and relocated to London. It was an experience that inured her to the cult of Stalin that swept across the allied world during the war and proved useful preparation for her time in Moscow. Also on her new beat was General de Gaulle and the Free French – opponents of Marshal Pétain's Vichy regime which, in collaboration with the Germans, controlled central and southern France and its colonial territories in Africa, Asia and the Middle East.

London
January 12, 1942

Dear Mary,

Seems to me I've been doing nothing but write letters the past week. Have heard nothing at all from anyone since Bobby was born. Please get someone to write me if you can't as I'm dying to hear.

News? Well I'm working but talks of that probably are boring. In case you're interested, I almost had my first scoop on Friday night. For a couple of hours things were really exciting – a Jugoslav political story – the censors wouldn't pass it. Today is Monday and the story still hasn't got through. Hourly I expect to get word.

Did I tell you I've been handed Red's old side job of the free governments? In between times I'm trying to brush up on past European history. I still can't tell a Rumanian from a Croat or a Serb. Tonight I'm dining with a Slovene (I think) just as a starter.

Thanks to Randolph I got wind of the sacked Libyan general being in town.[1] After a hellova lot of trouble I got hold of his address. Now all there is to do is to persuade him that he must see me, either on or off the record.

My battle with Inez Robb doesn't look as though it will come off. When I wrote you via Bob Low I was all set to combat her charges, now I've calmed down and decided to leave her alone. From various compatriots I've learned she's just waiting for me to rise. I won't give her that pleasure. She must be a very maladjusted female or something.

As our new cottage isn't ready, the three of us, Randolph, Pam and I went down to Lord Melchett's for the weekend.[2] Very pleasant. Randolph and Henry consider themselves great connoisseurs of wine and liquors. So on Sat. night son aged 17 got 6 glasses of drink, which we all had to identify blindfolded. The results were

1 Probably General Archibald Wavell, who was removed as Middle East theatre commander by Churchill in June 1941 and transferred to India.
2 Colworth House in Bedfordshire.

unbelievable. We were given vodka twice – most everyone called it gin once, whiskey the second time – other simple tasting drinks like rye, brandy, port etc. The old-time drinkers got but two right and a 19-year-old Eton boy guessed every one correctly. In case you and Shirley ever want to make some money off your friends – try that game – it's very amusing.

Jan. 13

Today I covered the inter-allied conference on what to do with Quislings after the war.[3] The various prime ministers spoke in French or bad English. The whole ceremony was rather fairy-tale like – in St. James's Palace – seated around a huge red-topped table, blaring lights, news-reels. Each old man read his speech (which had already been released). It all seems so damned unimportant and remote from the war. I was disillusioned to find that the new Jugoslav P.M. is a tiny shrivelled old man with a high squeaky voice. Give me Simovitch[4] any day!

Since I've been going around in free-gov't circles, I've found a very different Stalin feeling. (Different from Averell.) They distrust him and fear him and figure he's doing a good job of out-smarting the Americans and British. Talking to my boss about it this morning, I discovered that Joe Evans[5] of the *Herald Trib.* got himself thoroughly in hot water with Brendan Bracken for speaking against the future motives of "our brave allies." Is there any feeling like that at home?

Bestest love
[Kathleen]

London
January 19, 1942

Dear Mouche,

I got a letter from you dated Xmas day. I'm sorry you haven't heard from me. I seem to be continually writing people. I wonder if you've

---

3 Political and other collaborators with the Germans, so called after Vidkun Quisling, head of the Norwegian government during the Nazi occupation.
4 Dušan Simović (1882–1962), former general who served as Yugoslavia's prime minister 1941–2. He was succeeded by Slobodan Jovanović (1869–1958).
5 Joseph S. Evans (1909–78).

received a letter from me via Quent Reynolds. He took one and so did Bob Low. They both should have arrived by now, but I guess they'll let me know when they do hit N.Y.C.

I'd like to see Inez Robb's stuff. She's being a fearful bitch, I'm sorry to say. Most uncooperative and for a while caused me a hellova lot of trouble. While she's still here I can't work in the office, because I never know when she's going to start spitting at me. If only she'd be decent, I'd like to get to know her and learn a trick or two. She came here with strict orders to help me. Instead she's decided it's worth her while to try and tunnel me out of the organization. I must say I'm flattered! Unfortunately, everyone around Fleet Street and my office dislikes her intensely. In another month she'll be gone for good and a great sigh of relief will be had by all!

Pam's husband has arrived. We agree on nothing but get along fine. I get nightly lectures on the fact (an unarguable one according to Randolph) that women have inferior brains to men, or that Britain is heading for racial suicide. He's trying to marry me off to Brendan Bracken, the Min. of Information!

[Randolph's] a very likeable boy, with an amazing memory, good brain, and an equally amazing lack of human understanding.

I went down to see the P.M. arrive at Paddington and discovered that I.N.S. was unrepresented so I covered it. Driving back to Downing Street, Randolph plied one of the members of the party with all the questions I wanted to know while I just sat and tried to remember. Once at Downing St., I left them and rushed to the nearest Whitehall phone booth and filed the story.

Slight break – just returned from seeing the new Garbo film, which I enjoyed more than anything seen of late (come to think of it, I haven't been to a movie for ages).[6] It's snowing like the blazes. If I'd had a pair of skis this weekend I would have skied at Box Hill, near Dorking. It might have been fun! Instead Win. Brown – one of Averell's Lend-Lease stooges – and I went for a walk and found a lovely old church and graveyard, parts of which were 14th century. Someday I

---

6 *Two-Faced Woman* (1941), an American romantic comedy and Garbo's last film.

think I'll go to church there. It's quite near our new cottage. Perhaps the vicar will be as quaint.

My social life is [filled] with foreigners since I took on Red Mueller's job of covering the free gov'ts. Don't be too horrified, I'm not completely selling my soul for the sake of a story!

Oddly enough the people I used to go out with when I first came here have retired out of the picture. Some have moved on elsewhere, others I've become bored with or had to give up for various reasons. It's a funny life in that way. I have a host of casual acquaintances and a few quickly made friends. But being busy I don't really need friends, in a dependent sort of way. Last Saturday I was in the country alone. There was a good Victrola [record player] and some nice records and I enjoyed myself immensely. Sometimes I wonder why I don't do it more often.

I'm sorry your hopes of my coming home at Xmas were in vain. I'd have come like a shot, only I'm just beginning to get somewhere. When Inez leaves I'll get a lot farther. It would have been foolish to ruin six months of work just for a couple of weeks of pleasure.

Funnily enough, when I first came over I talked a lot about being serious about the newspaper business without being able to convince myself. Now I'm really beginning to like it. It lacks all the boredom of routine and at times is quite exciting. The next day, the fact that you filed a story an hour ahead of the other agencies doesn't mean much, but at the time it's fun. Besides, the people in the game (foreign correspondents, not reporters) are damned nice.

Maybe I'm wrong, but the next few months at home are going to see a wave of frustration. I'd just as soon miss it. There's nothing worse than being surrounded by a lot of people champing at the bit, raring to go, but with nowhere to go to. Here I can experience it vicariously. At home I'd probably be one of them. Thank you no.

I love getting clippings of friends' doings. They make me feel very far away, but without regrets. That doesn't mean I've lost interest in home – it's just at the moment I am lucky enough to be getting something else. Don't despair or worry about me Mouche dear. I haven't changed much. That's the last thing I'd want to happen!

My best love to you all,

Kathleen

London
February 3, 1942

Dear Marie and Mary,

Averell's back and now after 24 hours I wonder how and why I can like London when he's not here. While he bathed I figured out which of the three ways I wanted to wear my BEAUTIFUL green hat. Without a crown was decided upon and at last we set off to Max's. The three of us had a very nice very late dinner. Then the two of them rushed off to see the P.M.

Later on Averell and I again met here, and I was just getting him started on gossip when Randolph, clad in pyjamas arrived down, so we started off again on the subject of the Averell–Randolph axis.

The news that Shirley is about to become involved in this godforsaken war took me completely by surprise. Somehow I hadn't figured on it hitting family so quick. To say I'm sorry doesn't mean much – war is a bloody invention anyway. Now suddenly I feel almost ashamed: here I am sitting over here, in the whirl of excitement, while you all stay at home with the harder end to keep up.

Averell arrived home at that moment and we went in his room and worried about the supply of nylons he brought back. He's funny as the devil about his "stockings." Did I have them properly supported for size etc? It looks as though big-footed Mrs Eden is going to get a big lot. Averell brought back quantities of size eleven and a half, so now my job is to find women to fit into them!

My half a husband[7] is going back to the M.E. soon. We'll miss his nightly lectures. He spoke on the second day of the [parliamentary] debate and was brilliant, spontaneous and exceedingly tactless, but Winston was pleased and that's what matters. Quite a relief from the usual boring run of speeches. (I was there.)

Incidentally, I just discovered I have a very desperate need – PLEASE SHIP IMMEDIATELY – London has run out of any form of Kotex.[8] At the moment my supply is being smuggled from the American Red Cross hospital.

---

7 Randolph Churchill.
8 A brand of sanitary towel.

Any good books would be appreciated, too. Also a subscription to *Vogue* & *Harper's* & *Reader's Digest* would be nice. Which reminds me – I walked in to Worth today & bought a beautiful black evening number. So now I'll be able to vamp all the generals at Chequers this weekend!

Best love,
Kath

London
February 10, 1942

Dear Marie and Mary,

News? Singapore – Averell was amazed when I told him Fleet St., anyway the Americans, thought its fall inevitable and has for some time. But now that the end is near it seems hard to believe. I wonder what comes next, and why in the hell are we still holding out with a handful of men in the Philippines when the British can't with many thousands. There's something funny somewhere. Thank God for MacArthur[9] and our troops. The comparison though uncomfortable to the British should be healthy. The P.M. I know never expected the island to fall so quickly.

There's political intrigue going on at the moment. Outwardly the trouble is over the new production head. Beaverbrook has been made the head with responsibility for Britain's production but no powers to have his will enforced. He's not happy. Commons isn't happy about the gov't changes. The people aren't happy (Randolph says that doesn't matter – nothing but Parliament matters to him). The whole thing is a mess.

I found Chequers rather depressing this [last] weekend. It is depressing to see a great man tired and depressed. The war is going badly, and to top it all his ministers are doing all they can to crack down on him, individually and collectively, and try and get what they want. He hates criticism, it hurts him as it would a child being unjustly

9 General Douglas MacArthur (1880–1964), commander of US troops defending the Philippines, which fell to the Japanese in March 1942.

spanked by a mother, and so he in turn is being obstinate. He refuses to compromise with anyone.

In the background looms the new and potential strong figure of Sir Stafford Cripps.[10] The whole thing is rather a mess, this is the goddamnest time to get into party politics. It would be nice when we can really get to work and fight just the Germans and Italians and Japs and Rumanians and Bulgarians and all the rest.

I made a discovery this weekend – Winant has a sense of humor. That great mystery loves to be teased. I paid him a call Sunday morning (no one rises for breakfast at Chequers) and found him looking rather like a modest maiden sitting up in bed. For my benefit he half-covered himself with a wrapper. Anyway, I found a couple of his cigars on the dresser and as they smelled of perfume rather than tobacco, accused him of all sorts of things. He loved it!

Sarah was down there too, she's a W.A.A.F. now doing very hush-hush work and now about to go to an O.C.T.U. [Officer Cadet Training Unit] to learn to become an officer. Gosh she's a nice girl, her acting and dancing and all that entailed hasn't spoiled her a bit.

Best love to you all and many thanks for all the wonderful things.

Kathy

PS I'm running short of my face cream.

London
February 20, 1942

Dear Mary,

I come home at night gloomy, mad or depressed and then at various stages around my dresser mirror I find Bobby, always smiling and not giving a damn about what the Japs are doing or what the British didn't do at Singapore. It must be nice for you to have something constructive to think about other than the war!

The government changes story broke last night. You know all about that I guess. I disapproved of what I.N.S. filed as to the

10 Stafford Cripps (1889–1952), Labour politician, British ambassador to Moscow 1940–1. A highly popular public figure when he returned from Moscow in January 1942.

meaning of the changes (the significance) but as my services to give a "true picture" were not accepted or welcome by the stupid old night desk man, I retired home to bed and mentally wrote a piece, which I'm sure would have been sensational!!!

Today I got a wonderful break. A couple of days ago I phoned Sir Stafford Cripps and asked for an interview on Russia which I thought might make a reasonable mailer. We arranged the time for this morning and with last night's announcement of him as Lord Privy Seal and War Cab. spokesman in Commons, anything said by the dear man are pearls of the highest price. I saw him for about 10 minutes. He spilled a few platitudes about America and Britain sticking together and an hour later I.N.S. in N.Y. cabled congratulations how smart I'd been to have gotten the first exclusive interview with England's newest glamour boy. It's the first byline cable story I've had for ages, that's about all that's nice about it. No hard work was involved, it was just a lucky break.

I'm still sweating over a mail series on juvenile delinquency. Spent Tuesday night down in the toughest sections of London drinking warm and bitter tea with would-be delinquents, who have been enticed to spend their hours of relaxation in the local boys' club rather than at a pub or gambling.

Tuesday, Wednesday and Thursday I lived down at the MOI covering the conferences and hot communiqués, and playing gin rummy with the U.P. man, and today I listened while the stupid old Min. of Aircraft Production told us nothing new or stuff that we also knew but is too secret to use.

God only knows what's going to happen to the production of England now that Max is out, but as Averell says the war won't be won or lost by ten less planes a month. I suppose Max will wait until things get into a real chaotic state, then he'll make a comeback into the gov't. As a matter of fact, he really isn't well. He was very gloomy last Saturday night, he's scared about dying I think, so probably a sojourn in Florida will be better in the long run.

My chief informers on public opinion are Averell's chauffeur and the 18-year-old lift girl at the office. Both are desperately upset that he's leaving the government. He's the one fighting man outside of

Churchill and they like the way he goes around talking to the workers and being tough with Whitehall boobies.

Finally met Sir Walter Citrine[11] – head trade union man – at Cherkley on Sunday night. His wife looks like somebody's cook on a spree and Sir Walter is the acme of stupidity. I'm afraid I wasn't very polite. He was sitting around the fireplace, he was expounding on Russia and suddenly I woke up half hour later. He was still on Russia. I wonder what trade unions see in him.

I'm wondering how Quent is and when he's coming back and if you finally met him. My friend Red has finally turned up in Batavia after having been lost for some weeks. He ought to be able to get stories from there.

Please tell Uncle Roland that I'm investigating the Boys Club situation – that many of them have been blitzed and many more are very much functioning. They all seem to be self-supporting, but I imagine if his N.Y. club wants to send some money to one over here, that would be much appreciated. I could find a particular club for him, if he wants. Also tell him that after a very superficial glance at the juvenile delinquency situation (one day in court, talking to several judges and Boys Clubs leaders) I would say that the war hasn't given rise to anything more than a normal increase (30%?). I'm writing about three stories on the various angles, so you might show them to him when they finally come out.

February 23rd

Still no sign of the ambassador leaving so letter continues. New batch of gov't changes came out last night. Everyone is pretty pleased about Moore-Brabazon going out and Moyne and David.[12] In the latter case of course I'm prejudiced the other way, he's one of my pet

11 Walter Citrine (1887–1983), General-Secretary of the Trades Union Congress.
12 John Moore-Brabazon (1884–1964), resigned as Minister of Aircraft Production after saying that he hoped Nazi Germany and communist Russia would destroy each other; Lord Moyne (Walter Guinness, 1880–1944), Colonial Secretary 1941–2, then served in the Middle East, where he was assassinated by Zionists; David Margesson (1890–1965), Secretary of State for War 1940–2, scapegoated by Churchill for the fall of Singapore to the Japanese in February 1942.

British politicians, a delightful man, the acme of tact and diplomacy and has had a most difficult role of late due to his big part in Chamberlain's regime (he was Chief Whip of Conservative party). J. Llewellyn comes up a step to M.A.P. [Minister of Aircraft Production], the consensus of opinion is that aircraft production will benefit. Lord Moyne I only met once and he struck me as a very old doddery man. Cranbourne who takes his place in the Colonial Office is awful nice. Spent the night with him when Averell went to the Middle East.

Went down to the cottage on Saturday for a little rest and relaxation. Pam and Randolph are permanently there until he goes back.

Dined with Beaverbrook last night. He's asthmatic. I interviewed him, wrote the thing up then and there, he passed it. This morning I made some amplifications on own interpretations, with the result that he's raising the roof. Hope to hell he won't take it out on Averell.

February 23rd – at night

Letters written in bed usually prove to be unsent ones – I've written a good many – but can't remember ever having the will to envelope it next morning.

If only I were a Bill Stoneman[13] – a Quent or someone, I'd start educating the U.S. public on Britain's future hopes. J. Llewellyn heads that list. I want to interview him badly. I.N.S. isn't enthusiastic. Maybe I'll still do it.

Please write and tell me who U.S. knows in the Brit. gov't outside Bevin and Beaverbrook – what are they interested in? Inez Robb's articles were very simple – they dealt with what I figure are obvious facts. I wrote stories broadly on her topics months and months ago – but if you say there's interest I'll pitch in again.

Today Mme and Ambass. Maisky[14] gave a big cocktail blowout for God and his puppy dog. Every damned person who is anything or means anything was there plus wife. Men who I've met at Chequers,

13 William H. Stoneman (1904–87), foreign and war correspondent for the *Chicago Daily News*.

14 Ivan Maisky (1884–1975), Soviet ambassador to Britain 1932–43, famous for his socialising and politicking, especially in Churchill's circle. Agniya Alexandrovna Skipina (1895–1975) was his third wife.

Cherkley or around London – now suddenly produce wives – dreary creatures – but kindly and well meaning. I begin to understand why England's better halves are kept in the background and only produced on such rare occasions.

Mrs Ernie Bevin wears a handsome mink coat – it's new – whereas Mrs Anthony Eden's looks at least 5 years old! What fun one could have – dealing with celebrities in terms of how they treat their wives!

Tonight gave dinner for Alexander Korda[15] – he's intense, interesting and the intellectual movie man as opposed to Sam Goldwyn.

It was interesting getting Korda's fresh viewpoint. It must be amazing for ex-isolationists to know that the pattern of their future anti-British propaganda program is well known.

Poor Korda – he's philosophical enough not to be bitter by the way the Brit. receive his constructive ideas – I wonder if we at Washington are any less dampening! The whole subject is one of Averell's pets.

February 25th

Averell was a terrific success at a huge lunch today – I'm really extremely proud of him. He spoke to what's supposed to be a rather select group. General point of speech: "Churchill's place in the World today." Got in a lot of excellent points about American production, that it mustn't be belittled, and the significance of the Roosevelt–Churchill friendship.

Everyone was very complimentary afterwards. It was his first speech since he's arrived and the way it was received was very much a tribute. Randolph, who is always under the impression that the world has no great speakers other than the two Churchills, was quite bewildered that Averell hasn't spoken before and naively amazed that he was so good. Which, as a sidelight on Randolph, rather amuses me.

I imagine it's rather hard at home to realize the strength of Averell's position over here and what a wonderful job he's doing towards consolidating Brit.'s and U.S.'s production. He gets things done and

15 Alexander Korda (1893–1956), Hungarian-born British filmmaker.

still keeps friends, an interesting comparison perhaps to the Beaver. I've just been asked to do an article here on him for a British magazine! As I can't say the things I'd like to say, I won't do it.

I sat next to a stupid woman at the lunch, who is the wife of somebody who I guess is important. She couldn't understand why I ever wanted to come over here, much less stay! I dislike worthless people, worthless Englishwomen more than anything.

If it's easy to send parcels over here you might get together some things like my blue spring coat and anything else that's nice. My mouth waters every time I open an American magazine and see dress ads.

There's no point in making plans these days, but one thing is obvious: a trip home will be one-way.

My bestest love to you all,

Puff

CHAPTER 8

'AMERICA CERTAINLY ISN'T IN A WAR SPIRIT'

While the war was Kathy's constant preoccupation, for her the big news of spring 1942 was the Harrimans' move from the Dorchester Hotel to an apartment at 3 Grosvenor Square, a townhouse beside the US embassy. It was a 'serviced' flat, which meant that Ave and Kathy had access to the embassy's commissary. As well as bedrooms for Kathy and Ave, there was a small room reserved for Pamela Churchill's use when she was in town, though she expected to spend a lot of time living in the country with baby Winston. Later in the war, Pam moved into her own apartment in Grosvenor Square.

London
early March 1942

Dear Mary,

Wish you'd seen Max when he was in N.Y.C. Would have loved to get your reaction. I've learned a lot about English politics in general watching him at work.

Everybody knows that he and Averell are friends. I only hope that won't do him harm (Averell) with people now in the gov't. For God's sake don't tell Averell I said that.

But you can't be friends and confidants of everyone at the same time and Max has a lot of enemies. Averell's doing a great job over here. His position is one created entirely due to his own personality. Actually, I suppose he's got hardly any power or authority at all.

Last Sunday we motored over to Chartwell – the P.M.'s own place. The P.M. was there alone & he took us around his garden – showed us the brick walls he'd laid, the ponds & swimming pool he'd built and talked about what he was going to do after the war: Make a waterfall, "a big splash – not just a trickle." There at Chartwell, surrounded by his own things, the things he's created himself, one almost feels sorry for him. He's had to give up all his personal pleasures. The war's tiring & ageing him terribly, but he never lets up.

The gas rationing must be hell. I'm ashamed to say that I get more than that here (thank God). Covering stories by car is so much quicker and efficient. Buses and trains out of London take so long & then they end you up miles away from where you really want to go.

Marie-André always asks after you, as does Geoffrey Patterson – who turns up in London regularly once a month, invariably arrives in the midst of a crisis – so I have little chance to see him. I think he's the most persistent creature I've ever met and that's going some! I've also picked up a phony Polish count.

Here I come to the end of the page.

Bestest love,

Puff

London
March 6, 1942

Dear Mary,

Today the world was going so badly I got into another of my "moods" – that Averell usually can get me out of.

Early this morning I went to cover the arrival of the first A.E.F. [American Expeditionary Force] in London. They were a fine bunch of boys. We interviewed them in their barracks hotel. I stayed for a couple of hours – going from room to room. In one way I had an advantage over the journalists, being the gal in the group, but at times it was nip and tuck who was interviewing whom.

Such statements as "I hated leaving home but being in London is better than the frontline" kept hitting me in the face. America certainly isn't what you might call in a war spirit is it? Those boys were on what the censor would prefer me to call "staff" – they certainly have no more idea than the man in the moon what this war's being fought about – much less what's at stake. Don't let me get going on that score.

Batavia, Bandeong, Java as a whole is going, Rangoon too – they will probably all be gone by the time this reaches you. India and its seas too for that matter. Then soon we'll no longer be able to look forward to the Russian communiqués and say "well at least the war's going well on one front." Am I being a heretic? Are you wishful thinkers at home?

Tonight I dined with one of my favorite men – he's middle-aged, bald – so don't worry. A soldier by profession, capable, honest and full of common sense. My gosh he's refreshing. He's fairly high up in the operational side of R.A.F. fighter command, but still a nobody. He's one of my few friends that I can blow off steam on. Then he talks and fills me with confidence. There are so few people who honestly make it their job towards doing their damnedest to help win this bloody war.

March 7th

I'm again in bed. I've been doing so damned much typing of late you've gonna have to put up with my writing.

Yesterday I was in a bad way – soon I'll get used to thinking the world is coming to an end. Today I told the B.B.C. what I thought of their North American broadcasts – not much I can tell you – it helped cheer me up. After, I covered Oliver Lyttelton's press conference at the M of I, a good one I thought. Then came the routine military conf. The situations in Java and Burma were both so confused it's difficult at times to file quick flash sentences that are meaningful. Today was one of the hardest I've yet come up against. This afternoon I again held down the Ministry until it was time to go pick Averell up at Henry Luce's.[1] He ain't a very impressionable guy somehow – my God he's inarticulate. It was interesting though seeing what he thought of England – he had so few new ideas. The one real point we agreed on was that England is very socialistic – getting more and more so.

---

1 Henry Luce (1898–1967), editor-in-chief of *Time*, *Life* and *Fortune*, famous for a 1941 editorial in *Life* that declared the twentieth century 'The American Century'.

After that Ave and I went to a cocktail party given by our navy for three members who are about to return home and go on active duty. I met my first ensign there – an awful nice Harvard kid from Brooklyn. Everyone got very drunk as time went on – so finally I persuaded Averell to leave – on principle. I think I like our Army Air Corps best in the way of senior officers and the Navy youngsters. I don't know any straight army but I'm getting quite good now. I can tell people's titles from their pips and stripes – being different from the British I found it confusing at first!

What's Shirley look like in his uniform – or don't docs wear 'em – when will he be going overseas? How's the baby? I haven't heard from anyone since Ave brought letters. The mail must be slow these days. You never tell me if you read my cable stories.

Bestest of love,

Puff

Dorchester Hotel, London
March 13, 1942

Dear Mouche,

For some reason I'm busier than ever – covering the A.E.F. in London is a weekly duty. All in all they think the British are the friendliest nation they'd yet to meet.

A group of Nat'l Guardsmen from the Mid-West until now have been stationed in Louisiana. Comment on reception there was "they're still fighting the civil war down there." The Westerners resented being called damned Yankees. Here in London strangers stand 'em drinks at the local pubs, stop them in the streets & welcome 'em to England. The A.E.F. men get saluted by the Brit Tommy (their uniforms are like Brit. officers' uniforms) so they're very impressed & happy. They spend their spare time watching the guards change at Buck House – visit the Tower, Westminster Abbey etc. The English girls receive them with open arms. I wonder if this happy picture will continue. It's a good thing tho for Anglo-Amer. relations.

Today I interviewed Geoffrey Lloyd, the Min. of Petroleum on the stopping of all pleasure driving for the duration. From now on my car will have to be used strictly for business reasons, which means more training – I hate English trains!!

Finally, flat arrangements are settled – we move into No. 3 Grosvenor Sq. on the 1st of April. It will be pleasant!

How's Mary, the baby? When's Shirley leaving? What are your plans? There's so much I'd like to know.

Best love,

Kathleen

London
March 16, 1942

Mouche dear,

Getting your letter was most exciting – the 1st since Averell returned except for a Chicago one sent by boat.

Now that we're at last moving into a flat we'd very much like a weekly food parcel – tinned meat (or in glass jars) & cheese & an occasional jar of mayonnaise, tin of cocktail biscuits.

We don't need tea, & things like fruits come thru with the canteen service, though not too regularly. I'd also like cigarettes because canteen supply is very limited & they make very appreciated presents – Chesterfields preferably.

Thanks for the Robb clippings. As I never see any of my own, I'd like it if you sent things like Sikorski interviews, the Cripps one etc.

I'm working like bloody hell. We've lost 2 men to Cairo, another to Moscow, and so far they're unreplaced. Shorthandedness makes me the only roving reporter at the moment. Consequently, think I'll soon have to ration my evenings & go out only 2 or 3 times a week. Probably will be good for me, but I have so many nice friends that I so enjoy seeing. Having no age restrictions opens the field considerably.

This afternoon as a great concession I was allowed in on secret joint House session of the Anglo-American committee. Averell spoke wonderfully well – extemporaneously on Amer. production, reasons for anti-Brit feelings at home etc. The question period was excellent – questions intelligent and Averell answered them very well. All in all, it was a great success. I was exceedingly proud of him.

Rumors 'round London say Winant not coming back – Averell to be next ambass. Wonder if U.S. thinks so too.

Bestest love to you all – & please start packages coming soon as possible.

Kathleen

London
March 24, 1941

Dear Mary,

My gosh what a cute kid you've produced! I loved yours of Feb. 27th.

Think I wrote and told you that Averell addressed the joint Commons and Lords secret session last week. He made a short speech on production and Anglo-American relations and what should be done to forward them. During question period he was excellent. They were mad about him. He did terribly well. I was allowed in on it, which was nice.

Personal news: I'm about to develop a new boss. C.A. Smith is to become assistant chief, somebody called (forgotten the name damn it) is coming over to take charge, probably in about a month. So it looks as though the struggles have to start again!

The last few days have been spent talking to foreign-speaking press attachés and writing human interest occupied-country stories. Done well it would be a full-time job; as I have so many other incidental assignments it's hard to find the necessary hours. Of late I seem to have produced a boring number of clothes rationing stories – on utility clothes, coupon values etc.

Does Shirley wear a uniform? Is he the rank of Captain? Is he scheduled for the A.B.D.A. area or where?[2] I suppose your plans don't extend any further into the future than mine do.

Averell seems to be more rested than he was. He works English hours. Works in bed in the morning, goes to the office at about 11 and seldom gets home before 8:30. His secretaries get a

---

2 ABDA was the American, British, Dutch and Australian command in Southeast Asia.

great deal of sympathy from me but they don't seem to mind their extraordinary hours.

Just returned from a Biddle lunch – the Belgians today. As Averell says, we've been put on their "feeding list." Today he wasn't asked – guess the people weren't sufficiently important. But I picked up a new contact who ought to be worth quite a lot – a young guy, Under-sec. of Foreign Affairs. The under-secs are usually better than the higher Ministers of State.

Last week the Biddles gave a small "intimate" lunch (so said the invitation) for the King of Norway to meet our general and admiral and Averell. As time goes on I get more and more grateful to Mr Hubble for having taught me how to curtsy. It comes in kind of handy these days.

March 27

It's Saturday now and unfortunately the Germans broadcast the news of a British commando raid on St. Nazaire last night.[3] Nothing other than one brief confirmation statement has come out of the War Office as yet and probably won't until later this evening. Being general stooge and water boy I got to stick around until we're sure no further details are forthcoming.

Interviewed a just-escaped-from-the-Gestapo Norwegian yesterday. He says food situation most critical there. Butter is used as lubricant by Germans. His greatest value was amazing story of escape, which I wrote up at length.

Yesterday went to most boring Biddle lunch for de Gaulle. Huge affair in hot smelly room. As Bob Post[4] of the *NY Times* spent most of the meal being nasty, I didn't enjoy it one bit. As Averell was surrounded by French-speaking ladies I'm sure he suffered as much as I.

Alexander Korda gave an amusing dinner the other night – an odd mixture that led to interesting talk on lit. The Maiskys,

---

3 A large-scale amphibious raid on the St Nazaire naval dry dock in Normandy, during which the British suffered heavy casualties.

4 Robert Perkins Post (1910–43). Post was shot down and killed whilst observing a USAF bombing raid on Germany.

H.G. Wells, the Leslie Howards[5] and us. Maisky I like the way you would a baby teddy bear. I was put off Mrs M. the moment she told me she'd hate to have children. That's an unnatural point of view and anyway she's loud, is rather masculine looking but wears feminine frills and furs. She always gushes over me as though I were bosom pal no. 1 and I hate that. But to get back to the Korda dinner. H.G. Wells has a high squeaky voice and acts rather like a spoiled child who must have attention. I enjoyed meeting him but wasn't impressed. The Leslie Howards were just ordinary civilians with not much to say for themselves.

March 30

That St. Nazaire raid turned out to be something big didn't it. With things like that happening ever so often perhaps people will stop yelling about the impossible second front.

Domestic news centers around our apartment. Cleaners move in on the 1st and we as soon after that date as the place is presentable. Running a household by Harriman methods of being late and unexpected ain't gonna be so easy. Averell is adamant we eat our own food. He figures that if other people can live on their rations so can we. I figure that English people don't entertain as regularly as we do. Averell always has somebody business-minded to lunch and then there's usually three or four of us for dinner. However, that's a problem I'm going to turn over to our one maid. As a full-time job, I'm not too keen on housekeeping.

Speaking of food, I got a good interview with Woolton – Minister of Food – which included a scoop that luxury feeding in restaurants is to stop soon. I.N.S. wasn't much interested. I'm glad restaurants are going to have to cut down because whereas they don't consume anything worth bothering about, there's a lot of press talk about the Savoy hotel feeding and how outrageous it is. In case you didn't

5 Leslie Howard (1893–1943), British actor and Hollywood movie star, killed when his KLM flight from Lisbon to Bristol was shot down by the Luftwaffe. He was married to Ruth Evelyn Martin (1895–1980).

realize it, Woolton provides 80 million meals a week in catering establishments which can be had for ninepence or slightly more.

It looks as though I'm going to be up to my neck in commitments about A.E.F. entertainment, welfare etc. Mrs Biddle is the guiding spirit behind it and Bunny Carter[6] and the U.S. army welfare officer the chief dampeners. I'm afraid I'm not a great admirer of Bunny. He talks big but gets not much done.

My job is to find out what the troops want in the way of entertainment, particularly officers. So far all they've asked for is a list of girls they can take out. That involves all sorts of problems. I don't know as any organization, Red Cross or otherwise, can be responsible for a girl's safety with an American fresh on leave from Iceland or Northern Ireland!!!!

It was most exciting getting Mouche's wire saying that a coat and four dresses were on the way over. I'm so sick of my few dresses that I could scream.

London is a hellova place for clothes, even ready-to-wear jobs are about $100. "Utility" clothes of course are fixed price, but they look rather like Macy's basement models, only not so chic.

Please tell Mouche I stayed in on Friday night and read her *Saratoga Trunk* and enjoyed it a lot.[7] At the moment I'm involved in the Polish campaign in Norway, after that I've got me a Greek campaign book to read, presented me by one Mr Christopoulos, who seems to be great friends with all the Sun Valley Greeks. He's head of the Greek information bureau, and, as Greeks go, is very nice.

April 6

We're officially out of the Dorchester. If I'd ever foreseen the difficulties involved I'd never have been brave enough to attempt it!! Our maid who I hired got temperamental on Saturday and decided first

6 Bernard Carter (1893–1961), American banker who organised American Red Cross activities in Britain and served as an army intelligence officer during the war.
7 Edna Ferber's romantic historical novel set in nineteenth-century New Orleans and upstate New York. Published in 1941, the book was later made into a film starring Ingrid Bergman and Gary Cooper.

she did then she didn't want to come to us after all, so I went chasing around town trying to find her. Four washermen took three days to wash three rooms, small ones at that. So at the moment my bedroom is filled with kitchen utensils, liquor, canned food plus all my clothes. We are blanketless and not owning or being able to buy a can opener, I don't see how we'll ever be able to eat any of our commissary food! It's all rather amusing.

Easter wasn't very Easter-like. But it suddenly made me realize I've been over here damn near a year. We were in the country. Had a political warfare American to stay and Bruce Lockhart,[8] so the subject of conversation was mostly occupied countries and Russia. Most interesting. We did a lot of talking about planting potatoes and carrots, but no one seemed quite to know how one goes about planting a potato. Net result: no potatoes in the Harriman family garden as yet!!

India is subject of interest at the moment. Thursday I hiked me around to Amery,[9] Minister of State for India. He's an ardent mountain climber, skier etc. and general boy scout. Tiny and wizen to look at. Sits on a high chair with a footstool to support his feet. He talked off the record. Said there was still hope for success in India, but that Gandhi's support was never anticipated. Did you know that the Rajah states comprise one half of India and quarter of the population? You probably did, but I didn't.

Today I lunched with a tank corps major, who was full of amusing stories of rape and murder. He's stationed in the country that's full of Canadian backwoodsmen who are bored stiff and tend to get surly when drunk.

Marie-André writes that his tank corps is to be moved to southern Scotland and that English soldiers are to take their place. The civilian population are furious. They love their Poles, but hate those lousy "southerners," as they call the English.

---

8 R. Bruce Lockhart (1887–1970), British spy and special agent who was active in efforts to overthrow the early Bolshevik regime in Russia.

9 L.S. Amery (1873–1955), Conservative politician, Secretary of State for India 1940–5.

He (Marie-André) has developed a wonderful sense of humor, I only wish he could get off on leave more often. I'm sure he'd know how to plant potatoes!

Your package of lemon juice and sugar and cocoa arrived this morning. Ever so many thanks.

I must stop now and write a piece about 200 Free French women.

Bestest love to you all,

Kathleen

Petersfield Farm, Surrey
April 16, 1942

Dear Marie,

I haven't written for ages but I guess Mary shows you what she gets.

Harry [Hopkins] has been great fun over here. We're all down in the country today – me to get a bit of much-needed rest.

Now we're in a flat, life in London is heaven. It's so nice to get away from hotel elevators, waiters and keys. I enclosed a plan of it to Miss M. just now, but it's sunny & clean and overlooks Ave's offices. Don't you think about coming over? It would be such fun if you did. The people we see are varied and all interesting on at least one subject. If you had some kind of a job you were interested in to take up the daytime, I should think you'd love it.

Harry says you're involved in troop entertainment & hate it. Mrs Biddle has got me roped into the same thing over here.

I'm sitting in the sun now trying desperately to get brown & healthy – without much success!

Bestest love to you all.

Kathy

Petersfield Farm, Surrey
April 16, 1942

Dear Mouche,

The flat is lovely. Dottie Beatty has lent us some furniture – nice old tables etc., for me a double-bed, which is much too sumptuous for my liking – but very comfortable.

After much discussion and re-changing of plans, [we] have decided not to keep house but to use service – food is good & servants much better than anything hireable on one's own. So far everything is fine.

We had our 1st dinner party – in honor of Harry – and had among guests the Mountbattens. He's a terrifically striking individual & has been doing a wonderful job with the commandos. She's a hard-looking individual – wears a St. John's Ambulance Corps uniform. So far I've never seen him in anything other than Navy uniform! He's got the right to wear all three though.

My new boss is a piece of wet fish to look at & to shake hands with – but I've only seen him once & then we both eyed each other and talked to a third person.

I must stop now.

Bestest love,

Kathleen

CHAPTER 9

'THE HIGHLIGHT OF MY CAREER CENTERS NOW AROUND A MOST GLAMOROUS CREATURE, GENERAL ANDERS BY NAME, POLISH BY BIRTH'

Ave went on a trip to Northern Ireland in April 1942 and shortly after his return fell sick with what was later diagnosed as para-typhoid. Cables flew back and forth across the Atlantic as Kathy sought to reassure Marie that her husband would be OK. Clementine Churchill advised Averell to be patient and lie very still. Winston had caught paratyphoid. 'It is a horrid and tedious illness, but when at last it is over one truly is absolutely well again.' Ave soon recovered and finished his recuperation by spending a few days at Kathy's and Pam's country cottage. By June, he had recovered sufficiently to make yet another trip to the United States.

London
May 6, 1942

Dear Mary,

It's all over now but for the shouting – the past two weeks have muddled themselves into what seems now to be months and months of doctors, nurses, phones ringing and arrangements to be made for one and all plus my ordinary work. The latter has suffered considerably, as you might well imagine, because Averell seemed to like to have someone around when and if he woke up, or at least have someone in the room when he was half dozing.

Pam was wonderful, she did all the shopping and food-ordering end of our most efficient hospital. Slinging the name Churchill around we were able to get every imaginable implement and unobtainable food (liquid).

What she couldn't get, the army, the Navy and the marines got. Lord Gort sent oranges all the way from Gib! Lemons were swiped from ships on convoy duty, the Army transported them to London in special planes. The efficiency of the American forces is no. 1 plus, I can assure you. There was nothing they failed on.

Food for Averell's meals, that is soups, were done by Max's French chef, who came in especially from the country once a day. The chef, a frightening individual, is taken to having periodic fits during which he throws boiling water on those nearby. Thank God he has been fitless of late.

Averell's nurses were swell – Tony, Milly and Lilly by name. The Harley Street doc was quite horrified by the informality of our layout at first, but he's grown used to us and now sits and chats by the hour sipping sherry, after his duties by Averell are done. The other doc – the American Red Cross one – is heaven. I first had the misfortune of running into him as a member of the press, shortly after the three above-named nurses arrived in London after their tussle in the sea last summer. He hates the press and was most surly. Now he's a different man!

Life now is really fun. We sit and idle away the hours gossiping in Averell's room and laughing ourselves sick. He must be very strong, because the temp went on the down swing a day or so before we ever hoped it would. Poor typhoid bug (paratyphoid we think) wasn't given much chance.

I got tired of typing.

The highlight of my career centers now around a most glamorous creature, General Anders[1] by name, Polish by birth, C-in-C of Polish forces by profession. A year ago he was in the dark and damp of Moscow's most gruesome prison, Lubianka, wounded, half-starving.

1 Władysław Anders (1892–1970), commander of a Polish army raised from troops captured by the Soviets when they occupied eastern Poland in September 1939. Anders's army was evacuated from the USSR in March 1942 and became part of the allied forces that fought their way up Italy from 1943 to 1945.

When the Russo-Polish alliance came into being his cell door was opened. Russian officials saluted him, told him he was C-in-C, their ally and friend, and please to have his baggage ready in an hour. "I have no baggage" was his answer. But in Russia all great and important generals must have baggage, so he was bought shiny luggage and it, empty, was carried with him in state through the streets of Moscow to a grand apartment. He was washed, waited on, fed and saluted. 24 hours, and his enemy became his friend and ally! He's the only Pole in Russia to whom Stalin will talk! An ex-cavalry-general, his horses tried to stop German and Russian tanks in the early campaign. He's been wounded nine times, three times in this war. Wears all the Polish bravery medals. Is that sufficient build-up?

Now he's in London, a short business trip. When he first arrived, Sikorski (Polish P.M. and head general) gave a cocktail party, a cozy little affair for about 500 of us. A few press and many generals from nine countries. I met Anders there. He's terrific to look at, if you don't mind a shaven head and bad teeth. Anyway, after that party I decided I must get an exclusive interview but unfortunately we had an interpreter. It was a good interview. I.N.S. cabled it. My questions were intermingled with his flirtations.

Yesterday I had a second interview. This time alone in French. While hundreds of important admirers and associates sat in the next-door bedroom, we had a nice general chat about his home, his family and the war. He spoke of the dazed feeling about the sudden transition from prison (20 months of it) to complete luxury and importance. However, we don't write such stories these days. We, the press, must never let on or remind the forgetful what happened to the 2,000,000 Poles transported to Russia. This guy is their head. In the meantime he's fighting by the Russian side. Ex-enemies made friends by a greater foe.

Today and yesterday I tramped round to the free governments and collected shooting-up-by-the-Germans figures in the occupied countries. They varied from the Belgians' modest figure of 86 to the Yugoslav claim of 360,000 killed by any enemy hand, not in battle. Armed with these notes, I went to the office, added them up and did a piece on why the sum total was false. For some reason or other it was cabled out quick.

Met a Greek escapee yesterday. 40,000 died of starvation in Athens-Piraeus area alone during Oct-Nov-Dec! The Germans and the Italians hate each other as rabidly as the Greeks hate them! Italian officers, anticipating their end, have purchased mufti, to facilitate a quick getaway. A good meal in Athens costs $20. That's all in a story which you'll never see!

You asked about India. England is sold on the government's and Sir Staff's sincerity in trying to settle the affair.[2] Congress wanted to change the existing constitution. That would be impossible in wartime, take too long, even if basis of agreement were decided by various pressure groups. I went and saw Amery, High Commissioner for India, while talks were in progress. He said military situation would anyway be unchanged, but that civilian defense and order would be much improved if proposals were accepted. Two weeks ago Jinnah and Nehru announced their intention to rally the civilians.[3]

Paul Manning[4] of NEA [Newspaper Enterprise Association] has just returned from India. We lunched on Sunday. He told of the hopeless panic the night Calcutta got its first raid. Panic of screaming mobs whose one thought was to get out of town, fear of a people who for centuries have been educated that they're the scum, the animal life. Paul's comments rather contradict Amery's statements. He went to Burma too. The A.V.G. [American Volunteer Group] is the one American-angle story in Burma. Hence those pilots have been played up way beyond their performance.[5]

Last week I made two trips to "a London airport" – during the past year I've been there often, meeting or seeing Ave off. So the Wing

---

2 In spring 1942 Churchill sent Sir Stafford Cripps on a (failed) mission to India to win support for Britain's war effort from the country's independence movement leaders.

3 Muhammad Ali Jinnah, leader of the All-India Muslim League; Jawaharlal Nehru, leader of the Indian National Congress.

4 Paul Manning (d. 1995), American broadcast journalist, a close associate of Ed Murrow.

5 US pilots who flew for China during the Sino-Japanese War (1937–45), also known as the 'Flying Tigers'.

Commander in charge is almost a bosom pal. A useful one too – I can use his office phone and hence get my story filed first.

When Winant and Stark[6] arrived, I was there – half reporter and half reception committee. Being on both sides of the fence helped!

Today I lunched at Downing St. for the first time in ages. The P.M. was in great form – Madagascar battle starting, a tussle with a man who's running for Parliament and thinks he can sue the P.M. for libel. The garden out back was lovely – I almost got sunburn. If not Sun Valley, at least Downing St.!

I've suddenly thought – if Shirley comes to England, you ought to come over too. Can't understand preferring to go to Australia. The final showdown will be on the continent. I should think preference would be in the triumphant kill. Hitler, not the Japs, is what counts in the end.

Of all the horrible things – I'm off to a little town in Berkshire to superintend what England hopes will be the second set of quintuplets. I.N.S. has been filing stories in my name for the past two days, so now they figure somebody better be on hand to sign up I.N.S. exclusive rights for their first words of wisdom. God knows how long I'll be there. It seems a hellova story in wartime, but there's not much I can do about it. If the children turn out to be twins or triplets, that will be a lovely letdown for all concerned. Pop private has been granted two months' special leave from the War Office and the whole village is knitting for the kids. Suppose they all died unborn?

I'm off now to dine with one of the opposition – an A.P. man, who's an ardent Dodgers fan.

Puff

London
June 2, 1942

Mouche dear,

Got a nice letter from you this morning. So I run to answer via Averell who leaves in great state this afternoon. It's something to have a private transatlantic plane.[7]

6 Admiral Harold Stark (1880–1972), at this time US Chief of Naval Operations.
7 Harriman hitched a lift with American general H.H. Arnold.

I wrote Mary a letter a couple of days back of all our current news, therefore won't repeat. The second round of the Solomons battle ended in our favor, from reports, and that's the most exciting news we've had in ages and ages.

The new comment on the second front is: "let it not be too soon and too small." Quite a change!

There's no need to send any powdered eggs as I have quantities, bought at the embassy canteen last summer and we seldom use it, except occasionally in the country.

List of wants this time aren't very many. Of course, I always like stockings, and please this time send some lisle gunmetal ones and a couple of pairs silk gunmetal, for Sarah. She's in the W.A.A.F.s and so doesn't have much opportunity to wear tan stockings. She wears size nine and a half. Not too dark a color grey – if possible six pair lisle ones.

Mrs C wants some more chiffon handies, Mary C wants a small bottle of perfume. Mrs C says to make it an "unsophisticated smell"!!! (Suggest something called allure, dangerous, or another such name!)[8]

I need a new pair of glasses, some liquid rouge, as much soap as Averell will carry, some Kleenex, tin or two of Amolin and any good books. Books, more than anything, we miss over here. Paper shortage keeps many of the best from coming out.

Incidentally, if Marie has any bright ideas about hats either blue or black for winter consumption – I'd be thrilled.

England is rapidly becoming lousy with remote friends who keep calling up. My main difficulty is trying to remember who they are and where I've met them. Sun Valleyites are the most difficult to place!

My work has become the exceedingly boring routine of covering regular news. On quiet days I sit on my fanny and play gin rummy all afternoon, which is financially a most lucrative occupation. I'm about to work myself up into another of my resignation moods and as far as

---

8 Around this same time, Mary Churchill wrote in her diary, 'Looking at Kathy – slim – competent – sophisticated & exquisitely dressed – & at Pamela voluptuous & furred & Sarah romantic & strange-looking – I then looked at myself & felt miserable.'

I can gather pretty much all the other members of staff are about as fed up.

One of these days I guess the N.Y. office will wake up and discover that if they want any semblance of London coverage, they'll have to do better than send a man who gets drunk every evening at six and suffers from bad temper and hangover every morning, to be bureau chief.

I'm in a particularly bad mood this morning because the office says that perhaps they'll let me off at five this evening to see Averell off, but at this early hour they really can't tell.

Best love,

Kathleen

Please send some black long combs, also fake gold pin or clip to wear on suit lapel.

London
early June 1942

Dear Mary,

I got such a nice letter from Shirley about all your doings and a long one from you just after.

My own personal excitement is I've been offered (unofficially) a job with A.P.'s feature service. I by no means know if I want to leave I.N.S. – but it's nice to get offered a job by the rival syndicate. It may not come off so don't say anything. Quent and other outsiders have been wanting me to leave I.N.S. for some time, but the work I do there is fun and I'm really very attached to the organization. The Free gov't assignments are the most interesting and I'm sure I wouldn't be allowed to do that for any full-staffed outfit.

Last week when Heydrich[9] got shot at I had great fun with miscellaneous Czechs. It's rather fun, too, to see stories you've obtained appear days later in the London press.

Had lovely sunny day in the country – I'm almost feeling suntanned!

[Kathleen]

---

9 Reinhard Heydrich (1904–42), second-in-command of the SS and in charge of German-occupied Bohemia and Moravia, was attacked by the Czech resistance at the end of May 1942 and died of his wounds on 4 June.

London
June 11, 1942

Dear Mary,

Your divine profile photo arrived today – it's going to look mighty snappy in our living room.

Averell hasn't been gone long – but it seems like months and months. I've been out of town this week – to the main ordinance army center – the depot is 450 acres large and includes tanks, trucks, everything on wheels that the army uses plus spares. Was much impressed by the way the show was run. I watched tanks for Russia being "arcticized," tanks for Libya being desertized – by gals. They do all but the heaviest gun fitting. I rode in a Churchill tank, walked thru what seemed like miles and miles of bulk storage houses, and got rather bewildered by the effect of lack of standardization.

American stuff is handled there, too. The press party was laid on mostly for the Sunday paper gals. They were quite a bunch – mostly aging and very much of a closed clique. We got on fine though.

At lunch we were entertained by the A.T.S. officers. I sat next to the Commandant – Dame Regina somebody – who made quite a name for herself in prewar days as a suffragette. I asked her what she thought of the 33-yr.-old head of the A.T.S. Mrs Knox. Instead of answering with something nice or noncommittal – she got very pompous and remarked: "in the A.T.S., we don't discuss our superior officers."

Mrs Biddle is trying desperately hard to get me to say I'll do something in the way of organizing U.S. women over here into uniform (under her of course). She's irked as hell I've volunteered to do work for the U.S. soldiers' club here in London, rather than her officers' club.

Finally I broke down and went and visited [the Biddles] last weekend. We played loads of tennis, and by Sunday afternoon I was a complete dead bunny. So was everyone else except Tony [Biddle]. He's a very good tennis player – cuts and slices like mad – used to be Davis Cup ranking once upon a time. Other athletics indulged in at the Biddles are croquet, golf, softball and drinking.

FDR Jr. arrived in town – no interviews allowed. I lunched with him on Wed. and he was full of all the Wash. dirt, who was in and who wasn't. He said all sorts of nice things about Averell. Not being allowed to see the press – as a naval lieutenant – I had a few of the boys around informally to meet him. It was his idea, not mine, but he withstood the bombardment very well and I guess everyone enjoyed it and the Harriman liquor.

That night Max did us royally at his new London flat. He produced Little Max and the two boys got on beautifully. Aside from being about the most attractive British over here, Little Max talked very intelligently. I wonder how long his luck will last.

Big Max decided he wanted to go nightclubbing. We took him to the only really above-board joint in London and [he] had himself a whale of a time. Secretly I think he rather hoped the place would get raided! Finally, when he was convinced that he could cause no more commotion, he went home and Pam and I went on an all-night binge, ending up for breakfast at the Dorchester.

Two of the *Herald Trib*. men turned up for breakfast, so we celebrated with not much coffee and a great many milk punches. At the airport the punches were continued and then came the ceremony of Max and Frank exchanging R.A.F. buttons for U.S.N. ones and swapping a pair of gloves that had shot down ten huns for an electric razor. The plane arrived and Frank was off.

I had hopes of retiring to bed but the Russian treaty story broke and the office set me to work.[10]

Pam is Chequers-ing this weekend. I'm very jealous – Dickie Mountbatten is going to be there and I'm going down to the Strathallans.

Kathleen

London
June 27, 1942

Dear Mary,

Averell's been home for about 6 hours and during that time we've covered a good bit of territory – all the family news, the kids, and

10 The 1942 Anglo-Soviet Treaty of Mutual Assistance.

Harry Hop[kins] getting hitched.[11] For a while I almost felt as though I was home again.

First and foremost, I'm absolutely horrified about your remarks about Red. I mean that too. You imagining him as a brother-in-law, I can't get over it!! What in hell's name do you think I am. I'm not that desperate for a husband. Please don't mistake me, he's a good friend of mine, I hope he remains one but I certainly can't help it if he travels around the world and wishfully thinks that I'll consider matrimony or anything else for that matter. Averell says to tell you I'm playing for far bigger game!!

The loot was terrific. There was quite a gathering at the station to see the P.M. in – all sorts of cabinet ministers and uniforms and hundreds of press and things. The P.M. looked very well and all set to squelch anyone who's still stupid enough to think that he's about to fall. That over we rushed back to the flat and Averell opened the loot. It was almost like Christmas – one by one the stockings, the underwear, perfume, lipsticks, dress shields, letters, bobby pins, blouses, wrapper and finally the cigarette lighters came out of that famous old red suitcase that once belonged to me, went to Moscow, the Middle East and home across the Atlantic.

Now we're in the country. Averell's in bed having missed out on a whole night's sleep. They arrived at their British destination at 11:30 Washington time only to discover that it was breakfast time in Scotland. Apparently, he took a good bit of money off the P.M. at backgammon on the way over. I guess Winston didn't realize he was tackling one of the U.S.'s pros.

Now that Averell's back I'm suddenly realizing what a completely different life I lead when he's here. It's sort of like waking up from a dream or moving out into another world.

Averell's full of me resigning from I.N.S. – says they're such skunks about what they put out from London. Drew Middleton still hasn't heard from Wide World (A.P.) as to whether or not they want me, but even if they did I'd be in a quandary. I don't particularly want to miss

11 Hopkins married Louise Gill Macy (1906–63), a fashion journalist, at a ceremony in the White House at the end of July 1942.

out on the regular day-to-day spot news conferences and spend my time with women's features or any features for that matter.

Added to my new list of friends is the recently arrived managing editor of *Newsweek* – now Major – Joe Phillips.[12] He's terribly nice – a believer in the possibility of opening a second front almost tomorrow, that the British lack the offensive spirit (always have and always will sort of idea), an optimist about Russia – all of which I couldn't agree with him less. But it's nice hearing a different point of view every now and then.

Averell brought back Quent's new book. I've read a few chapters. It must be most boring for an outsider to read – that is the chapters about London. I thought the Sidi Omar dive bombing story excellent though. Dear old Quent, I think he's sort of lonely over here.

George, Averell's oil man, is a swell egg. The other night Geoffrey Lloyd gave a party for him (he's Minister of Petroleum), which included that bitch Olive Baillie and an awfully nice girl – ex-social whirler who's running a huge farm almost single-handed – and Chips Channon and Olive's feeble-minded husband (feeble-minded only when drunk). We saw a swell musical and then dined on a most un-austerity meal at Chips! He's got one of those huge Belgrave Square mansions – with palace-like dining room, beautiful glass table, chandeliers that burn candles and lots of gilt. It was most unwarlike and fun. For once in her life the Lady Baillie turned on the charm to me, husband did too for that matter. They're the people I spent my first England weekend with last summer – and swore I'd never go again. It was the first time in months I'd been out with the super London socialites. For one short inning it's fun – amusing.

That's really the nice thing about London – life is always varied. In wartime you get a unique collection. I'm lucky enough to get a glimpse at them all.

Since writing above I've seen the clippings Ave brought back. In case you're interested – one of the stories you marked as liking best was the underground factory one. I wrote the story but I've never been near an underground factory!

---

12 Joseph B. Phillips (1900–77).

I'm sleepy now, having just written another eyewitness story – W.A.A.F.s who made the 1,000 Bomber raid[13] possible. I wasn't there!

Bobby looks absolutely divine – baby Winston never crawled until after he walked – Nanny says it's not unusual. Pam says please hurry up and have a daughter. We think two years apart is about the right age for marriage. Hope you don't mind our settling your future daughter's husband now!

This is a bloody war all round – much worse for you than for me, even though we did almost get hit by a bomb last Sunday.

Incidentally, everyone admires your wedding pictures very much.

Bestest love,

Puff

3 Grosvenor Square, London
June 28, 1942

Dear Marie,

You've sent back Ave in the best form I've seen him in for ages. He sounds as though he had a hectic busy time, but looks wonderfully well.

My gosh it would be exciting if you came over.

Last night after Averell deserted me [to go to Chequers], I went out with my latest, most beautiful beau (he's very beautiful but not much else) all dressed up in the navy blue hat & purple ribbon. He was very impressed. I can't wait to wear the black velvet one with the pink flowers. It's quite the loveliest thing I've seen yet.

The dresses are divine. In a fit of generosity I've given Pam the blue one – am keeping the red. It'll be fun being twins.

I'm now working, fairly irregularly, but whenever I have a moment, at the information desk at the main A.R.C. [American Red Cross] club in London. There's a nice bunch of girls working there – all Americans, British-wed. The few staid English women who started out there have

13 In summer 1942 the RAF conducted three 1,000-bomber raids on Cologne, Essen and Bremen.

retired. They couldn't cope with the Doughboys' cracks & continually felt they were being insulted!!

See you soon I hope.

Bestest love,

Kathy

3 Grosvenor Square, London
June 29, 1942

Dear Mouche,

Averell got in on Saturday with the P.M. Much excitement. He told me all the news about everybody.

After all these years it's sort of hard not to think of you living at Arden or Locust Valley, but anyway you're still one of the family no matter where you live or what you do.

Tonight I drove around London after dinner. It still stays light until almost 11:30. We passed the Tower of London. Remember the first time you took us there? Instead of being 1941 it was 1924 – a hellova long time ago.[14] But all of a sudden I remembered a good many things. There are so many things I'll never forget. If you don't hear from me as often as I'd like, remember that a day seldom goes by that some association of our past over here doesn't crop up unexpectedly.

I hope you're happy in your own mind about the new arrangement. At times last winter when it was cold & dreary over here & dusk after 4 o'clock, I thought of you alone up at Arden. It must have been very lonely. Now you'll be able to go back to your independent life – like it was while Mary & I were at college. I always did feel you were happiest during those years.

Write me your plans. Will you be living at 74th street or will you take a larger apartment?

Your last letter arrived the morning after Tobruk fell. The day had been depressing – the press was disgruntled, the people in the streets stunned. Despite the fact that we've been told time & again

14 In 1924–5, Kathy, Mary and their mother Kitty spent several months in Britain and France.

since the fall of Singapore, Java, & all the rest, that the news would be bad all during 1942 – when the blow comes it's impossible to sit back & say "I told you so." (God only knows when we'll be able to hold the Germans this year.)

I came home Monday week after the fall of Tobruk and found your letter. There's a good many comforting things going on in the world & the things you wrote about is one of them.

The loot was terrific that Averell brought back – the earrings divine, the blouses just what I needed, the underwear I now have on. The stockings were a godsend. Before I forget it – I'd love the tweed coat please. Also, the Cheddar cheese sent in food parcels isn't very good. Plain Kraft cheese is nicer – that comes in blue boxes.

I'm distressed to hear about Shirley moving down to Fort Bragg, but the one consolation is that at least they'll be more or less together for a while longer. It has been awfully hard, even so, on Mary & Shirley having the inevitable parting perpetually hanging over them.

It's odd to think how different our lives have turned out, after having grown up with the same external influences. I often wonder when & where I'll settle down & start producing children. After the war is such a long time ahead that it's hard to think in those terms & I'm not one to even think of regretting anything I've done so far.

My best love to you Mouche dear,
Kathleen

3 Grosvenor Square, London
July 6, 1942

Dear Marie,

The pale blue wrapper, the perfume & the assorted gifts you sent suddenly made a hot June day seem like Christmas.

Now at long last I can leave my horrid, spotted Fortnum-Mason wrapper in the country. My beautiful new one is most glamorizing. Averell thinks it's most indecent. It is rather what you might call décolleté' but at least it's a safeguard against Averell having strange generals & assorted production fanatics for breakfast!

Coming back on the plane I gather war strategy was forgotten for some hours when the big boy discovered Ave knew a little about backgammon. The Harriman pocket was filled with several pounds at the expense of much sleep. He takes Mrs C on in croquet & Winston on at backgammon. No wonder they think he is a superman!

I was sort of hoping you might come back with him this trip. I do wish you would. It would be such fun with you here. There are all sorts of jobs to be done. Mrs Winant isn't up to much & Mrs Biddle has all the free governments to care for and in-between times she succeeds in doing a great job getting into everyone's hair!

The past weekend was spent celebrating the fourth. The Washington Club – where the enlisted men stay when on London leave – was opened officially on Saturday. Saturday night there was a dance – no liquor (or even beer as the Washington Club is financed by the Amer. Red Cross). Despite that it was a great success. Girls were imported from the 3 services & from the looks of some of them just off the streets. I wish more of the men were just normal dancers. They all seemed to prefer jitter bugging.

Somehow, I can't quite remember how, I got invited to continue celebrating by a Military Police Sergeant. We adjourned to the enlisted men's club in Grosvenor Square. The next morning at breakfast Averell got very fatherly. He still seems to think I'm not able to take care of myself – even with Americans!

July 8

Gave a wonderful party tonight – to entertain General & Mrs Nye.[15] He's second to the C.I.G.S. [Chief of the Imperial General Staff], which makes him pretty high up in the British army. Averell produced the most divine major general. He looks about 35 yr. old & couldn't be nicer. I fell for him immediately only to discover he moves out of London in a couple of days. All the best people seem to do that!!

July 14

The war's getting horrider every day. Down at the military spokesman headquarters they've run out of adjectives describing the Russian situation – though "hopeless" has yet to be used.

15 General Archibald Nye (1895–1967), married to Colleen Knox (1905–88).

We dined chez the Wooltons last night. He's Food Minister. Lady W & I had a lengthy chat while the men talked business. At this point I can't really remember what dinner when both sexes [talked] together is like!

Bestest love,

Kath

CHAPTER 10

'OUR GENERALS ARE A SUCCESS – UNFORTUNATELY THEY AREN'T VERY SOCIALLY MINDED'

The big diplomatic story of summer 1942 was Churchill's trip to Moscow. It was Averell's idea to go with him. Churchill's mission was to tell Stalin that the British and Americans had neither the troops nor the ships to mount a cross-Channel invasion of France in 1942, previous promises notwithstanding. With the Red Army retreating towards Stalingrad, this was disturbing news for the Soviet dictator. More welcome was news of Operation Torch – the imminent Anglo-American invasion of Vichy-controlled French North Africa. Churchill's talks with Stalin went badly and almost resulted in a breakdown of personal relations between the two men, but harmony was restored at a long, private dinner which finished up in Stalin's Kremlin apartment.

The build-up of American forces in Britain continued apace. America's Eighth Air Force joined the strategic bombing of Germany, focusing on daylight precision raids on military-industrial targets while the RAF continued its night-time area bombing campaign. In October 1942 Eleanor Roosevelt slipped secretly into Britain and then conducted a highly publicised tour of the country. Kathy was among those with the somewhat tedious task of reporting on the trip.

On the personal front, the big news was Kathy's decision to quit her reporter's job at INS and work for *Newsweek* magazine as a feature writer. Her move pleased those of her journalist colleagues who took a dim view of INS because it was part of William Randolph Hearst's

American media empire. Hearst was an autocratic proprietor, whose newspapers were renowned for their sensationalism and for their conservative and isolationist views – which were not at all to Kathy's taste.

London
July 30, 1942

Dear Mary,

It's been so long since I've written that I'm quite embarrassed. Actually I did start a letter the day Harry left then never got enough of it done to send off. London was pretty exciting while the group was in town. We saw a lot of the bridegroom and he was in the best of spirits. His one subject of talk was Louie. We went through every step of the engagement campaign time and time again, evening after evening. It's so nice that he's getting married.

There's a whole slew of visiting Americans here at the moment, lots of them to do with Averell, so he's busier than ever. Bill Bullitt,[1] ex-ambassador to France, was a great disappointment. I expected a world beater and instead I couldn't get over how much he looked like Orson Welles' version of W.R. Hearst. Perhaps that's a slight exaggeration. Ed Stettinius[2] I like a lot, particularly as he crashed thru with Virginia ham and some lemons.

Steve Early[3] was over here and great fun in small doses. We've played violent gin rummy and his last day in town I succeeded in getting £12 off him.

Our generals are a success – unfortunately they aren't very socially minded. The best of all is Clark,[4] commander of the 1st army. He lives out of town. He's terrific looking, tall, dark, and most ungainly. The P.M. calls him "our American eagle," which is most appropriate.

---

1 William C. Bullitt (1891–1967), the first US ambassador to the Soviet Union (1933–6).
2 Edward Stettinius (1900–49), US Lend-Lease official who later served as Roosevelt's Secretary of State.
3 Stephen Early (1889–1951), American journalist who was Roosevelt's White House press secretary from 1933 to 1945.
4 Mark W. Clark (1896–1984), who later commanded the allied armies in Italy.

Eisenhower is his Mutt complement (perhaps Jeff complement, anyway he's the short one), most genial and well liked by all. Spaatz[5] (head of U.S.A.A.C.) impressed me least of all. Perhaps though that's because he's fairly inarticulate, doesn't express himself terribly well. He's an ardent gin rummy-ite though.

Don't know if any of the above interests you or not, but I enjoy being tactless every now and then.

I'm working like the devil of late and I have a couple of good stories coming up. Max Aitken dropped in this morning and said that Whitney Straight, an American millionaire type in the R.A.F., ex-member of 601 glamour boy Squadron, is back in England. He was shot down over France last summer, twice escaped from prison camps and now at last is out. Anyway he's going to get me an interview. Hallelujah!!!! Max has been doing terrific things of late and is up for a D.S.O. [Distinguished Service Order], just got a high Czech medal and already has a couple of other ribbons. (He's Beaverbrook's son and heir.)

Another story coming up is an exclusive message from General Mikhailovich,[6] the guerrilla warfare Serbian, all the way from Jugoslavia, about the second front etc. etc. As we hope to have it signed by him, I don't get the credit, but that doesn't really matter. All I have to do in return for getting it, is to dine with a horrid little Jugoslav who's getting the story.

I almost resigned from I.N.S. a while back, drove down to the office in a fury, then damned if my car didn't break down on the way to Fleet St. It took me so long to get it going again, I was too late – had an appointment.

There's wild talk and speculation about the second front; people are betting like mad. Those who come in frequent contact with Beaverbrook are giving terrific odds, saying that there will be one this year. A while back I dined there with some people he wanted to

---

5 Carl Spaatz (1891–1974), chief of the Eighth Air Force and in overall command of the US Army Air Forces in Europe.

6 Dragoljub 'Draža' Mihailović (1893–1946), chief of the 'Chetnik' guerrilla army in Axis-occupied Yugoslavia.

impress, head of the *NY Times* included; he got quite drunk (Max) and after dinner gave us a long harangue on the second front, the whole works, and with much crashing of champagne bottles and thumping on the table. The scene was terrifying. He's quite a fanatic on the subject and seems to have lost all sense of balance. His line is that if we stop the Russian convoys (which are getting sunk anyway, he says) and used the ships that would be diverted [from] that route along with the supplies of tanks, aircraft and munitions, for the opening of a second front, we'd be doing more to help Russia. He's against maintaining the Middle East and seems to honestly believe that by landing a few divisions in France we'll be able to get Hitler to divert a goodly portion of his troops [from] the Russian front. Can't say as I agree with even one of his points, but it's interesting to see how his mind works. Apparently, someone got the idea back home that we've got millions of U.S. troops over here, which of course is all baloney.

The U.S. Navy is in town in a big way and London's turning itself upside down in its honor. You see them all over the place, sight-seeing like mad. So far their disorderly conduct has been nil, or practically so.

Randolph gets in tonight, so we're doing a rapid shift around. Sarah Oliver, the nicest Churchill daughter, is moving in with us and Pam and Randolph are taking her flat. It will be fun to see Randolph again, but I certainly hope he doesn't go around making any more statements about British soldiers being "enthusiastic amateurs" as he did in N.Y. The P.M. wants him to take a big part in Parliament, the prospects of which are terrifying.

London has been getting every-other-night raids. Unfortunately I can't get much interested in them – never having had reason to be frightened by bombing, the recent ones hardly do more than partially wake me up. The so-called secret ack-ack makes lovely-looking fireworks.

There's a hellova harrouche [*sic*] going on about the American Red Cross being in exclusive charge of U.S. troop welfare, which includes entertainment. They want to make British women who run the camp canteens and hostels get into A.R.C. uniforms, so that they, the A.R.C., can get all the credit. There was a big stink in London when the head man of the I.R.C. [International Red Cross] started on his campaign to get British women in American uniform and flatly turned down all British offers of hospitality. Now I think fast-working Eisenhower's got the whole thing under control.

Tonight Quent's movie about the Eagle Squadron opens, the Biddles are giving a party afterwards. Was horrified when I received my ticket for the show – 10 guineas a head – for charity. It amazes me sometimes the way the Biddles throw around money. God only knows how much they spend, entertaining.

I must be off now, write soon.

Bestest love to you,

Puff

London
August 10, 1942

Dear Mary,

Spent a very enjoyable weekend at Max's. There was just Pam and Randolph there and a few incidental people like Bruce Lockhart, but none of the usual bores. I got lots and lots of sleep, that came as a much-needed pleasure. The weather rained so we saw lots of movies and Pam and I drove around with Max, he playing the fool as though he'd never driven a car before in his life. It's amazing at times to think what simple pleasures he gets out of life! I trained up to town this morning and found that I'd have to wait an hour for a cab at Waterloo so I tackled the underground and found it just about as easy as the N.Y.C. subway once you set your mind to it. Now that pleasure petrol has stopped, I use my car only for work purposes. That means walking at night, which is a bore having been used to the luxury of a car.

This week I'm stationed from 11 a.m. 'til 7 p.m. at the Ministry of Information. The regular man is off vacationing. I seem to have picked a good week! India, Russia, Egypt is about to boil, to say nothing about D.N.B. [Deutsche Nachrichten Büro] and Vichy radio reports of Moscow doings.

After almost a month of wrangling, the Mikhailovich story came thru. N.Y. sent congratulations etc. so I guess they liked it. He said he figured a second front in the Balkans rather than in France would be most effective etc., on and on for 1,000 words. The last couple of weeks I think I put in a good 12 hours in one of the Jugoslav offices, all of which I now suppose is worth it!

Have just returned from "making the rounds" of the military advisers. In return for a Lifesaver,[7] one of the little men gave me a good bit of background information on why not to expect a push in Egypt on the part of the British – all of which makes a very nice little story – particularly as A.P. is writing that there will be.

The Indian authorities tend to play down the riot stories coming out of Madras city, Poona, Calcutta, Bombay etc. They say that in terms of Indian riots of the past the present ones are chicken feed. I think that A.P. has just put out a story saying that Martial Law is about to be declared in India. God knows who their source of information is.

Apparently there's trouble in Morocco, but I don't think we are interested.

The above written Monday – it's now Wednesday [August 12]. A terrible thing has just happened. The other day I was ordered to pay a visit to the chief U.S. Army censor and persuade him to let one of our stories through. Net result: the story didn't get thru, the British wouldn't pass it and I have to go dining some night with the U.S. censor. Just gave Leo, the boss, hell. He thinks it's funny, damn him!

I lunched with Mrs Churchill today – very pleasant – the Winants, my favorite minister (transport) one Lord Leathers and wife, who's also sweet, Col. Llewellin, Minister of Aircraft Production – in the days when he used to be a junior minister he was nice, now he's become most pompous and boring.

The other week Averell and I went out and spent the night with the Winants. They've got a house outside London, swimming pool, tennis court etc., but we were too late and the weather was too cold to make use of either of them. The evening was, oddly enough, rather fun. And I think I made some headway with Constance, who I hardly know at all. She and the Ambass. are a funny couple. If she had the

7 A brand of American confectionary.

chance, I think she'd like to be social, but as it is, they never entertain. I discovered, too, rather to my amusement, that she feels about the same way about Mrs Biddle as Mrs B does about her. I suppose women must be jealous, but it all seems too stupid to me.

Last night the Donovan[8] mission gave a party that I got unexpectedly roped into. Discovered one of the members is the pres. of Williams College,[9] so I had fun teasing him about not letting Bennington girls attend the classes of Williams' left wingers.

Had a wonderful lunch with Admiral Griffin when he was in town. He's admiral of our task force over here – and full of fun. Next time they come into port, he's invited me up to visit him!

Am home now. Just had a long chat with Rose, the maid. She's in love with the Ambass! "A lot of good it does me to fall for a man like him!" She's very pro-second front. We talked about it for a while. She doesn't think much about the government outside of Winston and Eden. "Too much red tape." She's decidedly pro-American, which makes me think of my own rather violent views on the subject of Anglo-American relations. They, as such, are being served up every morning noon and night in speeches and articles etc., sort of like a dose of cod liver oil. The average Britisher is going out of his way, all on his own, to make our boys feel at home, in his own small way. He likes to think of his actions as being spontaneous, not the result of government and official orders.

Sarah's been up a couple of times lately. It's fun having her here; though I miss Pam at times, she's a very good second. I'm giving a party for her on Friday night – to get her to meet some of our "nice, young American" boys.

At times I long to come home for a couple of weeks. There's so much we could talk about – my gosh it would be fun!

I was down at our bomber command last week for the day, doing the story on the W.A.A.F.s there. Got to talking to some little captain

---

8 William J. Donovan (1883–1959), known as 'Wild Bill', head of the Office of Strategic Services (OSS), precursor to the CIA.

9 James Phinney Baxter (1893–1975).

& he asked "haven't I seen you skiing at John Seesaws?"[10] Someone else was a Salt Lake man. Funny the way you meet up with people.

Best love to you,

Kathy

• • •

A most distressing thing has just happened. Your above letter was in my purse and enveloped. I came in after lunch just in time to get an important Admiralty communiqué read out. Your letter was the only available paper in my purse so it's scribbled on back. In case you're interested it was the very exciting one about the Malta convoy getting thru. Sorry though to have messed up the letter, but hardly think it's worth recopying.

Saw wonderful show last night – about the R.A.F. – tear-jerker if there ever was one. If produced in N.Y.C. would be swell propaganda.

My love to you both,

Puff

Aug 18

The Moscow story broke this morning – exciting isn't it? All the papers here carried a wonderful 3-some picture [Stalin, Churchill, Harriman] which I'm going to get framed.

There was great excitement the night Averell left. He had a stag dinner. I came in about midnight – most of the guests had left – everyone was scurrying around – then finally at about dawn he got off – in great spirits.

I must be off now.

[Kathleen]

London
August 24, 1942

Dear Mary,

Life is still varied and certainly never dull. The triumphant return of the prodigal father comes soon I hope. The one advantage of

10 A ski lodge in Vermont.

having him leave is the fun when he comes back. It's exciting every time.

Red Mueller is back, trying hard to get me to go work for him on what he calls the "family" magazine. Somehow I don't know as I'd like working for Red, or enjoy the stooge type of job a London office will have to do for *Newsweek*, however we shall see.

The past week not much else has passed one's mind outside the Dieppe raid.[11] The participants came back rather stunned. My landlord in the country was with an outfit that lost nine tenths of its men. Other sections, of course, had few or fewer casualties. The commandos did a superb job, each of three units took their objective and retired. I dare say you've been reading the stories. The raid should certainly give food for thought to the politicians who have been riding high on the immediate second front slogan. A continental landing will be no picnic. They got that in black and white. Though the raid was perhaps not as successful as some hoped, it provided experience for all. The air force provided an umbrella second to none. "Every bomber that came down to attack had at least three fighters on its tail, which rather took his mind off his target," was one friend's version. Quite different from Dunkirk.

Great excitement. The above was written yesterday in between chasing Al Jolson and the Lady Korda (Merle Oberon to you). They, plus others, have arrived over to sing to the U.S. troops. Arranged an interview with them for early evening and was just about to set out to get the stuff when Randolph called and said in five minutes he was leaving by car for parts unknown to meet the P.M. and Averell, so I canned everything and went off at breakneck speed in the Secretary of State for Air's official car – all done up with nice signs like "priority" and pink ribbons. We tore through the countryside, almost killing countless bicyclists and sundry children until finally neither of us could stand the strain any longer. We persuaded the driver to slow down to sixty in the towns, which hurt his feelings no end. He thought

---

11 A large-scale amphibious raid on the German-occupied port of Dieppe on 19 August 1942, mostly by Canadian soldiers, who suffered several thousand casualties.

we were terrible sissies. "The Secretary of State allows me to go 95. He has confidence in me." We got a flat tire and we were sure we'd arrive at the airport too late, but luckily the planes were late and we got there in plenty of time. Mrs C, a secretary and Portal,[12] Chief of Air Staff, had gone up early in the day and seemed rather amazed when we two turned up. We sat around for a bit listening to all the coded message signals coming in. It was all very exciting. Just after blackout time the first Liberator came into sight. The flare paths were lit up, a plane with flares on each wing went up and led them down. Just as they landed, the fighter escort came into view – first one squadron of Spitfires, then another. A few minutes later, the second Liberator appeared overhead and it was led down with flares. The P.M. and Averell were together and the C.I.G.S. (Chief of the Imperial General Staff) in the other plane.

We trained down in a "special" and had a wonderful dinner en route. Averell and I gossiped at dinner and then I had a nice chat with the C.I.G.S.[13] who gave all sorts of interesting tidbits about Stalin. He's a lot less tolerant than Ave. Tends to judge the Russians by British standards, so his version was interesting, but perhaps a little indiscreet to pass on. The arrival station was a mass of photographers and floodlights and important people, but dark enough so it was difficult to recognize anyone unless you had your back to the lights. I had great fun as everyone seemed to think I'd been to Moscow too!

Averell looked a little tired but seems fine today. He's just completed a very successful press conference. He'll give you all the dope.

I weekended with the Biddles – lots of gin rummy and tennis. The usual bunch of "Biddle babies" were there – Quent etc. His activities were however strictly non-athletic! Red was there. He seems much the same as ever. Seems amazed, for some exceedingly stupid reason, that I've changed. Amazed that I know certain am't about what's going on and have very definite ideas on certain subjects that are in disagreement with his, and what makes me laugh even louder – that

12 Charles 'Peter' Portal (1893–1971).
13 General Sir Alan Brooke (1883–1963).

I'm very good friends with all the American press. I don't think he likes the idea of me no longer being his stooge.

U.S. Air Force is going great guns and there's a lot of enthusiasm on that score. All the Americans who went on the Dieppe raid say one thing first: "My God, but those Canadians are fighters."

I'm back on my usual Ministry of Information beat, hence the typewriter change. Brielle's husband was killed in the Duke of Kent's plane crash and for a horrid moment I thought I was going to be the one to tell her.[14]

I think I have run out of news. Wouldn't it have been fun if I'd have been able to come home with Averell this time!!!!

Bestest love to you all,

Puff

London
September 9, 1942

Dear Mary,

Life is getting so damn complicated that I really don't know whether I'm coming or going. For this week and next, I got to produce a daily troops feature plus cover a regular beat – daily visit to U.S. headquarters, embassy and an assortment of service clubs. Needless to say I cheat on the clubs end of the beat like mad, cover them by phone – the office knows no difference so who cares.

Said office misbehaved badly yesterday. Wrote stupid story about the Dieppe raid being result of Stalin's threat to Churchill "you do something or else." I arrived in too late; story already had been sent off. However, it wasn't reported back in daily headline review from N.Y.C., so not much damage was done.

Tonight dined with Brendan and he showed us some wonderful night and day bombing newsreels and the Russian version of Moscow mission. All very very good. Bill Paley's comment: "Someone ought to tell Averell never to arrive again in Moscow unshaven." Part

14 Prince George, Duke of Kent, died in a plane crash in Scotland in August 1942. There was only one survivor among the fifteen RAF passengers and air crew. I have been unable to identify Brielle or her husband.

of newsreel was Averell's radio comment, which showed that he wasn't indiscreet in opening statement. The Lippmanns[15] were at dinner too. They're very nice. He's quite silent.

Went to Commons yesterday. Disgraceful performance on the part of the M.P.s. They most of them got up at one o'clock sharp to go to lunch even though the P.M. hadn't completed his speech. Stafford Cripps made a complete ass of himself and proved once more what a lousy leader of the House he is. As you can gather, I'm not much of a Stafford Cripps admirer.

I enjoyed the P.M.'s speech, but then I always do. It was received with a certain amount of apathy by the House.

Today Aneurin Bevan[16] shot his mouth off, called the P.M. a paranoiac. Aneurin, unfortunately, is a very good speaker. That's about his only good point though. I've had the misfortune to be bored by him many an evening at Beaverbrook's. He once was called the white-haired boy of the Labour Party – "our future P.M." That swelled his head considerably. He never got over it.

Dined with your friend [Dr] Stinchfield[17] last week. He's the most divine bit of unadulterated Americanism I've yet been able to introduce Pam to. We were both charmed by him. On Friday I'm going up to Churchill hospital to pay them all a visit, a professional one and will write the results.

Tomorrow evening I'm being most swell. Dining at Eighth Air Force headquarters with Tooey Spaatz – Major-General to you – just another gin rummy fan.

September 10

Had a great day today. I was working behind the information desk at the A.R.C. Washington Club, when up came two sergeants asking "where can we contact Quent Reynolds." They were two Dieppe

---

15 Walter Lippmann (1889–1974), influential American journalist and political commentator who specialised in international affairs. He was married to Helen MacGregor Byrne (1897–1974).

16 Aneurin 'Nye' Bevan (1897–1960), Welsh Labour politician who was later instrumental in the creation of the British National Health Service.

17 Frank E. Stinchfield (1910–92), leading American orthopaedic surgeon.

Rangers, 19 and 25 respectively, from hick Minnesota towns. One an ex-butcher boy, the other fresh out of high school. They were terrific. We chatted for ages. They talked about the beatings the Rangers take in training (they both love it). Praised the Canadians, the R.A.F., and the R.N. sky high, but sort of forgot to say much about their own guts. One told what it felt like, waiting to land on Dieppe beach, being able to see the massacre ahead and being frozen scared. "Then suddenly I got mad, real mad, and I forgot about being frozen and scared. All I could remember was General Laycock's speech: 'Hit Jerry, hit him bloody hard.'" Both boys had just been dehospitalized. They were swell kids and it gives you a mighty nice feeling meeting Americans like them. An hour after being with them I was at 8th Air Force headquarters. Quite a change of scene. Won 2 pounds 7/6 from General Spaatz. His partner was lousy though, so it wasn't a real moral victory. However perhaps I'll get invited down again.

It's 2 a.m. so I must stop.

Bestest love,

Kathy

London
September 14, 1942

Dear Mary,

Your blue dress is mighty nice – fits well and will be good for both town and country. Ever so many thanks.

Visited the Churchill Hospital in Oxford last week. I arrived there about noon and had to leave at 4:30 – got lots of good stories, viewed many patients and had a good, interesting, though unprintable chat, with a Miss Knowles, ass't chief nurse.

Your friend Frank [Stinchfield] took me around and left me to my own devices while he operated. Met Frank's colleague – Patterson – and listened while they talked shop. Most all their orthopedic cases are blackout casualties and bicycle accidents.

Was absolutely horrified at general feeling among corpsmen and nurses of complete and utter contempt for the British. "If Hitler knew what he was fighting for on this island, he'd stop tomorrow" was one comment I got. They seem to think the British aren't working and won't fight, and they're quite sincere in their contempt. I'm glad that feeling isn't prevalent among the doughboys who are training to fight with the British soldiers. I guess the riffraff and those physically unfit are the ones who end up as corpsmen. They always will be the ones to criticize.

Read a whole collection of *Herald Tribs* and *Times* that Ave brought back with him. Was slightly bewildered by the wealth of news and comment you still get daily. My gosh there's a lot that never hits the papers here – especially Pacific news and of course goings on in America.

It must be sort of hard for you to get used to being minus Shirley. In some ways a life that's not dependent on anyone is so much easier in wartime. I can't say I envy you – but then I dare say you don't envy me!!!!

My love to all,
Puff

London
September 23, 1942

Dear Mary,

A couple of days ago, I did the inevitable, resigned from I.N.S. I was quite pleased. Boss Leo Dolan was much upset, but I think I convinced him that the resignation was not due to any hard feelings, just that I was considering a better job, namely *Newsweek*. Now that they have a London office, it really makes more sense that I work for them. I can get the kind of information they want and the type of query work they require will be far larger in scope than what I.N.S. does. All of this is still up in the air, as no word as yet from Muir.[18] Averell and I have discussed the subject at length. He's keen I switch over and personally I'd much rather work for an organization I've got an interest in and respect for.

I went in and saw Red at his office the other day – told him I was considering the matter – he needs an assistant – and of course he's been asking me to join *Newsweek* ever since he got over. Right after that I walked across the street and resigned and the next day formally

18 Malcolm Muir (1885–1979), editor-in-chief of *Newsweek*.

tendered resignation. My dearest I.N.S. friend Tommy Watson (Englishman) had tears in his eyes when I told him. He's the diplomatic reporter – and older man – he's been my mainstay during the "difficult" periods when I.N.S. has what I call "misbehaved" – gone out on the limb with bad stories.

Yesterday at the Association of American Correspondents lunch for Eisenhower, Charlie Smith told a couple of people I was leaving and they one and all marched over and congratulated me.

I can't tell you what fun it is resigning from a job. Red was horrified that I did it so quickly, before the new job was cinched, but I figured once I'd made up my own mind to leave, there was no time like the present.

Despite all I do daily to stick up for the organization [INS], everyone's cracks about working for a pseudo-fascist press can't go without effect. Besides, I never did consider it as a permanent position. Quent and everyone else has been trying to sabotage me out for months and months, so now I hope they're happy. I know I am.

September 25

It's now Friday and I'm sitting in our cold and dreary Ministry of Information office trying to materialize a Free French exclusive – so far no luck. I.N.S. is trying to dissuade me from leaving so am more or less avoiding the office.

This weekend I was going to Scotland to [do] some shooting but what with having a wisdom tooth out (the most painless affair imaginable) and getting an invite to visit the Ronnie Trees at Ditchley, I didn't go at the last moment. The P.M.'s going to Ditchley – that's why we are accepting.

My bestest love,

Puff

London

October 9, 1942

Dear Mary,

Such fun I'm using up my last sheet of I.N.S. clipper paper. It gives me great pleasure. I got out of I.N.S. just in time.

Fun! Today Harry Butcher,[19] one of Eisenhower's aides phoned about a job with NBS.[20] One of their heads is over here enlarging the organization and apparently they have need of a woman and Butch suggested me.

Having spent five days in the *Herald Trib* office I'm awfully glad too that I didn't take up Joe Evans on his offer. They have five American correspondents on their staff who between them cover pretty much all the woman-angle stories.

I'm enjoying myself immensely with *Newsweek*. Red was away first part of week so I busied myself getting set towards accreditation of American army, which consists of answering who your dead aunt's mother is in triplicate and having all my numerous passes changed from I.N.S. to *Newsweek*. Another major task was binding up all the chair and desk legs with adhesive tape. First day at work I ran both my stockings. Red complained at result on his return. But adhesive tape remains.

Today being end of weekish I finally had to do some writing. Result three stories – Major David Sterling[21] (desert commando), Sark raid and binding of Germans, which probably won't get out, and a bitty of a fashion piece. Strictly Red's idea the latter one.

It looks as though the Germans have given up the taking of Stalingrad and are concentrating on taking something constructive in the Caucasus. In other words, business is looking up on the Russia front.

Last night, socially speaking now, we took Clemmie to see a hellova swell show – about the R.A.F. – and dined afterwards at Claridge's. That's Averell's first party in over a year. (Clemmie is Mrs Winston.) All in all it was most enjoyable and Mrs C loved it.

Elliott Roosevelt is over here as you doubtlessly know. I was sick the day he arrived but Averell sent him over to be entertained. He

19 Harry C. Butcher (1901–85), American radio broadcaster who served as Eisenhower's naval aide during the war. In 1946 he published a memoir, *My Three Years with Eisenhower*.

20 Could be MBS (Mutual Broadcasting System) or NBC (National Broadcasting Company).

21 Archibald David Stirling (1915–90), founder of the Special Air Service (SAS).

arrived accompanied by a cowboy-booted major and he's much nicer than I'd anticipated.

[Kathleen]

London
mid-October 1942

Dear Mary,

The excitement of the moment is Larry[22] in the vicinity.

His letter saying he was in England arrived the same moment as he in London – so we had such cause for celebration. First day here, I lunched with him and a rather dreary pal. For dinner I got hold of the Strathallans, we dined here and then went nightclubbing 'til all hours. Larry's again coming up tonight. Pam's giving a small dinner – Max Aitken and his girl, Jock Whitney[23] and Larry and me. Then tomorrow night I'm taking Larry to dine with Win Brown and those boys. I can't tell you what fun it is having him over here – he's enthusiastic about everything – the people he meets – so full of appreciation of what's being done here for Americans. I think he was rather amazed by the un-wartorn-ness of London. It's pretty neat and Americans are so used to empty lots, that in some districts it's difficult to notice bomb damage. He gets such a kick out of everything that it makes it all the more fun seeing him, getting his reaction. I hope he likes Max [Aitken] – because he's about the most attractive battle of Britain pilot alive.

Dixie Tighe[24] came to dinner last Friday – and she's a great gal – funny. One of these days I'm going to pluck up enough courage to ask if I can go along with her on a story. I'm so used to doing things on my own that I haven't the vaguest idea how an old timer goes

---

22 J. Lawrence Pool (1906–2004), surgeon who served in the US Army during World War II. Larry was Kathy's stepbrother through her mother's marriage to his father Eugene H. Pool after divorcing Averell in 1929.

23 John Hay Whitney (1904–82), American businessman who served as an intelligence officer for the US Air Force in World War II. He was distantly related by marriage to Averell's second wife, Marie Whitney.

24 Dixie Tighe (1905–46), American war correspondent, who worked for INS and the *New York Post*. Died after a stroke in Tokyo in 1946.

about getting a story. Dixie, I figure, would be about the best one to learn from.

I've just returned from an unofficial conference on the subject of how the First Lady's tour gets covered. It's going to be a madhouse – everyone wants to go everywhere it seems – thank goodness I ain't no longer with an agency. *Newsweek* will just be interested in her end of the week activities, I hope.

Incidentally, I've become a most expert apple picker, spent most of this weekend and last doing same. This week's work was hardest – the tops of the trees having been reached. Lord knows why I didn't fall once. The trees belong to our very nice landlady. In return for work, I get apples, onions, honey or anything else – pretty good pay!

I've been offered another job! Tooey Spaatz needs a private secretary. He's head of the 8th Air Force.

An abrupt end – but now's the time for this to be mailed.

Bestest love,

Puff

London
October 27, 1942

Dear Mary,

Sorry about size of the paper but it's all that's available . . .

I'll be God damned if I'll let a grandma like Missus R get me down, so I'm taking a moment – while she's off to too-secret-for-the-press-to-go-places – to repair a part of the physical and mental damage I've acquired while trailing her the past 4 days. She's reformed me, indirectly I must admit. I rise at seven, or a very little later, and as yet haven't had sufficient energy to go out for pleasure in the evenings. Last evening Winant threw an all U.S. bigwigs gathering. I was the only non-bigwig but I had a very nice time flirting with our starred uniforms and bald-headed ministers and ambasses. The whole of the daylight hours had been spent in the pouring rain following Eleanor from A.T.A. to A.T.S. station and depot after depot. The party started at 8 and ended for me at 5 minutes to 8, which meant less than 5 minutes to dry my wet head and stop my chattering teeth. The latter I did by downing a half tumbler of Scotch. The net result, I arrived at the party half-stewed, anyway, feeling wonderful. Today "we" inspected the National Fire Service, listened to a brass band, watched tunicked gals and men do amazing acrobatics, ride motorcycles in drill and go through flares – all very exciting I can assure you. After that we dashed to the other end of town and watched some civil defense squad go through a very gruesome and lifelike rescue scene.

October 29

Thursday. I've now caught my second wind. Yesterday we had the afternoon off while Mrs R saw the various heads and kings of the guerrilla governments. A much-needed holiday, I can assure you.

Today starting at 8:30 we set out to tour U.S.A.F. [United States Air Force] 'dromes and stations. We caught a fleeting glimpse of Eleanor at 12:30 then lost her again until 4 p.m. Must admit I didn't mind at all. We, the press, got dumped at a bomber airfield where there was a very nice little bar with excellent rye, then I made up to a major – a bore if there ever was one – and thereby got me a beautiful car ride back to London in lieu of a cold damp bus trip. So far it's not stopped raining once since Eleanor arrived.

Tonight I was writing my story down at the U.P. office when I discovered Ave and I were dining at No. 10, quite an (un)expected pleasure for me. Dinner was just the three of us. The P.M. in topmost form. He delighted himself and us with a discourse on Willkie[25] (likening him to a big Newfoundland puppy dog rolling in the mud, jumping up on a gal's white dress, knocking coffee cups off the table, on and on). He's such a wonderful man. I do wish you could know him.

American reporters are a fine bunch. Dixie Tighe is one of the funniest white women alive & wears very well. She's far more conscientious than I could ever hope to be.

We [reporters] laugh & joke and have a swell time driving to places. On the story we race around like mad in all directions, collecting names, quotes, local color etc. Then back in the bus we

25 Wendell Willkie (1892–1944), Republican candidate in the 1940 US presidential election.

pool our stuff. Almost all, that is – we're very cooperative about passing on innocuous information. Our best gets we keep well guarded.

Dined with Stinchfield last nite. I was too tired to make a nite of it, but I don't think he minded. He certainly likes you!

Bestest love to you,

Kathleen

London
November 1, 1942

Dear Mouche,

I'm afraid this won't be a very newsy letter, but I figure Averell can do that end. He's leaving tomorrow.

First and foremost, the food packages are wonderful. Some jelly would be nice as Averell likes it for breakfast. The corned beef and tinned meats are good and cheeses occasionally. Also a tin of pears would be nice now and then. Butter isn't necessary and cheese less often than meat.

Lipsticks, my non-allergic kind; the dope Shirley prescribed for me for cramps. Some wash cloths, cold cream for face only. Stockings for Pam and me, also four pair white ankle socks, 12 pair of dress shields. Face powder. Two cotton or linen baby suits (Winston is almost two and a biggish baby). Two sets of slips and pants, one white and one pink and two nighties. I also need a black or navy-blue slip and two bras. Girdles are hard to get here so if they're still obtainable in N.Y., one for Pam and one for me.

A couple of small bottles of perfume (some nice unsickly scent) would be wonderful for presents.

To mail over if possible. Hot water bottles. Sanitary napkins have returned on the London market so don't bother to send any more. I love chewing gum. The black low-heeled shoes are perfect for daily wear. But I still need a blue and a black suede or grosgrain for evening wear.

I lost my fake gold earrings – could another set be sent me?

I think that's about all, except two white long-sleeve blouses, one with biggest collar lapels.

There's little personal news – other than the usual work and play in the evenings.

Hope you see a lot of Averell, because that will mean he's relaxing in Arden. He's by no means completely back on his feet and the meeting in Washington with Lyttelton there will only add to his work.[26]

Best love to you all,
Kathleen

London
November 14, 1942

Dear Mouche,

It seems ages since I've written to you. At the moment I'm tired, having recaught my cold, but despite all that, plus my social life being shot to hell due to work, and no weekends, I'm having the time of my life. My God it's fun. At what more exciting moment could I have been left alone to handle this end of *Newsweek*! The office end of the work bores me stiff – Marjorie, the secretary, can't add or translate American money into pounds without making a mistake. She's not so hot on taking dictation – but somehow or other we're still intact. Pretty soon Mr Muir, the big boss, will leave and that will be one less headache. He's a bore second to none. I really get quite mortified taking him around to meet people. Instead of listening to these people – learning what they think – he talks about himself. When you keep him off the subject of himself, sometimes he's quite astute. What he thinks of me – I haven't the vaguest idea. I told [him] I hoped *Newsweek* wouldn't be worried about me taking over the bureau. His answer was: "that's your worry not theirs!"

One day I took him down to bomber command (American) to meet General Eaker.[27] We saw all the interesting rooms and things that press don't normally get to, which I enjoyed no end. Then went

26 In November 1942 Averell spent a month in Washington with Oliver Lyttelton, the British Minister of Production, discussing US supplies to Britain.
27 General Ira C. Eaker (1896–1987), commander of the US Eighth Air Force.

to a bomber station. Muir got stuck in the narrow Fortress passageway, which was really quite funny.

Today I spent most of my time trying to make head or tail out of Darlan's appointment as civil administrator of North Africa.[28] Cold bloodedly that means the Americans have set up a fascist state, which is in direct conflict to what we're fighting for. The havoc created among guerrilla governments is terrific. They and everyone else are wondering what the score is. Oddly enough, the Fighting French are among the calmest – they're taking the line "we'll do nothing to jeopardize Eisenhower's position."

I finally got a story written, came home here to bed and since I've been writing this I've had a series of seances over the phone with the censor, but I'm getting used to that.

I don't like the idea of having no more weekends because they used to be the saving grace of my existence – at least one day of health – but now I can't see myself going to the country by myself on Tuesdays!

Best love,
Kathy

London
late November 1942

Dear Mouche,

Your two novels arrived today. At this point I wonder when I'll get a moment to read them! Each day I've got to go thru every damned newspaper and periodical, but anyway I love having them. Please see that Averell brings back Ed Beattie's new book – *Freely to Pass*.[29] Also, if he will I'd much appreciate my possum fur coat. If I have to go on country stories this winter, I'll really need something to keep me warm. I was in a continual state of shivers on the Roosevelt story and

28 Darlan was in Algiers when Anglo-American forces invaded the French North African colonies in November 1942. In return for a truce he was named High Commissioner for France in Africa but shortly afterwards was assassinated by anti-Vichyites.

29 Edward W. Beattie (1909–84), American journalist, whose *Freely to Pass* (1942) recounted his experiences as a war correspondent.

that was by no means winter. My good fur coat isn't quite the thing to wear and besides it's beginning to show signs of age around the edges, so I do my best to preserve it.

A good friend of mine is in desperate need of a pair of garters. They are non-existent over here. Could you oblige. (Incidentally it's not women's garters.)

Also, I need some dress shields – "preservers" as they're called.

Best love,

Kathleen

[Mouche passed this letter to Marie, writing on it that she didn't know anything about men's garters.]

London
December 7, 1942

Dear Marie,

Averell says you're worried about my state of spinsterhood. Please don't worry as personally I can imagine little worse than being married in wartime.

Though I like to think my social life has been shot to hell, it hasn't actually. A few nights per week I can't go out due to having to work here late.

I've developed some new friends, sort of Air Corps people, but for the most part few people stay in London long. They move on to North Africa or disappear to other parts of the globe, so it's hard to keep the same friends for longer than a few months.

Frequently these days I get mad as the devil [because] women correspondents have to sit at home where all's quiet. Covering the war from military conferences perhaps gives you a better all-round picture of the war, but at times like these it seems awfully tame and monotonous.

Yesterday at Chequers I went out for a walk with a youngster, perhaps he's my age but he doesn't look it.[30] He was complaining he hadn't done a thing in this war – three weeks of not too hard fighting

30 Patrick Anthony Porteous (1918–2000), awarded the Victoria Cross aged twenty-four for his conduct during the Dieppe Raid.

before Dunkerque and then four hours at Dieppe – that's all. He wears only one decoration – the VC!

My bestest love to you all.

Kath

London
mid-December 1942

Dear Everybody,

This must be community 'cause that's the only way you'll ever [hear] how much I love my beautiful birthday presents.

Mouche dear your book sits by my bedside. I finished *The Prodigal Women* last weekend, which I enjoyed most terribly.[31]

I had lovely birthday presents galore – so many wonderful roses & other ultra-expensive flowers I could never afford to buy.

Did I tell you – overworked as I am – I love my work? Loren Carroll ex-ass't editor or something is over here for the O.W.I. [Office of War Information]. We lunched two days back and he was a great help, as I have really no idea what *Newsweek* likes or doesn't like. I haven't as yet received any answers to my letters. Damn lousy communications!

Joe Evans, head of *Herald Trib.* Bureau, is a great help on telling me what to do and what not to do in the way of running the office etc. On Thursday I was took to lunch by the Editor of the *Financial News*[32] – middle-aged – just what you'd imagine the editor of a strictly financial paper would be like. I gave him the works thru the whole meal (he's gonna work for us – do financial stuff) & then finally as he paid the bill, I got a little scared & asked that he please not judge *Newsweek* by me. "Do you mind if I do?" was his answer, which I thought was rather sweet. I suppose it's the first time in years he's lunched with a young girl!

One thing of interest I got from him: what is the margin between unemployment insurance & low wage pay sufficient to create the will

31 A novel by Nancy Hale (1908–88) published in 1942, which explored the lives of three young women coming of age in the 1920s.
32 The *Financial News* later merged with the *Financial Times*.

to work? This was re. Beveridge Report.[33] I gave him the works on subject of future Republican politics, which of course was cribbed straight from Averell – verbatim – so that interested him no end.

This week I've been up to my ears with the "Cliveden Set"[34] & air force stuff & the Darlan Affair etc. Now that I look back on it – can't remember what all that cable wordage was about!

Haven't done a scrap of Xmas shopping. I forgot all about Xmas cards too & can't think when I'll get a moment to look around for something for Averell that he won't want anyway.

I've run out of conversation. Goodnight. Merry Christmas to you all. Sorry my writing's so bad – but I've forgotten how to write properly.

Bestest love,

Puff

33 A British government report on social security written by the Liberal economist William Beveridge, widely seen as the progenitor of the British welfare state.
34 Named after Lady Nancy Astor's country residence, an aristocratic circle identified with promoting prewar British appeasement of Nazi Germany.

CHAPTER 11

'THE BRITISH AMBASSADOR TO MOSCOW – THE MOST DIVINE CREATURE I'VE MET IN A LONG TIME!'

Kathy's letters contain many amusing anecdotes about Archibald Clark Kerr, the flamboyant British ambassador to the Soviet Union. She gives the impression that they were kindred spirits and the best of pals. While there is no contemporaneous evidence that Kathy's wartime relationship with 'Archie' was anything but warm, in the 1980s she told her father's biographer Rudy Abramson that he was 'a terrible man', hated by Churchill, prone to lewd remarks, and whose designs on a young male war correspondent in Moscow had led to the reporter being dispatched home. She told me much the same story when I interviewed her in 2002, though not before asking me to switch off the tape recorder.

For Kathy, the political was personal, especially where her father was concerned. Hence the explanation for her changed attitude towards Archie may be more political than personal, since, as Frank Costigliola has pointed out, there was a degree of falling out between Averell and Clark Kerr over relations with the Soviets. By the end of the war, Ave favoured a tougher stance on negotiations with Stalin over the postwar order, while Archie continued to favour a more conciliatory approach.

London
January 4, 1943

Dear Mary,

My gloves are wonderful – ever so many thanks and the Xmas card with Bobby's picture is absolute heaven. We've already added the big photo Averell brought back with him to our array of pictures of Stalin, Churchill, Roosevelt and Ave that adorn the mantlepiece.

One thing which I'll probably expound on at greater length later on: Pam's younger sister, a hellova nice girl aged about twenty entered the A.T.S. at the beginning of the war. Anyway she was invalided out of the A.T.S. about two years ago.

I'm trying to persuade her to go to the U.S. She's going to see if she can get a job in Washington, some British department. Her family have all sorts of connections and there is a great demand for English girls. If her family decide to let her go, and she gets the Washington job, would you mind taking care of her the first few weeks?

She's an awfully nice girl, loves riding, outdoor things. She's shy at first. I discovered via Pam she was scared stiff of me for ages (not that that means anything).

I'm home now – went to bed for dinner as I think I've got a sinus on one side of my face. I didn't feel like coping with dining out, the fog and the blackout. Finished the Ilya Ehrenburg novel *The Fall of Paris*, which you should read.[1] Reminds me of my favorite André Gide book – *Les Faux-monnayeurs*.[2]

Put the mag. to bed tonight (Monday) – issue dated Jan. 11 – story about Vichy France – it's quite the most exciting scoop I've had yet. I was so scared *Newsweek* wouldn't appreciate its worth that I almost cabled you. 'Tis sad but the story will go unbylined – because Averell doesn't want anyone to think I might have gotten it from him. In case you're interested same issue should have a piece about Russian equipment, tanks, aircraft etc., uniforms and a few new tidbits about

---

1 A novel by Soviet writer Ilya Ehrenburg (1891–1967) published in 1942, which deals with the decay of French politics and society in the run-up to France's defeat by Germany in 1940.
2 Published in English as *The Counterfeiters* (1925), Gide's novel concerns the lives of a group of schoolboys and their teachers.

the Urals industry; a piece on German youth; a piece on Mrs Churchill; the Jugoslav government collapse, the Arctic battle, and that's about all I can think of – except my hardest story. An American woman was murdered by her son last week. There was little released about gory details etc. so I had to go around bribing janitors, interviewing girls who'd known the son – doing all the "routine" things one reads about in detective stories. 'Twas quite fun – a change to say the least.

I was quite pleased this morning to read in the papers that the Jugoslav government had reformed as I said it would!

Saturday night I went to the country with Win & Charlie (2 boys in Ave's office). I had a disastrous experience: we went in the field to see how the ponies were making out and I jumped up on the little grey half-Arab one & was fooling around when suddenly Poppy decided she'd have some fun – so off we went galloping around the field, swerving around corners at terrific rate. 2nd time round the field she decided she'd try & brush me off so we went under the low-hanging branches. At one point she slipped in the mud and almost went down. Needless to say I was scared stiff and practically fell off 99 times. Today I'm very stiff. Moral: don't get on bridleless, halter-less ponies just for the fun of it!

New Year's Eve was most gay and drunken. The party I went to had everything from a Crown Prince to a U.S. able seaman at it and was most genial, [lasting] to 3:30 a.m. I was dropped off by some drunken Guards officer. As he was most amorous, I jumped out of the taxi and came quickly upstairs without any "goodnights" or anything else. Two minutes later, the doorbell started ringing. Averell had heard me come in so we decided it would be fun if he answered the doorbell. He made a magnificent Victorian Father guarding his daughter's honor & the boy fled in terror, much to our amusement. God help me if I ever see him again!!

Tomorrow I'm giving a cocktail party. The British Ambass. to Moscow wants to meet the American press. He's a great friend of Averell's & I think he's quite the most divine creature I've met in a long time!

Best love to you and Bobby.

Puff

London
January 14, 1943

Dear Mouche,

You are an absolute angel. Ever so many thanks. It was fun opening our presents. London was really quite Christmassy; Averell and I enjoyed ourselves very much.

Thanks for Ed Beattie's book. I'm reading it now and like it a lot. I loved *The Seventh Cross*.[3] My God, it was depressing.

I had a very amusing dinner the other night. Geoffrey Patterson came up to London on leave. As I had avoided seeing him the last four times he'd been up, I figured I couldn't avoid it this time. So we dined. No sooner had the soup appeared on the table than he started proposing. The crucial moment and an earring fell into the soup with a splash. I burst out laughing, which annoyed him rather as he was all so serious as usual. From then on the evening became lighter and gayer, and I hope to God I've seen the end of him.

I have developed all sorts of new friends, mostly American, so in between working hours life is pleasant to the detriment of sleep.

When I get a copy of *Newsweek* these days I practically feel as if the whole damn magazine originated from the London bureau.

I get a great kick out of writing things up I know nothing about. This week and last week are centered around Russians. The advance is so rapid that I have given up coping with being able to spell the recaptured town names. However, pretty soon they will be entering familiar ground, particularly in the Caucasus.

My one New Year's resolution – please don't be horrified – was not to lose any more money in gin rummy, and I'm delighted to report it has been kept 100%.

I am going to try and wangle somehow to get to North Africa. Even Averell is sold on the idea. As you probably know from reading the papers, London's in turmoil over the North African political situation.

---

3 A novel by Anna Seghers (1900–83) published in 1942, which centres on an escape from a Nazi concentration camp.

I have a new source of information amongst Poles, who's got a glass eye, much scarred-up face – result of opening days of the war. Don't know yet how good a source he will turn out to be, but so far he has produced ample sufficiency.

Best love,

Kathy

PS A terrible thing – none of the lipsticks work – soon I will be desperate – as my original lipsticks stock is near to exhausted.

London
mid-January, 1943

Dear Mary,

Saturday night at Max's was fun – the British Ambass. to Moscow was as full of tidbits as usual and as nice as ever. He's got the great gift of telling little anecdotes that are most expressive. As he used to be ambass. to China and has greatest respect for the Chinese, was equally interesting on that subject. Sunday morning, Max and I went for a long walk. He's so damned nice when he wants to be.

Training up to London, somehow I got myself entangled with a couple of drunken Canadian soldiers, who most persistently followed me to my office, where finally after much talk and discussion I persuaded them I must leave & do some work. London's getting worse & worse that way. Such incidents are frequent & unavoidable if one travels alone.

Sunday night we had a raid, which I gather was played up in the U.S. as a veritable blitz. It was fun watching the new ack-ack – which is less noisy & more colorful, but I must admit I experienced no sense of being scared. As Pam was in the country I marched over to Pam's flat and found Butch already dressed and ready, wide awake, trotting around saying "guns going boom, guns going boom" which alternated with "no more booms, no more booms." He was quite unfrightened, more pleased at the idea of going out than anything else. Nanny, however, I gather hated the shelter, and somehow I don't blame her. Shelters aren't designed for luxury. Anyway, all went well and I came back to the apartment just in time to run into a couple of pajama-clad, senior U.S. officers tearing towards our shelter, well armed with gas masks and tin hats. I'm neither brave nor blasé over the combined dangers of bombs dropping and ack-ack shrapnel, but I thought that performance was mortifying.

I'm absolutely furious a U.P. man interviewed "the Scarlet Pimpernel" of Belgium[4] – a good interview & the Belgian boy in question is a beau of mine. Damnation I never thought of so doing.

Last night Pamela and I went to see the best damned movie – *Casablanca* – the script is full of clever cracks & tidbits. We both loved it. Then afterwards Joe Evans, *Herald Tribune* & Ed Beattie, U.P. came around for a session of gin rummy. Pam and I took them on. They're the most conceited rummy players – 2nd only to myself, with a result that after about 3 hours Pam & I were ninepence ahead. A moral victory if nothing more!

When these days are in the past, I'll have a memory of many an evening of hours and hours of gin rummy intermingled with talk of the war. Someday I hope you'll meet some of the correspondents here, you won't find nicer people anywhere. I sometimes get cold all over (not at the moment as I'm in bed with two sizzling hot water bottles) when I think of how close I came to not coming over. What comes next!!?

To get back to *Newsweek*, I'm getting better settled & now don't get rattled or befuddled when high-sounding queries come in – asking for U-boat tactics etc. Bit by bit the pieces of miscellaneous information take their place and at last I feel as though light's coming through. Lord knows my information is dangerously sketchy – but at least it's better grounded than that of the newer arrivals.

I'm going to stop now.

Bestest love,

Puff

PS Tomorrow I lunch at No. 10 Downing Street. Fun. Fun.

• • •

[Letter continues:]

---

4 Possibly Albert Guérisse (1911–89), a Belgian military officer who helped allied military personnel to evade or escape German captivity.

As areas of London got strafed & dive-bombed, Pam went down on WVS business and came in just as I was leaving for dinner and had a good case of hysterics. Pam reacts violently and emotionally to all things, and today being with people who were waiting to see if the next person dug out of the debris was their husband, brother or friend was just too much for her.[5] Perhaps I'm made differently, I know I am, but there's only a certain point – height of horror emotion that can be reached. I reached that ages ago and now everything is impersonal. It's better all round that way, I figure.

London
January 30, 1943

Dear Marie,

Averell's back safe and sound thank goodness, so now you know why you haven't been hearing from him lately. The louse came in one evening and said: "I'm going to Nordafrica to meet a Lend-Lease mission going over from the States" and me the sucker believed him.[6]

Averell arrived back with the First Sea Lord, Dickie Mountbatten and Pug Ismay plus other smaller fry and I've never seen such a bunch of dejected, dirty-looking men in my life. They came in an unadulterated bomber which at best is uncomfortable; this one was also very dirty. They'd slept in the bomb racks and were covered in mud, dust and matting.

I always get scared stiff meeting Averell, never quite sure whether he'll be mad or pleased. (Secret arrivals are supposed to be secret.) But after this last time, I don't think I will again as none of the other men were met by other than their chauffeurs and were most jealous of Averell who'd have someone to enthuse to on the long journey home. He told me all the dope that there was to tell, which of course I loved, so did *Newsweek* I hope. But unfortunately a great deal had to be left unsaid.

---

5 A reference to the German bombing of Sandhurst Road primary school in Catford, South London, on 20 January 1943, which killed thirty-eight children and six teachers. Chips Channon wrote in his diary that when he had dinner with Pam that night, she was in an 'emotional state' and 'much moved by the horror'.

6 In fact, Averell was heading to a Churchill–Roosevelt conference in Casablanca.

Averell's very lucky the way he gets in on all the good shows – it's nice too 'cause everyone says such nice things about him. Now for some time I've watched his position and prestige grow. It's unfortunate you can't come witness it as I can tell you it's very gratifying to see.

I had one slight diversion from the ever-lasting answering [of] *Newsweek*'s dumb queries and went out and watched the fortresses come back from their first raid on Germany. They had few casualties so the crews were in the best of spirits when interviewed. As I, with forethought, had attached myself to the wing commanding general (a bore if ever there was one) I got driven to more stations than the rest of the press. At one station, we were on the ops tower watching the B17s land when all of a sudden out of nowhere a squadron of Mitchells and Marauders came over hedgehopping and proceeded to beat up the airdrome, just missing hangars and our heads by inches. They buzzed around the Fortresses like a lot of angry bees and it was really quite funny. I laughed but for obvious reasons the general was mad as hell.

I lunched with Joe Phillips, ex-*Newsweek* man now head public relations officer down in Algiers, the other day and he made the encouraging remark that the next woman correspondent would only go to Nordafrica over his dead body. After that I almost gave up all hope. Now Averell reports that General McClure[7] (I used to be hostess for him when he was in London) says if Virginia Cowles[8] can go to the front when she's not even writing for the press, he sees no reason why I can't. So now I'm all pepped up again. All we've got to arrange now is to get someone to run *Newsweek* here and get Red out. I wish it were easy!

Bestest love to you,
Kathy

---

7 General Robert A. McClure (1897–1957), US military attaché in London and then head of Eisenhower's Information and Censorship Section.
8 Harriet Virginia Cowles (1910–83), American writer and journalist, later awarded the OBE by the British for her service as a war correspondent.

London
January 31, 1943

Dear Mary,

I'm getting a bad case of traveler's itch. Ave says I'm a fool, but I don't want to spend the whole war in London & the way things seem to be pointing, once an offensive starts somewhere I'll get seated with the London bureau of *Newsweek*. Thank you no! At the moment we're trying to buy Joe Evans away from the *Herald Trib*. Say nothing about it, but I've got all fingers & toes crossed. The novelty of bureau managing is beginning to wear off – scratching around & getting "authoritative" answers to New York's stupid queries gets monotonous, particularly when the story can't be told anyway. I hate the idea, the feeling, of being tied down – unable to leave town at a moment's notice if I get on a good story trail. All *Newsweek*'s stuff – from Fred in Algiers, Bill's from Moscow & Kennedy's from Dublin [comes thru London] & I'm the general clearing house for information. I suppose it's all very good training & all that, but at the moment I like the idea of getting away from the blasted desk for a day or two – away from the everlasting pile of newspapers that must be read & clipped.

We went to the country last night, stopping off to see Max en route, who was in top form. Then as the weather was lousy – too bad to even walk – we came up after lunch & went to see *Casablanca*.

Feb. 1

As I told Marie, André, according to Averell, is doing a swell job down in Algiers. He's Giraud's diplomatic aide and liaison between the British and the Americans.[9] Both the latter think he's terrific. And Ave says Giraud's success at Casablanca was due to André's diplomacy. That's pretty good as he only arrived down there a few days before the conference started. Already by the time Giraud was invited, he'd created an important position for himself. André was up here for a while before he went down, we saw a lot of him and he was

9 André Poniatowski (see note 5 on p.21) was aide to General Henri Giraud, commander of French forces in North Africa and successor to Admiral Darlan, who was assassinated in December 1942.

his usual charming self. His conversation was fascinating. He's the first Frenchman I've seen since the war who can be coldly unemotional about homegrown politics.

I can't tell you how exciting I think the above is. Averell says he's really a gift from heaven to the mess down there, where, of course, the scum of the scum are assembled.

I'm rushing off now in search of my monthly reckonings of German troops.

Best love,

Kathy

London
mid-February, 1943

Dear Mary,

What would adulterated envy be as compared to unadulterated? Anyway doesn't matter. I'm envious as hell of Sheila – who you'll now have seen. But I still expect to be home sometime.

Bob McClure (head of Eisenhower's A2) dropped in the other day for a brief visit & told me all about the trials and tribulations he's been having with women correspondents down in Nordafrica & [partly] sold me on the idea that the front line isn't the place for women. However, he'll do nothing to stop either Helen or Mary or me from going down. I suppose he considers us the orthodox correspondents who obey rules & regulations, as opposed to [those] who disobey P.R.O. [Public Relations Officer] (press) orders & make nuisances of themselves. But it does make me mad as hell that all female correspondents get damned because of a few bitches.

I got me a new boss – Joe Evans. He's been boss for 2 days, so we're still going through the process of reorganization. Having been on "night work" for the *Herald Trib.* During the past 2 years he finds getting to the office mornings very difficult.

Boss Joe is so nice, I wish you knew him. He's really the best bureau chief/correspondent combination in town & he'll give *Newsweek* a hellova boost, prestigely speaking.

Needless to say Red is mad as hell. Probably thinks I buggered the queries up to such an extent that in desperation they hired Joe – not that it bothers me.

My 3 months "experience" was great fun while it lasted but as a steady job single-handed was too much, particularly the time I got the flu & couldn't afford to stay in bed. Besides, I rather doubt it does *Newsweek* any good, in the final analysis, having Averell's daughter as bureau chief.

Went to the Commons last week to hear the P.M. [February 11]. He was in great form, however his announcement of Ike's appointment went ungreeted by even one "hear, hear" from his fellow honorable gentleman. Actually, Alexander's[10] back in his original job as C-in-C of the 1st British Army. I met him at Chequers – he's dapper, untalkative.

This is the first letter I've not typed for ages. My writing gets more & more unreadable. Even I have trouble deciphering press conference notes!

Give everyone my love.

Bestest,

Puff

London

February 16, 1943

Dear Mary,

I haven't heard from you for a coot's age, hence have no idea if you have received my various letters to you telling you about Sheila Digby (Pam's sister) coming over. As I've already told you she's a very good friend of mine and one hellova swell kid. I'm sure you will like her.

Sorry to be such a bother and hope you won't mind keeping an eye out for her.

---

10 General Harold Alexander (1891–1969). In February 1943 Alexander's command in North Africa was subordinated to a new configuration headed by Eisenhower, who had been transferred from the European Theater of Operations.

As you may or may not know, Joe Evans, former *New York Herald Tribune* chief here in London, has taken over the office here. A very pleasant state of affairs indeed. As much as I enjoyed my three months "experience" there was a little too much for one person to do, particularly as that one person completely lacks knowledge of such things as bureau running.

Averell's fine. Since he returned from Casablanca we seem to have done a goodly amount of entertaining, which I view with mixed feelings as it usually means we are kicked out of the main room before coffee is served and the men are too involved in their interesting talk to join us for some hours, after which time the party breaks up.

Best love to you and Bobby,

Puff

London
February 18, 1943

Mouche dear,

I've now joined the ranks of the employees, and it's a delightful change. My three months running *Newsweek* was fun but it was rather hectic. There are so many conferences, daily and odd ones, *Newsweek* sends an ever-increasing number of "queries" asking for impossible-to-get information about war materials on all fronts, leaving no time to write.

Red Mueller got absolutely furious when he heard Joe Evans, a very good friend of his, has overtaken the office and cursed hell out of both Joe and me via cable from Gib.

Actually, I'm glad as the devil Joe has taken over. He's a much more experienced man, got a good deal of tact, something which Red lacked almost entirely.

It's so nice too not having so damned much responsibility – before I had to do everything. Now I get complete entire days off. Yesterday was my first – a Tuesday and I had a lovely time, dawdling in the morning, lunching with a sweet little B-17 pilot and then as a final afternoon spree I went and spent the 200-odd dollars I made from U.P. covering Missus Roosevelt. I bought a very nice black suit.

Actually I couldn't be happier about things in general. The war in Tunis seems to be going badly. Thank God I gave the Italian alpine troops a big build-up last week!

It doesn't look as though chances for my going to North Africa will materialize. Due to the bad name that various females have given our variety of correspondents, women aren't looked upon in a very good light down there. If I went I wouldn't be allowed anywhere near the front, as the two that have been did so only by breaking all regulations laid down for war correspondents. However, when Joe Evans took over our London bureau, the editor sent me a little "we love you dearly Kathy" cable.

Averell gave a thoroughly swank party on Monday for General Andrews[11] – the new U.S. big boss – to meet the heads of the British services, service ministers and all the other war cabinet ministers. There was quite an array of gold braid.

Kathleen

London
late February, 1943

Dear Mary,

Got a lovely long letter from you this morning.

Sheila certainly seems very gay – Pam was getting worried on that score.

The correspondents gave a luncheon yesterday for General Devers,[12] the new big boss. According to him, he knew us in the West Point polo-playing days. I'd have liked it if my 1st impression was more favorable. He made a speech after lunch – the kind I imagine Rotarians make at gatherings. It compared badly with those of either Eisenhower or Andrews when they came to similar luncheons.

11 General Maxwell Andrews (1884–1943), US Army Air Force general who took over from Eisenhower as commander of US troops in the European Theater of Operations. He was killed in a plane crash during an inspection tour of Iceland.

12 General Jacob L. Devers (1887–1979), armoured divisions supremo, who in May 1943 succeeded General Andrews as chief of the European Theater of Operations.

However, I'm not a good judge of soldiers or soldiering qualities. He sure is "press" conscious.

I wrote Popsie about my going gliding the other day – which was an amusing experience, very noisy & bumpy until we were cut loose.

My only other out of the ordinary activity was last week when I was asked to be one of two guests on the Brains Trust. You sit around a table with a mike in the middle and questions are drawn out of a pile & if and when you want to speak you raise your hand. Needless to say I was practically in a state of fright for the first two questions – one on snobbery & another on why British clothes are lousy. After those I got slightly less scared & enjoyed it. Now I'm $63 richer – a hellova lot of money for little effort or time. The "regular" Brains Trust members I found stuffy, conceited & didactic. One – a Professor Joad[13] – opened conversation at luncheon before the broadcast with "which one of my books have you read?" When I told him "none" – he turned away in complete contempt!

Did I tell you *Newsweek* gave me a raise last month? I now get $60 a week, which is very little I think, but at least a $10 step up in the right direction.

I must be off now.

Best love,

Kathleen

PS I'm having my picture taken for *Mademoiselle* – to get Pam out of a jam.

London
March 4, 1943

Dear Mary,

Last week I succumbed to the luxury of staying in bed for a few days with a stupid very prevalent disease called gastric flu. It was nice to stay in bed though. I slept most all the time and look the picture of health and sunshine.

I can't tell you what fun it is working with Joe, he divides up all the work. I take Saturday afternoon thru Sundays and Tuesdays off and

---

13 C.E.M. Joad (1891–1953), British philosopher and radio broadcaster.

he takes none – a swell arrangement, which I imagine will last till spring. After acting like a spoiled prima donna for a few weeks, about his being removed without consultation as head of the London bureau, Red's finally come to realize that he's better off where he is.

Yesterday Admiral Stark, our head naval around here, gave a huge cocktail party for all the Brit and American press plus pretty much everyone else. As usual I enjoyed myself immensely, because at those sorts of parties you meet all sorts of mild friends and acquaintances.

Have I told you that we got a new Public Relations Officer for the Eighth Air Force in the form of one Lt. Col. Jock Whitney? Only yesterday he was a captain. Now he's very high and mighty. I have yet to have any dealings with him, so can't yet comment on whether he's good, bad or indifferent. However, we (the press) are most hopeful. Jock's a hellova conscientious worker & should do a top-notch job.

Pam gave a party the other night for Avie Clark which was lots of fun. Avie was continually complaining that he knows only "old women" (Pam and I are in that sphere) so [we got] Avie together with a nineteen-year-old girl. A very sweet kid and blonde and beautiful into the bargain. The evening was a great success. However, I think that at the moment Avie's prime interest is the war and flying, which is as it should be.

We had a short intermission. Some friend of Averell's just phoned, who sounds most lecherous over the phone. For some stupid reason he wants to meet me, and the only way I could get him off the telephone was by saying – yes. I spend half my time saying yes, and the other half trying to figure out a way of getting out of things. My biggest blunder was one time I said yes, I would represent America in some International Women's Organization. When I discovered their main desire to have me was for me to make a speech on International Women's Day, I galloped out of that thing quickly.

Had a lovely time last Tuesday, my day off, and went round with Sarah Oliver, the P.M.'s middle daughter, to a shop where she used to get her clothes in the days when she was an actress.

It was very sad Bob Post getting lost on the Wilhelmshaven raid. His wife had just come over to join him. Another quite good friend of mine – a pilot didn't come back too. Eventually, I suppose there'll be very few of the originals left.

More reports have come in about André doing great things down south. As far as I can gather he's still serving unofficially in the background, getting on well with all parties. In other words, doing pretty damn near the impossible.

There was an air raid last night, and I was out with two American bomber pilots. They were quite excited. It was the first time they had been on the lower end of a raid, so we hung out of our window for a while and watched the fireworks. Nothing dropped around near us. Lord knows why because they seemed to be directly overhead.

There was another raid at 4:30. I am ashamed to say I even slept through the ack-ack guns.

Give my love to everyone.

Best love,

Puff

London
March 8, 1943

Mouche dear,

You write such nice letters. I love getting them – particularly the ones that scold. I am awful aren't I – forgetting – not forgetting – but just not getting 'round to writing Aunt Cornelia?

I'm in a wonderful mood tonight. Appropriately after dinner I retired to let Ave & dinner guests talk & now I'm comfortable & in bed. The B.B.C. is forthcoming with some lousy music. But life as usual is pleasant. I sometimes wonder if I'll ever lose my pure joy of living. I enjoy almost every minute of it. Now that it's over, I wonder why I enjoyed the 3 months of hell when running the London bureau of *Newsweek*. These days when I split all the work with Joe, I wonder how I ever did all of it & survived.

Tomorrow I get another whole day off. It's well mapped out – fitting for new black suit – luncheon with an ex-Sun Valleyite now in 8th Air Force. Then I'm being good Samaritan & going to visit a friend who's been terribly ill with meningitis. He's way out of town at a hospital & a mutual friend needs cheering up.

Next on schedule for "day off" activities comes 2 cocktail parties.

The above is just a usual picture of "war-torn" London – just in case you ever think that we're roughing it!

March 14

It's now Sunday and I'm at the office waiting for the boss to arrive so's I can send off a story about why the Italian navy isn't and never will be commanded by a German admiral; why Goebbels has changed his propaganda to the Herrenvolk; and what the British reaction is to Standley's[14] statement in Moscow (privately the British are very pleased that at last someone has dared even unofficially to be tough back to the Russians). If Standley gets recalled, I wonder if there will be another attempt to get Averell to Moscow.

The last couple of issues of *Newsweek* we received are very encouraging. They credit London bureau with a piece I did on the Archbis. of Canterbury and they used all I sent on General Alexander. *Time* is still fighting mad at us for getting a statement out of General Eaker, which gives me a goodly amount of pleasure.

Most fun I had this week was an 8th Air Force sortie to see our (America's) latest fighter. We saw said aircraft, but can't yet write about it.

[Kathleen]

Chequers, Bucks
March 19, 1943

Dear Marie,

We came down here unexpectedly this evening. 1st just Averell was invited, then at the last minute word came that I too was expected.

The P.M. is in great shape. It's the first time I've seen him since he's been ill. Just Sir Charles & Lady Portal are here. Clemmie's at Chartwell, so everything couldn't be nicer. At dinner the P.M. recited famous speeches made by famous speakers on every which subject, told

14 Admiral W.H. Standley (1872–1963), US ambassador to the Soviet Union 1941–3, who on 8 March 1943 held a press conference at which he criticised the Soviets for not being sufficiently grateful for American Lend-Lease aid to Russia.

funny stories, and made what he called his "stained-glass smiles." I've never seen him clown so well before.

The movie this evening was *Desert Victory* (third time for me) and a Stalin to Churchill special on the capture of Field Marshal Paulus.[15] After that we took up the serious sport of a few rounds of bagatelle[16] – which the P.M. won hands down & now at 2:00 a.m. I've discovered that the voices below are making far too much noise for me to concentrate on sleeping.

The war's going well – if the general atmosphere of tonight is any judge. It's comforting to see him in good spirits, and nothing worse than when he's lost – tired or disconsolate. Then he sits with his head in his hands at dinner & refuses to talk.

Sunday [March 28] we again went to Chequers, which was nice. It turned out to be just the family circle & us. The moment we arrived Averell was whisked off to a secret chamber by the P.M. I figured all sorts of important things were being discussed. The hours passed & still they didn't appear. Do you know what they were doing? Playing bezique!!!

Dixie Tighe's latest, said after Averell's recent press conference: "For G. sake tell your father next time I have to cover his conference to wear a gas mask so's I can concentrate on what he's saying."

Best love to all the family.

Kathy

London
April 4, 1943

Dear Mary,

I'm very worried about something. It's such fun to worry about things you can't help, for a change. I'm getting very grey, around the head I mean. Are you? In fact now I've gotten beyond the stage of trying to pull the ones at my part out, there are just too damned

15 Paulus's German 6th Army surrendered to the Soviets at Stalingrad at the end of January 1943.
16 A type of billiards.

many. I was just wondering if perhaps you were undergoing the same signs of age. If so we can blame Averell.

Friday afternoon late I happened to casually mention to Joe Evans that I wish I were going to Algiers to cover the Giraud–de Gaulle meeting and that probably if I went I'd find I had a pretty good ready-made contact on the spot (André). He said he'd been thinking about the same thing so then and there we got to work. I failed in getting a place on de Gaulle's plane and then discovered I needn't bother about transportation until I receive permission to go from down there, so Joe cabled Bob McClure and now we're waiting. Helen Kirkpatrick and Geoff Parsons[17] got Admiral Stark to cable Bob. If Red happens to be in Algiers at the moment, which I think he is, I won't have a prayer as *Newsweek* already has above its quota of correspondents for that theater. If I thought there were really any chance of my getting there (it would be tomorrow or next day) I'd be excited as hell. Anyway it was a good idea. I feel I need a change of air or something.

This morning I went to General Eaker's for lunch and a little tennis. He's got a nice house for himself and staff just on the outskirts, one of those big villa affairs that you wonder why anyone builds. I arrived and was immediately shooed off to the court (a holey affair) with plenty of dust and not much back court room, and discovered to my horror I had to take on the general single-handed. He turned out to be a mighty powerful player, who lacked what I call a gentleman's serve and did his best to paste everything possible. Result, I countered with powerful swearing, calling him a skunk, a complete louse etc. which I suppose isn't quite the correct language to apply to one with the rank of major general. However, if he minded he didn't show it.

I arrived back here to discover that the ambass. was back in our midst. He's now firmly entrenched in our living room. I listened to about two hours of his conversation and then had to leave when things that little Kathy shouldn't hear came up.

---

17 Geoffrey Parsons (1879–1956), American journalist, *New York Herald Tribune*.

April 6

Spent most of this morning with the Norwegians getting (1) a story for *Newsweek*'s religion department and (2) a story for the science department on how the Germans go about making heavy water at the Rjukan factory, which recently was sabotaged.[18] This afternoon I've got to try and find something new to say about army–air cooperation, lessons learned from Tunisia. That one's going to be hard as pretty nearly each week since the battle of El Alamein we've filed something on said subject. Just last week I did about two hundred words. Repetition, I always figure, is a waste of time.

Last night horror of horrors Averell ditched me at the last minute and I had to go dine with the Swedish ambass. all alone (unescorted). Don't think the party was much of a success. The Swedish Ambass. made an anti-Russian crack which was overheard by Maisky (Soviet ambass.) [who] wasn't pleased. Dinner guests included a mixture of Norwegians, Swedes, me and the Maiskys plus a couple from the Foreign Office. Meal time seemed to be spent in me consuming large quantities of champagne. I kept catching either Maisky or Mme Maisky's eyes – one of them would lift their glass for a toast and we'd drink a silent toast to victory. Soon the Swedes caught on to the game, with the only positive result that one of the English ladies married to a Swede got quite drunk!

Love to you & Sheila,
Puff

Around the same time – early April – Kathy wrote to Mouche about being taken on a B-17 training flight:

The trip was a major success. I succeeded in accomplishing the impossible – crawled all the way up into the nose of the Fortress and out again and didn't get a run in my stockings. I sat up in the nose amongst guns and unmentionable instruments and got very bumped turning each way trying to keep track of the fighters coming in on

18 The famous 'Heroes of Telemark' Norwegian resistance raid on the Rjukan heavy water plant that was key to Germany's atomic weapons development programme.

us. It's an odd sensation, sort of like being inside a big fish that's in a fish bowl. The sky and the clouds float by, and as the fighters came in and rolled over on their bellies, they too seemed as though they were floating. The only noise is the noise of your own aircraft. Having nothing to compare it with, your own speed seems negligible until another aircraft comes in and even then you're not quite sure if it's he or you that is moving.

In the same letter, she explained her attitude towards Ira Eaker:

A very nice man and top of my list of those who should be "cultivated." That's a complicated way of saying something rather mercenary!!! But there's nothing quite so effective as far as reporting goes than cultivating generals. To get atmosphere etc., there are the junior officers, pilots etc. Combine both and you've got the proper mixture, but a very discordant picture.

London
April 13, 1943

Dear Mouche,

Our news centers around my being exceedingly mad at *Newsweek*. They distorted very badly some information I sent them about the Eighth Air Force – the importance of its effort. Needless to say all the Eight Air Force authorities are amazed at *Newsweek* attacking them, which puts me in a most embarrassing position as I know them all pretty well and they know I write the Eighth Air Force stuff.

My trip to Algiers has been sabotaged by Red, damnation, even for the future date if and when the two G generals[19] meet.

Had a nice mid-week interlude on Tuesday. Averell and I went out and spent the night with R.A.F. bomber command chief[20] at his home. The occasion was a birthday party – joint one for him and Eaker, which was very genial. Harris has a sweet youngish wife and cute

19 Generals Giraud and de Gaulle.
20 Arthur 'Bomber' Harris (1892–1984).

precocious child, who I taught how to draw cats and trees the next morning.

Tomorrow I'm off to visit a B-24 station to interview some boys that have been down in North Africa, and were here before the landings. They should have good comparison story. A *Newsweek* scoop, I hope.

Lunched today with my opposite number on *Time* and *Life*, while Joe and the *Time–Life* bureau chiefs lunched. Our lunch was most pleasant, the other one probably wasn't. We start publishing an edition over here next week.

I'm off now.

Best love,

Kathleen

CHAPTER 12

'HAVE YOU EVER BEEN CALLED A BITCH TO END ALL BITCHES?'

'Not really,' was Kathy's coy response to my suggestion that during the war she must have been 'hit upon' by lots of men. Equally deft was her sidestepping of a question put to her by a reporter just after the war, regarding a comparison between young American and Russian men: 'I think it's hopeless to generalize, don't you?' Talking to the Russian historian Vladimir Pechatnov in 1995, Kathy recalled the procession of handsome young pilots and sailors that had been dangled before her by Soviet intelligence agents. But not once did she bite.

We know from her letters that during the war Kathy had numerous ardent male admirers, including several high-ranking American and British military officers and politicians. Wartime affairs, especially between older men and younger women, were quite common; indeed, one took place under her nose! But there is no hard evidence that she had even a passing romance, let alone a serious boyfriend.

Most intriguing in this regard is Kathy's relationship with Alan Kirk, a married, fifty-something US naval officer she met in summer 1942. He is not mentioned in her letters but his name crops up in her appointments diary. Kirk served as US naval attaché in London from 1939 to 1940, accompanied by his wife Lydia and their three children. In April 1942 he returned (alone) to Britain to serve as Admiral Harold Stark's chief of staff. He lived in the Connaught Hotel, located not far from Kathy's apartment and the US embassy in Grosvenor Square. In February 1943 Kirk was recalled to the United States and placed in charge of the Atlantic Fleet Amphibious Force. That same month he presented Kathy with a pencil portrait of himself, inscribed, 'To Kathleen with best wishes'. The artist was Serge Rodzianko, a Belgravia-based Russian émigré who specialised in portraiture. Among his other subjects was the actress Vivien Leigh.

In July 1943 Kirk took part in the allied invasion of Sicily and a couple of months later was once again posted to London, where he was slated to command the US naval forces that would take part in the Normandy invasion of June 1944. He ended the war as an admiral and then embarked on a diplomatic career, initially in Belgium and then, from 1949 to 1951, as US ambassador in Moscow. His last diplomatic outing was to Taiwan in the early 1960s. Instrumental in that posting, recalled Lydia, was their 'friend', Averell Harriman, who was then Assistant Secretary of State for Far Eastern Affairs.

We don't know if Kathy met Kirk after the war but her encounter with him in 1942–3 seems to have had a lingering impact. She kept his portrait in her private papers. Kirk died in 1963, but after her own husband's death in 1999 Kathy placed a photo of him on her bureau, where it stood for many years, though the picture was of a pensive-looking older man, rather than the suave naval officer of Rodzianko's drawing.

Kathy finally got to go home on 5 August, when she and Averell sailed from Scotland to Canada aboard the *Queen Mary*, a luxurious Blue Riband passenger liner that had been converted into a troop transport. They were accompanied by Churchill and his entourage, the P.M. being on the way to a conference with Roosevelt in Quebec. Among Kathy's companions were Mary Churchill and Wing Commander Guy Gibson, the leader and hero of the famed 'Dambusters'.

While Ave politicked with Churchill and Roosevelt, Kathy caught up with friends and family in New York and at the end of August boarded the *Queen Mary* for the return journey to Britain, this time accompanied by thousands of Canadian troops. She shared a cabin with Joan Bright (Astley), a British civil servant who was the organiser and keeper of the Churchill Cabinet's military secrets. In her fascinating but unsung memoir, Joan remembered Kathy as 'dark, slim, vital and attractive', one who 'easily and without pretensions' mixed with the returning members of the British delegation. One night on board, recalled Joan, they all had to sleep fully clothed because of fear of a German U-boat attack. Joan and the Harrimans got on very well, both in London and again when they met in Moscow in 1944 and at the 1945 Yalta Conference.

Averell, who had remained in the US after Kathy went back to Britain, was under increasing pressure to accept the post of US ambassador to Moscow. He didn't want the job but Roosevelt needed to replace the incumbent, Admiral Standley, who was unpopular with the Soviets. Ave's two trips to Moscow and his meetings with Stalin made him the obvious choice, as did his efficient handling of US Lend-Lease aid to Britain, since henceforth most American military aid would go to the USSR, where the bulk of the fighting against Germany was taking place. Absent an accompanying wife, Ave would need Kathy's services as a hostess more than ever.

There is a story that when leaving for Moscow Averell broke off relations with Pam, a somewhat surprising note he wrote to Kathy being cited as evidence: 'Help Pam straighten herself out – poor child. She is in a tough spot. Tell her I am sure she will do the right thing if she follows her own instincts. Give her my best love. PS destroy this letter or keep it locked up.' The note dates from 1946, however, not 1943. Pam, who had divorced Randolph, was in the United States, as was Kathy, while Averell was leaving for Britain, where he had just been appointed US ambassador – hence his concern that the message to Pam didn't leak out.

The three-way relationship between Kathy, Pam and Averell continued throughout the war. Pam wrote many letters to the two of them in Moscow. And whenever Ave and Kathy were passing through London, Pamela was the one person they never missed seeing.

London
early May, 1943

Dear Mary

Popsie's about off – weather permitting – which makes me think how nice it would be if I were coming home too.

Marie-André is in town at the moment. Just before he came down we had a violent exchange of letters on the subject of Russo-Polish relations. Living up in the midst of Polish soldiers, you can imagine his feelings – they still apparently think the subsequent breaking off of relations with Russia is OK.[1]

I had a very enlightening talk with the ex-Russian ambass. To Poland[2] (he's also accredited to all the other exiled governments). He's a talkative individual (in French) so I got a lot out of him. We sat in his bedroom office, half facing a huge Russian map of Europe. The countries were all colored in light pastel shades, with the exception of Russia which was dark bright red. Russia certainly looked very big and ominous. The ambass.'s line was forceful – "our breaking of relations with Poland is a victory for the United Nations, not Goebbels. We have cleansed the ranks of the United Nations of Fifth Column elements, just as we cleared our army of Fifth Columnists in the purge." He gave incident after incident of antagonism, Poles against the Soviets. All of which gave the impression that a break-off was inevitable. When I left, I felt more depressed than ever, not only for Poland, but for all the countries that border Russia. You can't blame them for having the jitters.

Give Sheila my best love. I'm sending Mouche a list of "wants" & Averell is bringing you some pink 3 little pigs material, which I think is completely beguiling. Sorry it doesn't come in other colors, equally sorry there's nothing exciting to send from here.

My love to you,
Kathleen

London
July 5, 1943

Dear Mary & Mouche,

The clothes & general loot are simply terrific.

The black dress with pink trimmings is the prettiest thing I've seen – ever I think – and combined with Mary's hat a beautiful outfit.

---

1 The Soviet Union ended diplomatic relations with the Polish exile government in London in April 1943, when, following the exhumation by the Germans of mass graves of thousands of Polish POWs at Katyn near Smolensk, the Poles called for an international inquiry into the massacre, implying the Soviets were guilty of the executions.

2 Alexander Bogomolov (1900–69), Soviet ambassador to Vichy France 1940–1 and then to the exile governments in London.

The front of the dress is alluring, so I'm told, to a state of anticipated indecency (I still haven't got it right!) & as a result of it have gotten two new beaux. Also, Dr Evatt (Australian member of the War Cabinet) saw me in it one night and made the remark "My goodness Miss Harriman you have grown up!" Roy Howard[3] came to dine another night – 1st time I wore the dress & now he has gotten United Press to redouble its efforts to hire me away from *Newsweek*. So you see it's a very important new addition to my wardrobe!!!

Mouche dear, Averell tells me you gave up your own shoe coupons to send me the shoes. I am terribly touched & they are wonderful.

It's terribly nice having Popsie in our midst again. This last weekend he was able to get away Friday night to the country and get some rest. He lounged around & amused himself while I worked like a dog on hay-making. Result: today my hands are a mass of blisters & my fanny is sore as hell from bumping around on the top of a huge hay rack over an uneven field. The horse & I continually disagree on the subject of just how the field should be raked & it took a lot of pulling for me to win out!

Personally I think Quent's book stinks. The baloney about Dickie Mountbatten beats everything. I wonder how he gets away with it. But perhaps if you don't know all the personalities involved it makes cheesy reading.

Lippmann's [book's] the tops – Averell has now grabbed it.[4]

London's a mighty pleasant town with no blackout until eleven – no need for torches – & that coupled with the war going well puts spirits way high up. Then to wake up in the morning & find the sun streaming in the window almost puts me on the "too good to be true" level.

I lunched with Hugh Dowding (remember he visited Sun Valley in the days when he still had an important R.A.F. job) to see if he'd be interested in doing some signed articles for us. He's not as he's turned spiritualistic of all things. Lunch was fascinating in one way. He's

---

3 Roy Howard (1883–1964), American newspaperman famous for interviewing Stalin in 1936.

4 Probably Walter Lippmann's *U.S. Foreign Policy: Shield of the Republic* (1943).

perfectly sane mentally, but honestly believes in inter-communication between the dead & the living!

I must be off now. Goodbye for the moment & many thanks for the lovely things.

Kathy

London
July 18, 1943

Dear Marie,

I, at long last, got attacked by the Lady Cavendish[5] at a restaurant in Soho the other night (not physically – she just called me a bitch to end all bitches). Ever since I did a story on her & said she "still wears silly little bows atop her head" and *Newsweek* from the New York end put in her age at 42 (Jock says even that is politely shortening it) she's been going around telling all listeners what a bitch I am and how she's going to "break" me in London. At last she's had the courage to say so to my face.

Have you ever been called a bitch to end all bitches?

I unfortunately reacted wrongly – and laughed, which made Adele all the madder. She's certainly good on vocabulary when she gets going, and she was slightly drunk that night.

Kathy

RMS *Queen Mary*
late August 1943

Dear Mary,

The trip has been a lot pleasanter than I anticipated. Perhaps Shirley wrote you about his troopship across. It's an experience I'd not have missed for anything. The troops aren't Americans. They're quiet, don't shoot craps or play poker. Just lie in huddled bundles sleeping or reading. Walking anywhere you have to pick the way over legs and jumbled bodies. The ones on deck look blue around the gills & the ones below equally physically unhappy. They lie in the

5 Adele Astaire (1896–1981), who was married to Lord Charles Cavendish, son of the 9th Duke of Devonshire. Sister of Fred Astaire.

corridors, sit on the stairs and then every morning between 12 and 2 they change. Those on deck go below and those below come up for air. The quiet surprises me most. There's no singing.

At first I used to get embarrassed walking around. The language when a gal passes is imaginable – actually it's not. Going to dinner, the officers we dine with make bets with each other whose dinner date will get the most number of cat calls, hoots and whistles & obscene remarks!

First day out one of the naval planning captains organized PT (just good old setting-up exercises) for the "special party" – run by a marine sergeant. I didn't go, with the result that so many remarks were made, I figured I'd better. Can you imagine U.S. generals dressing up in slacks or shorts & sweaters and making figurative fools of themselves in front of their junior officers, staffs & little secretaries? I can't – but that's what the British do. We get up there on deck, freezing cold, and go through a routine of jumping and skipping and swinging arms and legs, then run relay races, much to the amusement of the troops on board and the crews on the ack-ack guns. It must be a nice feeling – not to mind making a fool of yourself in front of others!

We, the privileged, have three meals a day – breakfast at 10, lunch at 1, dinner at 8. Punctually. At 12 noon, cocktail parties start. Usually I have two before lunch . . . and then the same thing starts all over again at 6 p.m.! I can't stand pink gin, but that's what you get offered.

We started off all having a cabin to ourselves. Then the general in charge discovered 100-odd officers, some senior ones, sleeping in the corridors so he asked us to double up. "Roughing it," I share a cabin with a hellova nice War Office secretary & share a bath (which adjoins our cabin) with a girl next door.

Incidentally my disease has practically left me. So the hot climate must have had a major part in its not breaking out.

I glanced into Averell's suite – bedroom & sitting room – one morning, and now it accommodates 24 officers + more on the floor! Of course this is luxury travel – so I'm told. Thank god it hasn't been rough!

I'm running out of conversation. Obviously I loved my trip home. Bobby's snapshots stuck prominently on my mirror cause delighted comments from all – it was great seeing him.

Best love to you,

Puff

PS Read *The Fountainhead*, enjoyed it very much, though the whole idea of it I figured was phoney.[6] The idealist just plain doesn't win out in this world. But it's fun reading a book about one who does. It's worth you reading.

PPS *The Robe* stinks, I just plain can't get thru it.[7]

• • •

[Letter continues on a separate sheet of paper:]

I'm back in London now. Walking home in the blackout last night suddenly, more than anything else, made home seem terribly far away. London's the same old place. 1st night I dined at Pam's – she's overworked getting her club opened & now is confined to her apartment with a bad throat – which eventually will have to be operated on.[8] We had a lovely "getting caught up" dinner – Joe Evans, Jack Kelly & Ed Beattie. Ed got in a few hours after me. Joe's grown himself a horrible mustache that looks like hell. Very nicely he's decided I don't start work 'til the beginning of the week – because now that I've relaxed I've discovered how tired I am.

I'll write again soon,

Love,

Kathleen

6 A novel published in 1943 by Ayn Rand (1905–82), Russian-born American writer and libertarian philosopher.

7 A biblical novel published in 1942 by Lloyd C. Douglas (1877–1951).

8 Pam ran the Westminster-located Churchill Club, a recreation centre for high-ranking allied service personnel.

London
September 15, 1943

Dear Mary,

London certainly hasn't changed much. It's just like it was before I left. In fact I keep running into people who figured I'd been away for a week or two in Scotland, shooting and whatnot and never caught on that I'd gone home.

I got back to discover that the cook had left suddenly to go to the dying bedside of a son-in-law. Hence I've not been to the cottage yet. In fact it looks as though we're going to lose the cook and her sister if the boy dies. Then I'll have to go through the ordeal of searching for someone new. There ain't much point in worry tho because at this stage I don't know what Averell's plans are.

Last weekend Pam and I went down to Max's. Max is very dreary on the subject of the war, guess that's because he's got no hand in running it anymore. Anyway he got the assembled group all pie-eyed after about six rounds of drink. Result: conversation became exceedingly lewd, as it invariably does under those circumstances. I left Sunday and went over to General Eaker's for some tennis and what have you. That was fun too, on a level that makes me feel more at home. I met the new head of 8th Air Force bomber command, who's a hellova guy. The most human operational general I've run into yet.

Another pleasant surprise – Beek[9] came up for a night last week. We dined at Pam's and then came back here and spent hours talking about home. I gather lots of people have been trying to get him put on their staffs – sort of headquarters type of jobs, all of which he's turned down. It's nice to know he's in demand.

My bright green woolen hat has made a great hit. And my pet tiny Bergdorf hat – black lace one – I wear faithfully whenever I dine out. Your Zeus holder[10] is still the joy of my existence. It sits each night in a tumbler of Listerine, which keeps it from getting too high!!!

---

9 Beekman H. Pool (1909–2004), Kathy's stepbrother through her mother's marriage to Eugene H. Pool. He served as a US Air Force intelligence officer during World War II.

10 A brand of cigarette holder.

I finished the Marquand book this morning at the hairdresser and loved it.[11]

I'm about to go off on my first story on the W.A.A.C.s [Women's Army Auxiliary Corps], a necessary evil, which I'm sure won't prove much, but there's nothing else cooking around town.

Sept. 16

Too true – the W.A.A.C.s story I went on proved to have no W.A.A.C.s present at all. Typical of 8th Air Force public relations. Story turned out to be a tea party given by Eaker for the Lord Mayor of London. A very nice tea party and all that, the Lord Mayor asked the prevalent question "Was it true my distinguished papa was Moscow bound etc." Wish I knew. Anyway, I came home storyless. Nuts.

Lunched with the Polish Prime Minister – Mikołajczyk.[12] Lunch found me struggling to think what the hell I'd talk to the P.M. about. He asked all sorts of questions about American production, none of which I could answer. So I decided I'd better get the lead and do the questioning myself. After lunch we gathered the following tidbits: Mikołajczyk's very pessimistic about the possibility of any Russo-Polish rapprochement. He figures a war vs communism inevitable and it will be provoked by a combination of Russian encroachment on Anglo-American interests in Persia, Russian Balkan policy, and Russian pro-Japanese policy and lastly Polish Eastern frontier difficulties. He says no Polish government in London will or could agree to the idea of Poland being given Eastern Prussian territory in compensation for Lvov–Vilna being taken by the Russians. He says recent Soviet overtures to the Orthodox Church shows the Soviets have decided to use the church instead of the Comintern to win favor from Eastern European countries, particularly the Balkans (also Eastern Poles who primarily are bound by their religion, rather than the government). He figures the Germans will continue to retreat until they reach the Dnieper. As we walked out, I suddenly thought what a chance he's

11 John P. Marquand (1893–1960), US satirical novelist who explored upper-class life in America.
12 Stanisław Mikołajczyk (1901–66).

missed not inviting Bill Hearst to the little gathering. His was food for thought for any anti-Russian.

To change the subject slightly I ran into a little boyfriend of mine the other day who's just back from the African theater. Went on a couple of Rome raids to say nothing of Ploesti and Vienna. Re Ploesti he said that the raid beat anything he figured possible. The aircraft, as you know, flew in at lowest level and dropped time bombs. Everything was OK for the first elements over one given installation, but the later elements caught hell. The flames rose higher from the exploding refineries and storage wells than the aircraft so the planes just dove straight into the inferno of flames, dropped their bombs and never came out. The Vienna raid he called duck soup. That kid was in the R.A.F. coastal command before he got into the war. He transferred to a twenty-four squadron some six months ago and says that including officers and enlisted men only three boys remain of the original squadron.

Eaker lost a bet to the Secretary of State for Air, which was a dinner. It came off last night. 40-odd people, music & all the trimmings. It was great fun – even though people below the rank of general or air marshal didn't exist. I lunched yesterday with the Mountbattens. He's got a new gold stripe & has puffed up about two stripes' worth!

I'm off now lunching at Pam's club and then to the country.

Write soon.

Love to all,

Puff

London
October 11, 1943

Dear Mary,

This is written in a hurried rush and 3 days is [less] than I['d] like to dispose of a house, flat, a job and get packed and buy stuff. As it is I have a hairy air hat (fur and tweed which when pulled down covers all but my eyes). Eighth A.F. have produced flying boots and coat (fleece lined). Mrs Biddle has given me some warm undies and slippers. Virginia Cowles produced a jacket and so on, and everyone has forthcome with plenty of conflicting information. Some say 'twill be cold – others say not much colder than U.S. Everyone agrees that Russia should not be compared to any standards I've ever known.

So now I'm about off. Maybe due to bad weather I'll be put down in Oran – see Shirley. God that would be fun.

In most every way it will be sad leaving London – all my friends, *Newsweek*, etc. Needless to say I didn't have any inkling I'd be going with Ave until the passport department phoned just before he flew in.

When I asked him about my prospects going he said there were three alternatives – 3 days, 3 weeks, 3 months to leave. Later I read your letter and laughed. Everyone but me seemed to know about my future. One thing I hate the idea of – no women in Moscow – apparently there's one English woman at their embassy and no Americans. The general idea appears to be that I learn Russian. Mme Bogomolov[13] took it for granted I would and others say I should. She said seven months would be enough time. Nuts. Anyway, all in all I'm quite terrified (British understatement).

I have no idea what will be expected of me, I only hope there'll be no entertaining (as here) and that I'll be able to do some work. Here it was nice because if I was frank and made an undiplomatic remark or was indiscreet, it didn't really matter and at least I knew some people liked me. I thought coming over here – starting work for the press and all that, would be the last time in my life I'd be scared. Now crashing London seems like chickenfeed and my feelings at that time minute. However, I wouldn't give it up for the world and I mean that.

My arms have been punctured so many times I've lost count. The Navy doc who injected said when it was all over "Lady, you sure have been shot"– three hours later I agreed! I have to stop now and get packed. We're off to Chequers for the night which means I'm missing a nice 8th A.F. farewell party, damnation.

Love,
Kath

---

13 Lidiya Alexandrovna Bogomolova (née Chernyavskaya, 1914–2000), wife of Alexander Bogomolov. She later edited the French edition of the journal *Soviet Women*.

PART TWO
MOSCOW LETTERS (1943–6)

CHAPTER 13

'ONE OF THE AMAZING THINGS ABOUT RUSSIA – YOU CAN GET YOURSELF UNDERSTOOD MINUS A COMMON LANGUAGE'

Kathy departed London on 13 October 1943, flying to Moscow via Algiers, Cairo and Tehran, arriving on the 18th. The first person she wrote to was Pamela Churchill, initiating a stream of correspondence that overlapped with but was separate from her letters to Mary, Marie and Mouche.

Pamela proved to be an enthusiastic correspondent. During Ave and Kathy's first months in Moscow she wrote to them every week, and regularly thereafter. Pam's letters were usually addressed to the two of them jointly. In some ways they were similar to Kathy's: a combination of personal observation, political commentary and war-related news. The difference between the two women's letters was that Pamela's were invariably more about herself than anything else. Yet Kathy loved them, and often urged Pam to keep sending her 'wonderful' letters.

Averell's arrival in Moscow was timed to coincide with a meeting of British, Soviet and American foreign ministers – an important milestone in the development of the tripartite alliance between the three nations. This was the conference that took the first step towards establising the United Nations as the successor to the discredited League of Nations.

Kathy's day job in Moscow was working for the Office of War Information (OWI), preparing a weekly *New York Times* news summary for distribution within the foreign diplomatic community.

She also helped to arrange for the publication of a glossy Russian-language magazine about life in the United States, called *Amerika*. Aimed at the Soviet public, the magazine was launched in 1945 with a circulation of 10,000. Kathy's new role pleased Clementine Churchill no end: 'I'm so glad Kathy that you have a proper job now' – although, according to Kathy, she never was actually an OWI employee, her work in Moscow being purely voluntary.

The US ambassador's residence in Moscow, Spaso House, was a grand but dilapidated mansion, a twenty-minute walk from Red Square, the Kremlin and the city's three main hotels – the National, the Metropolitan and the Moskva. Acquired in 1934 by the first American ambassador to the Soviet Union, William C. Bullitt, its name derived from its location in Spasopeskovskaya Square, which was also home to the former Russian Orthodox 'Church of the Saviour'.

Kathy soon made her presence felt in Moscow. Less than a week after she arrived, Britain's *Daily Express* hailed the 'tall, keen-looking, quick-witted ex-journalist' as the new leading lady of Moscow's diplomatic corps. In January 1944, UP reported that Kathy had 'brought a big change in the atmosphere at Spaso House. She is there when a party begins and when it closes. Her energy is something to write home about.' Two years later, the head of *Time*'s Moscow bureau, the syndicated columnist Richard Lauterbach,[1] claimed that Kathy was the best-known American woman in the Soviet Union – with the possible exception of Deanna Durbin and Eleanor Roosevelt. Kathy was popular with US embassy staff, explained Lauterbach, because she did not act 'like a spoiled daughter of the rich, in spite of being rich'; popular with the Russians because she had made an effort to learn their ways as well as their language; and popular with her ambassador father because she had relieved him of many domestic and social duties, while at the same time keeping 'her thin but pretty mouth shut'.

1 Richard E. Lauterbach (1914–50).

Moscow
October 20, 1943

Dear Pam,

Just a week and a day ago we watched as you got smaller and smaller in the distance. Jesus that seems a long time ago.

Things here are a mass of conferences, talks, and little private discussions behind closed doors – Chequers on a busy weekend with lots of people coming and going multiplied by ten. I've discovered a few things I didn't know – we live at one Villa Spaso but the embassy is about five minutes away in the center of town. Apparently, Averell and Archie Clark had an argument last night whether his or our house is the worse.

The servants consist of two Chinamen (one's called Gin) and a motley lot of others. Looking after me is a Volga German. She speaks German, Italian, Spanish and Russian, but we get along fine. God knows how – but that's one of the amazing things about Russia – you can get yourself understood minus a common language. Frinstance the maid knows all about you and baby Winston and all the other people I have a picture of. She has five brothers and a sister – two are in heaven and three in Siberia (all Volga Germans were deported in '41). Try conversing in no known language sometime – it's funny how easy it is to catch on.

Flying into Algiers, Tommy Thompson[2] pulled out a "how to learn Russian in ten easy lessons" book. Page one and two consisted of the alphabet, which I learned mostly in about an hour. Tomorrow I hope to start lessons from a French woman or a woman who talks French, can't remember which. French however is a useless language. Russians apparently learn German or English but seldom French.

Today I went on a hair washing expedition armed with my own cake of Lux, hair pins and comb (next time I'll also take a towel). The Beauty Salon was in the National Hotel – two basins and a table for manicuring, and hair drying machine with two air arms. I got well washed and set – the set turned out to be a compromise between

2 Llewellyn E. Thompson (1904–72), Second Secretary at the US embassy in Moscow.

my way of wanting it done and the man's way of thinking it ought to be done. I paid the usual 100% tip and left with assurances that I'd be back next week.

Last night I went to a press showing of the battle of the Don Basin – a film on the order of the Stalingrad picture and every bit as gruesome. The director made a couple of long speeches before and after the film, which were informally translated by Alex Werth.[3] I was taken by Dave Nichol and Bill Downs[4] and afterwards we went back to the Metropol for dinner in Bill's room. Dinner consisted of very good sausage and black bread, vodka and some beans Bill heated out of a can. The restaurant situation sounds impossible as meals cost $50 a head!

News we get from the B.B.C., but already I've gotten the feeling of being completely cut off from the rest of the world. B.B.C. news minus newspapers is sketchy.

Eddie Gilmore[5] and fiancée came in during dinner. She's sweet looking, small and looks sort of like a scared bunny rabbit – which I guess she has got every right to be. Eddie talks Russian at a terrific rate and she knows a few words of English. The A.P. bunch in Algiers gave me a bottle of perfume for her as a wedding present and she was almost touched to tears.

We went overnight to Cairo [from Algiers] and arrived there in the broiling heat and dust. I was bunked at a Mr and Mrs Jacobs of our legation – thank God as I promptly got my usual ailment. I survived for a Kirk[6] luncheon and then retired to bed with hot water bottles and a huge fan. We were off again early next morning (got up at four a.m.) and flew 'til after lunch to Tehran (moral of that little ride – don't ever fly in altitude if you are susceptible to cramps – there's something about it that doesn't let any quantity of dope work). As Averell predicted, Tehran was much the same as Salt Lake to fly into – high mountains and plenty of dust in the valley. We all stayed at the commanding general's

3 Alexander Werth (1901–69), Russian-born BBC correspondent.
4 David M. Nichol (1911–2009), *Chicago Daily News* correspondent; William Randall Downs (1914–78), CBS correspondent.
5 Eddie Gilmore (1907–67), AP correspondent. His fiancée was Tamara Kolb-Chernashova (1927–80), a ballet dancer.
6 Alexander Comstock Kirk (1888–1979), US ambassador to Egypt.

house – a modernish stucco high-ceilinged affair – rented by the army from a Persian chieftain who lives in the mountains now and daren't come to town as there's a price on his head due to some pro-German instincts. I spent the afternoon in bed but got up for dinner with the local U.S. minister and wife – mostly so as to escape from the attentions of the general's aide – a persistent major from Kansas.

Last lap of the flight – from Tehran to Moscow – we (Popsie and I) rode with the Secretary.[7] Due to apparently usual formality, we'd taken on a Russian navigator and radio operator. About an hour out I received a formal note from Hull's pilot (the best in our A.T.C. [Air Transport Command]) that the pleasure of my company etc. I went up front and discovered that my arriving and being seated in the seat behind the pilot and co-pilot kept the persistent Russian navigator just that much farther away from the pilot. Apparently, the Russian wanted us to fly high, [Hull's pilot] not wanting the old man to have to fly any higher than absolutely necessary. For a while things were tense. Finally, as we neared the Stalingrad area and signs of battle were visible, things got very jolly. In the sign language we had the battle of Stalingrad fought out for us and by the time we'd reached Moscow everyone was bosom pals.

The armed guard of Moscow plus everyone else turned out and it was really quite impressive. Finally I awoke to the fact that Averell and Hull had left the airfield, but a familiar face – Don Nelson[8] – turned up and took me in tow and I arrived at Spaso House.

My love to you.
Kathy

Moscow
October 22, 1943

Dear Mary,

I'm all comfortably curled up in a big chair so I hope the non-typewriting won't bother you.

Due to the conference everything is chaotic – the Secretary is staying in what I imagine will eventually be my bedroom. Every

---

7 Cordell Hull (1871–1955), American Secretary of State.
8 Donald M. Nelson (1888–1959), chairman of the US War Production Board, who was on a trip to Russia.

available non-bedroom has a conference or discussion going on in it most every minute between times of the big conference – people run in and out and all in all it is like a glorified boarding house.

While this goes on I'm desperately occupied catching up on just what the O.W.I. has done in Russia, what it does elsewhere etc. Sam Spewack's[9] awfully nice. We have an impermanent office in the Chancellery.

Flying into Algiers I learned the [Russian] alphabet. Walking around the streets I pronounce all the signs on the houses and billboards to myself. People all stare at me so much anyway – due to fur coat and silk stockings – that me muttering to myself doesn't make me any more odd.

Our little house is something I didn't think was possible for an interior decorator and an architect to dream up. Bill Bullitt apparently had a hand in the interior decorating and for that I'm really going to resent him for the rest of my life. We live in a sort of slum area and cobbled stone streets, about five minutes by car from Red Square, the Kremlin and the two hotels for foreigners. Our garden consists of some leafless shrubs and a couple of dead trees. Averell brought his axe so he'll be able to occupy his muscles cutting the latter down.

But to get back to the home, general theme is Regency, with plenty of gold and black damask. Walls are white (dirty and in very bad plaster condition) and the designs are chiefly white sunflower; the ceilings vary – either just moldings or painted women and fish and things or both. The house gets entered unpretentiously at the side into the vestibule – monstrosity number one. This has great marble columns and is generally so dark you can't even decide whether a Russian, a Chinese, or a Finn has let you in. Up a small flight of stairs you find yourself in monstrosity number two – the Reception room – this has large Doric columns (white stone) and a chandelier to end all chandeliers that hangs down from the roof of the house. Ceiling is domed and fluted. Under your feet is a Bill Bullitt (so the

---

9 Samuel Spewack (1899–1971), American writer, sent to Moscow to work as a press attaché for the OWI, arriving at the same time as Kathy.

rumor goes) creation in the form of a sea-sick green, yellow, pink and brown carpet. ("Beautiful" the chargé d'affaires calls it.)

Ave's bedroom has the one fireplace so we expect to use it as a sitting room. His bathroom is about the size of my lovely yellow apartment in N.Y.C. In general furniture downstairs is solid gilt with plenty of designs which are useful to start runs in stockings. In every available corner, on every big table, there are heavy gold and black bric-a-bracs – which one of Ave's mission has named "the Ivan the Terribles."

Our trip up was most interesting. Algiers was wonderful. There were lots of press friends there. Butch and André (Butch is Eisenhower's naval aide) met us at the airport and we stayed at General Ike's villa, which incidentally was the least sumptuous of any villa I went into. We lunched at General Giraud's, [who] was genial but surprised me by his anti-Russian sentiments. Needless to say, de Gaulle is very pro-Soviet. André seems depressed but philosophical about "his general" [Giraud]. As he put it "if you were betting on a horse you wouldn't pick the one I have."

I paid a call on Bogomolov, ex-Soviet equivalent of Tony Biddle in London, now accredited to the French. He gave me an hour and a half lecture on how to get on with the Russians – actually was just a talk on the great Democracy.

Waking up in Algiers the next morning I thought for an instant I was back in N.Y.C. – the toots in the harbor were very Hudson River tug-boat like. Cairo I saw little of as I got my usual complaint and spent every possible moment in closest contact with a hot water bottle and fan. The weather was the hottest I've ever been into. Flying to Tehran was the best part of the trip. The country reminded me of Kubla Khan's Xanadu. I expected every minute to see the Castle and its meandering river appear beneath our plane. The mountains were barren, but interesting because every now and then a patch of green copper-colored soil would flank the usual reddish rock. Tehran was dirty and dusty. I spent most of the time in bed there too as flying at high altitude didn't help my trouble any and no amount of codeine seemed to help. Driving down to the airport next morning one of our party suddenly realized he'd forgotten and brushed his teeth in tap water – a drastic mistake as the plumbing system of Tehran is the simplest. Water runs down the main streets and in deep gutters. People wash, drink and relieve themselves in that water.

Last night I went to the ballet – *Swan Lake* – started at 7:00 and we got out at 11. It's quite a procedure, the orchestra is terrific and the ballet like nothing I've ever seen and very extravagantly put on. There were 4 acts and 3 intermissions of half hour each. During intermissions you parade around a huge ballroom looking at everyone and everyone else looking at you or just parade around the passageways. I apparently made my faux pas no. 1 by keeping my coat – not checking it at the door. It's illegal to keep it apparently – but no one kicked hard enough at the time for me to realize what they meant.

The streets are invariably crowded with mobs of men in uniform, women who all look old, and tiny kids. Everyone pretty much seems happy, smiles and laughs and the kids look amazingly healthy. (I hadn't anticipated any of this.) Coming up the way we did through the Middle East and Persia, Moscow by contrast is clean, the people clean and still, comparatively speaking, well dressed. Obviously, there's no one around who dresses like me, and even the American correspondents look pretty shabby and wan.

I guess for a while I'll do all my letter writing to you, so if you could send copies of what is interesting to people like my friends, aunts and family it might be good.

I gotta go now.

Bestest love to everyone,

Kathleen

Moscow
October 22, 1943

Dear Pam,

During the past 2 days I've seen Popsie at ½ mile distance – the other end of the table – at 2 meals & a couple of other times for a few minutes but he seems to be bearing up better than some under the stress of work. He's looking okay and gets to sleep before one a.m. anyway as that's the curfew time and everyone has to be home.

I started work with Sam yesterday. We're now permanently established in the Chancellery – in a room with a half-conscious State Department clerk whose sole reason for being here is to make a daily translation of the Soviet press to be put into a short cable for back home. You see we've all arrived here full of hopes & enthusiasm about the "New Deal" U.S. is going to get, but the Americans here are resigned & have given up hope. Sam & I finally got up and left the office after being conscious that our discussions were being quietly laughed at, and adjourned to the streets where we could talk freely.

The streets, the main ones that is, are wide – very wide, and the little ones off them are mostly cobbled. People in the streets are gay – the children healthy looking by Cairo or Tehran standards.

Today I had my 1st Russian lesson and discovered to my horror that Russian printing and Russian writing is completely different – or at least different enough to be really confusing. My teacher speaks French and she's living in a sweet little flat in a section taken over by the Theater folk (High Society in Moscow) not far from the Chancellery. Walking back I suddenly discovered I'd gathered quite a bunch of kids – following me they jabbered away, half at me and half to themselves. It will be fun when I get so's I can talk to them.

I've discovered that we have 30 servants here [and] run a laundry for all Americans in Moscow. Today I met the housekeeper, who is the widow of a rich manufacturing king (pre-Revolution). She used to have her own house – twice the size of this. Now she's a glorified cook. For some odd reason – her choosing – we conversed in French tho she speaks English. She ended up bursting into tears and remarking that she was so glad at last she had a female in the house to work for. Jesus, I suppose that means I'll have to eventually take over a part of the running.

It's sad thinking about you in London, but this is fun.

My love to you,

Kathy

Moscow
October 26, 1943

Dear Mary,

Averell got accredited yesterday – which means he and incidental staff took time off from the conference and went to see the President, all dressed up in their blackest suits. From others there, I gather Kalinin[10] told Popsie that he'd heard rumor had already spread around town about the handsome new American ambass. That apparently was interpreted as "a very friendly gesture."

Anyway, the result of Averell getting accredited meant that I had to start dropping around to meet all the various ambass. wives in town. Luckily there were only five. The list of those to see greeted me with coffee this morning (gentle hint from old timers that I get started today).

The procedure apparently is to drive up to their house in cold blood, present your card and then hope to hell they are either out or otherwise occupied. I had no luck today. My first choice, for no reason other than I couldn't pronounce her name, was Madame Ahi – Iranian. She never appeared but M. Ahi[11] greeted me in reception room number one and took me to reception room no. two, offered me a very strong Iranian cigarette and we got down to what I figured would be the killing of twenty minutes (minimum length of time for such a visit). As that was half thru in walked a daughter.[12] That helped conversation considerably, then just as I was about to say goodbye, tea, cakes and candy were brought in. For your information M. Ahi is small, dark and unhandsome due to scar on tip of nose. Daughter is at unfortunate adolescent age covered with hickeys and doesn't seem to use make up at all. Anyway, she was nice. Apparently, she made a slip because when she told me Averell and I had been the subject of much conversation at their dinner table, she got a very dirty look from Popa. That shut her up for a bit, in fact completely

10 Mikhail Kalinin (1875–1946), chairman of the Central Executive Committee of the USSR, the closest Soviet equivalent to a head of state.
11 Majid Ahi (1886–1946), married to Raissa.
12 Mehri Ahi (1922–88), who later worked as a translator of Russian literature.

until Popa got up and left us alone for "a nice girlish chatter." When I said I'd be working most of the time, she seemed sorry – figuring I'd be on the loose too – someone to do nothing with. Finally I said I must leave and she filled me with pleas of "please don't go yet" that were damn near pathetic. That was the end of call no. 1.

Next up list came Mme Fierlinger – wife Czech ambass.[13] I rang the bell at the right address – no answer – so the chauffeur went in and finally after five minutes succeeded in arousing someone. Mme Fierlinger came and got me out of a very chilly hallway where I'd been left to stand.

She's French – fortyish with badly dyed black hair so's it's red around the edges. We were getting along fine when in walked hubby. He's small with ears like Dumbo and apparently expected me to know all his American friends in Washington. Explained I'd never lived in Wash. but he still insisted on producing them one by one. That failed miserably. So we talked about *Goodbye, Mr Chips* (movie held here last Friday for members of the diplomatic corps, to which I'd not gone). M. Fierlinger said he didn't figure any woman would ever marry or love a man so meek as Mr Chips. (That I didn't think worth arguing about.) Then we talked about London, Czechs in London etc. That went better as both [had] been there during blitz period. In fact, I gather the blitzing plus returning for another seance in Russia has rather got Mme Fierlinger down. "She needs a change of air" was how her husband put it. "She's going to take a trip to Cairo in January." She rose at that immediately with a "you always say that but when January comes you'll say to wait until spring and then even when the war is over we'll still have nowhere to go." After that outburst, I resorted to the first subject that came to my mind – English-fashion – food. Mr F followed suit beautifully. He told and described the taste of each of the fifty varieties of bread the Russians had prewar. At the end of that I jumped up and left. Poor woman, I guess she's sorry she didn't marry a meek little man like Mr Chips.

---

13 Zdeněk Fierlinger (1891–1976), who served as prime minister of Czechoslovakia from 1944 to 1946.

I had meant to kill off the Dutch Mrs Ambass. but in a weak moment I told the driver to take me home. And here I be – waiting for dinner which is already an hour late. Everyone seems to be in, but they are conferencing or something.

Sunday night there was relaxation for all (except Bob Meiklejohn). Invitations were extended to big and little wigs to see *Swan Lake*. Suddenly Averell discovered Molotov[14] expected me in his box, so I went too – my first invitation. We sat in the "royal" box (can't think correct word), anyway it's a big one, first tier directly opposite the stage. The ballerina quite outdid herself and ended up coming out for a curtain call armed with two huge bouquets – one from each Forn. Sec (Hull did not go). Before there had been some discussion as to whether or not Eden should follow Willkie's actions and leap onto the stage and kiss the ballerina. The distance between stage and box in this particular theater made it impossible, so he was able to gracefully decline. When we first entered everyone in the audience stood up and clapped. We remained standing until they stopped clapping. I thought it would never stop. During the entrée acts we ate in a private room and chatted. It was grand great fun meeting them all – Molotov, Vyshinsky,[15] Litvinov[16] and Kornichuk.[17] I got stuck talking to K for nearly a whole intermission (in no known language) and just to meet casually [he] seems nicest after Molotov. M's got a hellova swell sense of humor and twinkling eyes. Kornichuk is youngish, nice looking and easy to talk to. However, we didn't discuss his wife or Poland – instead, his play which takes a crack at the generals (old school tie ones).

Last night the taking of Dnepropetrovsk got announced so at ten o'clock we had another show of fireworks, just as good as when they

---

14 Vyacheslav Molotov (1890–1986), People's Commissar for Foreign Affairs.
15 Andrei Vyshinsky (1883–1954), Deputy People's Commissar for Foreign Affairs. A lawyer, Vyshinsky was the prosecutor at the 1930s Stalinist show trials.
16 Maxim Litvinov (1876–1951), Deputy People's Commissar for Foreign Affairs, former ambassador to the United States and Molotov's predecessor as head of the Foreign Commissariat.
17 Alexander Kornichuk (1905–72), Soviet writer and war correspondent. Born in Kiev, from 1943 to 1945 he served as the People's Commissar for Foreign Affairs of the Ukrainian Soviet Socialist Republic.

took Melitopol. We were at the Brit. embassy at the time and some little Russki got the idea to take a picture of the ambasses, Forn. Secretaries and things with fireworks in the background. Good idea, except that everyone but me had a coat and I damned near froze to death.

Archie Clark Kerr is trying hard to make a deal with me – swap houses. He has one great asset over us – fireplaces in most rooms, but the general atmosphere of his place is too damned gloomy, in fact, by comparison, ours is a cheery little love nest.

Oct. 27

I came here anticipating to find a city made of wood and streets filled with unhappy, unsmiling people. T'aint so. True, the outskirts are regular half-split log houses of one or two stories. They have double walls with mud and straw between – an effective insulation apparently. The city itself is a mixture of oriental (church) and Greek and pretty much every other architecture down to the most modern. For instance the Lenin Library sports rectangular columns. The main streets are wider than anything I imagined possible in a city. Their effect is to dwarf the people on them and make the usual 6 storey house appear low and squat. Trolleys and trams are crowded beyond imagination. How you ever get out when you're firmly wedged inside is beyond me. People hang on so that all public transport looks like the return to New Haven after the Harvard–Yale game – & about that hazardous. Shops are deceiving – it's hard to tell what's a shop and what used to be one. Some have window displays – buttons, dolls, candy etc. but nothing to buy when you go inside. Basic foods and commodities are bought at government stores at controlled low prices but everything else is a free for all – and prices exorbitant. In fact money hasn't much value to the Russians – 100 roubles buys little (worth about $8 on our exchange).

Though the weather is still warm, people are bundled in layers & layers of stockings, sweaters, coats and jackets. Each layer visible through holes. Kids are the same way. All women wrap their heads in scarves or wear angora berets pulled way down over their ears (I walk around in a suit and raincoat and no hat), maybe there'll be more layers superimposed when the cold weather sets in. I wouldn't know. But the general effect now is a mass of shapeless humanity in browns, blacks and greys. Even at the ballet where the best dress is worn (and make-up if it's owned) you see no bright colors at all. Cops are ½ women and ½ men & traffic signals all still beyond me. Sometimes you seem to stop for a green light and go when it turns to red. At others you do the opposite. There is an ordered plan – but I've yet to discover just how and when it works. One rule always stands. Horns blow continually and no pedestrian ever pays the slightest attention to them. The blackout is moderate. Blackout curtains exist but it doesn't seem to matter whether or not they get pulled before sundown. Lights run down the center of all main streets so it's fairly easy to see (compared to London). Main hazard at night are the cars that run without lights. (The bulbs have died and owners haven't been able to procure new ones.) Procurement is a procedure which I haven't yet gone into. Food and everything is gotten in exchange for coupons.

Oct. 28

Averell seems to have the lovely idea that two weeks study and I'll be conversing по-русски (in Russian). In fact, last night, when we were again entertained by Molotov and co., at a Red Army Choir show, he was amazed that I didn't join in the jabbering.

Anyway, I've spent almost three hours today writing, spelling and pronouncing to myself till I figure I'm damned near the "crazy" borderline. Unfortunately, I've discovered I learn languages by sight, not ear, so that means for the moment I have to spend extra time reading – to get used to the sight and pronunciation of things in Russian writing. It's a hellova job and my memory stinks. I never could spell in English. Nuts.

Yesterday was the Iranian national holiday, today it's the Czechs, tomorrow the Turks and after that we go for a spell without any receptions I gather. Tomorrow Averell's giving a party – cocktails and buffet supper for the 3 delegations and I haven't yet figured out whether or not I'm allowed. Tonight I'm skipping out and going to a circus with one of the A.T.C. pilots.

1. The Harrimans at their Sun Valley, Idaho skiing resort, c.1936/7 – Mary, Marie, Averell and Kathy.

2. Kathy embarks on her journey from New York to London, May 1941.

3. Mary, Kathy's slightly older sister, who was the main recipient of her letters during the war.

4. Kathy's best friend Pamela Churchill, wife of Winston Churchill's son Randolph, and the future Mrs Averell Harriman.

5. Kathy and Brendan Bracken greet Averell upon his return from Moscow, October 1941.

6. Winston Churchill with wife Clementine and youngest daughter Mary.

TELEGRAMS
BUTLERS CROSS
STATIONS
LITTLE KIMBLE 1 MILE
WENDOVER 2½ MILES
PRINCES RISBOROUGH 3½ MILES
TELEPHONE WENDOVER 76-77

CHEQUERS
BUTLER'S CROSS AYLESBURY
BUCKS

Dear Mary –

Was it a hope? I always hoped – & wondered – to be in London the night we got into the war. Somehow it's been ~~[illegible]~~ more exciting – [illegible] here –

We heard the news of the bombing of Pearl Harbor – just like everyone else – over the 9 o'clock news – It took a while to sink in – the words had a too new association to – then there was a clamor. "What was that? Pearl Harbor – where's that?" Then Martin left to get a confirmation – Ave & Winant wondered – a rumor no doubt – It couldn't be true – but it was –

I don't remember much else of dinner – the P.M. had cheered up – he kept leaving to phone – Winant kept leaving – then finally we & the coffee pot were left alone in the dining room – I left, & the men came back to finish & talk –

I sitting by the fire place when Winant came in – "It's come at last – it's exciting –" Winant spoke of his son – "He'll be in it." Why in hell did he have to get personal at the moment?

Plans were made – Parliament called for tomorrow – Washington called – Winant was nervous he smoked down an all-night cigar in a short hour – "I'm glad we're together –"

"The light that flickered – the light that ~~shone~~ gleamed, the light that shone" perhaps he'll use that in tomorrow's speech –

"We must see our cinema." For a hour perhaps we did – Came down for the midnight news –

"Japan declared war on U.S. & Brit. Emp." Then 16 min. of news – P.M. pacing in dragon wrapper – Ave standing by fire place – Winant in overcoat turned up – standing at different places – puffing a new cigar – God save the King – Argument ensues – about yesterday or tomorrow in Singapore –

"The 1st day of war is always exciting."

7. Kathy's Pearl Harbor-day Chequers letter, 7/8 December 1941.

8. Agniya Maisky, wife of the Soviet ambassador to Great Britain, unveils a plaque to Lenin, March 1942.

9. Eleanor Roosevelt and Margaret Biddle at the American Red Cross Club in London, October 1942.

10. American women war correspondents, 1943. From left to right: Mary Welsh, Dixie Tighe, Kathleen Harriman, Helen Kirkpatrick, Lee Miller and Tania Long.

11. Sergei Eisenstein's 1945 drawing of Kathleen Harriman – the 'dollar princess'.

12. Kathy at a reception in Moscow, pictured with Averell and 'Moly'.

13. Kathy (second from left) at the Katyn massacre site, January 1944.

14. Polina Zhemchuzhina, in charge of Soviet textiles, wife of Foreign Commissar Vyacheslav Molotov.

15. Soviet diplomat Maxim Litvinov with his English wife, Ivy.

16. Kathy receiving flowers at the US Air Force base at Poltava, Ukraine, June 1944.

17. Kathy with General Ira Eaker in Italy, summer 1944.

18. Yalta daughters: Sarah, Anna, Kathy.

19. Elsie Marshall's family c.1914: 'Mouche' – Kathy's childhood English governess and one of her main wartime correspondents – is standing on the far right.

20. Alexandra Kollontai – Bolshevik feminist and Soviet diplomat.

21. Averell and Kathy land in Washington, DC, 14 February 1946.

22. Boston – Stalin's gift-horse to Kathy.

23. Kathy and Stanley Mortimer on their wedding day, 11 October 1947, together with Mouche (Elsie Marshall).

24. Spaso House – residence of the US ambassador to Moscow – where Kathy lived from 1943 to 1946.

Life here is very different from the London I left, but probably it's not much different from London when I first arrived and knew no one. At any rate I'm liking it a lot better than I dared hope.

The Conference is going well as far as I can gather. The Secretary's bearing up wonderfully under strain – so's Averell for that matter. In fact, Ave's doing a hellova job.

Oct. 30

I'm beginning to feel as though I've been here untold ages. Every spare moment I spend studying Russian and this week there have been parties & receptions every night.

Last night we had one for the three delegations – about 70 – and I suddenly realized what a great asset the huge reception room is downstairs. It will hold 200 people comfortably, plus huge tables for food and drink. The food situation for receptions is something incredible – canapes of caviar etc. then cold turkey, duck, chicken, salads, fish, hot beans, spaghetti & huge cakes and cookies. Such a layout appears to be a routine matter in Moscow. Then apparently we have a special patent for a punch. It tastes mild but creeps up on you and when intermixed with a couple of bottoms-up of vodka is dynamite. I found the party thoroughly exhausting as I tried to have a chat with every Russian I've met so far. It was easier here as a goodly number of our military, navy and State Dept can speak Russian so an ever-ready interpreter was invariably on hand. The same bunch of commissars and vice-commissars were on hand, and I have a hellova time remembering their names, their interests and occupations! But as the Russian sense of humor is very like what we're used to, it's not so hard to get on. However, I wonder if I'll keep on seeing them after the conference breaks up. Our party ended around 10 and some of the servants came up and played gypsy music and danced and sang. I guess they enjoyed it as much as we did!

I must be off now. If you ever hear of anyone coming this way, please have my skates sent and I'll wire you when I hear of anyone leaving for these parts.

Give my love to everyone and kisses to you,

Kathleen

Moscow
October 30, 1943

Dear Pam,

The conference has been a great success – far more so than people dared hope. Pug's been my [main] informant on Ave during the conference & he says for all purposes Ave ran the American end, coached Hull when need be and generally filled in. Despite this, Hull's being here made a great difference – apparently to the Soviets, title and age carry dignity. Dear Pug – he's been terribly sweet though not very well – his headaches have been bothering him pretty much all the time. He & Deane[18] have a lovely mutual admiration society and I gather they did a great job of selling and everyone's pleased. (Suggest all this part go no further than you – as far as reading goes – for obvious reasons.)

This week has been one party after another. The Iranians and Czechs both celebrated their national holidays – big receptions to which I had to go. They're as boring as you'd expect any reception to be, particularly when there's scarcely a familiar face in the crowd.

Last night we had a party for the three delegations. Today Archie has a party – all the same crowd plus the diplomats and press.

One evening we were all taken to hear the best Red Army Choir perform. The auditorium was tiny and sitting in the front row I thought for a while my ears would be blown off. The songs were numerous – an odd combination of war songs, love songs and excerpts from Stalinoid operas. Then there was dancing (good old Bear dance variety). Like all Russian shows it was very long, but very well done. Oh yes, I've also been to the circus. That however was slumming, not an official party. The circus is a one-ring affair – trained dogs (very good), 2 very tired and old horses, 3 half-starved male lions, some amazing Mongolian acrobats, then the usual clowns etc. Best of all I enjoyed the crowd. Kids, just like American kids, thronged the doors & a few lucky ones succeeded in crashing. They swiped seats, took unoccupied ones and were exceptionally adept at not getting

18 General John R. Deane (1896–1982), head of the US Military Mission and Ave's principal military adviser.

themselves thrown out. During the entire acts most of them smoked tightly rolled cylinders made up entirely of newspapers! For a circus, the audience was very unenthusiastic, but everyone watched with childlike rapt expression.

I'm beginning to figure out who is who & what's what in the way of personnel here. First comes the Chargé d'affaires (Minister) – Mr Hamilton[19] – he's white haired and very prim and proper, no sense of humor. One of the junior secretaries, John Melby[20] runs the house – organizes food and liquor for parties etc. I hated him at first as he continually wears a cynical smile (which I'm sure he's practiced long and hard in front of a mirror). He's very unenthusiastic about everything – bored & lazy outwardly but he gets things done. A week's hard work on my part [and] he's become slightly more human. Also staying at Spaso House is the agricultural expert – Doc Michaels – an older man who's lived in Russia since about 1900. He's the character sketch type – dry sense of humor, good store of stories, but would not utter a word unless he's in good company.

Hull's detective, one Mr Thomas, I find fascinating. He talks without moving his lips hence sometimes he's impossible to understand. Russia, he judges by good old U.S. standards. He doesn't like Russia, the R way of life & makes no bones about it. In fact, the thought they all might get snowed in here all winter terrifies him. The other day he inadvertently discovered that people who don't work in Russia don't get food. That he figured was the end. During conferences he sits in an outer room with his Russian "opposite number," drinking tea and vodka & swapping stories. I'd like to be in one of those seances!

Our weekly movie is going on downstairs. I went for the news & a Mickey Mouse. The latter had Polish captions which means it's [a] leftover from the Russo-Polish campaign! Maybe it was Biddle embassy property in Warsaw!

---

19 Maxwell M. Hamilton (1896–1957); later in the war he served as US ambassador to Finland.
20 John F. Melby (1913–92), Third Secretary, lived in Spaso House.

There's not much else to say. Wire if you hear of anyone actually coming this way & we'll let you know what we need most desperately. Ave says your packing was superb – not one bottle broken! Good work! Your lovely mittens seem to be mislaid but I remember packing them so I'm still hopeful they'll turn up. As yet the weather is only sort of freezing temperatures.

My love to everyone. We miss you.

Best love,

Kathy

Moscow
November 5, 1943

Dear Mary/Pam,

Things have quieted down a bit now, due to the departure of the delegation but as usual Averell continues to work at full rate. Meals are erratically spaced, but we are gradually getting shaken down to at least an air of normalcy.

The weather is lovely, not much below freezing, so I'm getting broken in slowly on that score. Meeting new people, they all warned me about the future cold but if Moscow isn't windy, which it apparently isn't, I'm not particularly worried that I haven't come equipped with top boots and what have you in the way of anti-freeze.

It still seems slightly odd, to see the familiar sight of countless jeeps and good old U.S. trucks galloping down the avenues. Aside from government officials' limousines, that's about all there are in the streets, but added altogether they make a goodly number. All driving full rate (speed limits are entirely ignored) with hands on the horn. The pedestrians seem impervious – they prefer walking in the streets as opposed to the sidewalks, so they walk on the streets, get honked at but continue walking. I suppose a goodly number get killed or hit, particularly at night when some cars don't have lights.

Another thing I'm mystified by is the system of cabbage and wood distribution. For a certain area, say an apartment house or a corner of a block – a given number of either cabbage heads or cords of wood get dumped on the street by a truck – the people come along and take them home. Who supervises that operation, I wouldn't know.

One gratifying thing is that my sense of smell never was acute. Moscow is full of a variety of odors, which I assume I don't reap the full benefit. For instance, though outwardly most apartment houses are comparable to any N.Y.C. suburb's housing project of the modernist variety, inwardly they're [a] mite primitive. To begin with you enter everything from an inner courtyard, which usually has an air of age about it, to say the least, no matter how new the front may look. Front door is usually a little door arrangement, which is lockless and frequently hard to find. Once you're inside you get the full benefit of Moscow smell number one – rotting cabbage. Stairways are invariably stone, unlit and very worn. Swell apartment houses sport elevators. These run when and if the electricity is turned on and that is spasmodic. Flashlights are an essential item for both day and night time. I seem to spend my time getting lost and since my handiest vocabulary to date is *Ya ne ponimau po-Russkii* (I don't understand Russian) or *Ya ne znau* (I don't know), I can't make much headway by other than the look for yourself method. To learn Russian is very like Latin, only there are 6 instead of 5 cases to decline, plus conjugation of verbs. I find the writing and reading easiest – it's a matter of memory work, but being able to discover when a Russian begins a word and ends another is still not among my accomplishments. My teacher optimistically says that getting one's ear trained is really only a matter of <u>months</u>. Nuts!

In the street everyone is in perpetual state of rush. I find that my walking overtakes only the oldest and most decrepit people. Maybe it's the cold weather or maybe it's that the people really are in a hurry to get into a particular queue where they'll doubtless stand for hours. That's something else about the Moscow population that amazes me. They will stand for untold hours and patiently to buy their cup of water and fruit juice, to catch their trolley or bus home or what have you. When it's hours they are dealing with, patience they've got, but when minutes are at stake, nothing, not even a two-ton truck, can stop them.

There's a lot of superficial bomb damage repair work going on day or night. Camouflage is being taken off etc. which in view of the supposed shortage of materials and labor at first seemed strange, but it's apparently just part of the general "victory is in sight" program to bolster up morale. In London the wear and tear of the war was fairly visible, but here it's unmistakable. There are no petty luxuries. Money buys nothing as there's nothing to buy at reasonable prices. I'm just beginning to realize that the good old Russian communiqués that deal in impersonal heroics and huge numbers of dead, missing and wounded, means something very personal here in the way of friends and family. When you get down to it, despite the teachings that the state comes first, the Russian still is a human being and funnily enough the government treats him as such – and so the reason for the periodic fireworks when a new victory is announced, and the dressing up of the bombed buildings.

While the delegation was still here I went on a sightseeing tour of the Kremlin. The room where the Presidium meets is most effective – varying shades of white with Corinthian columns set into the walls (these are fake white marble). Window drapes are yellow (an apparently favorite Russian color) and the lighting beautifully done. Each member of the Presidium has a desk and chair, plus an earphone in case he is hard of hearing. Desks are dark greenish brown wood and upholstery green leather. Maybe schoolroom-like furniture goes with marble and white and yellow, but not to my way of thinking. The lobby outside immediately struck me as a swell site for about six bowling alleys.

We went through several ballrooms – some dating back three or four centuries. Most were smaller than I imagined and except for the center buildings were broken up and spoiled by huge spare columns – a necessary architectural evil. All our tour was done without stepping outdoors but we went from building to building and finally ended up in the palace of Ivan the Terrible. This is entirely oriental in style. Rooms tiny, with badly restored wall paintings. The guide took us into what he called Ivan the Terrible's banqueting hall. The walls were covered with badly restored early Italian religious paintings. Then we were taken into the famous Catherine the Great ballroom, where Stalin now holds his banquets. It too was far smaller than I'd thought. The columns were an off almost pinkish white with slabs of malachite set in one side. Personally, I didn't like the bright green contrast with the pleasant pink and silver and gold effect given by the rest of the room, but apparently it's supposed to be terrific. I discovered too that the brocade on the walls was the background of all those pictures of the P.M., Stalin and Averell – the ones that look as though they're in El Morocco amongst zebra skins.

Love,
Kathleen

On the copy of this letter to Mary, Kathy scribbled:

> Sam upset by [Thompson's] and [Hamilton's] "attitude" towards him; like nursery governess. They stopped his cable telling of general war-weariness of Russians and that basically [Moscow Conference] meant nothing to them, that only military action on our part would impress them of our sincerity and wish to contribute to the quick end of the war.

On Pam's copy of the letter, Kathy handwrote at the end:

> After much delay I saw Madame Maisky yesterday. She's been "ill" after her long travels by truck from Cairo to here. She received me at the Spiridonovka – the house where the conferences were held, which is sort of the official entertainment place of the Foreign Office. She & hubby are living in great discomfort, to quote her, at the Hotel Metropol – where the foreign press lives, which is rather unusual. Important Russians are accustomed to being put [up] at another hotel. The press boys figure it might be a sign that he's not very well thought of at the moment. Anyway, I certainly got the impression that she misses her accustomed luxury living in London. She talked at length about "the great suffering of my people," which I guess she feels more strongly now that even she can't get a hot bath. Maybe I'm being cruel! She was really most cordial. But interestingly enough stalled when I asked when she could come and have tea. She smiled and asked that I let her call me because "I don't know how my health will be." In other words, she doesn't know if she ought to accept our hospitality!

CHAPTER 14

'MAYBE I'M JUST CRAZY, BUT I'M ENJOYING MYSELF THOROUGHLY – AND I'M DETERMINED NOT TO GET INTO WHAT SEEMS TO BE A HELLOVA RUT'

Tension and rivalry between the US State Department's professional officers and political appointees like Averell were legion. Rumours swirled that Ave was going to bypass the diplomats and run an alternative embassy from Spaso House, with Kathleen as his chief political adviser.

There was no truth in such rumours, but as Robert P. Newman pointed out, the Harriman embassy was quite different in style from that of Averell's predecessor as ambassador, Admiral W.W. Standley. In October 1943 John Melby wrote home that 'the new regime here is distinctly more on the big-shot side of life. The conversation is all Winston this, Tony [Eden] that, and Franklin the other. The White House has moved into the Embassy and the Department of State has moved out.' The apprehension and irritation were mutual but did not last long. The embassy staff got used to the Harrimans' 'non-state department ways' and Kathy and Melby became quite good friends. Twelve months later, Melby commented in another letter, 'I suppose one does not build great railroads for nothing. His Excellency can dish it out, but he can also take it. In my experience his daughter is the only woman I have ever known who could also do it and slug it out, a quality I wholeheartedly approve of in females, but seldom find.'

Moscow
November 9, 1943

Dear Mary,

It's nice knowing that letters are already reaching you. I wish I could figure out what makes most interesting reading. I personally run into something new about this country I'd never heard about or thought was different pretty much every day. This certainly is quite a town!

Today, three of the army boys and I went on a buying skis expedition for everyone. One of them had contacted a guy attached to the physical training section of the government and he took us out to a ski factory on the outskirts of town. We went in a huge palace affair that once belonged to some Prince, now turned into offices. Some of the Grecian statues were still standing in the halls, but the rest of the place was office-like, dingy and smelled like a cleanish riding rink.

We were taken up to a room where various types of skis and all equipment were on display and here I got a hell of a shock. There were jumping skis, cross country, downhill slalom, plus regular army skis. We were told to take our pick. The director of the place was upset because he figured we weren't taking the best. The Russians seem to have gathered the various types made in other countries, tried them out and used the ones they figure best for their own needs.

When I got back for lunch and told Averell I had purchased him a pair of laminated hickory skis with cable bindings, plus steel edges, he didn't believe me and I don't think does yet. Skis have to be made – in a matter of five days and for the boys who need boots they take about ten days. The price, being government-controlled, is unbelievably low – about 8 bucks for skis and edges! Now all we have to do is to find the semblance of a hill in this flattest of flat country.

Changing the subject a bit, Averell and I had ourselves quite a time on Sunday night – Nov. 7 – the 26th anniversary of the Oct. Revolution. Molotov & co. gave a huge reception for all the corps diplomatique at 8:30 in the evening. Invitations asked that either white ties or black suits be worn, which is the first time for the Soviets to suggest the wearing of the former. Needless to say none of the

Americans had a dress suit, so to make up for our deficiency I scrambled into my one and only pink and brown Hattie's dress. In honor of the occasion, all Foreign Office officials were dressed in their new dress uniforms. Molotov is the equivalent of a field marshal and rank goes down to one small star – the same as a second lieut. Uniforms were black, double breasted with gold buttons marked with F.O. insignia. Sleeves had a width of gold embroidery equivalent to an admiral. More embroidery on the velvet collars and finally at the shoulders were worn straps of gold and silver on which were embroidered rank insignia.

The general effect was inclined to be dazzling and needless to say each little individual Soviet was as proud as a little boy all dressed up in his new Christmas present fireman's suit. Later in the evening, Molotov asked me why I had been the only one not to compliment him on his uniform! Because I didn't like it? Archie Clark Kerr had managed to scrape together a dress suit, plus a borrowed stiff shirt from the Swedes. Together with his medals and best KCB red and blue ribbon worn horizontally across his chest and stomach, he managed not to look insignificant next to a Russian, but he was the only one not to. Obviously, there's much speculation about why the Soviets have given their foreign service officials a resplendent uniform. Some say so they won't get outshone by the Red Army uniform, others say it's so they'll stand out when compared to the diplomats of the other nations. No one knows, but one thing is certain: it's one more sign of them leaving behind even the trimmings of a proletarian government.

The reception marked the first time during the war that wives of officials were put on show and also the first time artists, writers, etc. got invited to an official function and were allowed to mingle freely with foreigners. After the reception was over, Averell and I were retrieved from some corner of some huge crowded room and along with the British ambassador placed in the first row with Molotov to listen to a concert. I, unfortunately, got the giggles at one point when a big lady singer dressed in ample blue velvet burped inadvertently while her introductory music was being played.

Present also at the party was Ambass. Sato and one of the Jap generals and a Jap admiral plus incidental staff. They and the Bulgarians were well surrounded by Soviet officials throughout the evening – a necessary protection against any not too sober Americans!

The drinking didn't start in earnest until after the concert when we were led into a room set aside for ambassadors. There were about five such rooms – with huge tables of food, drink and fruit – and little tables in the corner – one for writers, actors etc., one for generals, one for civilian officials etc. It was quite an effective way of getting people together informally with their opposite numbers. The food wasn't particularly good, being mostly cold and very heavy, but I ate all I could get my hands on as protective coating for what was to follow. Averell and Clark Kerr were immediately seated at a table with Mikoyan[1] and Shcherbakov,[2] the head of Military Intelligence. Mikoyan is famous for his ability to put any guy under the table, so I guessed that's why he was picked. He and Averell drank bottoms-up after bottoms-up in toasts to all the obvious things – in vodka. When I finally joined them, they'd had quite a head start. Fortunately for me, soon after I sat down the drink was changed from vodka to sour Caucasian white wine – but even it has a pretty high alcohol content! Our table was sort of the center of attention – just the three of us and the Soviets, who came and went. It was quite genial and at times very funny. Kornichuk – one of the Vice-Commissars of Foreign Affairs was there with his wife Wanda Wasilewska[3] (she's a very notorious Polish gal who heads the Communist Poles organization in Moscow). I'd been wanting to meet her as she's quite a figure (read *Newsweek*)! I'm afraid I was very disappointed. She's a big hulk of a woman with black short hair worn behind the ears with two big metal bobby pins. Her complexion is sallow and her personality as sour as can be. It was obvious she disapproved of the party, refused to join the gaiety or drinking and gave her husband unadulterated hell for drinking. Her

---

1 Anastas Mikoyan (1895–1978), People's Commissar for Foreign Trade.
2 Alexander Shcherbakov (1901–45), head of the Red Army's political directorate and director of the Soviet Information Buro.
3 Wanda Wasilewska (1905–64), Polish communist writer.

husband is a Ukrainian whose field of activity centers in the direction of Poland, the Baltic States area (so you see he's pretty damned important). Also, he's written a significant play,[4] supposedly by order of Stalin, making fun of the Russian Colonel Blimp generals, the bureaucrats and their inefficiencies etc. (Damned good, too – I've seen it.) Anyway, when Clark Kerr asked him if he ever read any plays by Shakespeare he caught on immediately and said "Oh yes, you mean the *Taming of the Shrew*." That subject, including the throwing downstairs, was used exhaustively, much to everyone's amusement, except Wanda, who finally got up and left.

Conversation was slightly difficult as only two interpreters hovered around, but they were extremely adept at carrying on the general cross-current of conversation. As time went on, I suddenly realized Averell was getting a worried look on his face – scared I guess I'd not be able to keep up the pace. It's hard to cheat at toast drinking, as you have to turn the glass upside down at the end of it and the drops of liquor that fall out are according to the Russian custom drops of misfortune you wish on the person you are drinking with. I can't remember what we talked about, though comparing notes the next day we discovered a number of significant things had been said, particularly about the Jap war. Then along about midnight the British ambass. rose to his feet for a toast with some difficulty, put his hand out to steady himself on the table, missed it and fell flat on his face at Molotov's feet, bringing a goodly number of plates and glasses clattering down on top of him. He was helped up quickly as expert waiters cleared the debris. Party continued. After that I turned to Averell and said "let's get the hell out of here" partially because I was beginning to get worried how much longer I'd last and partially because after we left the British ambassador [would] be able to go home. So after one long last toast to Stalin, Churchill and the President, Averell and I gathered ourselves up and marched solemnly out down the long hallway and stairs to the car. It was some party and I'm mighty glad Nov 7th comes only once a year. When I got to bed the room really started whirling. (A most unhappy feeling as the only way I

4 Alexander Kornichuk, *The Front*.

could keep from feeling I was lying upside down of the ceiling was by concentrating very hard on the light outside my window.) Finally I got tired of keeping myself awake so I got up, closed window, turned on the light and went to the bathroom and drank 3 glasses of very strong soda bicarb. That got me properly sick to my stomach and when I climbed back into bed the ceiling stayed in place. Next morning I was awakened by voices in the hall – Averell calling for bicarb seltzer and as none could be found he was not in particularly good shape. (Not that I was either but at least I was better than he!) That's about the end of that story.

Averell did himself proud, because the one thing the Soviets apparently appreciate is a guy who'll drink with them and be able to keep the pace & not show any effects. All the Moscow Americans were very pleased.[5]

At that moment I got interrupted. Averell blew in from Mokhovaya (the office) & with about 3 minutes to spare before expecting the Swedish ambass. got into one of his furniture moving moods. So we arranged and rearranged all three uncomfortable sofas in the living room until the carpet looked like plans for a tank battle. These had to be smoothed out hurriedly. Still no Swede arrived, then Ave suddenly remembered he told him he'd go and see him – rather than have the meeting here – so he rushed off.

Now it's after dinner. Ave's working with Chip Bohlen[6] (1st Secretary). Bob's rushing around typing and retyping cables and things and Mr Hamilton (chargé d'affaires), John Melby (junior secretary) and I are all in our separate rooms studying for our respective Russian lessons tomorrow. It's practically like school days all over again – homework & all that. Tonight I learned how to count, the days of the week, plus tomorrow's lesson, which is the genitive case (singular only) and such verbs as stand, sit and drink.

---

5 Ivan Maisky wrote about the reception and Clark Kerr's collapse in his diary, noting that 'Harriman and his daughter were also very drunk, but were able to "retreat" from the Spiridonova without incident'.
6 Charles E. Bohlen (1904–74), diplomat who served as the president's Russian interpreter during the war and later as ambassador to the Soviet Union.

Last night I was quite pleased – after dining with Cassidy[7] (A.P.) and Bill Downs (CBS & *Newsweek*) I went to a party given by a little Russian communist agitator boyfriend of mine and could get the gist of at least some of the conversation, so maybe it won't take me the years to learn everyone says it will.

The press here are a motley bunch of boys. Dave Nichol of the *Chicago Daily News* is the only one I really like & even he is dreary by London standards. Most of them, however, are semi-Russian like Shapiro (U.P.) and Maurice Hindus[8] (*Herald Trib.*). He's strictly party line and inclined to be surly. Cassidy of A.P. is a nice guy but rather boring. Downs is a good reporter but not overloaded with grey matter. I miss the genial London correspondent gatherings. Sam Spewack, however, is swell, full of ideas and good company. At the moment, at his suggestion I am tackling the large task of assembling U.S.A. editorial comment on the conference for the Soviets. Fun, fun!

I could go on writing for hours about this place. It seems to hit some people hard – gets them depressed, almost morose – Americans I mean, particularly the press! They live very secluded un-newsy lives and gradually get into a routine of filing a few words a day on a subject that will get thru the censor after a few hours' fight on their part. (That's no exaggeration.) Then occasionally they write letters to people like Stalin or Molotov complaining, go to diplomatic functions and that's about all there is for them to do – except to drink among themselves and sometimes fight. Their rooms are dreary affairs at the Metropol – with alcoves screened off for bedrooms. Furniture is dark, woodwork dark – black and red and gold being the main colors. The embassy boys living at the National Hotel fare about as badly. Me, coming here fresh and full of enthusiasm find the majority half dead by comparison. It's sort of the result of having "no" said to you so often and feeling that you're not wanted. Foreigners can mix with few Russians and then only a few set out for that job. Maybe I'm just crazy, but I'm enjoying myself thoroughly – there's

7 Henry Cassidy (1910–88).
8 Henry Shapiro (1906–91); Maurice G. Hindus (1891–1969).

plenty to keep me busy and I'm determined not to get into what seems to be a hellova rut.

We've had a smattering of snow the last few days and the moment the first flurry appears on the horizon the street cleaners, men and women, are out with their shovels and brushes. Apparently that goes on all winter!

Of course, we live in great luxury – hot water all day long – whereas the hotel livers get it one day a week and late Sunday morning. They have meal tickets and have to give one of their own up when entertaining a guest, so the plan usually is eat at home and go out afterwards. We have stuff in cans, beautifully cooked, plus delicious cold slaw and vegetables, which are a treat after English Brussel sprouts. In fact, the food we have is much better than London. Honest to God home cooking is mighty nice when you've been without it for a couple of years!

Goodbye for now,

Kathy

In her report to Pam about the Revolution anniversary reception, Kathy observed that, despite everything, Wasilewska and Kornichuk 'are madly in love with each other! An odd combination!' The letter – dated 16 November – continued: 'Re. our little conversation – warning about boyfriends, Averell asked me the other night who I'd like to have come live in the house with us! I think he was referring to that, but unfortunately [X] on seeing more of ain't no glamour boy, in fact no likely prospects are in sight at all. The State Department sure doesn't go in for sex appeal!' On the last page Kathy wrote, 'Pam for God's sake don't let anyone read this page before cutting out.' In a further handwritten note she told Pam about the treatment of Averell's boils, which was going well, concluding, 'Everything is working out very well. The process of the Foreign Service-ites changing to conform to Averell is great fun to watch. He's doing a good job of breaking their "bad" (stereotype) habits & soon the bunch will be almost human.'

Moscow
November 17, 1943

Dear Marie and Mary,

Averell, the skunk, is about to go off and leave me in the clutches of the esteemed members of our Foreign Service. That's just a little better than leaving me in solitary confinement in Lubianka prison! I'm sure I'll be well cared for in a comfortable formal way. You see they figure me as not much better than a freak. Anyway, I anticipate an interesting, perhaps that's an exaggeration, amusing is better word, time.

After a month at Spaso House, my ambition is to inveigle Sam Spewack into someday writing a play about the INSTITUTION. I'm sure the average American doesn't appreciate the potentialities, from the standpoint of comedy, of the [State Department]. Each day we add to our fund of anecdotes of the general attitude towards outsiders.

It's great for the sense of humor to suddenly discover that the number one attitude of the members of the Institution is that ambassadors are a necessary evil of our foreign service set-up. Ambassadors should be treated kindly and handled with the best of care, sort of like a great-grandfather or baby sister – better still a combination of both. Ambassadors are told what to do, and most particularly what not to do. Can you imagine Averell under this type of system? Or the consternation and bewilderment of the Foreign Service men at his complete failure after a month to fall into line? The tussle is great to watch. The senior members of staff will have their last gasp for breath while he's away and they know it.

Attitude number two deals with reports and cables. These are lengthy and usually manage to say nothing at all of importance. (If you don't say anything you don't get blamed for creating an impression which at some future date will be proven false.) So, to cover up this failure to say a damned thing worth saying, the writer resorts to verbiage. The guy on the receiving end can't understand what the hell the report is about, but since the words are strung at impressive length, he figures he should be impressed and to cover up his failure to be so, he files the report away and all is forgotten.

Frequently, however, cables telling of specific happenings are required. These are drafted according to strict formula, day after day, year after year. Since they are boring to read and extremely pompous, no one reads them, except Averell, who only reads them to tear them up.

Maybe it may not sound so, but this is a wonderful place, better than most embassies because here you live and eat with most of the staff, so you really get to appreciate every side and angle.

In the evenings, when we're not out dining with outsiders (who mostly are diplomats and not particularly appetizing ones at that), we have a gay old time at dinner. In fact, the conversation has improved no end. Even the deadliest, most straight-laced State Department guy made a mildly funny crack at Averell tonight. That we considered a major victory. Before lunch of late I've taken to mixing cocktails. Each day we experiment – vodka with sherry, vodka with wine, vodka with synthetic fruit juice. The result is good (not the cocktails themselves!).

But to get back to evenings – after dinner one bunch play something called bottle billiards, very seriously and the game lasts well on 'til midnight. Averell and I adjourn upstairs, maybe with a boarder or two. We converse for a bit then Averell and I settle down to the serious business of making me into a good bezique player. After that Averell goes to bed and I study Russian.

Incidentally, Russians call me Gaspadeena Garriman. If you pronounce it, it sounds like an old man clearing his throat.

It's getting late now so I must get to bed.

With much love to everyone,

Kath

PS On re-reading, I've discovered I'm in a very blasphemous mood. So please for God's sake read this letter and tear it up and don't show it to anyone.

CHAPTER 15

'THIS REALLY IS THE DAMNEDEST TOWN – IMPERSONAL AS HELL, BUT STILL RETAINS AN ATMOSPHERE AND MAKES A MARKED IMPRESSION ON YOU'

By the time Kathy arrived in Moscow she was an experienced war reporter and took a great deal of interest in the work and welfare of her fellow foreign correspondents. As Bill Lawrence of the *New York Times* recalled, Kathy was a good friend to the thirty or so 'unhappy correspondents' reporting from Moscow.

The foreign ministers' meeting that had brought Ave and Kathy to Moscow was merely the curtain-raiser to the main event – a conference between Roosevelt, Churchill and Stalin in Tehran at the end of November 1943. As Kathy relates, had Ave known that Churchill would bring his daughter Sarah along, she too might have made the trip to Tehran. Left to her own devices in Moscow, the swirl of engagements that had engulfed her when she arrived continued unabated. Her appointments diary lists meetings, shows, lunches, dinners, receptions and Russian lessons morning, noon and night. The only respite was when she was ill with a cold, or was laid up with mumps.

Moscow
Thanksgiving Day
November 25, 1943

Dear Mary,

Life in Moscow is proceeding according to plan and as pretty much everything I do these days is a novelty in one way or other, I'm enjoying it muchly.

For instance, a couple of days back I unsuspectingly went to lunch with the Mexican ambassador.[1] He's noted in Moscow for one thing only and that's his sex life. The stories that circulate all originate from him and don't need embellishing, which may give you an idea what kind of a guy he is. According to him he's exceedingly prolific and I guess the courses at his luncheon party about equaled the number of lady friends he keeps on call. (There were seven courses at the table plus a huge hunk of cake served upstairs with coffee.)

The lunch started at 1:15 and I left at 4:15, which is pretty damned good going for an ordinary social luncheon where no one cares a damn for anyone else or gives a hoot what conversation consists of just so long as it persists.

The only other gal at lunch was the wife of the Dutch ambassador. She's Rumanian, I think, has a cold sort of beauty, dresses nicely but isn't the type easy to warm up to. She hates elevators and hence has to trundle up eight flights of stairs to her Russian lesson. (She and I share the same teacher.) I guess it's lucky for her she doesn't live in N.Y.C. So much for Madame Breughel-Douglas.[2] (Good name don't you think?)

The rest of the luncheon party were ambassadors and ministers and whatnots. I never seem to be able to get titles straight as some biggish countries have only ministers whereas smallish ones have ambassadors. The result I usually get mixed up and produce the wrong title for the wrong guy. When we were in London, we had a "bore list." Here I think we'll have to have a list figuring the other way as there are too damned many bores to have it fun to count them. However, I have found one nice diplomat – that's the Norwegian ambassador.[3] He's a bit on the ancient side but then you can't be picky in Moscow. I took an immediate shine to him at the Mexican's lunch when the Mexican ambassador was [asking] for the third time as to Averell's whereabouts. The Norwegian took my arm and

1 Luis Quintanilla del Valle (1900–80). As a writer, he was associated with the Mexican avant-garde movement Stridentism.
2 Aga Iona Maria Berendei (1901–70), married to Baron Casper van Breugel Douglas (1896–1992).
3 Rolf Andvord (1890–1976), reputedly recruited as a spy by the Soviets during the war.

suggested we sit down and chat because he didn't "give a damn" about Averell's whereabouts. At first I figured that was just one more way to worm information out of daughter, but he didn't mention the subject again.

Another social experience was a hen party at the Persians. As I was given about a week's notice there wasn't much reason to refuse. So I went and discovered I was the only non-Eastern European or Chinese present. Conversation was exclusively conducted in Russian with some translation for my benefit. The raison d'etre for the party was mostly food. We sat at the dining room table and stuffed. Most of the girls were fat and pimply but nothing stopped them from downing about four slices of Persian pistachio layer cake (heavy and soggy) after a goodly amount of caviar and what have you. Conversation centered mostly around college as most of them apparently take courses. I guess they're all extremely well educated in the liberal arts and they speak French and English (after a fashion) plus their own language and Russian, but their general run of talk was mainly the lack of boys in Moscow colleges and the "nice" professors. I left early which doubtless was rude.

Also slightly adolescent in atmosphere are our navy parties. Lord knows why but the naval attaché's office is quite large. In fact, until the arrival of General Deane, the navy outnumbered the military attaché's office and the supply mission combined. Anyway, I've been to two navy parties. Both exactly alike. The girls were mostly Russian translators with a couple of movie actresses and girls who play the piano and sing. The routine seems to be alternating dancing to a gramophone with listening to someone sing and play some sort of concert music, but drinking all the time. Rough-housing is indulged in to a great extent between the boys while the girls look on, not particularly amused. No one seems to enjoy themselves very much, except those extremely drunk.

The evenings here at Spaso are more normal. There are usually at least four of us in and maybe a guest. After dinner we play bottle pool, a game at which I am lousy, but better than Sam Spewack, which gives me slight consolation. After a rousing game of pool we adjourn upstairs and the last few nights don't seem to get to bed until near three a.m. "We" however does not mean the entire ménage. Sam and John Melby are the only ones who don't retire before eleven.

Today being Thanksgiving I'm the one who's throwing the party – for all Americans in Moscow, which when you add the military and Navy to the embassy plus aircraft missions on down to two Jewish fur buyers and a priest, comes to damn near a hundred. The Soviet Foreign Office (who gives us food for parties, or rather gives us permission to buy food) was very sticky about liquor, so I'm scared to death we'll run out. What stocks we had we consumed while the Conference was on. However we do have some turkeys and hot dogs, so at least guests will leave unhungry, if not tight.

Maybe I haven't made life in Moscow sound as enticing as I intended. But by comparison to what I anticipated it to be, it's damned near paradise. Thanks to me studying Russian as seriously as time allows, I'm busy during the day doing either it or work for Sam. In fact, for the moment I'm taking a Russian lesson every day except Sunday. Three times a week from my French speaking teacher, and three from a little gal. The point of the latter one is "conversation." As she speaks a minimum of English I damn well have to [do] my own thinking.

Then aside from all that, this is a pretty interesting town, one of my favorite sports is just plain walking in the streets watching the people.

[Kathleen]

DAILY NOTES: November 19–28, 1943

Nov. 19: Was awakened at 5:45. Breakfasted with Averell and went out to airport . . .

Sat in during Hamilton's Russian lesson. Listened to fairy tale by Pushkin about goldfish. That took most of the lesson. Got idea of getting Deane's teacher for three days a week and had it arranged easily. Afternoon spent editing Moscow Conference editorial reaction, which made me realize how spoiled I'd been in *Newsweek*. Very boring.

After dinner went to navy party for French fliers.[4] 'Twas fun.

---

4 The Normandie Squadron was a Free French fighter squadron that flew on the Soviet–German front.

Nov. 20: Conversation lessons excellent idea. Movie this afternoon – [The Young Mr Pitt] – with goodly number of cracks at French. Asked Normandie officer if he liked the movie. He didn't answer. Cuban ambass. stayed for dinner. Seems very nice, but certainly very fond of himself.

Nov. 21: At Sam's suggestion, went to see *Wait for Me* at Arbat movie house.[5] Had great moral; light and sound effects lousy. We sat in box and downstairs audience sounded like a lot of rats in a loft. They rustled, conversed and appeared not to pay much attention to the movie. Some nice-looking army girls, but they were either alone or with other girls. Had tea with [Mme] Ahi, Jugo, Czech, Chinese were there; all hens. Talked Russian mostly. Czech girl is studying to be lawyer. They laughed and ate a tremendous amount. Reminded me rather of tea party at home, of Foxcroft vintage. Went to Navy party. Party didn't get gay until midnight, and then the girls didn't take part. They sat or danced, but never got gay Gaiety consisted mostly of rough-housing among naval officers.

Nov. 22: Lunched with Mexican ambass. Lunch wasn't bad, conversation ranged from skiing to Russian icons.

Nov. 26: Sort of the morning after. Yesterday being Thanksgiving, I was the one who threw the party. We decided that the party should be restricted to Americans and their wives, which meant that, not counting me, there were only two gals (both nice).

Personally, it was my first step in getting to know some of the clerks, the junior officers, etc., who have a very dreary time in this town. Most of them, up till the party, were inclined to be suspicious of me for something, but now that's all straightened out.

Lunch with Dave, Bill and Bill Lawrence at Metropol. They are just back from Kiev, and the first part of lunch was spent telling us of 1) the banquets they had to attend, food and drink they consumed, and 2) minute details of atrocity committed outside Kiev. They didn't know whether or not it was faked. Lunch was long, but I left without any feeling of Kiev. The boys didn't get it. Sam saw Henry Shapiro. He said "it is a dead city."

---

5 A Soviet war film.

Nov. 27: Dinner. Had press boys in plus York and Chase. I'm beginning to find me a place in this joint at last.

Nov. 28: I've now discovered that the best damned thing that could have happened to me was to have Averell leave me alone in this place. Discovered great feeling against the embassy on part of clerks. Now we are all fighting the same battle.

It's Sunday now, my one day that doesn't start off with a Russian lesson. Last night we had a few people in for dinner – some Navy boys who play bridge and the five press boys who missed the Thanksgiving party due to being in Kiev. Much to some people's horror I invited Eddie Gilmore's wife (a little Russian gal). I'd figured that it would be a nice thing to do, an obvious one, but apparently last night was the first time the embassy had accepted her.

Moscow
November 29, 1943

Dear Pam,

The best damned thing that could have happened to me was to have Averell leave me here alone. At the time when he left I anticipated a couple of weeks of mild hell – but, as in London, I've gotten into [the] swing [of] a bachelor existence. Averell not being here, I've gone out a lot – gotten to know the lower-ranking embassy staff, our Navy, Army etc. On Thanksgiving I threw an all-American party – cocktails, buffet dinner etc. which turned out very well. Pretty much everyone got plastered, talked a lot, so I learned a good bit about just what the score is here and why Spaso House ain't popular (all of which dates back to Steinhardt[6] days). So now I've set about trying to break the bad feeling down. In the evenings when I don't go out I sit around with the other Spaso House borders – play pool with them etc. and slowly they're getting used to me and my "non-State-Department" approach, all of which is to the good.

Then thanks to the general exodus of Americans with Averell, there are some stray Russian teachers around – so now I have about two hours of Russian conversation daily – which helps considerably

6 Laurence Steinhardt (1892–1950), US ambassador to Moscow 1939–41.

on that score. Now all I have to do is to get up enough courage to start talking Russian in public.

One necessary evil is the round of social functions. Frinstance yesterday I had to cocktail with the Jugs, lunch today with the Norwegian, tonight the Chinese. The Norwegian ambassador is the best of them, though slightly old (decrepit). He's new here and may prove worth cultivating.

[Kathleen]

Moscow
early December, 1943

Dear Pam,

The news of the second conference broke this morning. My little Russian teacher was thrilled and completely surprised. You can imagine with all the corps diplomatique rivaling each other for the best stories (particularly the Mexican and the Colombian) it wasn't much of a secret as far as the press was concerned.

It's unfortunate, but the American press boys are a pretty crummy bunch taken as a whole. It's too bad, because a good core of correspondents could get a lot more out of this country. Shapiro, U.P., is the best. He's good, but personally he lacks a sense of humor and he's the studious type. But then he hardly counts as an American. He's really more Russian.

I was mildly shocked when the boys came back from Kiev. I lunched with Lawrence (*N.Y. Times*), Nichol (*Chicago D.N.*) and Bill Downs and they were struck by two things mainly – the amount of food and number of banquets they were given at Kiev, en route there and on the return journey and, number two, they were worried as to whether or not they should believe the atrocity story they were told. 50,000 Jews killed and burned in a ravine just outside the town. None of the three got any feeling at all of the town or seemed to appreciate it was a great story. Shapiro was the only guy who reacted personally to the town, which prewar had a population of a million and now has 70,000. It's too bad the American press can't send its best correspondents. The bunch here are either tactless as hell, or so brow-beaten by the lack of information that they've lost all initiative. None of them seem to trouble to learn the language (except Eddie Gilmore who married a Russian girl). In one month I know more than most of them.

For the past week it snowed every morning, then sort of melted come afternoon. I'm still amazed at the way the old women come out in droves to clear the main streets. It's damned hard work with no end to it. They pile it up and then a truck comes along to cart it to one of the sewer centers. Sometimes little kids (four-year-old ones) help too. The traffic goes on, no one seems to get run over, Lord knows why, because it's nip and tuck whether or not a street cleaner is the variety who will give way to a car horn. So far the weather isn't much colder than New York in midwinter. But already I've worn out both heels of your galoshes!

I discovered the best way to figure out just how cold any particular day is to look out the window and see how fast the people are scurrying. We live in a little square. It's a pretty square. The kids play in it all day – either skate or make snowballs, or slide on a strip of ice. But even it has an air of frustration about it. The trees are half dead, the iron railing sort of tired and bent. The houses range from Victorian, factory-like red brick to little wooden cottages – these are made out of spliced round logs. Down one side street is a tiny church.

The funny thing about this town is that East and West have been mixed, but never blended. The Russians have copied Georgian architecture, Victorian architecture, French Mansard. Then, intermingled with all, are the Byzantine churches with their spires. Our chancellery is opposite the Kremlin and sticking out above the high brick wall is every kind and type of tower, minaret and dome you could dream of, left over from every century. Moscow is like the Kremlin, only less crowded, less grandiose, but the log cabins are mixed in with the old ornate and the colorless modern.

It's an impersonal town – people in the streets seem divorced [from] each other. Perhaps it's the wideness of the streets that make it so, and make all the scurrying figures seem so dwarfed. Every house I've been to, I've asked "who are your neighbors." No one knows. We know only that on our right live some N.K.V.D. boys.[7] Behind us is a

7 Narodnyi Komissariat Vnutrennikh Del (People's Commissariat of Internal Affairs) – the Soviet Union's internal security police.

crowded apartment house. But faces never appear in the windows. Washing is never hung out to dry.

Walking in the streets, people look on the ground rather than up (that may be because it is so damned slippery!). They stare at your galoshes and I stare back at their huge shapeless valenki [felt] boots. The military, of course, are beautifully dressed. So far I haven't seen one beautiful Russian. Hair is badly kept and through holey white long underwear you can [see] wool stockings, or perhaps another layer of long underwear.

Moscow makes an impression on you – mixture of dank smells. For all its apparent impersonality, it's got atmosphere. It's a town where foreigners get depressed because they can't become part of the town.

[Kathleen]

Moscow
December 24, 1943

Dear Mary,

I'm "unlaxing" in bed with a tray and a mild state of exhaustion. This is my first day completely out of hock and despite the fact that I was allowed up around in my room after about 10 days of mumps, my knees are still weak.

Last night I started wrapping Xmas presents at 10 p.m. and at 1:30 a.m. I finally gave up. We have 30 servants here at Spaso (females got a sweater, pair of cotton stockings and mittens and males two flannel shirts). Then all Russians at Mokhovaya (Chancery) got a case of canned milk – unwrapped thank God. Clerks got a carton of cigs and embassy officers a gold tie pin which, incidentally, I think you purchased in N.Y.C.

Yesterday afternoon General Donovan and dreary aide turned up in town (not unexpected) and they are house guests. Donovan brought Popsie a case of champagne!!!

Oh yes, today I've been addressing and writing cards to all the various "His excellencies" around town, we're sending them cigs, and families with kids canned milk.

Tonight we are having a party for U.S.ers. The usual variety of buffet banquet and liquor, particular accent on the latter. As usual there was the problem as to whether or not the boys should be allowed to bring their girls. I wanted females so that there would be dancing, but as the majority of the girls are out and out prostitutes it was decided against having any girlfriends – so that there would be no feeling between the men with presentable girls and those without. Much problems!!!

New Year's is another big problem and we've finally decided not to throw a shindig – as most of the Russkies have their own private family affairs in the country.

The tree is beautiful, it's nearly as high as the ceiling (3 stories). It, needless to say, has yet to be trimmed as the electrician has disappeared.

I have no particular personal news – as I think I wrote you shortly before I got the mumps, and for the better part of the past two weeks I've been lying in a dark room, one eye closed up due to the swelling and then both of them got red like a road map and unfocusable for reading – so I just sat and tried to get the radio to work. I feel extremely bitter on the subject of radio jamming. I approve of it in theory but the Nazis have good musical programs, and their news broadcasts are particularly amusing and interesting. The B.B.C., as ever, stinks from the entertainment standpoint. At this time of year U.S. is unobtainable and Algiers U.S. radio hard to get clearly enough for music. Since my eyes weren't usable I couldn't take Russian lessons so I've practiced on the gal who brought the meals. Now I can ask for anything from servants and get along with an atrocious American accent, regularly slaughtering the grammar (I talk using the Nominative, Accusative and Dative cases and say to hell with the other three [Genitive, Instrumental, Prepositional]). However, my vocab still doesn't function sufficiently for the drawing room. Apparently 3,000 words are needed for that and I'm nearer the 300 word state!!!

Bob Meiklejohn, luckily, has had mumps, so has General Deane. So they legally visited me and hence kept me from going crazy. Then Sam and one of the embassy secretaries said to hell with it all and came in daily. It remains to be seen if they get it. Averell, not having had mumps, figured it was beneath the dignity of one of the ambassadorial rank to contract such a disease so he stayed good and clear of my room and kicked me out of Bob's room whenever he found me there. (Bob has best radio and temporarily had a gramophone). We're having a flu epidemic here and literally all but me and one embassy guy have been down with it. After three days in bed, Bob greeted me one morning with "oh dear, I'm afraid I'm getting well." Some people have run a temperature of 105.

Dec. 26

We had a very nice newly snowing Xmas – and now in an attempt to recover, I'm going skiing.

Xmas eve we had a big party here at the embassy – with gypsies and the few "American" girls and a couple of un-attached females. It was a great success – with only one gashed eye (due to falling not fighting) which is pretty good, when mixing the services and adding a bunch of tough oil men. My knees were still on the shaky side but somehow they survived and so did I. For some reason or other one takes a worse beating at Moscow parties than any other parties I've hit yet – sort of combination of the tough vodka punches and then me being one of the few gals.

Xmas day we had to do the rounds of cocktail parties given by all the various people and so now I figure with some skiing today I'll last through tonight – the last of the Xmas festivities – the press boys' party.

Dec. 27

Our skiing expedition was a great success. We found a ravine not far out of Moscow and spent some hours clambering around it. The new snow is very dry and hard to pack – sugary with an icy base underneath which made it not what you'd call easy, but then I discovered I was the only one who tried to turn in it. The others all climbed to the top and schussed, invariably landing in a heap at the bottom in a ditch. However, we all enjoyed ourselves.

Last night the press had their party – stand-up dinner followed by a series of skits – take-offs on Americans and British – one of the best ones, and funniest, was a press conference with Averell. Subject: the weather in Moscow – and results: Averell said nothing. Lauterbach of *Time* played Averell and did a damned good job of it.

Result of our sending the various big shots in the C.D. [Corps Diplomatique] cigarettes has been most lucrative. Frinstance, the Turkish ambass.[8] retaliated with a gallon of eau de cologne for Averell and three cakes of soap for me. We can't figure out if the Turk figures I smell or whether he figures Ave's a pansy! Apparently all the ambassadors were very touched by our "thought." We also got large quantities of beautiful boxes from the Chinese.

Tomorrow I guess I go back to work, such as it is. For your information, there's no definite work to do as such, or anyway a minimum. The idea is to get U.S. pictures, stories and articles on our war effort into the Soviet press and magazines. In theory the Soviets think it's a swell idea – in practice they say yes to the U.S. material and then throw them in the waste basket. Sam is going home shortly. He says not permanently – just for a few months to get things organized – but I kind of figure once he gets back he won't return. He's an "ideas man" who hates the routine office business. After 10 weeks of trying he's got very little in the way of concrete results from the Soviets and the inactivity and generally invariable day-to-day stalling has driven him slightly crazy. What gets done in his absence I guess will depend on my willingness to keep plugging. There are advantages, because as Averell says being the daughter of the U.S. ambass., the various editors will have to be polite to me – in other words, they won't throw me out or refuse to see me. As you can well imagine, compared with *Newsweek* this job stinks, but I've got to do something to keep busy. But it's not easy to be enthusiastic about a job today that at best may produce results in mid '44. People seem to think it's important so I guess I go to work. One thing – it's a means of meeting Russians.

Can't remember if or not I told you – or if you know – but no Russians can come here to a meal or even a drink without permission from the top.

---

8 H.R. Baydur (1890–1955).

What I do need desperately is codeine as the dispensary here is very short so I don't figure I can rightfully deplete their supply. Put some in a capsule or something in a letter and they should get here quickly. After all, at most I use six a month. I need a parka too, for skiing. I suggest you cancel magazines to London and send, via the State Department, *New Yorker*, *Reader's Digest* and all fashion magazines as the Soviet women crave them.

The weather here is amazingly warm, hovering below freezing. The worst thing is that we've seen the sun three times since arrival.

Averell brought terrific loot from Tehran in the form of fur-lined boots (leather) and a grey fur hat to match my coat (possum one turned inside out) so I'm warm which is crucialest thing. However, your ski suit, which was inadvertently sent me, hasn't a wind-proof jacket and the sleeves are 4 inches too short! I've put on weight since arrival here!

This is boringly long and says nothing, but now I'm up again perhaps I'll get off a newsier one soon!

My love to you all,

Kathleen

Moscow
December 28, 1943

Dear Mouche,

I've completed a letter to Mary yesterday for Donovan and co. to take but weather unpermitted their departure.

At this stage I'm still trying to recover from the Xmas festivities, which started with our party on Xmas eve and continued until Sunday when we all went to see ourselves taken off by the Anglo-American press. Everyone was very impressed with Averell as apparently most ambassadors get a trifle sore when they're made fun of. They were surprised he enjoyed it. The press were very kind to me – all I did was to break up a press conference of Ave's at the most important moment by clamoring in on skis.

The much talked of forty-below weather has yet to freeze us so I haven't yet worn my lovely fur-lined Persian boots which Averell brought back from Tehran. It was sad we didn't know that Sarah

Oliver was going to be at the conference because then maybe Ave might have taken me along, not that I would have had a thing to do but it would have been interesting, but as it was I had me a fine time getting established in my new home, if you care to call it that.

This really is the damnedest town. It's as impersonal as hell, but still retains an atmosphere and makes a marked impression on you.

We live on a little square just off one of the main avenues. The streets off it are cobbled and therefore not cleared with snow so the kids skate up and down all day long. The smaller kids (under 5) play on their sleds, slide on the icy spots and make snow figures and generally seem very happy and contented. The school system is for boys to go to school in the mornings and girls in the afternoon. The rest of the time they seem to play out of doors. It's hard to tell actually how healthy the children are – they get black bread and cabbage and a little skimmed milk – as their faces are pinched by the cold and their layers upon layers of clothes make them look like bundles with legs rather than human figures. Every now and then you see wonderfully dressed kids – little 3- and 4-year-olds tottering along the streets in white rabbit fur coats with hats and earmuffs to match and the invariable scarf to cover up the cracks. Sometimes the coats are so bulky that the kid's arms stick out horizontally like a little fat scarecrow.

Last night I took [Mr X] to the circus or at least he took me, which is overrun by children. A bunch of them cornered us and asked us for cigarettes (they were smoking rolled paper) and when we said they were too young they answered right back with "we're old enough to work so we are old enough to smoke."

But to get back to [the] square – it's pretty in a frustrated sort of way, the proper setting for a Chekhov maiden aunt character – with a few smallish leafless trees and a tired bent railing. The houses around it range from two one-storey almost windowless cottages to red-brick flat-faced factory-like apartment houses with windows front and back but not on the sides. Then of course there is our mansion – built just prior to the Revolution and never lived in as the owner was murdered by an illegitimate son in the front hall as he walked in to take over. Outside it's Russia's idea of Georgian, with a garden in front and an inconvenient entrance that's wide enough for only one car at a time. Added all together it's an odd mixture, but I'm growing sort of fond of it.

It's now the crack of dawn next day – and I'm still sort of unfunctioning because for some stupid reason I never seem to get to bed before 2 a.m. and last night wasn't any exception.

Love to you,
Kathleen

Moscow
January 3, 1944

Dear Mary,

A good week has gone by since I wrote you and Mouche hurried notes for Donovan to take out. Since then we've been going through the usual routine of being called at 7:00, driving out to the airport only to return full up. Waking at seven is becoming a horrid habit, particularly since it doesn't get light until eight-thirty.

Today we're in a lovely state of affairs, but not unusual for Moscow. Yesterday something went wrong with the plumbing – there was cold water spasmodically but no hot. Today there is no water, the cellar is flooded and the whys and wherefores not yet discovered. As I told you, the Turkish ambassador sent Averell a huge bottle of cologne – well pretty soon it will come in handy. I went skiing yesterday, didn't take an icy bath and this morning we all had nothing more than a bottle of drinking water to wash in. Fun fun.

New Year's was very pleasant. We celebrated it by showing *Casablanca* and then having a quiet drink upstairs afterwards. I was supposed to go to a brawl given by the R.A.F., but didn't have the strength. Thank God too, because the next day I made my apologies to the three Britishers who had invited me. One thought I'd been there and the other two hadn't missed me anyway.

The French gave a party the other night for the new Normandy pilots – unfortunately all the originals have left so I wasn't able to give anyone hell for giving me the mumps. The party was quite amusing. I discovered a Russian colonel friend who faithfully comes to see

Donovan off every morning, plus a couple of others, who I practiced my Russian on. Unfortunately my good Russian teacher has been ill the past few weeks so my progress has been ungrammatical. Did I ever tell you about her? In the good old days, so to speak, she used to be a sort of unofficial teacher for the Corps Diplomatique – and then when the Soviets became isolationists her husband was shot (he had some translating job with the Germans) and she was sent wood chopping in Siberia. That happened in '36 and she remained in the woods until the Russo-German treaty when the Germans got her out. Nice but a hellova snob. She refuses to teach anything less than an ambassador!

Our skiing expedition was again fun. Some Russian kids joined us and one of them I started to teach how to turn. His idea of skiing was to climb to the top of the ravine, schuss and fall in a heap in the ditch at the bottom. We have a date next Sunday. Once you get away from the people who are scared of the bureaucrats, in other words out of Moscow, everyone is very friendly.

Averell's got a new car – more ambassadorial than ever – a large long hearse-like shiny Buick with a large State Department seal painted in gold on both back doors. The American flag, of course, flies up front. Averell's chauffeur thinks he's closer to God than ever before and now practically won't deign to drive me, at least when I'm with one of the "secretaries." When we're alone he teaches me Russian and is much more particular about my pronunciation than either of my teachers!!!

Speaking about servants, did I ever tell you the story of George Gross? He "works" for us – that is, he's had a stroke and can hardly move and sometimes can't talk. Well George is Polish. Come the Revolution he was pressing pants in a West End hotel in London. He saw the light and got transportation to Russia via America then Siberia. He finally reached a town where he saw some English fighting and figuring that the English would of course be fighting on the right side joined up. Some weeks later he discovered to his horror he was fighting with [Admiral] Kolchak against the Revolution so he started his trek around the world again and finally ended up in Moscow jobless. The American relief organization took him on as he spoke English but eventually his past caught up with him and he was sent to a concentration camp up near the Arctic Circle, where he pressed pants for seven years. Finally, one day one of the superintendents told [him] it was all a big mistake – he should have been released three years before. An American correspondent found George half starving in Moscow and he then became pants presser for the press, from there he became pants presser for some of the embassy and finally ended up as a full-fledged embassy employee. His greatest asset at this stage was that he could serve Scotch with a flourish second to no butler. On the liability side he was dirty, unwashed and slightly touched in the head – due to his rather shattering attempts to help the cause of communism. Now George is waiting to get admitted into a poor home – that's his last ambition – to die there. Though incoherent he remembers a lot, all the names of the people he's met etc. and keeps asking me how they all are. I make stories up and that makes him happy.

It's later in the day now. I worked this afternoon – believe it or not – which means trying for ages to get people on the phone (the phone system is erratic, sometimes it works sometimes it doesn't, more often the latter) for an appointment. The procedure from then on is that if you're lucky you get an appointment for three or four days hence, to be checked the day before the appointment. When that day comes you are stalled some more and so on ad infinitum.

Water system is still out. [In] true Russian fashion they found that the water worked in one basement room – so instead of tearing up the pipes that don't work, they tore up the pipes that did work to see why they happened to work. Whereas once we had one sink functioning, now we have none and the government won't provide a fixer until tomorrow at the earliest!!!

Latest rumor is that Donovan won't get off even tomorrow using Becky and flying straight thru. Becky, I presume I've told you, is Averell's C-37 – so named after the pilot's baby daughter. The name Becky is first written in English then Russian with a [pin-up] Varga Girl painted over it.

Now 4 days later they are off. So goodbye. Get Sam to tell you how Becky nearly became an international incident.

Love,
Kathy

Moscow
January 6, 1944

Dear Pam,

Averell and I have just returned from a diplomatic luncheon and in comparison a Biddle function is bliss – something to be remembered and talked about as "really great fun." If it weren't undiplomatic, I'd like to give you a sketch of each of the best of our fellow C.D.'s. Today the Mexican topped luncheon conversation by offering to produce me a Russian boyfriend (first time we met he offered to introduce Averell to a gal) so that I could learn Russian painlessly and quickly. Jesus what a man!! Conversations at lunch center around [one] thing – the difficulties of living – a mighty boring subject and inclined to be embarrassing to me as we live off American canned foods and get the best as far service and heat from the Buro-bin (the section of the Foreign Office that deals with diplomats' living problems).

Christmas, as I look back on it, was a mass of parties and drinking bouts, starting with our own show Xmas eve (for Americans) and ending with a press party complete with take-offs of the American and British dignitaries three days later. As my legs were still weak from being in bed, I spent most of the time trying to convince myself that I wasn't exhausted and as a result survived. For Xmas we threw what old timers said was a party second to no other. Actually it was very simple with gypsy entertainment but very gay dancing and singing. The party ended two hours after the curfew, with no fights and no mishaps other than Averell picking one non-embassy man up by the collar and guiding him quickly out the front door.

New Year's we had a nice quiet time – showing *Casablanca* after dinner and then having a nice time upstairs with the pick of the crop. That film brought back lots of nice memories, so we both enjoyed ourselves.

Jan. 9

A couple of days back was the Greek Orthodox Christmas – the day when Christ was supposedly baptized – so I took that chance to go to the church where the Patriarch (equivalent of the Pope) was officiating. Though the church was packed like an overcrowded stockyard pen, there was no large crowd outside the church waiting for a chance to see the Patriarch or hear at least part of the service. People queue up for bread, transportation, movies and pretty much everything else – except to get religion!

The congregation was made up mostly of women – a fair cross-section of age groups (I was surprised to see so many youngish girls), a smattering of men, mostly old, and a handful of children. The women wore peasant-like shawls and tired oddments of clothing and obviously belonged to the lower-bracketed workers – the ones who chip ice in the streets all day and do other thankless jobs for the sake of a food card. Apart from the female members of the choirs, I saw no well-dressed woman, even by Moscow standards.

Part of the church had been bombed so that most all windows were boarded. One wing had wooden supports and light came from electric candle chandeliers.

Floral decorations were limited to one small fur tree on the right of the altar (the outer one) and a few wreaths and garlands made up of cheap green and white daisies. Somehow they didn't look too appropriate on the beautiful, but ornate altar! The Patriarch and his long-haired and bearded cohorts looked most handsome and dignified in their gold brocade and bejeweled robes. There were about a dozen bishops and priests and page boys, or whatever you call them. The page boys looked about 20 and all three had collars of military uniforms sticking out over their robes. They appeared slightly ill at ease and certainly unimpressed and had to be coached during the ceremony.

We arrived at about ten, just as the service started (me and an embassy secretary and a Soviet interpreter) and were immediately led by church officials onto the outer altar which made us slightly higher than the rest of the congregation. A wooden stool was provided for me to sit on and when I refused it a more comfortable upholstered bench covered with a lace altar cloth was produced. I still refused, as no one is supposed to sit in an Orthodox church, so they brought out a small rug so that I could stand in greater comfort, or something.

As the service progressed and the church became more and more humid and stuffy – the combination of a few thousand people and abundant use of incense – most of the women around me went into a kind of trance. Many were teary and stood, their heads raised, and seemed to only half listen, half watch the ceremony. The little old women, who kept putting out and lighting the altar tapers, were the only ones who didn't seem dazed.

After about an hour and a half, the head priest of the church, who our interpreter called "99% politician and one percent religious" went forward for the sermon. It lasted a few minutes, was short and quite simple and very much to the point. His subject was the meaning of Christmas – he called it "a family day" – a day for reunion. He commiserated with his congregation, he realized, he said, that probably none of his congregation had reason for personal rejoicing, that at least some members of their family were away at the front if not dead etc. Then a few words about victory. Only the first few sentences were necessary before the first sobs came and soon they were general. The oldest sobbed and moaned hopelessly, the younger ones cried. The children just stood still. Everyone was moved.

Then came the blatant statement "the next collection will be for the Red Army." It was so damned cold blooded that it made me mad. The plates started around and I noticed a little shrivelled old woman right under me. She had two ruble notes in her change purse. One worth three rubles and the other one. She held one in each hand – maybe she was undecided, perhaps not – anyway when the plate came her way the Red Army got the bigger note.

After that emotional crisis, the congregation gradually relaxed back into a daze and some again became starry eyed and sleepy. The service continued – a perfection in music – the priests chanted and the two choirs echoed back and forth. It was really beautiful. No instruments, just voices – all perfectly timed. There are all sorts of prayers, even one to the government, as such with no names or the words "Soviet Union" mentioned, instead the seldom-heard word "Russia" appeared frequently.

When the ceremony adjourned to the inner altar, the embassy secretary went back too (females weren't allowed) and the head priest went so far as to push him forward into the inner sanctuary and even wanted him to stand right next to the Patriarch on the altar as his crew knelt for his blessing.

We left at noon, after two hours, the service about half over. One little candle woman thanked me for coming (we were the only foreigners). The crowd was separated by officials and we were ushered out.

Maybe I've been a little cruel in my description, because it is true that more and more Soviets are turning to religion due to the war etc., but somehow the way the church officials treated us, with complete disregard to their religious customs, gave it a phoney air. Their whole attitude seemed to be "You see we want to please."

Enough of that. As you can probably imagine, slowly and surely I'm learning to play bezique!!! We play nearly every evening when we're in and despite my previous ideas, I'm beginning to admit it's a fun game.

My best love to you,
Kathy

Moscow
January 14, 1944

Dear Mary,

I trust you awaken this morning feeling appropriately aged and dignified. It's sad you are not here – it would be a nice excuse to celebrate and perhaps invite some of the more dignified and delightful members of the C.D. to dine and wish you "happy birthday." Yesterday, lunching with the Greek ambassador I scored a major triumph – namely I survived a meal without the subject of "living problems" in Moscow being mentioned once. By chance I knew the Greek was accredited to Japan before coming here, so as a change he discussed at length the internment period, during which he and a little secretary had seen no one but each other and 4 Jap guards! These days I look back at Biddle luncheons and dinners and wonder how I ever thought they were boring!

Last night I had more luck. In the interest of furthering good relations with the Soviets, I had accepted an invitation. I met the leading Soviet novelist and his wife, the wife of a leading cartoonist and a wonderful old man who's best known for his children's books. Rather sorrowfully he told me he had written 40 serious books that no one had ever read. One of his main jobs is translating poetry. He had infinite charm and had the great asset of knowing England. Ivanov,[9] the novelist, looks like a larger, but less fat edition of Max Beaverbrook. He was more or less silent and incessantly moved the beads of a rosary-like bracelet. He says playing with beads keeps him from smoking and drinking too much. His wife[10] was delightful – a grey-haired lady, who is the best-dressed woman I've seen yet. We sat around the table drinking large quantities of tea and less vodka. Our hostess was the American wife of a well-known, but recently dead, playwright by the name of Afinogenov.[11] I gather one of her husband's shows has just opened in New York.

The subject of the Russian issue of *Life* that dealt entirely with Russia came up and unanimously they disliked it. First they pointed out that opposite a full-page picture of Lenin was a Campbell soup ad. That they thought insulting. Secondly they thought that *Life* was pro-German because it picked a rather beautiful girl for "Volga German" type and made all the other Russian nationalities look "feeble minded" in comparison. Third, they laughed at a series on "Moscow's most prominent ballerina" – a gal no one has ever heard of. People are so hard to please but I dare say I'd probably resent and laugh at the product of a Soviet magazine's picture story on U.S.A., particularly if it tried to be all inclusive.

I do hope my magazines start arriving soon and books too. Pam has forwarded those still coming to London but none have arrived yet. I took a batch of old *Saturday Eve. Posts* and *Lifes* over

9 Vsevolod Ivanov (1895–1963).
10 Tamara Kashirina (1900–95), formerly the partner of Soviet playwright Isaac Babel.
11 Alexander Afinogenov (1904–41), killed by a German air raid. He was married to an American dance teacher, Jeannette Schwarz, who renamed herself Jeanya Marling and went to live in the Soviet Union.

to Mme Afinogenov and she had an even older collection. It was almost pathetic the way her friends devoured them, borrowed them, promising to return them immediately. There's a terrific interest in anything American and the women clamor for fashion ads, even though most of them can't get material for dresses. The members of the artist set of course are very well off. They are, socially speaking, the blue bloods and are allowed to associate with foreigners (I suppose on the grounds that they will be least contaminated by foreign ideas) and most importantly the artists and writers get top food rations. I can't remember if I told you or not but you are given a food category. Army generals and commissars are at the top, artists and Army and heavy laborers next, then clerks, then other laborers, women, children and dependents at the bottom. In bread, the category ranges from 800 grams per day to 150, quite a lot even allowing for the fact that this is the real land of privilege.

New series of "regulations" have recently been put in on the subject of theater seats for the Red Army. Generals can only sit in the first 15 rows, officers must sit downstairs, and enlisted men must sit in the gallery. Frinstance, if a general can't get a seat far up front, it's just too bad. He damned well does not go to the theater. Another item, it's beneath the dignity of a Red Army officer to hang on to a street car. (This rule came in soon after the uniforms were changed.) Odds on that means he has to walk. This certainly is a great country for the strong.

Saw what I figured an odd interpretation of *Anna Karenina* the other night. The husband was dignified and you sympathized with him rather than with Anna and her lover. The lover was a little Jewish squirt with an ill-fitting guard's uniform and Anna was played by a 45-year-old woman. Resulting effect was a middle-aged woman trying to recapture the last bloom of youth and falling for a little gigolo, who incidentally wore pink nail polish. Needless to say I didn't particularly like it but I suppose the form fits into the present government's condemnation of home breakers. (It is now harder to get a divorce.) Another evening I saw *School for Scandal* beautifully done. Seeing plays is supposed to be a good way to learn Russian – so my teacher says – and as I don't have much time to study or do homework – I'm more than willing to oblige her by entertaining myself at the theater. Averell still hasn't gone yet to any ballet or play that hasn't been an official function. I'm hoping to break that down, because when I go out there is not much for him to do but work, and war or no war there's a limit to hours spent on work.

At the moment I'm as busy as hell – result of a minor breakdown of our secretary – which means I do the sort of paper-doll-cutting-like work and mimeographing etc. that is involved in getting a daily news bulletin out.

Today I had a most unsuccessful interview with my contact in the official culture (with a capital C) organization. I'm trying to arrange photo shows on various U.S. war effort topics and today I just wasn't in the mood to be politely stalled. Of course I was, but the gal I interviewed was made to feel damned awkward while doing it, which gave me a minor feeling of compensation.

The new *Newsweek* man has arrived. He came up and had a drink with us tonight and I don't think he's much good, but maybe he just creates a lousy first impression. I haven't much patience with correspondents who write <u>unhelpful</u> stories for the sake of a headline during the war.

I figure if I just write you, I'll have at least a type of diary which may be fun for me to re-read. Needless to say, I'm not keeping a diary (I guess I'm not the type and basically my personal thoughts ain't the secret variety) so please don't mind if I ramble on and remember a State Department censor is also being bored!

It's sad that Ira Eaker has been kicked out of the 8th Air Force.[12] I never did like Spaatz much. I hear too that our flat in 3 Grosvenor Square has been vacated by Jock and Lou Ordway. At times I get mad as hell at the idea of sitting in London for two years and then having to miss the final act. One lucky thing, Moscow life is so completely the antithesis that it doesn't make me much homesick for London excitement. This place is exciting too in its own way. It's friendless here but that's not really necessary and luckily I get some pleasure out of

12 In early 1944 Eaker was appointed Commander-in-Chief of the Mediterranean Allied Air Forces.

boring people. London had its advantages on that score – it sort of gave me a primary education.

I'm finished now on news, and damned sleepy (before I started this I had a 10–1 bezique session with Averell).

My love to you all,

Kathleen

CHAPTER 16

'THE KATYN FOREST TURNED OUT TO BE A SMALL MEASLY PINE TREE WOOD'

Within weeks of her arrival in Moscow, Kathy was witness to and an inadvertent participant in an outrageous hoax: the Soviet cover-up of the Katyn massacre. In spring 1940 the Soviets executed some 22,000 Polish POWs who had been captured by the Red Army during its invasion of Poland's eastern territories (present-day western Belarus and western Ukraine) in September 1939. They were mostly military officers but among them were a goodly number of police and government officials. The initiator of the killing spree was Soviet security chief Lavrenti Beria, but his proposal to arraign the Poles before NKVD tribunals with a view to trial and execution was endorsed by Stalin and the rest of the Politburo.

Several thousand of the murdered Poles were buried in mass graves in the Katyn forest, near Smolensk. The Smolensk area was captured by the Germans in summer 1941 and in 1942 they began to disinter the bodies of the Polish POWs. In 1943 they exposed the crime to the whole word, precipitating a breakdown in Soviet–Polish diplomatic relations. When the Soviets recaptured the area in summer 1943 they immediately organised to present the murder site as a Nazi atrocity. In January 1944 Stalin created a special Katyn commission headed by Nikolai Burdenko, the surgeon-general of the Red Army. Among its other members were top diplomat V.P. Potemkin and the writer Alexei Tolstoy, whom Kathy got to know quite well during her time in Moscow.

The Soviet show included an invitation to Western journalists to visit the Katyn site. According to Henry Cassidy, it was Kathy's idea that she should go too, and at Ave's behest John Melby also went. Prompted by Kathy's inclusion, the Soviets laid on a special train to take the correspondents to Smolensk. As Bill Lawrence wrote at the time, it was 'probably the most unusual press junket in the history of the world – and certainly of the Soviet Union'.

The trip took place on 21–23 January. Kathy kept copious notes in which she recorded her conclusion that the Germans, not the Soviets, were responsible for the killings. Among her annotations was the following observation: '1,355 Russ. Jews killed in Smolensk.' On 25 January Ave informed Washington that 'the general evidence and testimony are inconclusive but Kathleen and [Melby] believe probability massacre perpetrated by Germans'.

A month later, Melby and Kathy wrote separate reports about what they had witnessed. Kathy's report was more detailed than the letter to Mary and Pam that is reproduced below but broadly similar. As she noted at the outset, the press group was not qualified to judge the scientific evidence presented to them, and they were expected to accept Soviet claims about what had happened. Nonetheless, in her opinion 'the Poles were murdered by the Germans', the most convincing evidence being 'the methodical manner' in which the killings were carried out – a view shared by Bill Lawrence and other journalists who made the trip. Melby's conclusion was a little more circumspect: 'It is apparent that the evidence in the Russian case is incomplete in several respects, that it is badly put together, and that the show was put on for the benefit of the correspondents without opportunity for independent investigation or verification. On balance, however, and despite the loopholes, the Russian case is convincing.'

In a dignified testimony to a 1952 congressional committee investigating the Katyn atrocity, Kathy explained patiently that her conclusions had been based on the information available to her at the time. 'You had access to every side of the picture, which I did not have available to me,' she noted. 'I would say, having read your [interim] report, that my opinion is that the Russians did kill the Poles.'

Moscow
January 24, 1944

Dear Mouche,

This is just a belated way of saying I'm sorry I didn't send you a wire on your birthday. Fact is I forgot – what with the flurry of getting ready to go to Smolensk to see the murdered Poles.

Everything was super swell – a whole private train just for the press. I don't think even Averell could have gotten more for nothing! The trip was on the gruesome side but most interesting and I thoroughly enjoyed it & the chance to see some countryside other than Moscow for a change. I imagine one of these days I'll get around to sitting down and typing out for you what happened etc. At the moment it's a bit late & I'm too sleepy. As usual Averell & I played "just one more game" of bezique from ten until one. When things started getting hot here at the beginning of the Polish–Russian issue, we used to start playing bezique at one or two in the morning. My problem was how to stay awake until Averell got through work – Russia hours of work conflict with U.S. sleeping hours.

I've been doing a certain amount of skiing right outside Moscow – on Sundays & then occasionally during the lunch hour. One of our code clerks & a Norwegian secretary are both enthusiasts and not bad skiers, so we skip lunch and get some exercise clambering around one slope with the Russian enthusiasts. It's all very genial, but unfortunately no friendships made informally get followed up.

[Kathleen]

Moscow
January 28, 1944

Dear Mary [copied to Pam],

I'm in a stinking temper at myself for contracting sinus so this may turn into an unkindly worded letter! However, even sinus has its compensations. Last night I had adequate excuse to sup in bed and thereby missed a party given by some slightly moth-eaten Russians for the pick of the dip. corps. Averell went and apparently he was belle of the ball (that's not his version). He reports that by Moscow standards the party was a good one. But as you probably realize, our standards are nearing rock bottom!

One nice thing happened night before last – the much-awaited O.W.I. clerk turned up after a long trek by truck, train et al. from Tehran, all of which means that what I call my "paper doll cutting" activities can cease. Hitherto, I've had to prepare and send out to about 70 people in town, a daily news bulletin – which involves mimeographing and clamping together mimeograph sheets – not what you'd call stimulating to the mind occupation. Now the clerk will do it, and among other things I'll be able, I hope, to spend more time in the fruitless study of Russian. Speaking about Russian, I've discovered to my horror that it can't be translated word by word from English and come out respectably. When I do that, I can be understood but that's about all. However, luckily the French sequence of words and phrases in a sentence is nearly respectable when transferred into Russian. Once I tried going out with a non-English-speaking friend (Russian being our only known language) and it was really hard work. We went to the theater – was *Pygmalion* – which was easy enough to understand as I'd read the play, but the meal prior to theater plus conversation during the three half-hour-long intermissions was a damned exhausting procedure for both of us.

We've been out skiing couple of Sundays – and me a couple of times during the week – during the lunch hour. We've found a slope right outside Moscow, where most of the Russian enthusiasts go. Some bring slalom poles so we practice together and have a nice time. Apparently last Sunday, when I was in Smolensk, they had some slalom races – so maybe one of these days I'll be doing that. When Averell comes skiing we're quite a procession. One of his N.K.V.D. boys wears skis and gets halfway down the hill on his fanny mostly and spends the rest of his time trying to keep Averell in view with the minimum of movement on his part. The other two boys stand in greater dignity at the top of the hill.

Our Smolensk excursion was quite an event for me – being my first trip out of Moscow. The press department let me go I guess because they couldn't very well refuse seeing what the story was.

We were first going down there by car, but then plans were changed and a private train was provided – for us, two Foreign Office press officials and a bevy of N.K.V.D. The train was most sumptuous – clean – two cars with compartments and a diner. I had a compartment to myself and most of the others had three in a room. There was congestion only in the mornings – as 25 people for one john is quite a number, particularly when all the men shaved.

Though Smolensk isn't much more than 200 miles away we took a goodly 18 hours to get there – our speed at best was not more than 30 mph and we spent hours on various sidings while priority supply trains passed en route for the front. Smolensk itself hadn't much left of it – and compared to bombed English towns it gave the feeling of being completely dead and deserted. The town itself is on the top of the hill overlooking the Dnieper, with the railway station on the opposite side of the river. Back in July '41, the Germans took the town quickly but had to fight a long time to capture the railway station – during that fight about fifty percent of the damage was done – the rest was German demolition last autumn. Smolensk has a lovely old Kremlin wall – the third oldest in Russia – dating back to mid-16th century. The Kremlin wall is fairly intact but in the town itself there are only some 64 buildings now whole out of nearly eight thousand. The present population is about a sixth of the prewar figure and they were occupied in getting the railway station in order or getting on with their own business of fixing up shelter to live in. Driving down the street, you'd see stove pipes sticking out of ground-floor windows – the cellars are the only really livable places.

One thing surprised me – the Dnieper at Smolensk isn't much wider than the Ramapo, where we cross at Arden station. Somehow I'd figured it would be at least a second Hudson. We traveled around in a convoy of cars – two of which were American trucks – but everyone else drove in slow pony-drawn sleighs – tough work for the ponies as there was only a slight amount of slush on the side of the main road – the middle was bare.

After a short tour of the town we were conveyed out to the Katyn "forest" about half hour out. Being one of the main highways to the front, traffic was considerable and our driver spent most of his time sitting on his horn. Going out and coming back from Katyn – about 10 miles each way – I noticed four trucks that had been either turned over or badly ditched, which is a goodly amount considering the road itself was in good condition.

The Katyn Forest turned out to be a small measly pine tree wood. We were shown the works by a big Soviet doctor who looked like a chef in white peaked cap, white apron and rubber gloves. With relish he showed us a sliced Polish brain carefully placed on a dinner plate for inspection purposes. And then we began a tour to each and every one of the seven graves. We must have seen a good many thousand corpses or parts of corpses, all in varying degrees of decomposition, but smelling about as bad. (Luckily I had a cold, so was less bothered by the stench than others.) Some of the corpses had been dug up by the Germans in the spring of '43 after they'd first launched their version of the story. These were laid in neat orderly rows, from six to eight bodies deep. The bodies in the remaining graves had been tossed in every which way. All the time we were there, the regular work of exhuming continued by men in army uniform. Somehow I didn't envy them! The most interesting thing, and the most convincing bit of evidence, was that every Pole had been shot through the back of the head with a single bullet. Some of the bodies had their hands tied behind their backs, all of which is typically German. Next on the program we were taken into post mortem tents. These were hot and stuffy and smelled to high heaven. Numerous post mortems were going on, each and every body is given a thorough going over, and we witnessed several. If Shirley had been there we might have been able to understand a little better than we did – personally I was amazed at how whole the corpses were. Most still had hair. Even I could recognize their internal organs and they still had a good quantity of red-colored 'firm' meat on their thighs. You see, the Germans say that the Russians killed the Poles back in '40, whereas the Russians say the Poles weren't killed until the fall of '41, so there's quite a discrepancy in time. Though the Germans had ripped open the Poles' pockets, they'd missed some written documents. While I was watching, they found one letter dated the summer of '41, which is damned good evidence.

So ended the first section of our tour. All feeling as though our clothes still retained the smell, we trooped back to our train for a hearty meal. Afterwards we were bundled back to town, where the Atrocity Commission received us. We had a long session with them – lasting until about eight o'clock – had dinner and then returned for another two-hour session. The committee room was warm and stuffy and I was very sleepy. Being scared of falling asleep, I kept verbatim notes – and thus kept from disgracing myself. We were given every bit of evidence the committee had unearthed and saw some of the key witnesses and were allowed to ask them our own questions. We were shown all the various documents that had so far been found (the committee had only been working a week) which included some U.S. notes and six twenty-dollar gold pieces!!!

Finally the show ended and we came back to Moscow. We tried to persuade the Foreign Office press people to let us stay another day to see the town, but the train's schedule had to be kept, so we came back to Moscow. It would have been interesting to have talked to some of the town folk – we noticed that the marketplace was doing thriving business, but couldn't see what was changing hands, other than huge logs of wood. Quite by chance I spotted a hospital (a converted one). There were huge truck-like ambulances with red crosses painted on their sides and people being taken out of them. Conceivably it was a base hospital as the front isn't much more than eighty miles away.

I did get a chance to talk to one inhabitant, though. While we were being recited a speech about damage done to Smolensk's Lenin Library I sneaked off with the Christian Science Monitor correspondent, who speaks good Russian, and started questioning a bunch of inquisitive onlookers. We discovered that during the German occupation those who worked got 200 grams of bread a day, those who didn't and children got only 75, which is sort of starvation ration. They told us the Germans took everything of any value away with them and destroyed the rest, killed thousands of people etc. The peasant woman who did most of the talking, talked in a calm matter-of-fact way – just as though she were discussing the weather. These people certainly are tough. There didn't seem to be very many kids around the town but those I saw were sliding on the ice, playing with snow, just as they do in Moscow. I guess by now they are used to living in a destroyed town, but it looked pretty depressing to me. But cleaned up – all rubble had been removed – what remained might have been a historic ruin – just the shells of former houses with jagged walls, surrounded with a pink and grey brick fortification. The town proper is on top of a hill – so it must have been quite pretty – with the main road circling it and smaller alleys going straight up. It will be a terrific job rebuilding – someone told us "We hope the Germans will have to do it for us."

One other sidelight – back on the train as we had our fifth meal for the day (all identical and starting with vodka) and finally around four a.m. a bunch of us started singing Russian and American songs. When the train stopped in a station or siding or something, the senior-ranking Soviet official with us asked us to stop. I guess he figured it wasn't sufficiently dignified for slightly maudlin voices to be heard coming out of a private train. Then the moment the train resumed its motion, he once more loosened up and became natural and gay again.

[Kathleen]

Moscow
January 31, 1944

Dear Mary,

Rumor has it that an aircraft is soon on its way to the outer world which means mail can go off. Please tell Marie she wrote us very fine letters indeed via Archie C.K. They are the first we have received since the beginning of Dec.

It's sad about not getting Xmas packages – or the case with my ski things – but the anticipation is exciting.

At long last we finally entertained formally last night. Due to the Supreme Soviet being in session, Molotov was unable to come as he had to make a speech, so minus their big boss the Foreign Office people were a lot less stiff. We invited either men or women of note and asked them to bring a husband or wife as the case might be. The procedure of inviting Russians amuses me slightly. A list is sent to the protocol department of the F.O. and they let us know which of the people we want to have are OK to invite!

Last night a good many officials and people like directors of movies etc. turned up with wives. Most all the females were elegantly, if not chicly, dressed, and they almost invariably wore their hair (usually dyed) high in front and long behind – sort of à la Ginger Rogers, which eyed by an American, gives a tartish impression.

Our merchant king's palace lends itself very well to a reception. We cleared out the movie room and had little tables so people could sit while eating, which proved very successful. For supper I bagged what I thought looked like the most genial Russian couple – he turned out to be an N.K.V.D. bigwig and both could understand a little English. That coupled with my stinking Russian meant word by word interpreting wasn't essential. Then I discovered a very nice Commissar for Public Health who talked French and a couple of genial movie directors – all new to me – so all in all the eating session was successful.

Of the actresses and ballerinas we invited one came – a swell gal – middle-aged – who plays all the heroine leads in the Tolstoy–Chekhov type plays. She was a great asset and charmed all the single diplomats of South American vintage.

We had an unpredictable orchestra – 10 pieces which include tuba and a lot of brass (we'd asked for a five-piece orchestra consisting mostly of strings so as to have a background of music). As it was, the band started with a military march after about three quarters of the guests had arrived – a nice blaring Soviet march – and was very hurt when we said "no" they could not end the party with a repeat.

After the guests had fed themselves, some danced and I spent a good bit of energy trying to get stiff generals and admirals to dance with me – some would, but some refused!

Due to our special request, the American press remained sober for a change and refrained from cornering the guests for interviewing purposes – something they are apt to do, unless told not to. As it was they were well behaved. In fact, with the exception of a British correspondent and Tolstoy, who always gets gaily drunk anyway, the party was amazingly sober.

Incidentally, if you all want sort of honey gossip of our life here get in touch with Bill Donovan. He'll love to take you out on the town if he is in N.Y.C. and you'll get all the kind of information that's too long to write.

Just before I started this, I had two Russians in for tea – neither of whom I like particularly – but one is a party member, the other a private citizen who works on the side for the Y.M.C.A. institute. One talked English so I asked what the hell was the reason for the *Pravda* rumor about Britishers negotiating peace. Reason may amuse you – it does me as it's evidently (obviously) the "party" line: it was done so as to help Churchill, and incidentally Roosevelt, combat the reactionary groups in Britain and U.S. who wanted a negotiated peace! When I said no such groups existed, they both smiled between themselves, unbelieving, and I figured being their hostess I'd better not get too nasty. The Russians sure have an insolence I find hard to take, but I'm learning!

Bestest love to you,
Kathleen

Moscow
January 31, 1944

Dear Pam,

Archie arrived back yesterday after what sounded like a grisly trip "over the top".[1] They were all air sick, the oxygen system broke down, and some of the people were really quite badly off.

This morning after breakfast Averell and I spent a wonderful hour or so reading your letters together. It made me awfully homesick listening to your daily doings. By comparison, Moscow ain't even a wee bit gay. There isn't anyone who's worth cultivating as a friend and what little entertaining we do, or have done for us, comes under the heading of effort with a capital "E" – certainly not pleasure.

Your rug is wonderful – and will be perfect if and when I ever go on another trip like the Smolensk one. Incidentally, I'm enclosing a

1 Reference to the flight from Tehran to Moscow, which crosses the Caucasus mountains.

copy of a letter I wrote Mary on the subject of our trip. I suppose by now you're getting a lot of rehash in the press about it. But I certainly found the evidence very convincing.

Last night being the President's birthday, we found an excuse to finally entertain formally. We had nearly 150 people – the first time we had the diplomatic corps around en masse, plus a goodly number of Russians. We invited various officials and members of the "arts."

All in all, a good many of the Russians seemed very nice, very genial. It's sort of unfortunate that we can't really get to know them informally. The Maiskys didn't come. In fact, he seems to be very much in the background at the moment. One swell girl came – an actress – middle-aged (I'm being a little cruel). She was very gay and decorative and I thought extremely nice and the diplomats of South American vintage fell violently for her!!!

[Kathleen]

Moscow
February 1, 1944

Pam Honey,

Another [letter] on your letters. It sounded very sad – one farewell party after another. The good group seems to have disbanded. It must be horribly lonely for you now.

Today we got a lot of O.W.I. pictures from London, which included one of baby Winston & the American G.I. Get your O.W.I. contact to produce you one if you haven't seen it. Also some of the Tehran & Cairo Big Three photos have some good pictures of your friend – Brendan can probably get them for you.

Last night we dined with the Dutch ambassador and his Rumanian wife. She's the cold beautiful chic type, speaks about 10 languages, 5 perfectly, is a doctor in her own right. One of those females who make me feel very ignorant. It was very pleasant by our rock-bottom Moscow standards. They're the only really nice couple in town.

Oh dear, I hope I'm not making Moscow sound too dreary. Socially it's a deadly bore – but on the other side it's very interesting and has its compensations occasionally. Actually, I'm enjoying myself in an odd sort of way, as there's really no one I'd want to call a "friend" or even want to see once I left this place – which is the real test. Compared to London or home, I guess I'd honestly hate it. But everything here is completely & entirely new and that alone makes it worthwhile.

Since I started this a little Russian communist friend (party member who still carries Lenin's colors but personally enjoys the liberties & privileges of the chosen few) with a gal – who, incidentally, works on the side for the N.K.V.D. – came in for tea. Ever since I returned from Smolensk they've been trying to get hold of me.

I'm ending now as it's time for this to go off. If Averell doesn't get a letter written, don't be angry. He's been terribly busy the past few days with work & added to that has to attend meetings of the Supreme Soviet.

Bestest love to you,

Kathy

CHAPTER 17

'THE PRESS RETURNED FROM LENINGRAD A COUPLE OF DAYS BACK FULL OF GRUESOME TALES OF THE SIEGE'

The year 1944 saw a series of Red Army victories, beginning in January with the lifting of the German–Finnish blockade of Leningrad. German armies had reached the outskirts of the city in September 1941, Hitler's order being to erase the Soviet Union's second city from the face of the earth by a combination of blockade and bombardment. The Germans' thousand-day siege of Leningrad was aided by the Finns, who had reoccupied territory lost to the Soviets during the 'Winter War' of 1939–40. During the blockade, some 600,000 civilians died of starvation and disease.

Moscow
February 8, 1944

Dear Mary,

Where is Shirley now? We gave ourselves a private movie showing last night of newsreels – "the latest" for distribution among "Soviets" and we saw a batch of medical outposts – which made us wonder if he's moved over to the mainland. I got me a nice invitation to visit General Ira's new headquarters, which I guess is Algiers – and get filled up with tennis and sunshine. Wouldn't it be fun if I could go and drop in on Shirley into the bargain!

In the way of work, my "paper doll cutting" activities continue. Now we have a clerk to get out the daily news bulletin, so I'm now involved in filing pictures – thousands of them.

Great news! We have a new member of our lovely little group of diplomatic corps in the form of a minister from Ethiopia.[1] He's very black, very hinkie and quite tiny. Averell says he's "sweet" whatever the hell that means.

There's not much in the way of excitement to report. We lead nice orderly sedate lives. Our one real source of enjoyment and fun is Bob. Of late he's decided against learning Russian on the grounds that it might futurely prove reason for his being sent back here and that, of course, he says he would never do. Dear Bob, I've gotten very fond of him. He loves life only when it's ordered and to schedule. So Averell's habit of working until way past midnight horrifies him to the core. However, he enjoys being teased about his Republican conservatism and that helps make up for some of his discomfort. He lives next door to me – on the other side of my closet – so each morning he pounds in and wakes me in time for the 9 o'clock B.B.C. News (frequently he oversleeps). The last few days he's decided to stop hoarding a couple of cans of orange juice – so now he wakes me with a glass – which is the height of luxury by any standards.

I've found me a new buddy in the form of a Czech girl. She talks a lot of Russian and little English, so every now and then I have her to tea and call that "studying Russian" – infinitely more enjoyable than translating sentences like: "When you go to a tailor, what do you ask him?" and such like.

Couple of days back we gave a small reception for our mission of doctors, the British penicillin man[2] and the Soviet scientists who've been taking them around. My attempts at conversation were lousy. Daily I learn and relearn Russian words but still I can't even do a decent job of passing the time of day socially.

---

1 Lorenzo Taezaz (1900–47), formerly Ethiopia's representative at the League of Nations in Geneva and said at that time to be the most significant black diplomat on the world stage.

2 Howard Florey (1898–1968) was actually an Australian pathologist, who shared the 1945 Nobel Prize for the development of the first antibiotic. He was part of an Anglo-American scientific expedition to the USSR, where he met Zinaida Yermolyeva (1898–1974), the leading Soviet microbiologist.

I went shopping the other day for ordinary dish towels – the cheapest findable cost 10 coupons and the equivalent of $1 apiece. Silk stockings cost 5 coupons and range from $2 up to $5 (this is at the diplomatic store, where prices are controlled and very low and reasonable by open-market standards). Thank God we don't have to try and set up a house here and buy linen and china and what have you. Our bed blankets, thanks to Admiral Standley, are Navy ones, with a few army khaki ones thrown in. It will certainly be wonderful to sleep under cream-colored blankets and unscratchy sheets once more!

Goodbye to you.

Best love,

Puff

Moscow
February 14, 1944

Dear Mary,

Yesterday, being Sunday and a day of rest, when to all outward appearances the embassy closes, Ave and I went skiing. Just as I was comfortably tired of climbing back up our hill (which we share with about a hundred others), a bunch of really good skiers came out well armed with slalom poles so I joined in and ended up so tired that I could hardly walk. They insisted on setting the tightest slalom I've ever tried to get thru and that, added to the icy, rutting snow conditions and my absolutely stinking skiing, made things not too easy for me. I don't think I ever managed to make one run without either falling flat or at least taking out one gate. There were a couple of damned good girls – as good as the best in America, and some top-notch men. They were very genial and talked slowly so's I'd be able to at least get the gist of their conversation. It turned out to be an invitation to enter the Moscow slalom championship next Sunday. It remains to be seen if I so do. Ave may not want me to enter as I'll obviously do badly. With luck I'd come in near to last, without I'd certainly be last – something that wouldn't bother me in the least, but he may not want to have me make a fool of myself.

This morning I spent a goodly amount of time getting a driver's license. Our procurement agent assured me it would take only a few minutes. Oddly enough, no questions asked about my knowledge of traffic regulations. Then they decided it might be fun to go driving in a nice "American" car. They were charmed at my ability to turn around in a huge wide street without having to back – plus being able to back into a parking space, with the net result that for a packet of Chesterfields I got a license.

Last night I went to see *Othello* – and it's completely delightful. The stage settings were elaborate to a degree, acting terrific and of course the language completely unintelligible. It's one thing to be able to understand conversational Russian and quite another to get more than an occasional word out of Russian Shakespeare. The play started at seven and ended four hours plus later. I went with the British second in command of their embassy, the Netherlands ambass. and an R.A.F.er. All three are experts on Shakespeare so they rivaled in complete recitation of the main speeches.

Our plumbing is once more on the blink – this time thank God we have cold water if not hot, so I suppose I shouldn't complain. Actually, I wouldn't mind, only the cold water is so damned cold that I can't even wash my hands without their going numb.

The [press] bunch here sure are the damnedest guys I've ever run into. The other evening at a cocktail party three of them attacked Averell on grounds that he was not looking after the interests of Americans in Moscow, namely the correspondents. In other words that he hadn't asked [for] Stalin's interference on story matters!!

Bestest love to you all,

Kathleen

PS Tell Marie Ave's fine – works too hard, takes no exercise, hasn't used his axe even once, but seems to be bearing up fine.

Moscow
February 16, 1944

Dear Mary,

Today, after a good many attempts, I went and visited a school – a girls' one. Apparently when the education reform went through last fall, schools were broken down into boys' schools and girls' schools. As I'd anticipated, the school I visited was an extra-swell one – it looked to me like what you'd expect the average U.S. town public school to look like – only nice and new. There were large, light windows with curtains, tiled or evenly wooded floors, clean freshly painted walls etc. I was told it was an average-sized school – 800 girls ranging from 8 to 18. Most of the children were extremely well dressed by Russian standards – far above average. I was told it was a school for the surrounding district, about 50% being the orphans of Red Army men (presumably high-ranking officers).

I listened to one class – in English. The teacher spoke with a passable accent but talking to her afterwards, I discovered her vocabulary is rather limited. Some of the girls were almost impossible to understand, but they all knew their lessons very well – which consisted of verb tenses in conditional sentences, a passage from *David Copperfield* etc. It was quite interesting but the best part was afterwards. A group of about ten had been rounded up to ask me questions about American education – how it worked etc. Aside from our educational system they wanted to know if schoolchildren could go to movies and the theater without a teacher (they can't here, not even with parents' permission); what school kids at home were doing to help the war effort (thank God for O.W.I. pictures on that subject); what kind of organizations there were for school kids (the Girl Guide variety), what they did etc.; what Russian movies were popular in America, which were shown (I was stumped on that one); what punishments there were for bad children; whether uniforms were worn; whether they could write to American school kids; whether Russian was taught in schools and so forth. They seemed pleased to hear that basically there's not much difference in systems.

As far as I can gather, schools here are very strict and the main reason kids aren't allowed in movies is so as to avoid truancy. (Even college students can't go to the movies or theaters without written permission from their teachers!) The younger kids have classes just in the morning and the older ones from 9 'til 3. One meal, consisting of tea and either candy or crackers, is served in the middle of the day. They call it "breakfast." Tuition costs about 200 rubles, but the children of Red Army men get educated without any charge. Orphans of army men also get clothed, if their mother can't buy them clothes. Due to inflation, 200 rubles is approximately the equivalent of two packets of Chesterfields!

In a couple of weeks the so-called Red Army Day is celebrated. Each class is getting up a poster – with pictures and a story telling of the glory of the R.A. I saw some of them and they're damned good.

The older girls wore dresses or skirts and the invariable Russian variety of gaudy "Austrian sweater." Half wore high heels and the rest wore the Russian valinki (high felt boot). The school was well heated. They get a medical inspection at least twice a year, however I didn't see one girl wearing glasses. A couple in the English class were very near sighted. I imagine by now I've bored you enough on the subject of education. One more thing – in line with the Soviet policy to return the women to the home, girls now get taught sewing – cooking they'll eventually get taught, but momentarily, due to food situation, that's not possible.

Last night I went to the Moscow symphony – the orchestra consisted of both men and women – the women wearing a dinner jacket and black skirt. It was really very pleasant – but an oddly mixed program, which intermingled Bach with operatic overtures and modern Russian music.

Yesterday Averell sprung the question "what embassy would you consider the least desirable to dine at?" I guessed like mad and when I gave up he said I just hadn't guessed bad enough. Finally it turned out we're eating chez the Afghans on Friday. This place is fun though as an experience. However, I can't imagine how anyone would ever take diplomacy for a career. It involves too damn much tea and cookie pushing.

Unfortunately, I can't persuade Averell to take an interest in either the theater or the ballet, which is sad because I'm sure he'd enjoy it if he ever made the initial effort (he goes only when he "has" to). He's just started on a new recreational project – that of reading *War and Peace*, but I don't think he's gotten very far yet! After dinner, he and the first officer and one of the secretaries have violent games of a thing called bottle pool. Sometime during his life Averell learned to play billiards – because he's got a mass of tricky shots and expressions up his sleeve.

[Kathleen]

Moscow
February 19, 1944

Dear Mary,

The press returned from Leningrad a couple of days back full of gruesome tales of the siege, during which the regular population got a ration of about 5 oz of bread daily and not much else. Apparently, those who were willing to exchange their household effects for more bread or meat on the black market were the ones who survived. They had quite a system – a good painting would be worth so many ounces of meat, a piece of furniture that could be broken up into firewood worth so much more etc. During the worst period there was no water, electricity, fuel or transportation. Adding to that, most all the windows had been blown in by the shelling and bombing, so life wasn't what you'd call very bearable.

The press visited an engine repair factory that, although it was only four kilometers from the German line, kept operating despite almost daily shelling. It wasn't unusual for workers (mostly women at that) to die of starvation at their machines. There they got double the Leningrad bread ration (equivalent to two and a half slices of bread daily) and occasionally a little muddy soup.

Then I gather the boys were taken on a two-day Cook's tour of the cultural monuments of the city. They saw every inch of the Winter Palace and various other museums. Though all the museum pieces had been removed prior to the siege days, the press got an earful of what wondrous collections once were on display in the rooms. Needless to say that didn't interest them much.

En route home I gather the great Mr Cassidy of the A.P. and Ed Angley of the *Chicago Sun* decided in a drunken moment that they could walk to Moscow faster than the train, so when the train stopped at a siding they got out and started to "walk to Moscow." Luckily the engineer spotted them and stopped the train and picked them up.

[Kathleen]

Moscow
February 22, 1944

Dear Pam,

Now let's see what you'd like to hear about our social life perhaps? High spot last week was an evening chez Afghan ambassador.[3] He's here minus all signs of a harem. I'd hoped we'd have beautiful orientals come out with the coffee and do a dance – or don't Moslems go in for that sort of thing outside of Hollywood? Despite the lack of decorative females, the Afghan had himself quite a fair-sized dinner. In other words he was killing off all the people he owed meals to. Our group included him, his silent son (adolescent age) and some of his embassy officials, the entire Persian ambassadorial family (Averell sat next to pimply daughter number one at dinner), the Ethiopian and us and the Dutch. We had a seven-course dinner, which was delicious, and languages were mixed. I discovered that the Ethiopian spoke French, but was hard to get talking on anything of import. He's the terribly shy type. (Later we discovered he thought I was Averell's sister, which Averell thought was wonderful!) The Persian boy being about 22 or 23 considered himself very much a man of the world and as a matter of fact is extremely well educated. He's an engineer, fresh out of college, speaks beautiful French plus I guess a dozen other languages. We discussed poetry, music, jazz, and finally I discovered that he thought Kipling's "If" the most semi-moving poem he's come across in English (his knowledge of English literature is by no means limited). That fact floored me a little. But maybe we and the Iranians don't think quite alike.

Moscow
February 23, 1944

Dear Mary,

A major event occurred this morning – sun came out for 10 minutes and that was mighty nice to see. Bob is beginning to despair of the weather ever getting really cold, not that he enjoys 40° below zero weather. It's just that he wants to be able to tell the "grandchildren"

3 Sultan Ahmed Khan.

someday about his life in Moscow and be able to boast about the cold. Thank goodness I haven't gotten to that stage yet!!

Today is Red Army Day so the flags are flying in all the main streets and tonight we go once more to a huge Soviet reception. One of our less gallant members of the press asked Clark Kerr if he wouldn't please put on a pass-out scene similar to his November 7th one for the benefit of the newer arrivals of the press. Archie apparently didn't think that remark one bit funny!

The Foreign Office phoned me on Saturday to say that Mme Maisky wanted to call on me. So I allowed as how I'd be "in" on Monday at five. We had a very pleasant chat about her household problems and how much I liked Moscow. Then oddly enough she started on the subject of all things – the Poles – wasn't it true that all Americans supported the Soviet position? I'd been properly primed to answer that one, in case it was asked. So I said my piece and then I asked her if she thought the problem was soluble (the problem was settling Russo-Polish relations). She figured it was soluble, but really not very important! I thought that kind of interesting, but unfortunately she refused to expand. She's the gal who, so London rumors had it, the N.K.V.D. sent along with Maisky to keep him in line. Somehow, now that I'm in Moscow that story just doesn't make sense, but it's interesting to think that I once thought it possible.

Sunday I went ski racing and I think Averell ended up almost more nervous than I was. It was a lovely grey snowy and cold day, but despite that quite a number of people turned up to clutter up the hill. There was an Army Band that played anthems and even good old U.S. college songs. The race for the kids came first, then the girls and finally the men. All three had a separate course, so's the ruts wouldn't get too bad and for the girls it was about a 45 second run (two runs on the same course). There were ten girls in the race and I finished fourth but somehow one of the girls got given penalties, so in combined times I came in third. Legally I should have been fourth as there was three girls who were a good deal better than I am – two professional instructors, the girl that got the penalties being the best in Russia, so one of her ski club mates told me. She certainly was a good skier, beautiful form etc. but she lost her head or something and tried to go too fast. The gal that won it skies about like Gretchen Fraser.[4]

I went down the coast like a middle-aged pregnant woman – skis ungracefully a couple of feet apart, but somehow in that position managed to angle myself thru the flush without mishap. As far as technique went, the men who placed were comparable to U.S. amateurs, but I've never seen such good kid skiers. One boy of 15 yr. placed fourth in the men's race – his time being only a couple of seconds behind the winner. The Red Army men, girls and boys all wore red sweaters, which was most effective, and any kind of pants. However, my costume was much the chicest. It consisted of your grey pants, held together by safety pins as the zipper was gone bust, my own ski boots and cap and a brown Navy sweatshirt with a white hood that's about four sizes too large. Everyone else has sewn on their numbers – mine was pinned also with safety pins. Anyway, I didn't make a fool of myself and the Soviets seemed very glad that I competed – so all was for the best.

That's about all the news I've got for the moment.

Bestest love,

Kathleen

Kathy's skiing success was reported by Moscow's evening paper, *Vechernyaya Moskva*. Her prize for coming third was a trip to the Caucasus but the Soviet authorities wouldn't let her go. The American press also reported her feat, noting that the times of her two runs were 49 and 50 seconds, while the Soviet skiers ahead of her were about 10 seconds faster.

4 Gretchen Fraser (1919–94), US Olympic skier. Fraser was closely associated with the Harrimans and their Sun Valley ski resort. She won gold and silver medals at the 1948 Winter Olympics in St. Moritz.

CHAPTER 18

'MADAME MOLOTOV IS A SWEET LITTLE THING, PLAYS THE HARP, IS MIDDLE-AGED, WITH LARGE QUANTITIES OF BRAIDED UNDYED BLONDE HAIR'

Of all the Soviet grandes dames that Kathy met in Moscow, perhaps the most intriguing was Polina Zhemchuzhina, Molotov's wife. In Russian her name means 'Little Pearl' – a derivation from her birth name, Perl Karpovskaya. The daughter of a Jewish tailor, she met Molotov at an international women's congress in Moscow in 1921. Molotov was Stalin's right-hand man and in the 1920s and 1930s Polina rose to the top too, playing a major role in the development of the Soviet cosmetics and perfume industry. She then ran the food and fishing industries but fell out of favour and was demoted. During the war she was highly active in the Soviet Jewish Anti-Fascist Committee, a role that led to later accusations that she was a Zionist. In 1949 Polina was purged from the party and exiled to Kazakhstan. Molotov was forced to divorce her and they were not reunited until after Stalin's death in 1953.

Molotov's predecessor as Commissar for Foreign Affairs was Maxim Litvinov. Like Polina he was a secular Jew, as was his English wife Ivy. A renowned international diplomat before the war, the temperamental Litvinov resented his subordination to Molotov and there were ongoing personal and political tensions between the two men, which sometimes spilled over into relations between their two wives.

The ranking Soviet wife that Kathy saw most was Agniya Maisky, who complained that her husband Ivan was in bad odor in Moscow because of the failure of the British and Americans to launch a second front in northern France in 1943. Since he was an appointee from the Litvinov era, he was not Molotov's favourite ambassador, while Stalin complained that Maisky talked too much and had gone a little too native while he was in London. And Stalin no longer needed Maisky's undoubted skills as an interlocutor with Winston Churchill since he now had his own private correspondence with the British PM.

Moscow
February 27, 1944

Dear Pam,

Mme Maisky finally got around to re-paying my call on her last November. She arrived beautifully gotten up in a purple velvet suit and pink lace blouse (but Russian heavy stockings), which made me feel very un-chic, being in an ordinary sweater and skirt. We had a very genial chat about sweet nothings. As usual she asked me about the 2nd Front and said that Maisky was blamed for not being able to bring it about while he was ambass. in London. If that's true, it's very interesting. The one amusing incident was when she asked me how I liked diplomatic society. I said I like some but not all, so she laughed and said "yes, I'm lucky now, I only have to see you and Mrs Balfour." Realizing then that she'd made a break she added "but of course you two are my friends!"

We've had an inordinate number of big parties the past week, starting with the Red Army Day shindig. Molotov, in his capacity as 2nd head of Defence Committee, was host. [Marshal] Budenny turned out to be just as bewhiskered as his photos and very genial in a big burly bear sort of way. The party followed the same order as the November 7th party, with a much less noisy concert. As usual, Popsie and Archie and I were seated up front with the Molotovs, Voroshilov, etc., and the remaining C.D.'s were left to their own devices. Mme Molotov is a sweet little thing. She plays the harp, I gather. Is middle-aged with large quantities of braided undyed blonde hair. It might be fun one of these days to try and see if I could call on her. Like M, she talks no known language, so our conversation was needfully limited except when the Litvinovs could interpret. Mrs

Lit.[1] seems very nice, much more natural than Mme Maisky. It's sort of sad that we can't really get to know any Russkies informally. But apparently even in the days of St. Petersburg, the diplomats were not allowed to associate with Russians.

I was amused to read about the discussion with Madam Chiang at your dinner table! And also that "some people" thought I'd reached the wrong conclusions at Katyn. I wish you'd amplified it, giving names! I wonder how Marie-André is getting along these days. His associates sure did a good and thorough job poisoning his mind against our friends. Do you ever see Red these days? I bet he's got interesting comments, because he's enough of an opportunist to see which way the wind will blow.

Today being Sunday I enjoyed waking up and turning over and going back to sleep and then finally ringing for breakfast in bed. After breakfast I amused myself by reading a Pushkin short story. It's amazing how few words you need to know in order to get the gist of the story. Personally I find Pushkin far more compensating than either *Pravda* or *Izvestiya*! Averell is working today, so we didn't go skiing. Last Sunday was the Russian championship and luckily I was able to compete without disgracing myself. I took the course like a middle-aged matron and came in a bad fourth on the combined times of both runs. Ave's hoping that postwar we can get a men and girls team to come to Sun Valley.

All my ski buddies couldn't be nicer and more helpful and hospitable. But I don't suppose I'll ever be able to see them off a ski slope. The girls are the first Russian girls I've met who aren't the fast type or the wives of important officials. Isn't it stupid that I can't get to know nice Russians?

Last night our Navy gave a big party – buffet supper & dancing. They had all their gals' friends and everyone else's too. One was a rather sweet ballerina (a new one on me, I'd not met her before). I discovered in talking she'd been wounded by shrapnel in the bombing of Riga. Her family moved to Leningrad before the Germans

1 Ivy Low Litvinov (1889–1977). Her husband died in 1951 but she remained in the Soviet Union until returning to England in 1972.

got to Riga and were there during the siege. She was the only one in her family who didn't die of starvation. Now she's not well enough to dance, so she teaches. Can you imagine watching the slow starvation of each member of your family & being outwardly unaffected? She's a gay little thing, about my age, with only sad eyes to show. Jesus, but these people are tough.

Couple of nights ago, one minister, who lives with us, gave a party (sole reason – to spend his entertainment allowance). About 50 of us started at the circus, came back here for dinner, where we had 8 gypsies – 4 men & 4 girls. They were damned good & great fun and stayed on until about 3. When a gypsy isn't singing, she's an ordinary-looking gal, but the moment she gets into song, her whole face lights up, becomes animated & appears beautiful.

This has gone on plenty long enough.

Bestest love,

Kathy

Moscow
March 4, 1944

Dear Mary,

I'm in a lovely mood tonight – after two months of stalling and delaying, but always being polite, the Soviet agency I deal with crashed through this afternoon with a plan for me to put on a bombing photo exhibit at the Red Air Force Academy. Whoopie!

You know it's really got one great advantage – my job that is – I'm interested in it only because it's something to do but knowing that nothing I'm doing is vitally important to anyone, I don't have to sweat mentally or physically every time V.O.K.S.[2] stalls; that being so, I get all the compensations and none of the liabilities. Since no one has ever done any of my kind of work before here, no one expects anything or blames me when the Soviets turn me down. As the general run of embassy people don't put much faith in the O.W.I., it's all the nicer when I get somewhere.

2 Russian acronym for the All-Union Society for Cultural Relations with Foreign Countries.

Another thing constructive came thru today. For a month I've been trying to get the Commissar of Public Health to let me present some few thousand cans of milk to a refugee kids' hospital. Averell dreamed up the idea, spoke to the Commissar about it, later I repeated the request by mouth, phone and letter – and now on Tuesday I'm being taken to two hospitals. So you see, life has taken a turn for the better, but you can also get an idea what it takes in the way of patience to get even the smallest things done.

Now I'll get down to the really important news: our Xmas presents arrived last Saturday, all in one fell swoop. Averell and I had such fun opening them. My pearls and earrings are divine, blue navy sweater is perfect. Thanks so also for the ski pants, jacket and galoshes. The weather has turned very warm, the snow has almost gone, but I'm hoping the winter will return so I can snap on my skis. The wool stockings will get worn the next time I get out of Moscow, maybe too that will be soon. (I was slightly horrified at the way *Time* carried my first excursion with the press – 18 men and one girl was typically inaccurate and more importantly not my idea of the proper way to write up such an important story as Katyn atrocities.)

Along with the Xmas presents came a nice batch of mail. Your Xmas card of Bobby has taken its place along with various shots of the Atlantic Charter meeting, the P.M., Averell and Stalin, the Tehran Big Three, and the President, on Averell's mantlepiece. So you see he is in good company.

There's not much of interest in the way of news. The past week I've had the average ration of lunches and cocktail parties and dinners.

What more to gossip about? Today we had our usual Saturday afternoon movie *10 Gentlemen from West Point*. Receiving guests I inadvertently forgot and said just "hi" to the Mexican ambassador, instead of the more correct "good afternoon your excellency" but it didn't seem to bother him much. Unfortunately, he seated himself right behind me at the movie. He laughs at the slightest suggestion of a joke and lets out such a spray of saliva that my neck got quite a washing. After the movie, Ave wanted to talk turkey to the French air general, so I was stuck with his dreary wife and one-eyed daughter for tea. To help out, I invited a Russian English-speaking director and his movie actress wife plus some other Russians to have tea too. When we adjourned upstairs I discovered no one knew anyone else and introducing everyone around I got all their names mixed up and made a hell of a mess of it. I wonder why it is but I even draw a name blank when it comes to introducing someone like Bob. Perhaps Shirley can explain that one scientifically. It's a damned annoying (to say nothing of embarrassing) mental difficulty of mine.

Moscow looks dingier and drearier than ever now that there's no snow. Now the people, the huge streets and tiny solid sidewalks make one mass of dirty grey. Some government buildings and reconditioned public places have been painted glaring red or the favorite Soviet yellow and white combination. These stick out like sore thumbs, glaringly new and almost grotesque next to their war-worn neighboring buildings.

We're all still searching for the proverbial Russian beauty. She doesn't exist to my knowledge – not walking around the streets at any rate. Some women have a certain passive, peasantlike beauty. But I've yet to find a face with expression & life in it. Most of the women are short, square and completely shapeless due to their bulky clothes.

Did I ever tell you about my little boyfriend who lives in the village next to our ski slope? He's a wonderful friend – a bright little kid with an invariably dirty face. Is about 4 feet high and I suppose 12 years old. He tells me he's 18 but that's just to convince me that he is old enough to smoke American cigarettes (even the five-year-olds clamor for "papiarosa"). He doesn't own skis himself, but he follows me around, up and down the hill, tells me when Averell is looking for me (how he knows I'm sure I don't know) and in every possible way makes himself indispensable.

Usually I take lunch out with me & don't eat it, so I give it away to some of the local kids. My little friend always refuses it – perhaps he's too proud to admit he's hungry. Many of the kids are but he rounds up the neighborhood children who are poorest – the ones who have to stay indoors during winter because they don't have shoes or coats, some pathetically pale and sick, and chases away the better-clothed kids. Once there happened to be an army officer standing nearby, so none of the kids dared come near me. They all refused food that day.

This is a strange country isn't it? Even the kids are on guard about being too friendly when officials are present.

Goodnight to you.

My best love,

Kathleen

PS A new problem is just beginning to loom up. My hair is growing terrifically fast here so most all of my perm has been cut off! (After learning that one's apt to get skin diseases at the "beauty salon" at the National Hotel, I wash my hair myself!)

Moscow
March 8, 1944

Dear Mary,

A couple of days back I learned that at last the O.W.I. man was en route from Tehran. He's been "arriving" for some weeks now, but – to get to the point – he came in great shape – well equipped with a badly broken leg and is now installed in a Russian hospital. The god damnedest things do have to happen! It all happened on the last day of the journey, at the Stalingrad airport, when a girl (child) fellow passenger got stuck in the 18-inch mud. She cried to her family for help but they didn't seem inclined to go to the rescue of their loved one, so our over-gallant Mr Nelson sprang to the aid. While he was in the process of extricating her, the mud suction gave way all of a sudden and she came out with a jerk and they both fell over on his leg. The local airport nurse fixed him up with a splint and he came on up to Moscow on schedule and had his leg set here. I went over and saw him yesterday and he's in fine spirits, sort of the belle of the ball at the hospital, and not in overly much pain. But it will be a longish time before he is any service to the Moscow edition of the O.W.I.

Yesterday I went out with the head of the children's department of the Commissariat of Public Health and had a very interesting time visiting a babies' hospital and then an orphans' home. She phoned just before coming over to pick me up to say that she's discovered that her interpreter couldn't speak English, so could I provide one and as luck would have it our Navy doctor was free and anxious to go.

As he knew all the obvious medical questions to ask, our trip was twice as interesting.

The hospital, as I'd expected, was a very swell one – housed in a pre-revolutionary mansion, well equipped with marble staircases etc. but had nice big airy rooms with some 65 beds. Illnesses were mostly pneumonia, ear troubles etc., but none looked terribly sick. The most pathetic was a little girl who'd been evacuated from Kiev when the Russians recaptured it. Her mother and father had both been in the army and during the two years of occupation, she'd lived with her grandmother. They had to walk some 6 miles whenever they went in search of food – bread was all that was ever available, so the child is still suffering from starvation. She was horribly thin, with huge joints and distended stomach and the doctors can't persuade her to eat. She was about three years old, with a crinkled face with huge soulful eyes. She just looked at us in a dazed sort of way and made no effort to move or talk to us.

The most interesting thing about the place was the kids themselves. They were very friendly, loved to be picked up and played with. None was shy and all those about two years sat at a little table and fed themselves with no help. All of which compared very sharply with all the children's homes I visited in England, where the shy ones outnumbered the friendly kids. Here they seem to teach the kids to stand on their own feet much earlier and not to be frightened. Perhaps you, as a child psychologist, would be interested. I for one was most impressed. Even the under-six-month babies love to be picked up, and laughed when you bounced them.

The kids had a wonderful collection of toys, mostly all made by the nurses themselves out of oil cloth, but their playpens were very professional, nicely made with good paint. There was one big nursery for kids who were convalescing. Apparently, realizing that children outside of hospitals get less food and even less care, the hospitals keep them on until they are completely well and in fact a good deal healthier than the average Moscow child. They all get five meals per day, consisting of soup, black bread, milk and mashed meat and vegetables and a lot of fruit. Mothers are allowed to come visit their kids and of course those who are nursing their babies came in and out all day. Apparently

Moscow's mothers donate some 4,000 liters of milk daily to kids who are on their own. They just go to their local hospital and suckle any baby that happens along. Milk donors get extra food, just the same as blood donors, which of course makes it extra attractive.

The one awkward part of our visit went along with the inspection of the kitchen facilities. Thanks to the invariably overwhelming hospitality, doctor and I were both faced by 6 plates of various slops and mixtures and expected to down them all. Somehow, I gagged them down and after much farewells we set off to place #2 on our list – where of course the whole eating performance was repeated.

The orphans' home was equally a smallish mansion well marbled. But there the gilt had been removed and paintings of children's subjects painted on instead. The children range from a few days to three years and all looked very healthy and extremely happy, but better behaved than any bunch of energetic kids I've ever seen. The younger ones all had their heads shaved so it was impossible to tell boys from girls. The older ones enjoyed about two inches of hair all around, but still that didn't help me any. Their toys – electric trains, tractors, soldiers etc. – were all American and their sweaters were all either A.R.C. or Russian war relief – dreary dark blue and maroon. We were told that the kids belonged to dead Red Army officers, presumably high-ranking ones, who have mothers who are either dead or working in places where they can't also care for their kids. One thing is certain, the Soviets are certainly taking the best possible care of their children. Due to the war having gone on for three years, the birth rate has fallen considerably, so they're doing their damnedest to conserve what kids they have.

[Kathleen]

Moscow
March 10, 1944

Mouche dear,

I'm in bed so I'm afraid you'll have to put up with my handwriting – which now due to writing in Russian has deteriorated measurably.

It was a wonderful surprise to come up after dinner and find a nice pile of parcels and letters on my bed. It's so wonderful getting things from home. I don't imagine I'll ever get to thinking of Spaso House as "home." It's too much like a boarding house.

I've written Mary about my more recent doings – so I'll not repeat. As I'm not keeping any kind of diary or anything please persuade her to keep the letters as sometime I might get amused re-reading them. If I wrote a diary I'd never get around to writing letters or studying Russian. Averell & I play bezique almost nightly & I usually end up too sleepy to do other than go to bed. He seldom goes out – I go out quite often for one reason or other. Unfortunately, he refuses to go to the theater (which is excellent). There are all kinds of plays – comedies, which are the easiest to understand, but the tragedies & Chekhov variety are the most interesting and the best. As part of my "I'll try anything once" activities, one evening I went to the local vaudeville. It stank in every sense of the word – but it is one of the few theaters that satirizes the government, which is something of interest.

We spent one pleasant evening a couple of days back at the Norwegian ambassador's. "Pleasant" of course by our Moscow standards because usually the dinners Averell gets to go to are deadly. But this one consisted of the British ambass., us and our host and the rest Russians. I sat next to an oldish painter and we rivaled to see which one could speak the other's language best and finally gave that up and relapsed into French. You know the Russians are such nice people. If only we could get to know them – then perhaps I might be able to understand them.

The evening after dinner, Averell got explained the Russian character by [Alexei] Tolstoy, the [most prominent] author here now – or at least the one who is in best favor (he's a nephew of Leo). A lovely complicated conversation – translated from Russian to French by Tolstoy's wife and then the last lap was my job. It was quite interesting as he was trying to explain why the Russian can be an idealist as well as at the same time a complete unpredictable scoundrel when dealing with everyday life. The mixture can't be rationalized but he was trying to explain it in terms of history. He's done a play on the subject and wants to get it translated into English for production in America.

Our one other Russian evening the past week was when a movie director gave us a private showing of his latest film – even he admits it's lousy – but it came under the heading of interesting and the people there were pleasant. As a return gesture, on Monday we're giving a showing of *Casablanca* – for him and various others of the artist group.

Time passes very rapidly here. I never seem to be able to squeeze all I want to do into the days, but that's an asset more than anything else.

My love to you,
Kathleen

Moscow
March 14, 1944

Dear Mary,

Unless I'm once more forgetful, I've got me a letter to you sitting in my office desk. There's a pouch leaving tomorrow, so I might as well bring it up to date. The alternative if I don't is to study Russian. I prefer to write to you – compliment I hope!

Last night we had a moderate party for a couple of film directors and some other Russians – a painter, pianist, author variety and their females. The point was to see *Casablanca*. It made my 4½ times seeing it, but as I had to spend my whole time interpreting, I didn't have much time to enjoy it. I sat next to a girl who beside wanting to know what the people were saying, wondered why Elsa was in love "with that horrible black-haired man" instead of her husband?

Before the movie we had invited Tolstoy and wife to dine. Despite the fact that we also had one of the embassy officers present for translation purposes, conversation went from Russian to French to English. It worked fine, except for once when Averell told me he couldn't understand something Madame Tolstoy had been translating into French and I unfortunately hadn't been listening. It was quite embarrassing. It's a lovely habit of mine – not listening – usually I can get away with it, that time I sure didn't. Can't remember if I ever told you about that couple or not. He's a nephew of Leo Tolstoy, an author and playwright, who has seen the light in recent years and hence now enjoys the position of being the favored good author at the moment. Unlike his colleagues, he is allowed to associate with such as us. In fact, I imagine he's ordered to. He's an enormous roly-poly man, about 60 with long hair on the sides but bald on top. He prides himself as being "the most glorious drunk" in Russia and he certainly is a very pleasant one. His wife is my age (his 4th I think), pretty in a stolid sort of way, and very earnest. Like most cultivated Russians she speaks perfect French and a little English. She tries to henpeck him about drinking but without much success.

After the movie one of our embassy pianists started things off and one of the guests – a concert pianist – volunteered and forthcame with extremely good jazz. A painter with an unpronounceable name sang Spanish songs. We danced and all in all it was a very nice party.

I went on the second lap of my tour of hospitals yesterday – a maternity one this time, called a "birth house" here. I again took along our Navy doc who turned out to be quite an obstetrician and told me later we'd gotten a lot of previously unknown material about things such as prenatal and postnatal care.

The hospital was a huge ex-mansion once used for barracks, later as a church, then a residence. We saw the works and the whole thing was very orderly and efficient. There were pre-labor wards for women just starting, or waiting for labor to begin. The second stop was the "birth room," a large room filled with operating tables. As many as twenty women can be in it at one time, all at varying stages of giving birth. Mild sedatives are given, but due to the acute shortage of anesthetics nothing more. (Most all operations, including amputations, are done under inadequate local!) All the women are carefully examined when they come in and bathed. The ones who are ill or look as though they'll have trouble are put in wards according to their illnesses. Babies are wrapped in swaddling clothes and have individual cots, something I'd not anticipated. No men are allowed, but each bed has a phone for "morale reasons." I made a point of asking a good many mothers what their jobs were – most were either engineers, government clerks or Red Army. The health officials who accompanied us took great pains to explain that the hospital like all in Moscow was a regional one. But the head dr said it wasn't and being the best in Moscow took special patients. However, I was interested to see that by no means all of the women lined in the waiting room were well dressed (by Russian standards). Abortions are illegal here except for health reasons. We saw some of those cases – mostly all advanced T.B. patients. The sick are cared for but bedside manner don't seem to exist! With one exception (a lung specialist) all the docs. were females. The nurses were an assorted bunch of all ages, with a variety of intelligence in their faces. We were told all women go to hospitals to have babies. There's no midwifery as in England and of course it costs nothing. We, as usual, sampled the food. "The regular meal" consisted of chicken, cold sauerkraut, onions and carrots (raw) and pancakes. I can assure you no Russian outside a hospital gets a meal like that unless he's a general or a commissar!

It's encouraging to find things like that hospital, because it's nice to be able to see things well done (& fairly done) and not completely swamped by the bureaucracy.

I'm getting sleepy now.

My love to you and Bobby,

Kathleen

Moscow
March 19, 1944

Dear Mouche,

As far as magazines go I'd like the *New Yorker* & all the various fashion magazines, as the Russian women – even though they can't buy clothes – love to see them better than anything else.

Last night Averell & I were subjected to an official ordeal in the form of a "closed" performance in the largest theater in honor of the 100th anniversary of Rimsky-Korsakov's something (presumably death or birth!).[3] The show started at 6 and we were ushered into Box No. 1 along with Clark Kerr, the Afghan ambass. (Dean of the Corps by virtue of seniority) & the entire Iranian family + a vice-commissar & daughter. I had halitosis to the right of me, halitosis to the left of me (combination Persian & Russian) and Mme Ahi's 250 pounds of fat

3 Rimsky-Korsakov was born on 18 March 1844.

pressing me. Our box was right on top of the brass section of the orchestra – hence from the musical side about the worst seat in the theater. The show began with an hour and a half of speeches on R-K, which even if I'd been able to understand them would have been boring. With questionable politeness, Averell & Clark Kerr got up & left after an hour of them and went outside to smoke. The head Vice-Commissar of Foreign Affairs, M. Vyshinsky sat on the stage with the musical notables. He got up and stomped out at the end of the second speech & never returned!

After the speeches, we (the Dip. Corps & all the F.O. officials) were fed on tea and choice tidbits. A good 10 minutes before the end of the intermission, Clark Kerr & I decided to go out & take a look at the rest of the audience marching around the corridors – and to our horror found the entire Corps, headed by the Japs, trailed us thinking it was time to return to the auditorium!

Our enjoyment of the concert was slightly impaired by our inability to hear any instruments other than the brass sections, so with an entire act of *Snow Maiden* still in the offing, Averell & I left, figuring our duty was over.

One night last week, I returned from the theater to discover that one of the protocol officials of the Foreign Office had phoned saying he wanted to call and deliver a wee gifty from Mme Molotov. He arrived in due course & presented me with a small cigarette holder. She thought my gold Zeus one too masculine, so now she'd remedied my lack & I can smoke like a lady – Russian standards! It was very sweet of her I thought.

Bestest love,
Kathleen

CHAPTER 19

'SHOSTAKOVICH SEEMED A NICE GUY, BUT VERY DEFINITELY AN INTROVERTED GENIUS TYPE'

The composer Dmitry Shostakovich was among those evacuated from besieged Leningrad but he began work on his famous Seventh ('Leningrad') Symphony while still in the city. He moved to Moscow in 1943, where he completed his Eighth Symphony, dubbed the 'Stalingrad' by the Western press.

Ave and Kathy's host at their first 'unofficial Russian dinner party', Alexei Tolstoy, had made his name by publishing a novel about Peter the Great that cast him as the progenitor of a Russian/Soviet patriotism. During the war he worked on a series of plays about another of Stalin's tsarist heroes, Ivan the Terrible.

On the eve of Russian Orthodox Easter 1944, Kathy was able to observe an 'Old Believers' service. The Old Believers were a split-off from the Russian Orthodox Church who preferred the church's original liturgy and rituals to those adopted in the modern era. The Soviet state was militantly anti-religious, but there was a significant reconciliation during the war when, in September 1943, Stalin – himself a former trainee priest – met with Russian Orthodox leaders and agreed to end the communist crackdown on the church, a tolerance that was also extended to other religious currents, Muslim as well as Christian.

Moscow
March 22, 1944

Dear Mary,

You sure are the God damnedest lousiest correspondent I've ever known! If it weren't for Mouche, who has been an angel about keeping us up on family news, we'd have received no recent news other than letters written Thanksgiving time!

Our poor Mr Nelson is having one hellova time with his broken leg. It has slipped twice and so now as a last resort they have strung him up on pulleys, which isn't overly comfortable. So it looks as though it will be a long time before we have the inspiration of his presence in this office. Have I told you about the O.W.I.'s latest acquisition? It's a little Russian who John and I call "the Termite" and who the clerks call "Friday." He answers to both but most readily to a dog-calling whistle. First day here he got some Russian who speaks English to write him out a list of necessary phrases written in Russian writing, but supposed to sound like English. For the first few days, he'd come into the office, shuffle through his little batch of fling cards, until he came to the sentence he wanted. Then with great gusto, he'd read them out loud. "May I go to lunch please" and "I want to go home please" were of course his favorites. Now he's learned them by heart, but he still can't tell the difference between Miss, Mrs, or Mr. He calls me first one then another, quite indiscriminately. Our clerks have great fun with him and every so often tow him into our room so that his eloquent English can be translated. Needless to say, frequently I'm also helpless – perhaps it's his Moscow cockney – anyway it's very different from what my teachers use. His main duty is to deliver the daily news bulletin but to date he's not quite up to the task. He gets lost around the town (so he says) or any rate gets himself properly mislaid. We are also in search of a chauffeur. So far we've interviewed two – one we subsequently discovered was fired by the Swedes for drinking and the other fired by a commissariat for cracking up two cars.

Last night Averell and I got invited to our first unofficial Russian dinner party – quite an event. The Tolstoys gave the party in their dacha – country house to you – about half an hour out of town.

Shostakovich and wife[1] were there, a very nice theater director, an architect and another couple and Tolstoy's ex-secretary, who spoke excellent English and acted as interpreter. Hors d'oeuvres alone in quantity were equal to a big meal by our standards. And after them came special meat and cabbage pastry, soup, fish, and a huge roast of pork with vegetables and finally ice cream. There was an abundance of wines and toasts throughout the meal.

Shostakovich turned out to look about 21 years old (he's over thirty), with very heavy glasses and more concentrated nervousness than I've seen in any man. He continually wiped his face, rattled his fingers, or squinted his eyes. His wife is a young little thing and like a good number of Russian girls, didn't look too clean. Shostakovich drank considerably during dinner and then decided he didn't feel like playing for us after dinner (something I didn't blame him for in the least) but finally he did – part of a concerto, second movement of his eighth, and a children's poem. I can't say I get anything out of his things (my loss) and his eighth is worse than the others. He seemed a nice guy, but very definitely an introverted genius type. Quite the opposite, Tolstoy revels in exhibitionism. In his own house he's at his best, being able to talk as much and as long as he wants. Toasts at dinner were mostly sentimental in variety, as opposed to the government officials' preference for witty ones with plays on words. After dinner, Tolstoy spent his time sitting or lying on the floor on his stomach expounding on any subject that happened into his mind. He's really a very lovable soul. His secretary was charming and unlike Mrs Tolstoy[2] has a very refined face. She told me she learned her English from a governess when she was a child living in Leningrad. Maybe her family got purged. Anyways, she went to the Institute – college to you – and later became Tolstoy's secretary. She was a lovely person, with a nice sense of humor and a complete lady – something very rare for us to have the privilege to see. It's really stupid that the only Russians I see are the girlfriends of the Americans – funny that I'm not allowed to meet nice Russian girls. I don't mean to be

1 Nina Varzar (1908–54), a physicist.
2 Ludmila Krestinskaya (1906–82), a screenwriter.

snobbish, but it would be nice to be able to get to know some girl who wasn't just one of the girls around town.

The Tolstoys' house was very swell. It was given to him by the government about ten years ago as a reward for a book he wrote, the last of a trilogy, in which he saw the light. The rooms were comfortably big, with nice fireplaces and lacked the usual bric-a-brac. It was simple, with all the modern conveniences.

We're having all sorts of upsets in the Dip. Corps these days. As far as I can figure, now that Simich[3] was repudiated by the Jugoslav gov't and is recognized by Tito as his ambassador, we don't recognize him. All of which means that his two daughters don't feel they can come to the movie on Saturday, which is tough luck for them. I wish they'd asked me if they could come, then I'd say yes. Apparently it isn't protocol, or something, for me to take the initiative and invite them.

I think my Alabam is going to [get] married. I suggested to Averell that I send for Alabam and I thought [he'd] bust! He always hated Alabam on the grounds that I spoiled him (personally I think it was because he disapproved of Alabam's original master!).

I'm running out of conversation, so I'd better stop.

Best love to you,

Kathleen

Moscow

April 1, 1944

Dear Pam,

Last night we dined with the Czechs and as per usual Archie was there. Dinner was like most others – the three of us and the Tolstoys, a very nice painter (old man) and charming (also old) wife, what is called here "an academician" (he's the foremost historical writer in the Soviet Union), Pierre Cot,[4] and the French Nat'l Committee representative here – a horrid little man with a twitch.

Averell of course sat next to Mme Fierlinger – a French lady who speaks no English, so he had trouble making conversation. I had

3 Stanoje Simić (1893–1970), later Tito's foreign minister.
4 Pierre Cot (1895–1977), left-wing French politician, former air minister.

Tolstoy next to me, who talks very little French, not enough to be able to express his extravagant thoughts anyway, so he kept calling to his wife across the table to translate for him, which disrupted her conversation with Fierlinger (the Czech ambass.). Averell kept calling to me for help at his end, so all in all it was rather amusing. Archie speaks very nice French, but like me is embarrassed about talking Russian. Only the Czech ambass. had all the necessary languages under control! Dinners in this town are really complicated. As a result, Averell decided last night he ought to get someone in every morning to talk French to him, which if he'd ever do it would be a swell idea. But you know how often his ideas materialize! Particularly when there are cables to draft, more to read and people to see.

One morning last week, Averell, I suppose having nothing of interest to do, decided suddenly to turn up unexpectedly at the office, where he had not been for over a month and decided he'd like to call in some of the clerks whose names sounded familiar, to see how they were getting along. The clerks came in, full of complaints of their hot-waterless hotel, overwork etc. Then from other sources (me and Bob) he got some dope on how some of the officers are very haughty to the clerks, treat them like dirt (which is something that continually horrifies me), so his next step was to pep talk the officers. On top of that he decided we'd give a party here at Spaso for all clerks and enlisted men in the military mission. The next day, most of the clerks came trooping into my office wanting to know what the hell was up. Officers had called them in, had asked about their problems and gripes in general and the clerks were damned suspicious. They figured this was a little soft soaping pre a big storm. It was all very amusing.

Our party for the clerks came off in fine form. Russ Deane and Admiral Olsen[5] and our Counsellor were the only officers present and I borrowed the wife of one of the Canadians to help me out on the female side. We had hot dogs, ice cream and chocolate cake and vodka punch so everything went well and warmed up much quicker

5 Clarence E. Olsen (1899–1971), head of the naval section of the US Military Mission in Moscow.

than I'd anticipated. The party ended with *Air Force* (the B-17 movie), which went down big.

Last week, another amazing thing happened – I finally persuaded Averell to go to the ballet – a good one in which both the Moscow main ballerinas were dancing. He went and thoroughly enjoyed himself. Maybe someday I'll be able to get him to go to the theater, which is even superior to the ballet (some of it).

A while back we had our first informal dinner with Russians. Tolstoy and wife invited us out to their dacha (country house) about 20 kilometers out of town. We went and discovered that they had gone to a terrific effort to put on a real show for us. There was an architect there, a theater director (absolutely charming) and the Shostakoviches. He's very young looking, pathetically nervous (always fiddling with his hands) and slightly odd looking due to very thick lenses. After dinner he played for us – part of his latest concerto and part of the new eighth symphony, which was all very enjoyable only I can't honestly say I like any of his music (my misfortune) or begin to understand it, but it was very interesting meeting him and hearing him play. His wife was the ineffectual sort, quite young. Moscow gossipers say he wants to divorce her, but that night they were very cozy.

The dress – the red washable one – sounds divine, but I'll be wiring you on that subject. I want to try and find out what our plans will be for the next few months before I start ordering clothes.

Incidentally, I'm in desperate need of a perm. I asked the wife of the Dutch ambass. to please bring me one from Cairo and she, being completely lacking in a sense of humor, answered: "How can I do that"!

Bestest love to you,
Kathy

Moscow
April 6, 1944

Dear Pam,

Don't know what Ave had written to you, if he was too security minded to mention the fact that he's gone off for about a week's trip up north, with our admiral. Just forget I told you! I think it will do him a world of good to get out of Moscow and away from the daily routine of State Department work. Except for our nightly bezique games, he seldom relaxes and always has a ready excuse when I suggest to go for a walk or something.

Then he's got that damned fetish about not going to either the theater or the ballet, that it's frivolous and not in keeping with his war effort.

As far as I can gather, our chances of returning to civilization before the warm weather comes are nil. So perhaps you could send me my beige coat, as all I have here is my Russian "shouba," a fur coat and a raincoat. In other words, nothing to wear when I want to look respectable when spring comes. In the way of other wants, I'd like my white pleated American tennis skirt and tennis racket and I guess white socks and things like white cotton gloves and my high-heeled evening shoes.

The black and white evening dress got worn the other night, when we entertained for the Soviet ambass. to Canada.[6] For your ears only: the Soviets might serve their diplomats well by running a course in etiquette for their wives. As most of the gals are of peasant variety, they have no idea how to act at a dinner party – particularly how to eat. It puts the poor girls at a terrible disadvantage and makes them just doubly self-conscious and shy. Mme Zarubin is far better than most, but she did things like drinking coffee with the spoon in the cup, and using the wrong forks.

I'm off now – it's a day later – & I'm taking a "visitor" out skiing.

Bestest love to you,

Kathy

Moscow
April 7, 1944

Dear Mary,

Ave went off on a spree for about a week, which will make a nice and much-needed change for him. Last week he was laid low with a sort of neuralgic tooth, and being a stoic he refused to take anything

6 Georgy Zarubin (1900–58).

to help the pain, which I thought stupid, but he had completely recovered before leaving on his trip. Bob is having a field day. Ave's farewell orders were that Bob had to have a good time, go out sightseeing, go out every night and do no work except stuff that he can't for security reasons put off on the other secretary. So now Bob's in his seventh heaven. He's planning each day and keeping strictly to schedule.

The Moscow ballet enthusiasts are in a whirl as there's a new man here from Leningrad who's better than anything Moscow can produce. Added to him, there's a new 18-year-old girl, who's supposed to be terrific, for a young girl that is. I saw her in *The Nutcracker* the other night, and was only mildly impressed. She's got an unfortunate figure – very long legs and short torso which makes her look funny when dancing. Last night I went with three of our new arrivals (colonels) to the unclassical ballet theater, where the heretics, who don't believe in the stereotype form of dancing, perform. We saw their best ballet, which I'd seen before and I must admit that the second time the general emoting of one and all performers gets rather on one's nerves. Added to that, the theater is cold as the devil. However, I went well prepared with little socks, a scarf and a shawl to put over my knees and a flask of vodka. For once, we did not suffer from teeth chattering!

Tonight the Navy docs entertain, tomorrow the embassy clerks are entertaining me, and on Sunday I go ballet-ing with one of our generals, so you see life is very busy, one way and another!

Interestingly enough the Sov. press department got a Russian press girl who works for I.N.S. to tell me that she thought they "would not turn down" a request, if I made it, to go on an excursion to see the "new Polish division."[7] I didn't bite and sure enough the head of the press department crashed thru with an invitation the day before the show. As I was due to be ill, I didn't bite, and aside from that I imagine there would have been, diplomatically speaking, much debate about the advisability of my going anyway. But the fact that I was invited was interesting.

---

7 Pro-Soviet Polish People's Army that served as part of the Soviet armed forces.

Last week we gave a small dinner for the newly appointed Sov. ambassador for Canada, one Mr Zarubin, who used to head the protocol department of the Foreign Office. He and wife and three other Russians came, plus two Canadian couples and some of our own officers. Ave was laid low with his tooth at that moment, so didn't appear, but the party went far better than I dared hope. After dinner the men played pool, which the Russians enjoyed no end, and us five gals had a little hen party. The wife of the Canadian ambass.,[8] being Russian, speaks fluently, so was a great help at interpreting for me, when I got stuck, which was frequent. Neither of the two Russian girls spoke a word of English even though one had lived in N.Y.C. for a year and a half while her husband worked on the Russian World's Fair exhibit. She however was very sweet. The other girl, as far as I could gather, never opened her mouth except to say Yes or No. Both were very shy and more or less at a loss as to what to do when.

Our Mr Nelson is still hospitalized and I'm beginning to despair of his ever being up and around and fit to work. His leg is taking a long time to set. We've heard that Sam Spewack isn't returning, which is sad but it was something I anticipated.

A Bennington Alum. bulletin arrived a couple of days ago, it was fun looking thru and seeing what everyone is doing. I was quite horrified by a Foxcroft news sheet that Mouche sent me. I hated the sound of it [and] didn't like what it has to say about the place going military.

I must be off now.

My love to you all,

Kathleen

Moscow

April 12, 1944

Dear Mary,

Today our office has an acute attack of spring fever. Spring isn't really here yet, but we figure it should be. The cobblestones are showing in one corner of our Spaso square, so maybe if we don't get

---

8 Olga Buergin (1897–1990), married to Canadian ambassador L. Dana Wilgress (1892–1969).

another storm soon, we'll soon be having green buds and grass. The women who clear the snow off the streets are madly shoveling the snow back into the middle of the streets, so that the sun can get at it and melt. This morning I nearly got stuck on a side street there was so much slush. People are now clearing the snow and the ice off their roofs. It comes down in big clumps and could be damned dangerous if one ever hit you. Last Sunday, walking over to the Canadians for a hen tea party, I got hit by the tail end of one and arrived looking rather dirty and in an exceedingly bad temper. Having a hen party in Moscow is quite an achievement. There were seven of us – most of them British press department secretaries, who I don't know at all. For some reason they never seem to come to our weekly movies, a couple looked nice. (But as usual I remembered no names.)

Last night we went to the gypsy theater, expecting to be entertained by just dancing and singing and instead got a full-dressed Pushkin play – partly in Russian and partly in gypsy. The theater was tiny and stank to high heaven, even by Moscow standards, but the show was quite amusing – had a couple of murders and one man died of a broken heart, but unfortunately no nice dancing.

Russian Easter is this Sunday – but we celebrated last Sunday. We weren't allowed to have any fresh eggs for weeks before so Cook could collect enough so that each of us could have two. She stayed up late at night for days before painting each one with elaborate designs. Then on top of that we had the Russian special cake and cream pyramid dessert for lunch. As far as I can gather we're going to celebrate both Easters. At midnight this Saturday I'm going to the Old Believers church (I've already seen the Orthodox service) and afterwards I'm going back for midnight supper with one of the Russian employees, which should be very interesting. As far as I can gather, the members of the Old Believers Church (the officials) aren't as politically conscious as the Orthodox Church. We shall see.

Yesterday at lunch, our little procurement agent came barging in during the meal with a huge wooden box filled with week-old ducklings that he bought on the open market. He was exceedingly proud of them and is still convinced they'll live to a ripe eatable age. At the moment he's got them installed in the furnace room with a big pan of water. I tried to explain that they really shouldn't swim now, but he insists that they want to swim and he wants to make them happy. We've made Bob, being the only Navy member of Spaso, in charge of these and all future ducks, but so far he hasn't taken much interest in them. Time to eat them is too far in the future for him to care.

It looks as though I'm going to have to do some work for a change now.

Bestest love to all,
Kathleen

• • •

Next day – now that foaling season is nearing, I discovered the Muscovites drive mares whether in foal or not, and don't seem to mind making them drag heavy carts. I wonder if they'll let the foals travel along behind the carts come late summer. But I suppose since women work until six weeks before childbirth the way the mares get treated isn't amazing.

One interesting item I discovered from our Mr Nelson: the Red Army men on his floor of the hospital still think that the second front won't even come off. They call it a gag to scare the Germans, but say that it doesn't fool the Red Army!

Moscow
April 18, 1944

Dear Mary,

Averell's returned from his trip up north. I gather he had a wonderful time and found it pleasant to get away from the officialdom of Moscow. He was full of enthusiasm for what's being done up there. He looks better and is full of ideas of making more trips more often.

The day after he returned a new ballet opened – Tchaikovsky's *Sleeping Beauty*. The heads of all diplomatic missions were invited and of course we went. As usual we sat in our same box on top of the brass section on top of the orchestra – the lesser diplomats got better seats, from the musical standpoint!

When it finally came to leave for the ballet I was not dressed so we finally got off in a flurry at extra-high speed. Just as we neared the theater (coming up the one-way street the wrong way), our chauffeur slowed down for some inexplicable reason and stopped on the wrong side for nearly a minute. Just as I was about to ask what the hell he was up to, I noticed a car bearing the Jap ambassador's flag drive away. My estimation of Mashcoff went up immeasurably. Our chauffeur may be lazy and arrogant as the devil about driving people other than Averell and me, but he's certainly diplomatic.

The ballet was a new one – played for the first time in a good many years – so everything in the way of costumes and scenery was new. I must admit they were god awful – thousands of colors, extravagant and without taste. The ballet was extra long, with many dances without point and the good ones lacked anything new. Each ballerina did the same old twirls and leaps. The ballet here doesn't seem to allow its stars to develop new techniques and steps, all of which makes it very stereotype and classical. Maybe I've been seeing too many ballets of late and am tired of the same old thing, however the music was most pleasant.

Between the acts we were led to an upstairs room for the usual tea and sandwiches. We stood around to gossip among ourselves, or I practiced my lousy Russian on the officials and their wives, all of which is an exceedingly boring procedure. Me and five of the ambassadors stood around and chatted like schoolchildren about the merits of the star man of the evening – the husband of our Russian teacher. I don't imagine any of us actually thought he was good, but we all remained faithful and were loud in our praise. Parts of this life here certainly are inane.

Except for a couple of diplomats, most are subnormal in intelligence by ordinary American standards!

Saturday night, being Easter eve, I went to the Old Believers church. We were not allowed back of the altar, but we stood in the crowd just near it, where there was an open window, which helped me no end. Our church was packed. Every person had a lighted candle and I spent a goodly amount of time anxiously watching to see that my clothes wouldn't get set on fire. We were so tightly packed that I couldn't get my hands up from my sides.

The service apparently goes on for twenty-four hours. We arrived for the beginning of it. The congregation brought pots and plates of food to be blessed by the priests and kept coming and going. Prayers were chanted and some sung, with a negro type of swing, sometimes with the congregation joining in. Unlike at Xmas time there were a fair proportion of men present – some young men but few uniformed ones. Main trouble was that I could only half concentrate on listening and enjoying the service. Keeping your feet under you was a major operation and keeping in time with the swaying congregation a necessity if you didn't want to get swashed under foot. Then I found myself looking in the head a few inches away from my nose to see if I could see fleas, lice and what have you. For some reason or other I collected no souvenirs of that variety – most everyone had a freshly washed head for the occasion, and apparently the type of lice that live on clothes found my fur coat unappetizing.

We left the service about 1:30 and I went back to dine with one of our messenger boys. He's a man of about 35 I guess, educated, a lawyer, and an authority on icons. I guess he was on the wrong end of the Revolution, hence that's why he's running errands for the American embassy. He had a lovely-looking wife and their one-room apartment was exceedingly attractive, if you like nice Russian things. I don't particularly, but that doesn't mean anything. It was beautifully clean, the furniture in good repair and I was fed a wonderful meal, interspersed with lots of vodka and wine. I left at 5:15 – seemingly far too early by Russian standards! It was daylight outside and already people were beginning to queue outside the newly opened "commercial" stores. You can buy all sorts of foods in them without a ration card for an incredible sum of money. I guess opening them is a scheme to get some of the millions of rubles out of circulation and bit by bit get control of the present inflation.

Sunday, Averell and Bob and I and two secretaries went out to our dacha. It's about 20 miles out of town in what the Russians would call the forest – a tree grove. Trees are what I call telephone pole trees – pine to you – but they're the variety that are very tall, very straight and don't have any greenery or limbs except at the top. Our property Averell paced and estimated at three acres. It's really very nice, surrounded on three sides by a wooden wall, contains our house (modern stucco), a goat house, a cook house (our house in true Russian style has no kitchen), a Turkish bath house, a greenhouse and a farmer's cottage. The one hitch is that nothing works – no water, no electricity, and telephone facilities only on days that aren't damp!

The main house was built for an N.K.V.D. bigwig who subsequently lost his neck. It's very nice with three big living rooms downstairs and one bedroom, and three more bedrooms upstairs, lots of big windows for mosquitoes to use and a nice porch. We sat and sunned ourselves and ate a picnic lunch and then Averell, much to the horror of our man who lives out there, started to shovel for exercise. The Russian just couldn't understand how anyone, much less an ambassador, would shovel snow for the pure fun (or exercise) of it. Between us we built a sizeable snowman which later we christened "lady" due to bumps and made a series of bets on how long she would last. There's still about two feet of snow there. Oh yes, our other assets consist of one pig, three big rabbits and five babies. Did I tell you that here in Moscow we have thirty baby ducks? All in all Sunday was well spent. I even returned with a slight suggestion of sunburn.

I'm running out of conversation. Yesterday in desperation about the state of my permanentless hair, I cut a goodly quantity off. There are three of us females in the diplomatic colony who are trying to persuade the others to try a Russian permanent. The wife of the British minister got herself one in Tehran recently, so we're all mad at her! I wash my hair Sunday night, look respectable until Wednesday and no longer. After that I rotate between putting it up so that it looks unbecoming but neat, or let it hang. I guess when I get too straggly looking, Averell will let me go to Cairo or Tehran!

Best of love to everyone,

Kathy

CHAPTER 20

'THE P.M. IS IN FINE FORM, AS HE ALWAYS IS WHEN BATTLES ARE RAGING WELL'

Films featured centrally in the life of Spaso House. There were twice-weekly screenings of American films, documentaries, newsreels and cartoons – one for Soviet guests, the other for members of the foreign diplomatic community. It was a tradition inaugurated by Averell's predecessor as US ambassador, Admiral Standley, who saw it as a way of insinuating American culture into the USSR. The shows were organised by John Melby, but Kathy's hosting was their heart and soul. Ave and Kathy's dinner invitees were often treated to private viewings of a Hollywood movie. John, Kathy and Ave were keen to visit Soviet film studios, but while the Soviet film commissar was amenable, Molotov's Foreign Commissariat was not.

Kathy must have met most of the major Soviet filmmakers but was unfortunately inattentive and unretentive when it came to people's names. So we don't know if she was introduced to the most illustrious Soviet director, Sergei Eisenstein, who was world-famous for his innovative montage techniques and for silent classics such as *Battleship Potemkin* (1925) and the patriotic epic *Alexander Nevsky* (1938). She was certainly on his radar: in 1945 he drew caricatures of Kathy (with an elongated neck à la Modigliani), and in his fragmentary, unfinished postwar memoirs he alluded to her as the 'dollar princess'.

At the end of April, Averell flew to North Africa for a meeting with Edward Stettinius, Roosevelt's Secretary of State (successor to Cordell

Hull), taking Kathy with him. They then travelled to London, where they dined with Churchill and Eisenhower, visited Beaverbrook and met up with Pam, leaving for the United States on 5 May. They returned to Moscow at the end of that month, again via London, where they had lunch at 10 Downing Street and spent the weekend at Chequers.

Kathy and Ave arrived back in Moscow on 1 June, just in time to visit the US–Soviet air base at Poltava in Ukraine and welcome the first participants in Operation Frantic, a series of raids on Germany by B17s, which then 'shuttled' to the USSR for refuelling before returning to their home bases in Britain and Italy.

Kathy came back from abroad with her usual 'loot', including some silk stockings which she gifted to Mme Maisky. Agniya returned the goods, however, together with a note: 'I do not require stockings. I have plenty of my own. Good stockings are so precious these days that I am sure you will find someone among your American friends who will need them.'

En route to Algiers
April 29, 1944

Dear Pam,

It's hard to believe but I'm sitting in an aircraft. Jock's asleep opposite, Ira's working and Ave and Shirley are talking down the other end. We're en route to Algiers. It's all too good to believe. Sort of like waking up from a dream finding yourself back once more with friends.

We're going to meet the White-Haired Boy[1] at Marrakesh and then 'twill be decided whether or not we make a quick trip to Washington. As you can well imagine, if it's possible (God knows Ave will do his utmost to make it possible) we'll drop in on you. Jesus, I hope so.

Our trip out came sort of suddenly and we've been travelling pretty rapidly. Left Moscow on Wed. (rose at 3 a.m.) and made Cairo that night at ten – something that's almost a record – we flew some 2,700 miles!

1 US Secretary of State Edward Stettinius.

At Cairo we were galloped off to a dinner party (weather hot as hell and then I discovered Ave had been expected but not me). We stayed with General Giles (he used to be with Ira in the U.K.) and left at the crack of dawn with the idea of making Naples that night, but we were grounded in Tripoli with bad weather. Tripoli I thought charming. The airport was a combined Anglo-American affair, with a nice villa for V.I.P.s, single bedrooms and baths and very clean. (One funny thing: the bathrooms consisted of a tub, basin and men's loo and I had a hell of a time finding a female loo in the place!) The C.O. was British and took us to Tripoli to dinner. The town has a certain charm – particularly the old Arab part built in the days when the Turks had Tripoli, but the modern Italian buildings look sort of shoddy – built of paper. It's sort of a dead city now – few ships use the harbor and the town's [filled] with a motley mixture of races. 'Twas most interesting flying over the desert – we saw El Alamein twice and could follow the line of battle clear up to Benghazi – tanks, trucks, aircraft are still scattered throughout. It was great fun seeing it all.

We got up to Ira's next day at lunchtime & stayed with him – the Castle Coombe[2] boys were all there. Ira's as sweet as ever & it's wonderful seeing Jock again. Seeing them all made me realize how much I miss having friends in Moscow. Our "acquaintances" there are most unsatisfactory. After dinner last night Tex got started on trying to locate "the family" in Italy and by some stroke of luck Shirley was up visiting Larry in a hospital just outside Naples. So Tex and I went out cross country around midnight to find them. It was almost too good to be true seeing Larry & Shirley again. We took 'em back to Headquarters & sat around in my establishment getting caught up. Then this morning Ira told Shirley there was loads of room in his plane, so he's still with us.

M.A.A.F. [Mediterranean Allied Air Forces] headquarters are lovely. Offices are in a huge palace, but the officers all live in tents and prefabricated houses in the park. I was given Air Marshal Slessor's house, which was heaven – sitting room, bedroom and bath. The Italians had built up lovely little gardens. Last night at dinner I picked

2 US Air Force base in England.

two magnolias to put in my hair. I saw Bill Hearst – same as ever – having a hellova time finding someone to write his stories for him!

I'm beginning to run out of news. Ira wants to play some gin. He seems busy and says that in scope of operation his job is now bigger than the U.K. one, but that's sort of rationalizing I figure.

Jock seems to like his liaison work and glad to be out of the PROing. His tent is fixed up nicely. Pictures and books, 2 air chairs. He's made it look like a home and showed it all off proudly.

I'll stop now and I'm crossing all fingers that soon we'll be seeing you.

Bestest of love,

Kathy

Chequers, Aylesbury, Bucks
May 27, 1944

Dear Mary,

I'm sitting in wonderful English sunshine watching Averell get beat at croquet by Mrs Churchill.

London has been wonderful. It's so nice to know that you have got lots of good friends. For your information I've had two proposals – one each night. We've seen all our 8th Air Force friends – they gave us a dinner party. Gosh, they are a nice bunch. Ira is here and we are going down with him.

As luck would have it we had engine trouble soon after Washington and landed at the first stop with a prospect of 48-hour delay, but we discovered that a bucket-seated transport was hard on our tail so Ave and I went on it, leaving Bob to pick up the pieces and baggage. It was quite comfortable – we lay on the floor among crates in sleeping bags. The crew was thrilled to death for a chance to see London and to carry passengers instead of freight. I woke up at about 1 a.m. and went up and sat in the co-pilot seat and had a wonderful breakfast of an orange and an egg.

Now we are down here. The P.M. is in fine form, as he always is when battles are raging well. Curtin (Prime Minister of Australia) is the other guest. He is delightful, very human, quite the opposite from what I expected just having read political stuff about him. He's not sharp and scheming, but has the quiet assurance of a great man and talks in terms of common garden sense. So different from Evatt, his Minister of Exterior Affairs.

I'm upstairs now. Ave's "running through the pack" with the P.M.

Yesterday at the hairdressers I learned that Marty Hemingway[3] had just arrived in town and sure enough just as I went under the dryer she phoned from the hospital (Ernest had 52 stitches in his head, the result of a car crash) so after lunch I went around and saw them.

He had a huge towelling affair around his head but otherwise was his same self. Her head is shaved à la *For Whom the Bell Tolls*, which I didn't think becoming. It was fun seeing them again. I like Marty, she'd make an ideal casual girlfriend.

Baby Winston is in bed with German measles. Incidentally he is Bobby's weight and height. He asked about Bobby – who he calls "Kathy's little boy" – and was furious I'd not brought him a photo.

A major incident occurred in the London duffle bag – the maple syrup broke all over everything.

We lunched [at No. 10 Downing Street] – first lunch in town, a foursome, which turned out to be the most fascinating luncheon I've ever attended. Someday I'll tell you about it. Oh dear, I'll miss all that side in Moscow.

By chance I had tea with my bestest British boyfriend – the Marshal of the R.A.F.[4] as he's now called. Damn but I don't have any Soviet Marshal friends!

I miss you like hell.

Bestest love,

Kathleen

---

3 Martha Gellhorn (1908–98), American writer, journalist and war correspondent, at this time still married to Ernest Hemingway.

4 Charles Portal, who was promoted to Marshal of the Royal Air Force in January 1944.

Moscow
June 4, 1944

Dear Mary,

There's nothing like landing back in Russia with a bang to help against that bad let-down feeling. This time we certainly did it. In fact I'm not really down to earth yet. Thanks to the Russians holding us up in Tehran, we got here Thursday afternoon. Gen. Deane met us at the airport and driving back to Spaso said that he was leaving immediately for "air base." Ave said he'd go too. I just sat quiet and held my breath. Finally home I found an opportune moment and suggested perhaps it would be a good idea if I went too. He looked as though I'd taken him by surprise (as if he didn't know that I'd been living in the hopes for the day when I'd see our aircraft land on Soviet soil), but in no time flat I convinced him that there were nurses down there so's being a female would be no problem (press females weren't allowed down). Besides, I'd promised our ex-host [General Eaker] that I'd be there to see him land.

We arrived at said airfield amid the cheers of the assembled Air Corps and press, who'd heard that we'd not be back in time to make it, and were hustled off by the commanding Soviet general – one Siberian called Perminov – to a concert given by the Soviet equivalent of USO for the assembled G.I.s and Russians on the base. The concert was held in the roofless, wall-less remains of what must have been a largish building. The stage had been fixed up with a roof – but we sat in the open on long benches. The audience was very enthusiastic – cat calls and whistles from the G.I.s and clapping and stamping from the Russians. Apparently one of the first difficulties we ran into down there on this American–Soviet venture was the cat calling. In Russia any form of whistle is the prime way to insult an entertainer and get him off the stage!

After the concert, I spotted a nurse and went up and asked if I could spend the night with all of them (four) in their tent but unfortunately in true Soviet fashion, the Russians at a moment's notice had laid on a regular suite for even me in their end of headquarters. Not wishing to insult them or hurt their feelings we did as we were told.

Russian hospitality is something that still floors me. Our suite was certainly no exception. We had curtains on the windows, sheets made of the same rough material, cloths on our table and to top it all huge jars of dahlias and irises on our tables – all this in the midst of complete devastation and nothingness. My God but they must have worked to get the rooms ready for us – that's the part of Russian hospitality that hurts, but to them it is so necessary to prove how welcome you are.

Come ten-thirty a dinner had been laid on by Perminov – about fourteen of us – half American and half Soviets. I thanked God that dinner turned out by Soviet standards to be a sober affair. Vodka flowed but each could determine the amount he wanted to drink. Toasts were not all bottoms-up, and even the Russians drank little in anticipation of all the work yet to be done.

I was close on to being pooped as we'd gotten up at four-thirty in Tehran that morning, been flying all day and from Moscow to the base I'd had to converse to a high Soviet official. As our command of the other's language was about equal it had been an exhausting affair, particularly as I hadn't thought about talking Russian for weeks. I wanted desperately to sleep, but figured it might offend him. Luckily I had Quent's book along, so we read the chapters on Russia together and that helped conversation along nicely. I blessed Quent for using translatable language in his anecdotes, but undoubtedly slaughtered them all.

At dinner we had a couple of interpreters, but I sat next to an air force general who was determined I understand his Russian. Our meal was hors d'oeuvres and more hors d'oeuvres. Finally some stew appeared which the Russian next to me volunteered as being "cow." I told him he meant "beef" but he insisted that he meant cow – "the kind that you milk." It tasted good anyway.

Our suite was guarded day and night by an armed and bayoneted Red Army private. Ave's N.K.V.D. boys even faithfully followed him every time he made an excursion to the privy – a procession that made us both laugh whenever it occurred.

Aside from the fact that I damned near froze to death, I slept wonderfully in between wondering why Ukrainian cocks crow for hours on end and what the hell a full orchestra (brass band) was doing playing in the yard. When I finally got up next morning, I discovered that the gal given the job of looking after my every need and want was really in earnest and expected to follow out her duties to a tee. She followed me to our own "bathroom." She held my tooth mug while I brushed my teeth, followed me back to my room and stood waiting for me to dress. Second trip to the bathroom, I figured I couldn't possibly shake her off, so all modesty forgotten, I stripped and sponge bathed myself while she chatted about her family, the war, the Americans etc. Later I tried to give her a pair of stockings, she thanked me profusely but never took them even though I laid them hopefully by my packed suitcase. Apparently all swaps of gifts are disallowed on the base, and that included me, which made me sad because she looked thrilled at the prospects of owning a pair of stockings. I guess her conscience got the best of her.

As conferences were going on all morning, I wandered around the camp and chatted with the boys. Morale was sky high, firstly I guess because that day exciting things would happen and secondly because our boys in Russia are sort of a pioneering group, but despite all, the ones I talked to have a great feeling of friendship and respect for their Soviet opposite numbers. It was genuine and very nice to find, particularly as there's little grounds for common conversation. Each shows the other how to do a job using a few words and lots of signs.

We were driving out to the field when the first bombers appeared as specks off in the horizon. It looked like thousands, then suddenly the first squadron was overhead with its welcome roar. Jesus but it was exciting – more so than anything I ever saw in England. Ave said he didn't think he'd ever before been so thrilled by anything. The general was every bit as excited as we – only being Russian he showed it. He bubbled up over with joy and started to throw his arms around Ave and kiss him.

The first Fort landed and taxied over to us and out stepped our ex-host from Naples and there standing informally in the rain while bombers continued to circle and land one after the other, we had a very impressive spontaneous ceremony. Our big boy presented Perminov with a Legion of Merit. In return he and I were given huge bouquets of flowers (a usual Russian custom when a general enters a town victorious). Russ made a short radio speech. Then we stood around for a while, everyone swapping short snorters signatures,[5] pictures were taken etc. and the bombers continued to land.

It certainly was a wonderful day and I don't imagine I'll forget it for a long time. Most of all the Russians were impressed by our bombers being in formation after a long bombing mission. Apparently theirs never are, and they appreciated the skill of our pilots – the skill of our bombardiers too after they saw photos of the damage done to the targets. So all in all the shuttle bombing has made a great impression on them and it's certainly a big step forward to proving that god dammit we all can do a job of work together.

June 9, 1944

Since I started writing you all hell broke loose in France. We heard it first from the Germans' news broadcast and were down at a Moscow airport seeing people off when Russ's aide drove up with confirmation from Washington. After that I went to the office and we spent most of the morning listening to all the various broadcasts. Gosh it was exciting.

Unsuspectingly, I went over after lunch to my Soviet Cultural-Relations friends about a photo exhibit. We did little work that afternoon! 3 of us – 2 Russians and me – consumed the better part of 2 bottles of cherry brandy, all drunk in toast bottoms-up. I don't like having a hangover come 5 p.m. but that day it was worth it. My Russian friends said that their phones had been ringing all day – people swapping rumor stories of where the landings were, how big etc. They were all out in their enthusiasm and being the first American they'd come across I got the brunt of their hospitality!

Funnily enough, Eddie Page,[6] that evening celebrating at the one newly opened restaurant was grabbed by the Russians and asked "are you an American?" Russians came up and toasted him all night

5 Inscribed banknotes – customarily exchanged by people flying on an aircraft together.
6 Edward Page (1905–65), US diplomat who bought a car with Kathy.

long. It's funny the way the public gives us complete credit for the invasion – not the British or Canadians. No one toasted them at all.

I guess now I've more or less settled back into the routine, starting today with a hen party at the Mexican embassy. The ambass.'s American wife and green-eyed daughter are now in our midst and I have a feeling will be very problematic. Missus Quintanilla is attractive looking and ultra-ultra social. Daughter is pretty, talks a blue streak and loves "boogie-woogie" dancing. She wants to have dancing parties every week – looks like trouble to me. She is about 19 or 20 years old. I went there for tea – the usual group of gals: Persian, Dutch (new arrival aged 15), French (cross-eyed and pitiful) and me. Oh I forgot a Czech.

Moscow itself with spring on our hands is a transformed city. The trees and parks are green. The people are out of their sacking winter clothes and everlasting felt boots. Now they look more human, almost gay. Our embassy has had its windows that were blown out put back. The downstairs hall now gets sunlight for the first time. Before there were no windows at all, just beaver-boarded blank holes. Now, though it is 7:30, I'm sitting on Bob's porch pretending to sunbathe.

Our head cook nearly died of nervous prostration when I gave her 24 hours' notice that we were having a 50 people reception. (I nearly died too when Ave told me to lay it on as it's very hard to get the necessary food, to say nothing of getting it cooked.) Everything turned out OK however. I did the shopping personally, so the Russians cracked through with everything I asked for and the party was the best we have ever had of that type. Our guest of honor was our ex-host of Naples and the Russians turned out about 20 strong of Army and Air Corps generals. We had a couple of British, the Canadian and Australian ambasses and that was all in the way of foreigners. We had invited one N.K.V.D. general & he turned up and all the Russian Army were very cold to him. He sort of stood apart and did not join in the little groups, no one asked him. I noticed it and got him to join my table where there were two generals (Air Corps) [who] without being rude more or less ignored the N.K.V.D. fella. Funny! I guess however it's obvious the army might be jealously cold to the N.K.V.D., who are the real power over here – but it was the first time I had had reason to notice it.

The sun has gone down now so I have to go in before I freeze.

Best love,

Kathy

PS The Elizabeth Arden package never was packed so please get some wax for removing hairs over to me as soon as possible.

Harper's Bazaar and *Harper's* are arriving but still no *New Yorker*. Your shopping has been very much appreciated by all.

Moscow
June 11, 1944

Dear Pam,

I'm enclosing a copy of Mary's letter [about] our trip to the Ukraine. Gosh it was thrilling. Flying down there too was very interesting. It's the 1st Russian countryside I've seen that's homelike – rolling country, fertile, great patches of different-colored greens & browns. From the air the villages that weren't caught by the war looked far more prosperous than anything around here – or what we fly over en route to Persia. Thatched roofs & little gardens. Occasionally in the larger villages there were picturesque churches – with their rounded domes. I was sorry we couldn't have gone down there by train – gotten off at the stations and really had a chance to see the countryside & the people.

3 days in Russia and I got what I thought was hoof & mouth disease. However, much to my disgust our dentist informed me that I'd got scurvy – caused by malnutrition – so now I take loads of vitamin something pills & am trying to get rid of it! The problems of living in Russia.

Staying with Ira was swell fun. Larry & the gang dined with us and were like kids getting their loot from home. Jock added to their "bottle" equipment, which was awfully sweet of him I thought, because even though he has liquor, which they don't, his stock isn't too good.

I must go now.

Bestest love,

Kathy

Moscow
June 14, 1944

Dear Mary,

Well I'm back again in the Moscow rut! However, it's a much pleasanter rut thanks to the sunny weather. We have badminton and volleyball in the evenings. I don't play the latter! So far I haven't tennised but hope to soon. After we returned from the air bases I was up to my ears getting things ordered and out of chaos for the bombing photo exhibition. That was some chore, but thanks to our having here a col. who used to draw the futuristic and streamlined cars and aircraft for *Esquire* (& also designed jewelry) we were able to brighten things up with some drawings which he did to perfection.

While I was away the Soviets decided that our exhibition could be displayed to the ordinary public as well as "technically interested people." The reason of course was obvious, but unfortunately no one here did anything about the necessary processing to make the exhibition more human and less technical, so I had our Air Corps up to their ears locating stuff like flak suits, flying suits etc. The Soviets wanted all the smaller things and loose-leafed pictures put behind glass because they were scared people might swipe them as souvenirs, but I finally persuaded them I didn't care a damn if things were swiped.

The show opened with a bang on Monday – much ceremony & many guests and officials. The head of the Soviet organization for Cultural Relations with Foreign Countries (called pure and simply VOKS) made a speech, Ave made a speech and thank God I had to do nothing more significant than cut a piece of red ribbon that led into the exhibit hall. Everyone was very complimentary, that's to be expected, but our new air general said it was okay. The British however were furious [and asked] why in the hell hadn't we asked them to put some pictures in it etc. Actually, the only reason we got permission to run an exhibit in the 1st place was because the British had had one last year. It's the first time I've come up against the British being anti-American here in Moscow, & damn it I don't like it.

It was fun having Ira here. In my 1st letter I couldn't mention him by name until after he returned to Italy. Tex & 2 other officers I know well came with him. Jock unfortunately couldn't wangle it, as shuttle bombing isn't in his sphere of activity. Ira went down very well here. The Russians liked him a lot – his direct and frank way of approach – & his trip did a lot of good.

The initial raid, the fall of Rome & subsequently the invasion has rather put Eric Johnston's[7] neck out of joint because it's meant that the press boys haven't been at his feet crying for stories about "our future president." The Soviets' hospitality is beginning to wear him down – drink and food at every factory & place he visits etc. He's now gone off to Leningrad. Ave's just gone off to meet the Vice-Pres.[8] in Tashkent so Spaso's now more or less empty of V.I.P.s.

Last night I went to the opening night of a new show at the gypsy theater – a swell one – lots of music & singing & dancing. The play itself was easy to understand. I get a kick out of going to a play I know nothing about and being able to understand it.

Can't remember if I told you or not but in honor of the 2nd anniversary of the signing of L-Lease to Russia, Mikoyan (Commissar for Foreign Trade) and 3rd big shot in Russia sent Ave & me "modest" (that's what the card said) gifts. Mine was enough baby caracal (30 skins) for a size 40 coat. My fur expert friends say it's the cat's whiskers of caracal, that is if you like it! Anyway, I'm not going to turn it over to Sov. furriers & will wait till next trip home to get it made into something.

Ave got the remains of 1,000 pound Polar Bear. It's so huge that it takes up nearly the entire floor space of our upstairs sitting room. Its outline is enhanced by a piping of felt-color "shocking." We'll have to build a new Sun Valley hotel around it! From Molotov, Ave received a piece of china, which I've not seen, but I gather it's a man riding on

---

7 Eric Johnston (1896–1963), President of the US Chamber of Commerce, invited to visit the USSR by Stalin, who told him that had he been born in the United States he too would have been a businessman.

8 Henry A. Wallace (1888–1965), who visited the Soviet Far East on the way to China.

a wolf with a naked woman in his arms, with plenty of snakes and dragons. Wonder where we'll put it!

Later same evening

My little communist friend came in for a drink before dinner. I've not seen him for three months & most decidedly we can get on better now. One way or another, I can get him to understand me and vice versa. However, it's mentally torturous for me putting my own ideas into simple Russian. I gave him one of your gaudiest ties and he immediately donned it and was most pleased.

He wanted to know two things about America – was Roosevelt going to be reelected and why do the great artists like Chaplin have to be the subject of a big scandal?

We've just received back the "passed by the censor" 1st edition of the O.W.I. magazine,[9] so I showed it to him and asked for comments. The most interesting thing of all was that his comments and suggestions tallied amazingly with the Foreign Office's – the party line makes all men think alike! The general idea being we should bring Russia and Russian influences more into the articles. 'Tis a wonderfully naive thought that we'd use our magazine to propagandize Russia to the Russians – but that's what the party boys hope we'll eventually do!

My friend, like all the other Russians, was immensely interested in the material but he couldn't help but laugh at some of the language. He suggested that a man with a current knowledge of Soviet Russian could lighten up the language no end. When I said that a Russian editor would be difficult to get, he answered "not now that the 2nd Front was open!," which is probably true.

This evening there were only three of us for dinner. Afterwards we went to a park & wandered around among the people. I noticed a building that intrigued me because it had been built around 3 trees – they'd not been cut down and their heads stuck out of the roof! We were amazed to find a large sign saying "Cocktails" in just that [Latin] script. The bar was upstairs. Two bewhiskered

9 The magazine *Amerika*. The first issue, priced at 10 roubles a copy, was published in January 1945 with a print run of 10,000.

"doormen" greeted us & God damned if we didn't find ourselves in a bar, attractive too. A semicircular affair with tables on the outer side of the room. It wasn't crowded, so we sat down and downed a "Moscow" cocktail apiece – mixture of vodka and cherry brandy. The place had obviously just opened and the barmaids mixed each drink as if it were part of an important chemical experiment. (Russian cocktails invariably contain at least 5 different kinds of liquor & equally invariably are horribly sweet.) The place reminded me of a rustic Canadian Pacific Railway bar. Eddie Page said it reminded him of Finland. It certainly amazed us all. Moscow's going gay. If other places like this have mushroomed up, it will be terrific. Three drinks and it only cost us $7.00 – that's not bad at all.

[Kathleen]

Moscow
June 19, 1944

Dear Mary,

Oh dear this office is a madhouse and there's so damned much work to do I don't know whether I'm coming or going, so I'm giving up and writing you. Thanks to the shuttle bombing, the landings in Normandy etc., the Soviet press is using a lot of our pictures, all very nice but means I have to keep on my toes and remember what we have to hand when they ask for things.

I'm sure you'll be pleased to know that my scurvy is having difficulty surviving the doses of pills I am taking. I presume I wrote you that I discovered to my horror I had it shortly after we returned. It's a nasty disease, you feel as though your teeth are about to fall out.

Ave got back last night with a terrific amount of loot – perishable goods in the form of fruit (even melons) and such things as an embroidered dressing gown for him, a rug to hang on the wall and a series of embroidered hats, one particularly beautiful one given him by a local bigwig for Marie. Now he's back he says that it's too bad I didn't go along too. A hell of a time to tell me!

On Saturday the Becky plane crew (Becky's Ave's Liberator) gave a party-picnic that lasted for thirty hours straight out in the country. There were about twelve of us, me the only female, and practically the only one who didn't pass out at some stage of the game. They're a nice bunch of kids, but when they go on a binge, they certainly do a thorough job of it.

Did I tell [you] that my *Harper's Bazaar* is arriving, so my Russian female friends are most happy. Also Melby says to tell you that your choice of tobacco was excellent and thanks very much. It certainly stinks up our office nicely!

Help, murder – the Foreign Office has just phoned to say that Madame Maisky will see me tomorrow at four o'clock at the official F.O. reception house. I tried to get her to come out and see me, to relay messages from Mrs C etc.

Goodbye now,

Kathy

Moscow
mid-June 1944

Dear Pam,

Your letters written for June 3–11 were fascinating. Sitting in bed reading them last night, made my missing all the thrill not seem so bad. I think Ave felt the same way. I was stupid to dread coming back here – because now that Ira et al. have left, life has returned to the Moscow normal routine, I've realized that I'd forgotten the compensations you can receive being here.

I'm in bed tonight, no particular reason except that my scurvy makes my mouth uncomfortable & unconversational & to top that I'm getting a cold. While Ave was away in Tashkent seeing the Vice-Pres., the Becky crew had a picnic-party. Somewhere along towards the evening one of the enlisted men threw Charlie (who's a full colonel, but much beloved by his crew) into the stinking canal that runs by our dacha. Eventually they threw me in too, clothes & all, so I guess that's where I got the cold. But the picnic did me a lot of good – getting away from the stuffy dignity of the State Department. They all got rather drunk & hence talked a lot. Except for our new co-pilot, they've all done their ration of combat missions either in the German or Pacific wars.

Yesterday, thanks to Eric Johnston, we were subject to an inordinately boring ordeal – a formal luncheon given by the organization that deals with cultural relations with foreigners. The Soviets there represented the pick of the artists. There were toasts and more toasts. The Soviets each started out being humorous but invariably their ending would be deadly serious. Unfortunately Bill White (author of *They Were Expendable* and *Queens Die Proudly*), who's Eric's PRO, made a shatteringly stupid speech about freedom of election in the U.S. etc. For a while the Americans at the party were sweating with embarrassment & the Soviets equally so. Can't think why White did it – he wasn't drunk. Lunch lasted 'til 7 pm!

While Ave was away the weather suddenly turned warm and nice so I spent most of the middle of each day basking in the sun and did work at other times. The only thing that suffered was my Russian lessons & I have got a nice suntan. My legs are dark enough now so I don't have to wear stockings in the daytime.

I've been to the theater a few times recently – gypsy play with plenty of dancing and music & amusing plot. Another evening I saw an expert production of a Goldoni play (Italian 18th century) with a top-notch cast. It's fun going to a play and being able to understand the plot even if I do invariably miss the significance of the jokes.

Did I tell you that my little communist pal is back in circulation. He's come here once and in a couple of days I'm going out to his dacha to dine. He's so damned earnest & friendly that I can't help liking him. The British want to send him to England as he's one of the young up and coming writers – so I'll let you know if he does and you can meet my Russian "beau" (God forbid!).

Bestest love,

Kathy

Moscow
June 26, 1944

Dear Pam,

For your information, I think Ave's made great progress with our Friend.[10] They seem to be on a far more friendship, confidant basis, which really is quite exciting. Ave is without a doubt from what I can

10 Presumably Stalin.

gather liked by him and most importantly trusted. So maybe our little seance in the isolation ward has proven worth it, will really mean something in terms of more than just the war period. Ave seems very pleased, but unless he mentions this to you, don't comment in your letters.

Litvak,[11] a Hollywood director now colonel in the Air Corps, is with us, a pleasant change from the usual run of guests. Being the director of *Battle for Russia*, the Soviet movie folk here have received him with open arms and being a Russian himself by birth and a fluent speaker in Russian, he's been able to answer a lot of idle and unidle questions about movies, war ones and general ones. We had a small party here one night – showed the invasion newsreels and an excellent film telling the story – preparations and operations – involved in the two first landings on New Britain.[12] The Russians were spellbound by both and afterwards they sat around Litvak in a circle, like children, and plied him with questions. One guest told me he'd never seen Russians act so naturally freely in front of foreigners before.

One amusing thing happened. You know here that most movie actresses marry movie directors and from then on out play the lead in their films, well that night we had the pick of the directors, hence all the more renowned stars (a pathetically frowsy lot, but nice). Both the men and their wives were intrigued by my sunburn, wanted to know where I'd gotten it, was it the "style" in America to burn yourself brown in summer. I'm wondering now if they're going to start sunbathing too!

Another evening after another showing of the above-mentioned movies, the Tolstoys came upstairs and had a drink with us. Mme T. wanted to know all about the little things in America, what were people wearing, doing, thinking etc. She too was almost pathetic in her search for news of the outside world.

---

11 Anatole Litvak (1902–74), Russian-American filmmaker, notable for his anti-Nazi and wartime propaganda films.
12 An island off the coast of New Guinea, occupied by the Japanese in 1942 and invaded by US marines in December 1943.

I saw Mme Maisky the other afternoon, but it wasn't particularly productive. She received me at the official F.O. joint instead of her own flat. Perhaps that's why she wasn't very free and easy. I left after the protocol prescribed 30 minutes and had the feeling she heaved a sigh of relief. She kept telling me how happy she was now to be settled down to the routine of Moscow life, seeing her friends among the intelligentsia (that's the word she used), but none of it really added up or rang true. But then no Russian will ever complain, much less to a foreigner. I really felt sorrier for her than I have before. And also glad that I was born an American, not a Russian!

Just in general life is far pleasanter here in the summer, occasionally the days are sunny. It's light until nearly midnight and dawn at three. We play badminton or the men play volleyball in the evenings before dinner. My garden is coming up nicely, only unfortunately my seeds are all producing pink flowers – no matter the variety they all seem to be shades of pink or purple. Better luck next year, God forbid!

Incidentally, General Burrows[13] was furious at me for telling his wife that I saw him only at parties, the ballet, opera etc. (which is true) because it gave her the idea that he was being very gay and in his letters he'd written that he did nothing but work. Apparently she wrote him about it and he didn't think it was a bit funny!

Last letter I forgot to tell you about an amusing little episode at Caserta. After dinner I told Ira how much I appreciated his going to all the trouble of collecting the boys for dinner etc. (you know the line) when he started in with "you know I've never had a sister, I've always wanted one ..." You can guess the rest. His little speech was pathetic it was so corny. But anyway that makes us relations or something doesn't it?

Goodbye now,

Kathy

---

13 Montagu Brocas Burrows (1894–1967), head of the British Military Mission in Moscow.

Moscow
June 26, 1944

Dear Mary,

Without doubt the best day of the week is Sunday. Yesterday I kicked all males off my sun porch and sunbathed, washed my hair and just generally relaxed. Averell worked all morning and suddenly decided he wanted some exercise in the form of a nasty game called volleyball. I've only ever played it once and that time succeeded in spraining my wrist, breaking two fingernails and just generally getting my hands and arms sore, so I get my exercise playing badminton and gardening. Eddie Page and I have gotten ourselves together a mighty fine flower garden. Already some of the flowers are blooming – the unfortunate thing is that our colors have turned out to be varying shades of [shocking] pink, purple and more pink.

Anatole Litvak blew in a couple days back with newsreels of the invasion. One evening we gave a small party for Litvak to meet Soviet movie directors etc. and showed the pictures while he gave a running commentary in Russian. They were all very much impressed. Very few Russians have ever seen movies of the Pacific War and one man told me afterwards that he figured our war against the Japs looked more difficult than their war with the Germans at any time of the year!! Being Russian he wasn't being funny, he meant it. After showing the movies we fed the bunch and they gathered around Litvak and plied questions about Hollywood, every possible aspect.

Last night after the movies we had another one of our three language sessions with Tolstoy and wife. As time went on Averell got sleepier and sleepier and I found his yawns very catching. Madame Tolstoy was having a progressively difficult time translating her husband's flowery Russian into French. She was getting sleepy too but Tolstoy was on top of the world – discussing his favorite subject, the Russian soul. In between times he consumed large quantities of Scotch – taken almost straight – without any real effects.

This evening *Sun Valley Serenade* is opening for general consumption around Moscow. I'm hoping to get there as I never saw the whole thing in English.

Best love to you,
Kathy

Moscow
July 3, 1944

Dear Mary,

At this stage I think I'm going mad. Tomorrow's the 4th of July. Ave's having a party for Molotov here in Moscow & at the same time we're entertaining all Americans at the dacha – a picnic with baseball etc. and beer. The number now adds up to something like 150. A half of the arranging goes to me, plus the worst part of trying to think what others might have forgotten to do!

Canada had its *Bolshoi Prazdnikh* [Big Holiday] on Saturday (Independence Day or whatever it is now called). Anyway, feeling original, they hired a big boat and we went boating down the Moscow canal. To my horror I found myself included in a select little party of bigwigs in a room up front, surrounded by glass windows so all others could look in as they walked around the deck. I sat between Tolstoy and the Vice-Commissar of Foreign Trade, a very nice man who lived abroad a certain amount of time and speaks good English – one of my favorites – so it wasn't too bad. Lunch over, a few of us started dancing on deck to a piano, alternating with a gramophone. It was quite genial but exhausting as the deck was sticky to say the least. There was a big turnout of Russians, all the usual members of the "cultural" set plus Foreign Office officials. Ave's and my one advantage over most of the other members of the diplomatic corps was that we know them all. I made one new delightful friend in the form of a minor Foreign Office official, Vyshinsky's second interpreter, a young boy with a shaven head whose specialty is American slang. He got quite drunk and was amazingly free and easy besides being funny. He danced abominably but was proud of it (I mean he thought he was good). Assurance is something unique in a young Russian, that is when he's with a foreigner. This guy certainly had it.

The party over, I progressed to the flat of one of our secretaries, where a good group had assembled, the more genial people who'd been on the boat. I dropped in for a while, but tactfully left as it grew more drunken. The Russians all got absolutely stinking. I worked on the husband of my Russian teacher and did such a good job apparently that I'm in the doghouse. Going home he fell most of the way down the stairs. He being a ballet dancer, it might have been serious.

Russian parties may sound sort of silly to hear about, but at the time they are lots of fun. It consists mostly of everyone playing the fool, getting drunk. That evening Moscow's best ballerina took off Leningrad's best ballerina doing the dance the Leningrad gal had done the night before. Having seen the performance made it seem all the funnier. My God but they hate each other!

[Kathleen]

Moscow
July 6, 1944

Dear Mouche,

This present business is getting sort of embarrassing. Between us Ave & I have accumulated in the last month a huge bear rug, the wherewithal for a fur coat, a piece of monstrosity china, a valuable Icon & an old silver box inscribed with my name & a little message about "her Moscow friends who sincerely & earnestly love her" or something to that effect. The box came on the 4th of July in a specially made box – American flag on it (painted) & the date – a nice touch – they got the date wrong – had 14th July painted instead.

Our [4th of July] picnic was purely for Americans at the dacha & was plenty big enough. Every possible thing except the weather went wrong at the start. Necessary passes to play baseball didn't come through at the last minute. The beer didn't arrive on time & I had to start people off drinking vodka punch, which adds up to dynamite. I bypassed the former misfortune by getting the navy boys to build a raft out of empty gasoline barrels. Instead of crossing the canal onto government property (military) by a guarded bridge, we swam or crossed by the raft and kept the various [Soviet] officials happy by doling out beer.

All the people seemed to be happy. We provided delicious picnic food & sports if they wanted it. Simultaneously Ave had a luncheon for Molotov here in Moscow, which also went well. Climax of the meal was our own fresh strawberries – which apparently were much appreciated.

The picnic started at 12:30 & lasted until 8:30 – or at least that's when I left with our enlisted men & clerks in a huge truck. Some of the officers stayed out longer [and] all got absolutely pie-eyed on weak Russian beer. They went around collecting the half-filled bottles that had been discarded & had themselves a real party. We were pulling them out of jail all the rest of the night!

July 10

Your letter, filled with amusing clippings, was great fun to read.

I'm fast becoming a worthless worker. My schedule is terrific – days when the sun is out I just plain don't go to work and sit in the sun. Result, I've read every damn book on Russia in the house.

The nice thing about Moscow sunshine is that when it does come out, it is so weak that it doesn't make me break out and I don't even have to cover my lips. I had a hard time in Italy even just sitting on a porch, to say nothing of Tehran, which made my lips swell up. So you see there are all sorts of compensations for living here!

Last Saturday we "killed off" all the worst members of the diplomatic corps for dinner – a wonderful time because our weekly movie that night came at 8:30 so there was no chance for boring conversation. The movie that night was a particularly good spy story in which the hero pretends he's an Iron Guard member. The audience loved it and laughed like hell, so did I. The only person who wasn't amused was the wife of the Dutch ambass. A Rumanian lady, nice but completely lacking in a sense of humor. She sat next to me and snorted with disgust and occasionally let out a "most exaggerated, most exaggerated"!

Yesterday, Sunday, we spent a wonderful day sitting on our lawn and playing badminton. Averell and Bob have recently taken it up and Ave particularly is getting very good. As usual he has the scientific approach and invariably objects to my style of playing, which is anything but scientific – particularly as I don't give a damn whether I win or not. That's not too good when we're partners.

I've got me an appointment with an earnest Russian girl, so must be off.

Best love,

Kathleen

Moscow
July 17, 1944

Dear Mary,

In future years when you're thinking of a nice summer resort where there's sunshine and not too much heat and no need to dress up, remember Moscow. For summertime this is the best city I've hit so far. I suppose it's the comparison to winter that makes the town seem so nice. It really is pleasant.

Yesterday we went picnicking on the outskirts of town to a monastery – built in the early fifteen hundreds and added to in time of Peter the Great. One building was [a] two-storey tower affair, quite small. That's where Peter put his wife after he got bored with her "to spend the rest of her days praying and crying." Thank God I didn't live in those times! It was all quite interesting, particularly as I've just finished the first two volumes of Tolstoy's (our friend) life of Peter (the others have yet to be translated). The monastery overlooks the Moscow river, some of our party went swimming, but the water was a little too smelly for me to get up much enthusiasm.

This past week seems to have been one succession of parties. General Deane gave a dinner of 22 for our new air general to meet some Soviet military bigwigs. For some reason or other he asked me too and it turned out to be far more fun than I'd hoped. The meal itself lasted from seven-thirty 'til ten and there were speeches and toasts throughout. I got away with only making two of them, which pleased me as I hate having to do that sort of thing. We adjourned to the movie room and saw *My Gal Sally*, one of our regulars that we pull out on such occasions. Unfortunately, as I had the two most important guests next to me on the sofa, I had to sit thru it again, but it was amusing getting their reaction. That party over, I progressed to a Russian birthday party and finally got home around five.

Another night I went to the new restaurant that's opened in the Moscow Hotel – Moscow's bestest hotel, where the party members and other favored ones are allowed to live. We went after dinner – me and some of our Russian-speaking translators and clerks. Going there for a meal, it's easy to run up a bill of a hundred dollars per person, but we only drank. (My bottle of sour beer cost about eight dollars, I think!) Imagine the center room in Grand Central Station filled with tables and with drapes along the wall and you'll have a rough idea of the restaurant (it's not that big, but it gives the impression of being huge). There's one orchestra that plays only Russian music, but from one until five a real honest to God jazz band plus evening-dress singer performs.

The girls are everyone's property. If a man decides he wants to dance with a girl he goes up to her escort, bows formally and asks permission. Being the only foreign female present, I don't think I even was allowed to sit out a dance (which thank God are short). As the evening wore on we had quite a big gathering at our table, mostly directors of big factories, all of whom are well able to spend thousands of roubles on an evening's entertainment. The most interesting guy was an Air Corps major, who had received the Hero of the Soviet Union star twice, which is most unusual. He was a youngish kid but had been in the Air Corps for some years. He turned out to be a bombardier and had been on most all of the Soviet bomber raids into Germany, Rumania, Poland etc. The one trouble was he was punch drunk [and] drunk, hence very hard to understand. He sort of muttered through his teeth and didn't like talking about his exploits. His one ambition was to get to one of our air bases and meet some of our bomber crews.

It's funny, odd that is, that the government allows a place like that to go on – where Russians can mix as freely with foreigners as nationals would in any other country. Perhaps it's an experiment. It's fun going there anyway.

July 21

Just as I started this letter we got word that some sixty thousand of the prisoners taken at Minsk were to be marched thru Moscow. At the time it was all very interesting to be able to see the types of men that the German Army's now made up of, but later and the more I thought about it the more depressing it seemed.

The Russians had weeded out the prisoners and we saw only the unwounded ones. They walked in batches of about a thousand and were headed by horse-ridden militia and flanked by foot militia with rifles and bayonets. For a while we watched the procession from a second-storey window at a place where the crowds were particularly dense. People had been warned by radio throughout the early morning that they must be orderly, not jeer or try to get to the prisoners, so they were on their best behavior and did little more than push. Actually, even talking between themselves they were little other than curious, none of our people heard jeering talk – they just stared at the Germans and the Germans stared back. After a while we went down in the streets and parked the car along the edge of the boulevards and watched the prisoners as they walked by. We saw few older men – mostly the ages seemed between 18 and 35. They looked fit. The weather was warm and they were walking fast but not sweating. Each carried a tin can and many water flasks. The uniforms were complete and aside from dusty in good condition. Those walking barefoot carried their shoes or boots. Some looked glassy eyed and shell-shocked, some were glum and refused to look at the sights of Moscow, but the great majority walked along quite unconcernedly chatting among themselves and pointing out things of interest as they passed – one of which was us in our American-flagged car.

We didn't see many blond Nordic Germans and the French embassy folk said that the Alsace-Lorraine troops all seemed to spot them and shout "vive la France," "vive de Gaulle." As we drove away we saw a little gathering of glum Japs – out to watch the spectacle too!

Watching those prisoners, we speculated on how many would ever get home again, see their families. (The Russians expect to have as much of their reconstruction work done by Germans as possible.) Perhaps none of them realized just how [tough] their future is. It's not particularly nice to think about. But enough of that.

Last night Averell at last broke down and went to the theater. The director of that particular one had pleaded and pleaded with him to come and in a weak moment he said yes. For a second time I sat thru a five-hour performance of *Othello*. I'm sorry I saw it again because first time you miss most of the flaws. Averell enjoyed it, but he found five hours of it rather stiff going!

Another evening which turned out great fun was when I went to a concert given by members of the ballet school. Mostly they were dancers aged about fifteen to eighteen. The girls did some of the main ballet dances with great seriousness, but unfortunately none of them had enough poise to be able to take curtain calls with dignity. Actually, dignity is about the most noticeable thing that the present generation of Soviet women and girls [lack]. I guess it's something they've never been taught – if it's teachable.

On the fortieth anniversary of Chekhov's death the Soviets put on a seven-hour affair at the big theater. Ave and I arrived two hours late and still had to listen to speeches. We stayed for one act of one play and part of a musical and reciting section, when thank goodness Ave dreamed up something to do in the way of work and we left. It's certainly lucky that Averell doesn't take that part of his job too seriously!

With luck I'll go out with this letter. It remains to be seen just where I'm going to. I've got my fingers crossed that it's further than Capri. But Averell treats my ideas on traipsing around the war with reservation, which I imagine is sound. But every now and then I get an urge to get a trifle nearer to the war than Moscow salutes!

Best love to you all,

Kathleen

CHAPTER 21

'WHAT SURPRISED ME MOST WAS TITO'S HANDS, THE HANDS OF A PAMPERED POLITICIAN RATHER THAN A GUERRILLA CHIEFTAIN'

Kathy's bout of scurvy earned her a recuperation trip to North Africa and Italy in summer 1944. In Italy she met the communist leader of Yugoslavia's partisan army, Josip Broz Tito; indeed, it was through meetings with American and British officials in Italy that Tito gained recognition as the political as well as military leader of Yugoslavia. By the time Kathy arrived the allies had invaded Italy and occupied half the country, including Rome, which was liberated in June 1944. Kathy's visit coincided with the launch of Operation Dragoon – the allied invasion of southern France on 15 August – the counterpart of the Normandy D-Day landing of June 1944.

When Kathy returned to Moscow, the Warsaw Uprising was in full swing. In early August, Polish nationalist partisans rose in revolt in an attempt to seize Warsaw from the Germans before the Red Army liberated the city. The revolt failed, as did the Soviet attack on Warsaw. Churchill and Roosevelt wanted to supply the insurgents by air, but Stalin – well aware that the revolt was against him as well as Hitler – thought it a waste of resources and refused to allow American and British planes the use of Soviet air bases for refuelling. Averell was outraged by Soviet intransigence, believing it to be a deliberate ploy by Stalin to enable the Germans to wipe out the anti-communist Polish resistance, venting to Washington that the Soviets were 'bloated with power and expect that they can force their will on us and all countries'. His secretary, Bob Meiklejohn, wrote in his diary, 'It is just a case of cold-blooded murder, but there is nothing we can do about it. When the full story of this incident comes out it will certainly go down in history as one of the most infamous deeds of war. Beneath all their veneer of civilisation, the ruling elements here are nothing but a highly intelligent and ruthless gang of thugs and murderers.' In a later diary note, Meiklejohn confessed that at a Spaso House reception he had been strongly tempted 'to drop something on Moly's skull from our balcony'.

Harriman's anger, if not Meiklejohn's, proved transient. In September the Soviets changed their mind about allowing Anglo-American planes to ferry supplies to Warsaw and began dropping their own supplies to the embattled Poles. Stalin admitted to Averell that he had misjudged the insurgents' motives. Red Army efforts to capture Warsaw continued, but finally ended in failure in October. During the uprising the Germans killed 200,000 Poles, razed the city centre to the ground and deported the surviving population to concentration camps. Not until January 1945 was Warsaw liberated by the Red Army.

Tehran
July 27, 1944

Dear Marie,

I'm off at last on my spree – 1st lap complete – and I'm sitting practically in the nude sweltering in Tehran's hottest weather. Shower no. 1 hasn't done much good but I guess soon I have to pull myself together and put on one layer of clothes for dinner. But for the moment the generals are conferring downstairs so I'm better off out of the way.

Ave is very happy with his new minister – George Kennan[1] – and as usual is working too hard. Ever since his trip to Tashkent he's had one of the usual forms of dysentery on and off. Most all of Moscow has it. I started 2 days ago and in terror stuffed myself with sulfur drugs etc., because Becky is certainly not well equipped to handle a disease like that!

1 George F. Kennan (1904–2005). In his memoirs, Kennan wrote of Kathy that she 'served with casual graciousness as mistress' of Spaso House.

At this stage I'm not too certain just where I'm going – anyway to visit Ira and perhaps London. Excuse: to talk Joe Phillips into joining us in Moscow to run the magazine.[2]

Kathy

En route to Casablanca
July 27, 1944

Dear Pam,

If this gets delivered to you by Russ it will mean I'm sitting somewhere sore as a wet hen. At this stage there's still a chance Ira will be in your neck of the woods long enough for me to join him there and come back.

Left Moscow yesterday. Ave seems in good shape considering he's been having mild forms of gyppy tummy off & on. Perhaps it will do him good to be minus me for a while. Remember our conversation last trip thru London?

My writing's too jiggly to make much sense.

Pug will have a friend leaving for Moscow soon – in the form of General Burrows. He's with us now.

Bestest love,
Kathy

Villa Moss
Casablanca
July 29, 1944

Dear Pam,

A hurried note. We got delayed by bad weather – one day – & now Ira wires he's leaving U.K. tomorrow night. It's damned disappointing.

Herewith is a wee gift that Ave got you in Tashkent. I got one like it too.

Casablanca is absolute heaven – sunshine with a breeze. Swimming pool, tennis court, good food [and] genial company. It's certainly the

2 *Amerika*. In the event, the magazine was produced in the United States and copies shipped to the USSR.

best possible place to get stuck in. I wish Ira could bring you down. You must be having a nasty time.

We did the unbelievable & flew from Tehran to Casa in one day – 23 hours. The last five were at 16 to 17 thousand feet. We had no oxygen, so most everyone, excluding me, fell ill. I felt quite normal until we arrived at the airport, then I promptly passed out in Russ's arms with a good attack of the "bends" – cramps in stomach & joints. After about an hour I was as good as new but at the time it was sort of a nuisance, aside from being slightly embarrassing!

I'll write from Italy.

Bestest love,

Kathy

Villa Moss
Casablanca
July 29, 1944

Dear Mary,

I'm lying in bed smoking with yards of mosquito netting draped around and over me which gives the situation a danger angle. Life is heaven at the moment except I got me a new neighbour who snores, not steady like but unpredictably and that is almost as exasperating as the four-engine aircraft that comes shooting over our roof every so often. No planes flew to the U.K. last night so tonight there's a double ration worth.

Russ and the gang left this evening for the U.K., leaving me behind. Much as I'd like to go to England, two night flights for one day there seems foolish. So I'll bask in the sun all day tomorrow and Ira will pick me up the following morning. It was sad saying goodbye to the Becky crew tonight. They won't be coming back. Russ is going to try and wangle them a B29 job. To fly over Tokyo is their ambition. It's sad saying goodbye to people you like and knowing you'll never ever see them again.

I came back here to Villa Moss in a decided sentimental state of mind. Luckily I found a good cure. I re-read my favorite chapters of *Low Man on a Totem Pole* and that fixed me up fine.[3] Yesterday I re-read Gide's *La Porte Étroite* [*Strait Is the Gate*] – something I guess

3 A book by American humorist H. Allen Smith (1907–76).

I thought was swell while under Mr Fowle's Bennington influence. Yesterday I pretty much thought it stank, it being all about a girl who loves a man so much she decides she mustn't marry him and hence make her love unpure. The Villa Moss has a lovely incongruous library! Moss, I gather, was a big newspaper proprietor both here and in Rabat and some town in the S. of France. He completed his house in 1938. The German Armistice Commission were the first requisitioners, then Gen. Patton and now the A.T.C. run it as a V.I.P. joint. A captain called Blacky does the running and he certainly does a swell job. The food's terrific, all kinds of melon and fruit. If only the water didn't have to be chlorinated! Bath water runs two hours a day.

Our party on the Becky turned out to be most congenial. Russ and Obie – our Moscow general and admiral respectively, and naval Doc. Max Hamilton, our retiring Minister Counsellor, Gen. Burrows, the British Chief of Military Mission in Moscow, his and Russ's aides and a Navy kid (U.S.) from Murmansk with a badly broken leg done skiing last winter, and a weedy clerk who's going home on leave. Burrows in Moscow is a most dapper Guards Officer and very correct in everything, including bright green uniform pants, which is part of his Scots Guards semi-dress outfit. Here in Casa he went around in grey flannels, no tie and bedroom slippers. We told him he was letting Kipling down – letting the U.S.ers be better dressed in the colonies, but he figured that was a good idea.

I'm hoping desperately that Shirley will be visiting Larry again. It may be sort of odd visiting MAAF headquarters, I guess I'll either hate it and feel in the way or like it a lot.

I'm sleepy now.

Best love,

Kathy

Caserta

August 2, 1944

Dear Pam,

That's the toughest luck I've ever heard – you coming down with Scarlet Fever. It must be a nasty disease. I guess the trouble is that I'm not around to keep you in tow!

I wouldn't think that the Melchetts' would be the quietest place to be in now. Ira's stories of the buzz bombs don't sound very nice. I hope you'll be keeping out of London. Do take care of yourself.

I was dreadfully disappointed not to make the U.K. As it was I sat in the sun at Casablanca and sunned by the swimming pool, played a little tennis & ate a lot of wonderful fresh fruit & food – the likes of which Russia doesn't have. I had one whole day after Russ left during which Admiral Standley turned up. I thought him rather senile. He was most secretive to me about his present job, which made me immediately think he's joined Bill Donovan's boys! He asked me a lot of trivial questions about Russia and didn't seem the least interested in anything important, which I thought odd. To top it all he was rather pompous with the other guests at the villa. I remembered him as such a sweet old soul. It was quite disappointing.

Ira arrived early Monday morning. We delayed a little and then set off for here but got only as far as Tunis, where we spent the night. I'd never seen the town before. It's lacking in personality completely. Cross it off your list of places to visit.

Everything here is divine.

Bestest love,

Kathy

Caserta
August 7, 1944

Dear Mary,

I've just returned from weekending in Capri and it's every bit as lovely as it's cracked up to be, sunshine all day, moon (full one at that) all night. I advise that you and Shirley take it in on your second honeymoon.

The island itself is like a camel with the middle bitten out, lots of unclimbable limestone crags that dip sheer into the sea. The fertile land is filled with vineyards and orchards. The town of Capri starts at the water in the middle of the island (the bitten-out part) and scrambles up the slopes. Narrow steps lead everywhere – roads are cobbled and lined either with trees and high old walls or the houses. Buggies and ancient Italian motors rival with jeeps. In many places there's no room to pass. The townhouses are faded reds and yellows with an occasional blue – and their gardens, overcrowded, fall into each other, intermixing every imaginable bright color. The streets are all cobbled and all day long the inhabitants toil up and down with their loads on their heads. Flat ground does not seem to exist.

The island is now taken over by the Air Corps and all the big hotels are filled with pilots and crews in need of a few days' rest. We stayed at the villa turned over to Ira. Beautifully located high on a hillside on a point with southern exposure, high windows, terraces and very comfortable – but not too attractively furnished (owner was Italian), Greta Garbo & [Leopold] Stokowski had a mild affair there once.

At dinner we had an orchestra playing softly in the next room and afterwards, too, while we sat out on a terrace watching the moon come up. It was really too good to be true. It's sad there was no one there I liked! Our gang consisted of a handful of visiting generals, a couple of colonels and Larry. Ira came over for one night.

The beach is pebbly and very small, but I thought it was wonderful, being the first sea I've bathed in for years. The sun was wonderful and the atmosphere the most relaxing of anything I've ever known.

There were dances both nights. I missed the first and went the second night and enjoyed myself immensely. The kids were sweet. Larry only stayed one night, but he was an angel. I carefully coached him and played the part admirably of chaperone!

He came up here to dine my 2nd night and I went and lunched with him next day. After lunch Larry took us sightseeing over areas he and Shirley had toured. It was hot as hell, dusty but very amusing. We saw some interesting Greek relics, to say nothing of Roman ones, with a volcano or two thrown in. It's sad that Shirley isn't in these parts of the world.

I had a lucky break today after we arrived. A travelling general was going off on a day's tour and Ira fixed it up so's I was included too. We saw an Air Evac hospital aircraft being loaded with wounded. They fly to N. Africa, then England. American wounded go from England to

N.Y.C. nonstop. We were flying in a B-25 – terrific speed. It took 20 minutes to go from Caserta to Rome.

The point of our outing was to see the first cage P.O.W.s are brought to. Doubly interesting for me having just seen the 60,000 Germans captured at Minsk.

We talked to a pretty scruffy lot of Germans – no arrogant ones at all came in while we were there. However, they do apparently exist. 30% of the Germans captured are still ardent Nazis but the number of them who've become defeatists grows. The ones we saw belonged to the latter group. Amazingly enough, they gave the impression of being far less suited for military use than the Germans I saw in Russia. The clothing was a mixture of a variety of uniforms, whereas the Moscow ones were all identical uniforms – it was quite the opposite of what I expected.

Coincidentally, standing apart from the Germans were a bunch of 11 men and boys in rags. Upon questioning they turned out to be Russians – so I tackled them, they being able to speak but a few German words. They crowded around and seemed delighted to be able to talk their own language. One blond 30-year-old man acted as their spokesman. They wanted me to tell the authorities that they didn't like being caged with the Germans. They'd deserted the Todt [forced labour] organization a month back and had been partisans, they said, in the hills around Florence. As the allies neared they slipped over our lines and surrendered. They wanted to fight with us – they were our friends, they hated the Germans, etc. All had been captured in the Don bend area spring of 1942. None had seen Germany proper but had worked throughout the Balkan countries. I asked if they wanted to go home. They hesitated and said "if it was possible." Until the Soviets proclaimed that they'd not shoot their own P.O.W.s all the Russians we'd rounded up in Italy were scared stiff they'd be sent home and shot.

That day I managed to see a certain amount of Italy. Except for the shelled and bombed areas, life looked very normal.

I have to stop now,

Kathleen

Caserta
August 14, 1944

Dear Pam,

When I think of how close I came to [missing] this little excursion, I almost shudder in horror. In many ways it's been the most interesting 10 days I've ever experienced. Jeepers but you'd have loved it too.

Thanks to Russian being passably like the various Jug languages, I've seen a lot of Tito – one night here at Ira's & all the next day on Capri. The latter was one of the conferences at which "military & political matters were discussed" (according to the B.B.C.) with Bill Donovan & co. (me local color).

Bebe & Ben[4] arrived last week & since their arrival Ira & I have taken them on at bridge nightly, long, long sessions. At first I was scared stiff as Ira is very good. Both of them are very proficient as well. However, so far so good. We play for what I call very high stakes & I'm about $100 ahead. Needless to say, my gin rummy winning vs Ira is also successful.

It's now the 16th & I leave tomorrow. Returning from Rome [we had] Ira's C-47 to ourselves, so we toured the whole area, circled and recircled the main points of interest.

I loved Rome but at the moment am too tired to go into that. I think a swim's in the offing!

I didn't wire Ave that you were sick as my only means were army channels & I figured that wasn't too good an idea – anyway he'd just worry.

My bestest love to you,

Kathy

Sorry about the non-typing – but I no longer follow my typewriter! Ira sends his love.

Cairo
August 18, 1944

Dear Mary,

Ave must have been green with envy having to sit in Moscow while I went to Italy, unsuspectingly to watch the invasion build-up.

4 Bebe Daniels and Ben Lyon, whom Kathy knew from London.

Unfortunately, Ira wouldn't let me fly over the beach-head but I guess his reasons were adequate. It was a temptation to stay over three more days so's I could land in France, but my conscience or something got the best of me. I'll write you more fully of my stay – saw the P.M., a lot of Tito and co., Rome, & added together my two weeks have certainly been about the most interesting and fun I've had this war.

Best love to you,
Kathleen

En route to Moscow
August 20, 1944

Dear Mouche,

At this stage I've more or less lost all sense of time. I left Italy three days ago and now we're about two hours out of Moscow. My lovely little excursion is over – it's certainly done me a lot of good – sunshine, good food – to say nothing of the fascinating time I've had. I can't quite get over how lucky I am to be able to travel as I have the past three weeks.

I arrived in Cairo just in time to get dressed and washed and go to the opening night of *This is the Army*.[5] Egyptian society was there in full force and I felt about as like a waterless fish as 'tis possible. The females wore $400-looking dresses – very chic and long – and the jewelry was something I've never seen the likes of. I was the only one in a short dress! The men were fat and frog-like looking – they are the very wealthy non-working Egyptians. I found all extremely boring, but was interested in seeing the rich of a neutral country. After the show we progressed to a dance – smallish and select (I went with our commanding general of Middle East, with whom I was staying). King Farouk was there and he was certainly by far the nicest Egyptian man I met that night. Gossipers say he is very anti-British, and hence playing up the Americans versus the British. Anyway, I soon got very bored at the dance, very sleepy (two hours' sleep the night before) and was beginning to despair of the King ever leaving

5 American wartime musical comedy, directed by Michael Curtiz.

so that other guests could retire – the King didn't leave – so I did – out the back door.

Next day I shopped like mad and spent all of my $250 gambling profits from Italy playing bridge and gin on material for upholstering Spaso and Mokhovaya.

Our General Giles is very much of a social duck, so second night in Cairo again saw an Egyptian social gathering. I was glad not to have a third night in the offing – our army folk at Tehran are nice so I enjoyed last night far more – being Saturday there was a dance. I went to be polite and considering all things had a nice time. At least I didn't get stuck!

At 3 a.m. this morning I was up again, starting on this last lap. For some reason I'm on a Soviet plane, not our own B-17. But I'm glad to have had the chance to make the trip this way once. It looks as though it will be 14 hours instead of the usual 7. We stopped in Baku for customs. I alone was not ransacked. We were supposed to stop at Stalingrad but we haven't. Flying with the Soviets is full of surprises, the DC-3 is jammed with luggage of all sorts and shapes, kids, beds, army officers and females. I have a seat but not all do. The weather is not very good so we are flying Soviet fashion below it – along the treetops – instead of U.S. fashion above it – makes the scenery more interesting anyway. The traces left by tank battles, artillery shell holes, dug fortifications, are all visible. These leftovers seem so remote from the physical horrors of war.

I'm getting as hungry as hell as I was told that to bring my own food was unnecessary. Breakfast at 3 a.m. – cheese, black bread – and tea at 8 at Baku. Now it is well on to the afternoon. Perhaps sleeping is the best pastime.

My love to you,
Kathleen

Moscow,
August 20, 1944

Dear Mary,

Well, I came down to earth with a big bump today, nice and hard, courtesy of Soviet pilot, at the Moscow airport. Apparently, my arrival was unanticipated but by chance one of the third secretaries was down to meet the plane, so he was able to give me a slight preview of what has been going on during my absence. Anyway, it all adds up to a very bloody time for Averell. God knows, it has been difficult before, but I gather the last bit has topped all, both unpleasant and worrisome. Adding to working troubles Ave's ulcers have cropped up again. So he feels lousy and can't do anything about resting up. Thank God I'm not American ambass. to Moscow Russia! Bob with glee spelled out the nightly sessions, which is all very well but Ave's beginning to show the strain, weighing only 160 lbs. I wish to hell Marie were here to make him take care of himself.

I can't remember ever getting such a kick out of a short visit to a city as I did Rome. Unlike either London or Moscow it doesn't take knowing for its atmosphere to attract you. I was there only a day and a half, but I loved every single minute of it. The extravagance of St. Peter's was too bewildering, but I'd been forewarned by a little Italian who went along with us to act as Baedeker that it was difficult to appreciate first time. I'd not expected to find such a profusion of marble of all colors in big squares and oblongs in between the paintings, the statues and mosaics. Result, I was surprised and a little disappointed that nowhere was there simplicity that gives a church or a cathedral a feeling of reverence. The Sistine Chapel I really loved, I could have stayed there for hours – watching. I give up trying to say more. Something that struck me was the smallness of the Palazzo Venezia – one has seen it so many times in newsrooms – Mussolini on the balcony haranguing the crowds. We found some lovely little Byzantine cloisters in off-the-way places, something I'd also not expected to find. But it is the sudden unexpected vista you come upon of lovely squares with their fountains, a church at one corner and at times a view in the distance of a Roman ruin – that gives the city its real charm and makes me feel I want to go back.

The city, of course, is filled with G.I.s on leave. Each army, each air force has taken over a big hotel for their boys. It's sort of a Cook's tour done wholesale. I stayed at the M.A.A.F. hotel – hot and cold water, even bath towels provided. Food was army, but the fleas were definitely Italian. Despite a flea powder and every other precaution, I got more than my ration's worth during my one night there!

En route back to Caserta, Jimmy and I were the only ones in the general's plane, so he took it slowly via Anzio, Nettuno and Cassino. The town of Anzio isn't badly bombed – about a third of the town is damaged, but that's all – but the land between it and the first hills some twenty miles inland is completely potmarked with shell holes. Piles of ammunition still lie around – the area is a maze of slit trenches and tank emplacements. A very few farmhouses escaped being knocked down and burned, but even these are still deserted. An occasional crop still tries to grow and cover up the tank tracks that run thru it. Farther down the valley, towards the Pontine marshes, everywhere the farmers are burning their grain – I suppose to try and reestablish the land. About half the marshland is badly flooded – deeply flooded, so that only roofs are visible above the thick water.

We came on Cassino suddenly and I didn't recognize it as a remains of a town. It bears no resemblance to anything living. Like a deadly disease of yellow callous the rubble spreads upward, as though trying to meet the rubble of the monastery on the top.

The narrow valleys running up in the area between Naples and Rome are checkered with battle scars, some areas are dead, others completely peace-like and filled with thriving crops and villages. The contrast is almost unbelievable.

Best love to you,
Kathleen

Moscow
August 30, 1944

Dear Mary,

Due to my principle of not working when there's no conceivable constructive thing to be done, I've taken the day off. One of the Soviet translators is sick, so mine has been borrowed by the embassy. Only solution I guess is for me to learn enough Russian so's I can do my own translating – something I don't relish the thought of, though I restart Russian lessons in a couple of days.

Life here at Spaso functions at an ever-increasing tempo. Ave has almost nightly excursions to the Kremlin but he's bearing up well. The news is certainly wonderful and people here are far more optimistic about the date of the end of the war than they were in Caserta.

Last Saturday I went out to a senior officers' Red Air Force Academy in connection with the bombing exhibitions we are running (damnation, Ave's just given me a job of work to do, so I got to stop).

Next day

Maybe my short absence from Moscow has made me naive or something. Anyway, quite unsuspectingly, I went to my place of meeting to go to the Academy, anticipating the whole thing would take at most two hours, that no food or anything would be given etc. (it was morning). However, I was given the works – at six p.m. I got home, my hangover well on the way. The Academy turned out to be a very sumptuous place, equipped with tennis courts, indoor theater, etc. There were generals galore and despite the fact I'd originally asked if I could bring an air force officer with me to help out on answering questions and the request was politely turned down, I was snowed under with specific questions – details on bombing altitude on various targets, new equipment etc. For a while I thanked God for my recent Italy trip, which had filled me in on that theater, but when questioned about the Jap war, I was completely stumped. It was interesting however what they wanted to know. Interesting, too, that they were using an exhibition as an excuse for getting an American out there – unofficially.

The general in charge of the Academy was a last war fighter here and very genial. The usual meal of many courses and much wine was laid on and the Soviets initiated three separate toasts to the advance of our army in France. For the first one, one officer asked if I could explain just how far they had advanced. A map was even produced. Another thing they wanted to know was how did Hollywood make black ice, such as they saw in *Sun Valley Serenade*! Their enthusiasm was quite childlike. As lunch progressed on into the afternoon, with more and more toasts, my host finally decided that come coffee time, my toasts should be made directly in Russian, which was quite a stumbling block. It limited me in subject matter considerably! Finally I was allowed to leave, after the car had been filled with two armful bouquets and a huge basket of more flowers. It remains to be seen if any of our officers get invited out! I'll put my money on that one being no. This certainly is an unexplainable country.

Yesterday the correspondents returned from Lublin where they had a hellova interesting time – heard bits and pieces of the story of the uprising in Warsaw, had a good interview with Morawski, plus saw the latest atrocity story, just outside Lublin at a camp called Majdanek, which was one of the main Gestapo slaughter houses. Estimates of victims run down from 2,000,000 and include some twenty-two nationalities. Bill Lawrence compared the camp to an American production line – the victims for a particular day were first completely unclothed, made to wash in a shower room with 72 water spigots, then moved down the passageway to gas chambers where they were killed. After that the bodies were inspected for gold fillings and some X-rayed if they were suspected to have swallowed capsules with information. In the nearby field, three small blast furnaces were used to cremate the bodies, the ashes removed to fertilize the surrounding country. The correspondents were then taken to huge warehouses, one contained nothing but shoes, old discarded ones, considered not worth shipment back to Germany, all of every size and shape. The estimated numbers ran into the hundreds of thousands. From there they saw the warehouses where the clothes of the victims had been sorted while awaiting shipment back to Germany. Articles were carefully categorized and stacked. Women's corsets, nail files, shaving brushes, suits etc. on down to the room which contained nothing but children's toys and games. I'm sort of glad I wasn't there to see it. Bill Lawrence, the biggest sceptic among correspondents here on any horror story he sees, told us about this with tears in his eyes.

[Kathleen]

Lawrence reported to the *New York Times*, 'I have just seen the most terrible place on the face of the earth – the German concentration camp at Majdanek, which was a veritable River Rouge for the production of death.'

Moscow
September 1, 1944

Dear Mary,

I hate writing stale personal news, but if I don't put it down in a letter I guess I'll forget it for good and all.

If I remember correctly, I wrote you after my first week in Italy, at any rate before I could mention the fact that an invasion was coming up. It took no imagination to discover that. Naples harbor was filled with every type and kind of warship, troopship and landing craft. One day coming back from Capri we saw a squadron of L.S.T.s [Landing Ship Tanks] sailing out to their rendezvous point. It was quite spectacular. They are hideous oblong objects with cranes and derricks that stick out, making them look like a lobster on its back. Headquarters people were flying all over the countryside – at least Ira was – inspecting everything. Tex disappeared and went in with the paratroopers, and he'd still not been heard of by the time I'd left. Jimmy Parton[6] went in with a glider group and was back the next day with a fine story. I was told that I had to be a good girl and not to try and wangle anything, so I figured I'd better do as ordered.

Did I tell you Ben Lyon and Bebe Daniels turned up at Caserta? They were about to embark on a tour and were a very genial asset. She and I shared a house and had a lovely time. It's wonderful to run into a congenial female that you can talk to about nothing at all. Such an animal doesn't exist here. Anyway, after their arrival, we used to have nightly bridge sessions, me and the general against them. Something which at the start scared me stiff as the general is very good and they both vastly better than me, besides that stakes were not low. Thanks to my phenomenal luck in holding cards, I escaped with my skin plus a good many dollars.

Tito turned up one night for dinner along with about three staff officers plus a lovely-looking young female interpreter. Nice eyes and sweet smile. She talked very good English and had great poise in a shy sort of way.

---

6 James Parton (1912–2001), historian, journalist and aide to General Eaker.

Tito himself is small and heavyset. Very handsome with a strong face. Slit steel-blue eyes that were cruel and hard looking but when he smiled or laughed, as he frequently did, his whole face lit up and made him appear less forbidding. What surprised me most was his hands – they didn't fit in at all, being smooth and well kept, the hands of a pampered politician rather than a guerrilla chieftain. On his wedding finger he wore a big crystal-like ring, with a female setting. Language was a problem but I soon discovered that I could understand most of what was going on between him and his interpreter (of course it helps to hear the English version at the same time!). Jug and Russian aren't too far apart. So I gulped down some sherry to give me the lacking courage and started tackling some of the officers, all of whom knew some Russian anyway. Tito himself speaks excellent German and some Russian, he having lived here for a good many years. He's a good answerer of questions, does it directly without hedging, but seemed to lack the creative imagination to expand. He's very literal, with a good sense of humor and likes about the same kind of joke a Russian would. In other words, he's very easy to talk to.

For years I've heard Pam and Randolph talk about Fitzroy McLean – the British brigadier who's attached to Tito, so I was very glad to meet him too. He's absolutely charming and full of fun.

Bill Donovan gave a daytime party for Tito and another bunch of his officers the following day on Capri at Mona Williams's[7] Villa. For some inexplicable reason I was invited too. This time Tito's son – youngster, who's lived most all his life in Russia, was in the Red Army and lost his arm in defence of Moscow, was along, also Tiger, Tito's mongrel police dog. And of course the two guards. They form a very essential part of the Tito setup. They go where he goes, in the same room and presumably even the can. Each is armed with a revolver, plenty of ammunition belts hung every which way and a sub-machine gun, held most of the time at the hip. Anyway, on Capri they relaxed slightly more, were allowed to sit when one started to look wilted. They were very genial looking, joined in the conversation

7 Mona Strader (1897–1983), American socialite, married to multimillionaire Harrison Williams who owned the villa Il Fortino.

when questioned and invariably laughed at all jokes. However, they eyed the OSS naval guards – laid on all over the Villa property – with complete distrust, and never let go their guns.

The Royal Navy lent Bill their bestest launch for the day so the trip to Capri was about cut in half – less than an hour. Bill was not apparent during the whole day there. He appeared for lunch but retired directly afterwards, leaving McLean and me to cope, while in the corner of the terrace a couple of OSS colonels conferenced with a Tito officer (the reason for the excursion). Later I discovered that Bill was inside, not conducting similar conferences but studying German. (He studied Italian while visiting us here in Moscow last Xmas.)

During coffee we had our one incident – one of the three small dogs that belong with the Harrison Williams setup got loose and came out to investigate, friendly-like, what was going on. Tito's dog made a lunge and nicely under everyone's feet a rather one-sided dogfight began. Soon Tito himself joined in the fray, trying to separate them. He succeeded only at the expense of a goodly number of coffee cups and plates. The dogs apart and not really hurt, Tito removed his dog's leash, marched him off to the corner and gave him a very hard beating. There was much howling, but apparently that's a usual occurrence, according to McLean. Personally, it made me feel very uncomfortable – like husband and wife quarrelling in public. That over we resumed our chatter. Swimming unfortunately was not allowed, "for security reasons" I guess, neither was a tour of the island, which Tito very much wanted to see. I thought that very stupid, but didn't figure I should butt in on an OSS show.

Finally we returned Naplesward, interwinding our way through the minefields of the outer harbor and thru the ships that kept assembling. At the docks, we discovered that little Tito and the dog were not invited out to dine – Bob Murphy[8] was the host – so I was asked to take them back home (near where I was living) to a hunting lodge colloquially known as "the Dog House." Tito and party were already

8 Robert Murphy (1894–1978), US diplomat, Roosevelt's troubleshooter in North Africa and Italy, later worked as a political adviser to General Lucius Clay, governor of the American zone of military occupation in Germany.

established in their various cars, when we started to make for mine. The dog refused to go. He howled and barked and did some more howling, so the son had to go for help. Tito's gunman tried to get the dog into the car – no soap – so finally Tito himself was bestirred. More beating and he ordered the dog into the car and we quickly slammed all doors and spent the next hour trying to hear ourselves think above the resumed howls. Poor little Tito was very embarrassed.

The next day was D minus one, so Ira went off and I was left more or less to my own devices, which gave me time to see Larry and do some sightseeing. A particularly hot afternoon we went to Pompeii and Herculaneum. The latter is far better preserved, but few people seem to take the trouble to visit it oddly enough. That day, too, I lunched with the P.M., who was in a very swell villa overlooking the bay. As I walked into the vestibule (having successfully overcome the British and American MPs [Military Police] guarding the villa) four very sour British naval officers and strange-looking civilians greeted me with stony glares. I felt like crawling under the table. A little sergeant finally appeared and asked what I wanted. When I said I was invited for lunch, he didn't believe me, at any rate repeated his question. So I asked for one of the private secretaries. He disappeared and I was left once more with hostile glares descending upon one. One came from a British full admiral, who later admitted he was on the verge of throwing me out, when the P.M. appeared and most cordially kissed me, thereby establishing my right to be there. I can't remember ever having felt so uncomfortable or embarrassed.

The P.M. is always at his best on the eve of great battles, or when they are going well. The Falaise Gap was beginning to be closed, S. France was about to be invaded, so he was in top form, intermixing the past with the present and refusing to be troubled by dark or unpleasant thoughts. He accused me of trying to pull a Virginia Cowles in coming down to Italy (Virginia and Marty Hemingway both got caught trying to get to S. France illegally – same tactics as they tried in Normandy – by the end of the war they'll have been kicked out of every damned theater of war!) and when I said I'd arrived in complete innocence he still didn't believe me! I'd hoped that perhaps he'd brought either Sarah or Mary along, he usually does. But he said they were both too busy. Mary's now on the coast, in an ack-ack battery still. One day her outfit got eight buzz bombs. Which reminds me, I hope to hell I hit England before they've stopped. That should be included in my education!

'Tis time to finish up. I've been waylaid several times while writing this. Don Nelson and Pat Hurley[9] are with us – they decided to drop off and pay U.J.[10] and Co. a visit en route to Chungking. They couldn't possibly have picked a less opportune moment to turn up. Everyone [is] too busy to take time off to entertain vodka visitors, who really have no reason for coming anyway. (I'm being undiplomatic, so don't repeat.)

Goodbye now,

Kathy

PS Many parts of this letter are indiscreet, particularly para about Wild Bill. Please be careful what you show to who.

Moscow
September 10, 1944

Dear Pam,

Are you one of those people who can read my handwriting? Can't remember. But it's a rainy Sunday & I'm nicely settled in bed – no mood to try coping with a typewriter on my knees. Today the Army started off at 10:00 a.m. for an all-day boating picnic, swimming etc. As I have a 2-day old curse, I rolled over and went back to sleep.

It's difficult to write any news from these parts at the moment. Things are sort of bloody. [Ave's] busy as the devil. He & Archie spend hour upon hour at the Kremlin, sometimes two sessions a day. Ave's very optimistic about the end of the war. What happens then I wonder. It's funny but I've never been able to seriously think of that

9 Patrick J. Hurley (1883–1963), American politician, appointed US ambassador to China in 1944.
10 'Uncle Joe' – the nickname for Stalin used by Churchill, Roosevelt and other Western allied leaders.

mythical date "the end of the war." I still can't. Here in Russia it's even more difficult to.

Our nice minister – George Kennan – has his family here. Sweet wife – Norwegian – but for all outward purposes perfectly good American – & 2 kids, daughters aged 9 & 12.[11] The Dip. Corps has grown extensively. My 2 weeks in the outside world got me way behind on who's who. There are at least 20 new faces.

Unfortunately, Ave thought it better that I not ask to go with the press boys to Lublin, Poland – something I'd have liked to do. Though come to think of it the horrors of Majdanek would probably have kept me awake for nights.

I don't think I told you about Cairo. I stayed with the local C-in-C – an old social skirt chaser – but better to stay with than some of our State Department folk! (A close choice!) I arrived from Italy early one evening & had just enuf time to change & bathe & was hustled off to the opening of *This is the Army*. It was Egyptian benefit night. The women are chic and beautiful to a degree that made me want to crawl under the table. I was the only female not in evening clothes. Their jewels were absolutely fascinating – the most beautiful I guess I've seen. Emeralds, rubies & diamonds all beautifully set. After the theater there was a dance and I was intrigued many of the women went home first & appeared later in completely new outfits, plus a new set of jewels. Their husbands are all like bloated frogs. They're wealthy, non-working & worthless – very hard to talk to – hence I really hated the dance.

I did my duty by the Sphinx & the Pyramids. However, it was too hot & dusty to do more than look out the car window. I was rewarded with 5 large flea bites!

Sept. 11

This is just a finishing up of a longer letter I wrote yesterday. I trust we'll be seeing you soon. God knows Ave needs to get out for a refresher course, or whatever you want to call it. Some of our people

11 Kennan was married to Annelise Sorensen; their daughters were Grace and Joanie.

need their heads to be knocked together. The more I think about it and read, the scareder I get about the forthcoming peace. Maybe living here accentuates it.

Bestest love to you honey,

Kathy

Moscow
mid-September 1944

Dear Mouche,

It is hard to get interested in writing home these days because I keep anticipating that we'll beat any mail home. I've been doing that for so long now, that perhaps I'd better give it up! However, I do get infinite pleasure out of thinking and planning future trips.

We are seriously lacking in juicy items to make Moscow seem like a real pleasure joint. The summer left us in early September and already we're starting on the job of getting storm windows put up, the inner windows sealed etc. No heat yet, so the house is continually sort of cold and damp so our guests shiver and look longingly at their coats, wishing it were polite to put them on. The poor Rumanian armistice delegation came up in summer clothes and nearly died of cold. The armistice signed, Ave decided it would be a good idea and a friendly gesture to have the group around for tea that afternoon. He told me to look out for two members particularly – one as having a skin disease in his hair and the second one as looking "typically Rumanian." As the first group came in I noticed no skin disease, so I made for a dapper-looking man with well-padded shoulders and a slightly flashy pinstripe suit – my idea of a "typical Rumanian" – based I might say on Hollywood. Short conversation made me realize that I definitely hit the wrong guy, this one being sort of a minor secretary. What I was in search of was the head of the delegation – a supposed commie. I finally located him and he turned out to be most uncommunistic and very genial. His beautiful wife was also along – well dressed with the sheerest possible stockings. Again, not what I'm used to in outward appearances of communists. As a whole the delegation was very nice and most grateful to Ave for being hospitable. If we ever get to go to Bucharest, I guess we'll get a friendly reception . . .

Our house is becoming more boarding house like. Our guest rooms are never empty, what with travelers from the outside, and now I'm putting up all female nurses that are arriving in groups of two from the air bases. They remain for 24 hours and now I've got their schedules down to a system – so's they can hit all the high spots in that time. Some of the girls I already know from my visit down to our base, and as a bunch they couldn't be more genial or appreciative. Breakfast in bed is included in the schedule – which they like after months and months of tents and community army living.

George Kennan, our minister counsellor, has his wife here now – a small Norwegian girl and two cute kids – ages 9 and [12] who play all day long in our garden and are beautifully behaved. Last week I took them to the children's theater here and had a terrible time keeping up a running commentary on what was happening on the stage (which took great concentration on my part) besides answering the umpteen questions the 9-year-old plied me with such as "The bear isn't a real bear is it?," "How can the goat come to life when it's been eaten?" I inwardly cursed the lack of logic in fairy tales!

Must stop now, my love to you,

Kathleen

CHAPTER 22

'THE MOST EXCITING THING IS THAT AT LAST I'VE MET STALIN'

Churchill's second wartime visit to Moscow, in October 1944, is notorious for his percentages agreement with Stalin. Churchill arrived on the 9th and that same evening slipped Stalin a piece of paper on which he had scrawled percentages of British and Soviet influence in various countries. In return for British predominance in Greece, Churchill conceded control of Bulgaria, Hungary and Romania to the Soviets. Yugoslavia he designated a 50/50 Anglo-Soviet sphere of influence – an arrangement unbeknown to Tito. When Churchill suggested they burn the piece of paper, Stalin supposedly said, 'No, you keep it.'

The Americans were vehemently opposed to spheres-of-influence deals and Churchill's conversation with Stalin would not have taken place if Averell had been present. It wasn't until several days later that Churchill told Ave what had transpired, and Roosevelt was having none of it. Besides, the main purpose of Churchill's visit was to reconcile Stalin and the Polish government-in-exile in London, with whom Moscow's relations had reached rock bottom following the Katyn incident and the disaster of the Warsaw Uprising. Churchill's mission failed, but there were some quite productive discussions about military matters, including future Soviet entry into the war against Japan.

Kathy spent a lot of time with Churchill while he was in Moscow, but her biggest thrill was seeing Stalin in the flesh – first at a reception in the British embassy and then at the Bolshoi Ballet's performance of *Giselle*, where she also had dinner with him and other Soviet bigwigs. Churchill departed Moscow on 19 October, and around the same time Ave and Kathy headed home and did not get back to Moscow until early December. On the return journey they stopped off in London – where they saw Churchill, Pam and the rest of the gang – and Paris – where Kathy visited her Aunt Frances and the Poniatowskis.

While they were away, Lillian Hellman arrived in Moscow, where she was met by Sergei Eisenstein. During her prolonged, arduous journey via Alaska and Siberia she contracted pneumonia and became so ill that George Kennan, Ave's deputy, felt duty-bound to aid her recuperation by putting her up at Spaso House. Thereafter she was an intermittent boarder at Spaso until her departure from the Soviet Union in January 1945. Within Spaso it was an open secret that she started an affair with John Melby. Evidently, Lillian, like Kathy, appealed to Melby as a woman who could 'slug it out'.

Because of Hellman's left-wing sympathies and communist connections, Melby's security clearance was withdrawn postwar and he was dismissed from the State Department in 1953. But as Robert P. Newman has shown, during the various internal inquiries that preceded his dismissal, Melby's former boss, Averell Harriman, was one of his strongest supporters.

Moscow
October 13, 1944

Dear Mrs Churchill,

It would have been absolutely perfect if you were here now. Averell and the P.M. are playing bezique – it's almost (but not quite) as nice as being at Chequers!

The P.M. lives in a very luxurious "dacha" outside Moscow. The woodwork is very fancy – all types and colors, but the chairs hard! The dining room, also sumptuous & [the walls] have four photo portraits [of] Stalin, Lenin, Marx & Engels – appropriately – to remind one that this is Russia!

Last week Averell told me Molotov had announced to him with great pride that you were coming to Moscow. I am sorry you couldn't. Last evening a reception was held and genuine regret was expressed by all the Soviets at your absence, [by] Molotov and Maisky particularly.

The P.M. looks wonderfully well. He's very busy. Tonight there's a moment's relaxation and I do hope he beats Averell. My bezique isn't good enough.

It's wonderfully exciting having friends from England here. In fact, it's almost as exciting as though we had made a trip out.

Averell joins me in best love & regrets that you're not here.

Kathy

Moscow
October 16, 1944

Dear Pam,

Moscow is such a nice place when friends come a-visiting. The past week while Ave and the bigwigs have been conferencing, I've been entertaining or being entertained by the littlewigs. It's great fun to take freshly arrived people to the theaters or shopping – their reactions are so enthusiastic. Everything is so new to them.

Ave is thriving under the long hours of conferences and more conferences plus his own ambassadorial work, Lord knows how come, but he is. The American press boys are naively pleased at the reports they have been getting from outsiders about the part Ave is playing in the conferences and the weight he's pulling. He's been in on pretty much everything, plus of course has seen a lot of the P.M. in between times.

The most exciting thing as far as I'm concerned is that at last I've met U.J. I was beginning to despair of that ever happening. A couple of nights back, a special program was put on at the big ballet theater – one act of a ballet, some singing and the Red Army Choir, for once a well-chosen program and not five hours long! Ave and I were invited to sit in the royal box. The P.M. arrived late, with U.J. coming in some minutes afterwards, so the audience didn't realize they were there 'til the lights went on after the first act. A cheer went up (something I've never seen happen here) and U.J. ducked out so that the P.M. could have all the applause for himself, which was a very nice gesture. But the P.M. sent Vyshinsky out to get U.J. back and they stood together while the applause went on for many minutes. It was most impressive – the sound like a cloud burst on a tin roof. It came from below on all sides and above and the people down in the audience said they were quite thrilled seeing the two men together. Perhaps that may sound odd to you, but that night was the first time probably most of the audience had ever seen either man. Stalin hasn't been to the theater since the war started and for him to go with a foreigner was even more exciting. Between the acts we went into a sit-down dinner at which Molotov presided. About 12 of us, all of which was very exciting for me. There were toasts to everyone and Stalin was very amusing when Moly got up and raised his glass to Stalin with a short conventional phrase about "our great leader." Stalin, after he'd drunk, came back with "I thought he was going to say something different about me!" Moly answered with a rather glum: "It's always a good one," which I thought was very funny.[1] Ave said that Stalin was exceptionally gay. He did have a good wit and looked as though he was enjoying his task as host to the P.M.

The first time I saw U.J. – at your embassy (he came into the room where we all were for a few minutes) – he seemed like a man in a daze – not much expression at all on his face, very cold and distant. But at the dinner he smiled – particularly by squinting his eyes – a good deal and seemed quite like a human being. Of all the horrible things, Ave figured I ought to make a toast in Russian, which the P.M.'s interpreter coached me on – so's I'd be sure to get all the right words in the proper tenses.

Last night I'd suggested that those who had nothing better to do should come around to us after the ballet. They came 50 strong & most stayed until after 3 a.m. I was exhausted but they seemed to enjoy themselves. Even the C.I.G.S.[2] got genial after a few whiskeys. The high spot for them was when Ave brought in the ballerina they'd all seen dance that night. All your generals crowded around her like

---

1 Joan Bright Astley, who accompanied Churchill on his trip to Moscow, recalled that Kathy told her that 'at one of the many toasts to "Marshal Stalin, the great leader", Molotov said *sotto voce*: "We're tired of that one; think up another"'.
2 Field Marshal Alan Brooke.

little school boys (she's no beauty & a good 35). Later in the evening Ian Jacob[3] came up to Pug & announced proudly that he'd had "courage" enough to ask Semonova to dance!

I'll write again soon.

Best love,

Kathy

At the bottom of this letter Averell wrote a PS:

Dear Pam, Kath has exaggerated my role, which is that of a "humble observer." Kath made a hit with U.J., from his cordiality to her. She was the only "gal" in the box & at the supper. We are counting on visiting U.K. on our return journey.

At the bottom of a retyped copy of this letter, Kathy wrote:

Litvinov asking Russ re *Look* article is it true that Ave has $100 million. Russ said he didn't know. Did he earn it or inherit it? & why if he did how could a man who had $100 million look so sad!

Toast to the Big Three – Holy Trinity – Stalin "Churchill must be the Holy Ghost he flies around so much."

Moore Crosthwaite[4] getting sore at Ave for making a big entrance for Semonova at our party.

Claridge's Hotel, London
late November 1944

Dear Mary,

It sounds none too good the prospects of seeing the France boys – thanks to the push. They're all very busy. Averell doesn't want to get someone to have them ordered to Paris since things have been on the move – a week ago it would have been OK. Damnation.

3 Ian Jacob (1899–1993), British army officer who served as a military assistant to Churchill's War Cabinet.

4 Moore Crosthwaite (1907–89), British diplomat.

However, via the Paris office of *Newsweek* I've sent Shirley news of our whereabouts.

I've had great fun – seeing friends etc., press & otherwise.

Love,

Kathleen

En route to Cairo
November 30, 1944

Dear Pam,

I fear that my pen won't work, so you'll have to put up with a dull pencil. We're over the desert a few hours from Cairo. Seems odd to remember that once upon a time I got a kick out of watching for battle scars. Them days are gone!

I enjoyed every minute of our short stay in Paris. Our hotel had hot bath water. There was an absence of heat but still my bedroom was no colder than my Moscow one.

Dropped in on the Poniatowskis just as André was leaving – he's with S.H.A.E.F. [Supreme Headquarters Allied Expeditionary Force]. Marie-André was in town on leave – so I saw them all. Aunt Frances had laid low "doing nothing but waiting" for the 4 years, said she thought her friends & relations in America had probably forgotten they all exist! & was like a child opening his first Xmas stocking with duffle bag I brought with utilities. They "managed" as far as food goes but all are very thin and well dressed – like everyone in Paris. They live in a tiny sitting room on the top floor with a small stove for heating. The Gestapo visited them once but found the bedrooms too small for their personal billeting needs so moved in on other houses down the street. Constance is very pretty – painfully shy. By contrast Marie-André was an extrovert. They haven't yet come out of their shell. I wonder if they ever will!

Dined that night with Geoff, Helen & others at Geoff's girlfriend's apartment.[5] She's American, ex-actress of sorts in Hollywood. Her last of 3 husbands was a Frenchman – killed before '40. I don't want to make her sound dubious. She was a hell of a fine girl – full of life –

5 Geoffrey Parsons, Helen Kirkpatrick and Drue Leyton (1903–97).

late 30s I imagine. Helped some 120 airmen out & had other underground activities. She was taken up once by the Gestapo & eventually got out thanks to a faked "cancer" operation. While Helen & others talked about the latest political scandals (all new to me) I talked to Drue about her experiences etc. It was all fascinating. She was full of tales too about the artists and their life & just Paris in general.

My love to you,
Kath

Moscow
December 9, 1944

Dear Mary,

Our trip back this time was the most fascinating ever. Our first evening in London, we dined at Number Ten [with] the Edens and Mary C who's now a full captain. Incidentally I discovered to my surprise that Beatrice [Eden] now has Alabam. Poor dog – a new move for him, but at least it's a country home. Dinner was very pleasant as the P.M., after a long and tiresome cabinet meeting, was in an unserious mood (much to Ave's annoyance). Beatrice, just back from Paris was full of the latest gossip and tales, which he rose to beautifully. He loves to play at mimicking – himself among others. Mrs C looked desperately tired, I thought, and quite haggard and ill. I guess people forget she's mid-60s when they make her do all the committee work etc.

Joe Evans, Ken and Zeek were in the town. The latter (your great friend) was very dour and mad at *Newsweek*, having been fired on one minute's notice. They were all rather amazed at *Newsweek*'s way of handling not only the elections but the war coverage. Ave had a short chat and that fixed that up fine. We had another dinner spent listening to Portal and Spaatz talk about all the kind of things you can't write about, both amusing and interesting – the kind of thing one misses so much here.

Pam was in fine form – full of work at her club. Baby Winston was sick in the country so I didn't see him. We had a chat on the phone though – which wasn't too productive!

I stayed awake one night for about an hour (very hard) waiting to hear a buzz bomb, but the all-clear went without anything happening. Next night I slept through the whole damned thing, which annoyed me very much indeed. I wanted desperately to hear one once. The V2s make a big bang – there's no warning so it doesn't bother those who aren't hit. I went out and looked at the result of one the next morning. A very deep hole (a church was cut in half – small one) and not as much blast effect as the V1s. I felt like a skunk standing there idly watching – just sightseeing – while the people who had been bombed out rummaged around in the debris for their bits and pieces that were left. Jesus but the Londoners have had a hard time – for four years now. And they look just as hard and placid as ever.

It took practically no time flat to get to Paris and we went out of our way to fly down the Cherbourg Peninsula. It's one flood after another. Some towns lay flat, others untouched. All wrecked tanks etc. have been cleared away. We flew over the Renault works which stood out markedly, being the only thing hit for miles around though I must say we'd done a good job, once upon a time, on the field we landed on. No attempt had been made to rebuild the damned installations either.

Joe Evans had told me that I'd probably have fun seeing Geoff Parsons and that things would be quite changed – none of the Ps involved (passes, proposals and propositions). 'Twas true. I wrote you about our dinner at his girlfriend's. I'd planned an evening for me to see the new nightlife but we left Paris Sunday afternoon (we had one night there) and didn't come back, so that was the end of Paris. I can give you only second hand from Bob who went to several [shows] all three nights he was there. He really was on the loose in a big way. Anyway, as you may know Bob's pretty damn particular when it comes to the female figure – he says the girls who performed were very much up to scratch. Champagne was served everywhere, but no food.

I didn't anticipate all hats to be as extreme as those pictured in *Vogue* – but they certainly are. The females are fantastic, bicycling along, skirts way above their knees, full-sleeved and skirted coats and huge high turban hats. Have you heard the story of why the milliners made them? Apparently the Germans rationed the amount of cloth to go into any one article of clothing – a maximum that is – but they forgot all about the millinery trade. Consequently the hat makers started piling all the material they could into hats as a little sign of resistance. God help us if N.Y.C. milliners take up the Paris style (they probably will though next year!). Shoe soles were all almost exclusively wooden; however, I noticed Constance had nice red leather-soled ones that look quite new. The Bois was filled with women with their kids, many of the latter dressed in rabbit fur coats. Everyone invariably had a huge poodle, a fat chow or police dog. None went in for the small species that eat much less. Perhaps if I'd remained longer I'd have found signs of hardships and real sufferings. But just from my one morning driving and walking around I was fascinated by how well, sleek and placid the majority seemed. It all came as a shock. Despite what we've heard and read, I still couldn't quite believe four years under the Germans could leave a city population so outwardly unchanged.

A couple of days have passed – the planes still aren't going but I am, this time to the Caucasus, I hope. To a music art etc. festival to last 10 days. The whole thing came up late last night – the invitation that is and I may leave tomorrow. I'm now investigating the chances of perhaps skiing (we went out for a few hours on Sunday). It may mean I'll be away for Xmas but it all sounds rather fun, and a chance to see at least a bit of Russia outside of Moscow.

I lost my two shades of gold cigarette case in Paris (fake one) and the tortoise shell one got broke in packing. Could you please send one to General Sidney Spalding.[6] If Bergdorf has any more of the flat case variety – they cost about 20 dollars I think – that would be perfect – otherwise anything.

My love & Merry Xmas to all.

Kathy

---

6 Sidney P. Spalding (1889–1988), involved in Lend-Lease supplies to the Soviet Union.

Moscow
December 13, 1944

Dear Mouche,

I forgot to tell Mary to tell Marie that her friend Lillian Hellman is a great success here. She's loads of fun. The Russians like her & the embassy secretaries have most all fallen madly in love with her! There's great competition.

When I wrote Mary I was all set & ready to leave for Tiflis in the Caucasus. That was yesterday – now for the usual unexplained reason the Soviets are giving me the run around. So it looks as though they don't approve of my having been invited. All of which is sad – Ave said that 18 years ago he & Mummy spent Xmas there!

My love to you & Merry Christmas.

Kathleen

PS None of your magazines have come but the Eliz Arden leg shaving wax did while I was away.

Moscow
December 23, 1944

Dear Mary,

We are in a flurry of Xmas preparations. This year Ave gave each American in Moscow a bottle of bourbon and we, in a fit of enthusiasm, decided each bottle should be wrapped and beribboned as well as carded. It took 4 hours – two of us working full time (production line technique). Poor Lillian, who hates wrapping anything inadvertently turned up the last few hours and was set to work. The number came to over 200! So you see your rolls of 50-yard ribbon came in very handy. Today they were distributed. Tomorrow we have an Xmas party for 220 Americans plus some imported females from the British and some Russians. Lillian's suggestion was that we fly in 50 Powers models[7] for entertainment purposes, instead of the usual greasy gypsies. The orchestra, all laid on and everything, has now decided it can't play. Nuts, nothing ever runs smoothly.

---

7 Female models who worked for John Robert Powers's New York modelling agency.

Two nights ago Russ Deane gave a 50 people seated dinner party here – for the Russians to meet a couple of new generals who came in with us. The main disadvantage of Russ's party gatherings is that I have to go, Ave's I can sometimes skip. Our tree has its lights on now. Miss Koon's decorations get done tonight. Our electrician has a very tricky arrangement – the lights go on and off all [the] time. The Russian servants came in last night to see our handiwork. I told one little old man to blow and then the lights would go off. He did, they went off and soon everyone was trying it. Each time the lights went off faithfully to schedule. They were as charmed as kids and I think some still think the blowing did the trick!

Of all the terrible things, last evening Ave inadvertently accepted a big dinner party for the diplomatic corps by the New Zealanders, thinking it was a reception. I didn't discover we were going until too late – so we went. A horrible affair. I was so cold my teeth started chattering. On one side of me the Swedish minister made some disparaging remarks about the Allied armies under Eisenhower, to which I took offence. I decided not to be too rude back and instead refused to talk to him again. It was a very long dinner.

The heating situation seems far more acute this year. The weather's a lot colder and there's no fuel. We'll be OK when and if we get two heaters functioning. I don't however see how the average Muscovite stands it.

I must stop now – a Pole I used to know in London has just returned from Lublin and is coming to call. My nose needs powdering.

My love to you,

Kathleen

Happy birthday!

Moscow

January 2, 1945

Dear Marie,

Your undies are much too swell for Moscow, but they're wonderfully warm & have been put straight to work. Thanks so much.

We opened all your packages Xmas morning – Ave & me, with Lillian doling them out to us. She's been a great asset here & added loads to our enjoyment. She lives in my sitting room, on a day bed which she swears is comfortable. The other vacant room means sharing a bath with a man and is as cold as hell as the heating doesn't seem to work down one end of the house.

Ave's New Year's resolution is not to work too hard! It lasted until 11:30 this morning. It's late now & he's still out conferencing, cables to write when he returns I guess. But the resolution was a nice idea anyway.

Moscow's not much different from last winter – a new show – a take-off on American "vodka visitors." Lillian's got 2 coming up. The ballet I've succeeded in avoiding except for twice. Averell's beating me like mad at bezique.

A little man (Swede) just out from Tokyo lunched the other day. He had a fine case of jitters, which I thought a most comforting sign. Moscow was peace on earth to him!

A Polish friend of mine, left over from London, came calling unexpectedly. He stayed hours – at the end of which I was exceedingly glad of one thing – that I'm not a Pole!

I must stop now – ever so many thanks – you made Xmas be most cheery.

Best love,
Kath

Moscow
January 2, 1945

Dear Shirley and Larry,

Though I've been back in Moscow for a month now, I can still write about how nice it was at home! It takes a long time for the benefits of those trips to wear off! (Don't worry I appreciate how lucky I am!) We had so many nice silly times together. I think perhaps best of all were the female lunches at the Newport. Everyone looked so smart and chic, compared to me in my Moscow clothes that hadn't gone to the cleaners!

Eugene[8] was better than I've seen him in ages. I dropped in on him almost daily at 121 E 60 as it's two floors below my dentist – where I

8 Presumably Eugene Pool, Larry's father.

spent many an hour! Then dined and lunched a few times at the Drake. *Bloomer Girl* is the best show I've seen in years. Charlie Engelhard[9] and I went – did the town afterwards and had a hangover lunch next day at the Plaza, with Jamie included – champagne and fowl – very hangoverish and Charlie-like. He's a captain now, still teaching Frenchmen and in a very bad state mentally. He got mixed up with some free-love communists awhile back and hasn't yet gotten over it. I did answer a few questions about the communism part though – Russian style. He believed me, but doubted if his friends would though.

This is sort of rambling – but it adds up to an attempt to tell you that home's as wonderful a place as ever – though I did bite a number of fingernails listening to Mr Dewey charging FDR with the killing of Americans.[10]

We arrived at a very damp and cold Paddington station one morning at 5 a.m. and found Beek and Pam running down the platform to greet us. Beek had been "ordered" up to London on business unknown to him. I guess he had a few bad minutes until he discovered why. He stayed for a couple of days – his birthday included. We had great fun.

Then we went over to Paris and what with a "push" going on Ave said strings couldn't be pulled (or at least shouldn't) to try and get you both to Paris. As it was we ended up with only one night there – just time enough for me to see the Poniatowskis and a few other friends. Both big and little André happened to be there too. Aunt Frances seemed to think it odd that all the family at home hadn't forgotten them – wondered why I just dropped in without phoning etc. She's sat around waiting for four years, saving a home for her husband and Marie-André. It must be a blow for her suddenly to discover that such things as furniture and rugs don't mean much to either of them anymore. As a contrast that night I dined at the flat of

9 Charles W. Engelhard (1917–71), businessman and racehorse owner who served as a bomber pilot in the US Army Air Force. Said to have been the inspiration for Ian Fleming's Goldfinger character.

10 Kathy's trip home coincided with the US presidential election, in which Roosevelt defeated Thomas E. Dewey.

a girl who'd had a job in the underground getting airmen out. She was so very much alive and certainly the better off for her four years of work. Anyway, if you were to go to Paris, do look up the Ps [Poniatowskis] at 23 rue Octave Feuillet (not far from the Bois). You'll find it interesting, if not amusing.

The rest of the trip in France we spent inadvertently at our Eisenhower's C.P. [Command Post] (inadvertently for me, I thought we'd go for one night and we ended up staying two days). Ave went galloping off with [General] Patton seeing things and had himself a fine time. There wasn't anyone there except a couple of W.A.C.s [Women's Army Corps] and Kay Summersby[11] (who I know well from England) and the general. People kept coming and going all the time. Like Moscow, I poured tea and sat people in front of a roaring fire, before they were sent off again, out into the mud and the cold. That C.P. was certainly the simplest and most unelaborate I've ever seen – trailers for the men and rooms in the house for the gals. Only excitement – I damned near got killed by a G.I. in the bushes with a machine gun – badly scared anyway!

After that we adjourned to my old stamping ground in Italy. Larry – we flew over Anzio again, and I hardly recognized it – looked most unbattle-like, grass growing, wrecks all cleared. Seemed incredible, for so short a time.

We got stuck in Tehran for four days thank God and I retired to bed with by that time a lovely runny cold and a few other things. Don't ever go there if you can help it. We had to on account of Oil Concessions and the what like, otherwise we'd have landed in Turkey – Ankara, which I'd have liked to see.

There's not much news to tell about Moscow. We've skied a couple of times, but there's practically no snow. I'm still chief drinker of sweet wine and cakes in the interest of culture. Lillian Hellman is with us for

---

11 Kay Summersby (née MacCarthy-Morrogh, 1908–75), Irish-born member of the British Army's Transport Corps who served as Eisenhower's driver and assistant. She published a memoir about her time with Eisenhower, and reputedly had a romance with him.

the moment – a very cheerful addition to our household. She's got all the boys on their ears and adds greatly to our laughter.

This is long enough. I'll stop. My love to you both.

[Kathleen]

Moscow
January 13, 1945

Dear Mary,

The New Year has brought a new horrible regulation: In the office by 9:30 – that's about 15 minutes after daybreak. The sun never comes up so as we can see it, which just adds to the general dreariness and cold. As far as temperature goes it's never been really bad, but it certainly is penetrating. I dined with Joe Phillips the other night and was comfortable only because I wore long underwear, sweaters and skirts and things. Thank God for our central heating, even though it's only tepid. At least the house isn't damp.

We entertained in a big way last night – a farewell, thanks party for Lillian Hellman – all the people who entertained her, plus some members of the cast, directors and what have you, of [Hellman's] *The Little Foxes* and *Watch on the Rhine*. They I thought were a rather frowsy lot, but the others great fun. We'd anticipated a dreary evening of culture and conversation. But things didn't happen that way at all. The liquor livened everyone up, the rugs were pulled back and we brought down the gramophone and the Russians had a swell time trying to tango, rumba as well as fox-trot. My feet suffered considerably. One Soviet poet – now famous because he wrote the national anthem – turned out to be the fastest worker I think I've come up against in any country anywhere. Until he got too drunk to handle with comfort, I thought him really very nice. One female who plays the lead in *Watch on the Rhine* tried hard to get me to dance with her but that was really the only embarrassing incident.

A painter who presented Ave with two watercolors sometime back – a swell old man – asked if he could see where they were hung, so I brought him upstairs and showed him (they're in Ave's room). He decided he wanted to autograph them, so with much trouble we got them down off the walls. Next problem: what should he say. Would "love" be alright? I said no and then volunteered that "best regards" might be appropriate. (He was determined that the inscription should be in English.) Next I had to write out "best regards" which he tried to copy, unsuccessfully. All in all it was quite amusing.

The movie we showed was Deanna Durbin's *His Butler's Sister* and the three songs she sang in Russian brought the house down – though there was much laughter about her pronunciation. Both Litvinov and Maisky (sitting next to me) cried (or at least sniffled) at the sentimental parts, which I felt was rather sweet.

Our Sundays recently have been profitably spent skiing out at a little village where Eddie Page and the Kennans have half a dacha. It's absolutely minute, but large for a peasant cottage. We take an already cooked stew, warm it up and nicest thing of all our landlady washes up afterwards! It's an ideal arrangement. I have my eye on a dacha in the same village – for summer use. The skiing resembles nothing relating to SV [Sun Valley]. But it's fun. Last Sunday I inadvertently fell into a slit trench that was too narrow to move in and had a hell of a time getting out!

Jan. 19

The dust gathers on this letter as I try and collect more news that's worth the writing. There's not much prospect of letters getting out. No planes have been near us for weeks. Soon I'll get to thinking I'm on a desert island that's visited twice yearly! Even Air Chief Marshal Tedder[12] in desperation took to a train!

Can't remember or not if I told you that Tex McCrary in all seriousness offered me a job. The letter arrived about Xmas time and the job was to start January 1. As far as I can figure out he and his general don't agree on many subjects – result many bloody rows. Tex wanted me to come down and be his buffer. Some fun! Ira wrote at the same time, all pepped up at the idea. I'm not that desperate yet.

We're now off to a cocktail party in honor of a delegation of Parliamentarians. Lord preserve us from having a delegation from Congress. These so far have been fairly tame.

12 Arthur William Tedder (1890–1967), Royal Air Force chief, who served as Eisenhower's deputy.

A comedy about an American millionaire's visit to Moscow has been the only show I've seen for ages. Ave went too and set the whole cast in a dither of excitement. Most of them kept their eyes on him all the time to see how he'd take the jokes and cracks. All in all it was very amusing. The American looked like Davies[13] – grey hair and black eyebrows, but that we later discovered was the actor's natural garb. He told us he studied with care two newsreels – the only two he could find. One of Eric Johnston and the other Wallace when on their recent trips here. He did a damned good job. Anyway, we enjoyed it.

Jan. 21

Moscow has gone wildly social over the British MPs – two big receptions, one by the British embassy and the other the Soviets plus a couple of command performances at the ballet and the Red Army chorus plus lunches and late parties. By far the most attractive is Lord Lovat.[14] He's going to U.S. after this trip on a lecture tour or something. I've told him to look up Marie and Aunt Carol. Personally I think he's charming – the rest are rather dreary, but at least they're behaving themselves.

I must go now.

My love to you,

Kathleen

PS Frances Balfour may look you up when she comes to N.Y. She's the wife of the British minister here, who's being transferred to Washington. I know her well and she's awfully nice.

13 Joseph E. Davies (1876–1958), US ambassador to Moscow before the Second World War.

14 Simon Fraser, 15th Lord Lovat (1911–95), British soldier.

CHAPTER 23

'THE PRESIDENT IS ABSOLUTELY CHARMING, EASY TO TALK TO ON ANY SUBJECT. THE WAR IS SELDOM MENTIONED EXCEPT ITS LIGHTER SIDE'

Roosevelt wanted a second summit with Churchill and Stalin but the meeting was delayed until after the November 1944 presidential election – which he won by a landslide. Roosevelt hoped the gathering would take place in Scotland but Stalin insisted on Yalta in Crimea, which meant that it would take place on Soviet soil and that he could travel to the venue by train. Stalin hated flying and had not enjoyed the journey to Tehran. Fine for him, but a tough trip for the ailing Roosevelt.

Kathy was invited as a companion to Roosevelt's daughter, Anna Boettiger. Ave wanted to fly to Yalta well in advance of the conference but was stymied by the weather. Instead, at midnight on Sunday, 21 January, he, Kathy, Meiklejohn and Eddie Page boarded a train. They were joined by Frances Balfour (wife of British diplomat John Balfour), who was on her way home. The group arrived in Yalta three days later, the train having passed through Orel, Kursk, Kharkov, Pavlograd and Zaporozhe. The conference venue was Tsar Nicholas II's magnificent fifty-room Livadia Palace, which had been badly damaged by the Germans but repaired by the Soviets as best they could.

The Yalta Conference, or Crimean Conference as the Soviets called it (4–11 February 1945), was an altogether grander affair than Tehran. The delegations were larger (seven hundred British and Americans alone), the agenda wider-ranging and many more decisions were made. Whereas Tehran had been mainly concerned with prosecuting the war, Yalta focused on winning the peace. The most fateful decision was the final agreement on the establishment of the United Nations. While the UN's structure and functioning had been hammered out at the 1944 Dumbarton Oaks conference in Washington DC, there was continuing controversy about the voting rights of the permanent members of its Security Council (Britain, China, France, the Soviet Union and the United States). Stalin wanted unanimity on all security decisions, whereas the British and Americans preferred majority voting. The agreed compromise was that Security Council resolutions could be passed by majority vote but each of the five permanent members had the right to veto their implementation. As Kathy recorded, Roosevelt was very happy with this outcome.

When news of the conference broke it was hailed as a triumph for the anti-Hitler coalition. Kathy shared the euphoria, and was still floating on it when she flew back to Moscow on 12 February.

Yalta
February 1, 1945

Dear Mouche,

We left Moscow about 10 days ago – to come down here to Yalta and get things in order for the conference. Ave's now left to join the bigwigs and I'm just sitting, relaxing and enjoying myself.

Pre-Revolution Yalta was the resort spot of Tsars and Grand Dukes, so palaces were plentiful. Unfortunately the Germans destroyed most all of them when they pulled out of the Crimea, so that now hardly a house at all is standing. The needless destruction is something appalling. There wasn't much real fighting around here at all. The Germans and Rumanians just burned and looted everything in sight.

The palace where the Pres. is to live was built by the last Tsar – overlooks the sea, with high snow-capped mountains behind. Beautiful old trees and grounds. The furniture was all looted and everything else too – but the Soviets have brought in modern stuff, which if not appropriate is at least comfortable. The Americans have three houses – the palace and two other buildings. Washing facilities are practically nil. (Mrs Boettiger and I share a small room opposite the one complete bathroom). Only full generals and the admirals and chiefs of state get rooms to themselves. The rest are packed like patients in a ward.

The British palace is a mixture of Gothic and Moorish architecture – equipped with a baronial hall and all the trimmings.

U.J. is living in the palace once owned by one of the men who killed Rasputin. It adds up into quite a picture.

The other afternoon I went and called on the sister of Anton Chekhov (writer). She's now about 83 and is charming, full of life and thrilled to be meeting some Americans. We're having a hellova time finding out about the pre-revolutionary history of this part of the coast, as the Soviets seemed very reticent on the subject. Even Miss Chekhov was – also about what happened during the year and a half of occupation. The natives who work around the palace here at Livadia don't seem to know anything either – they're certainly old enough!

All the Moscow hotels have been stripped of their staffs, furniture and plates, china, kitchen utensils – to look after us. I wonder what the poor folk in Moscow are doing. Besides that, the country nearby is being scoured for such things as shaving mirrors, coat hangers and wash bowls. I guess they're just being "requisitioned." We found one ashtray that advertises a china factory by appointment of 5 Tsars!

Yalta
January 30, 1945

Dear Pam,

As you probably know we ain't in Moscow. After having sweated for weeks trying to get the Becky up to Moscow to fly us down here, we finally took to a train. So far our party holds the record – 800 miles in 65 hours. Which means the train averaged about 15 mph. Those who have come here since have taken four days. We were stopped, sometimes for hours on end – had a chance to take a walk around Kharkov – which is far less destroyed than most big towns. The train dumped us in Simferopol and we drove over here to Yalta – 3 hours – a snowstorm & mountain roads.

The British palace belonged to a Grand Duke and was built by an English architect – half Gothic and half Moorish. It's got a baronial hall and all the trimmings. What struck us most was a huge champagne cooler – the size of a bathtub. Joan Bright figures in desperation some of your V.I.P.s will take to bathing in it! She came over to us last night for dinner but was off again at crack of dawn to Sebastopol to meet your ship. I haven't a damn thing to do but relax and enjoy myself, which is heaven. The weather's almost spring-like but rainy. Hopefully we think that by next week when everyone has arrived it will have rained itself out.

Mrs Boettiger, the Pres.'s daughter, is coming – which is the reason I was able to come and stay for the show. Ave says she's a "Peach."

The layout is really lovely – high mountains with snow caps that border the sea – rather like Italy, with countless little villages perched on either sides of the winding mountain roads. Our people are all in a palace grounds – one palace and two large houses – built by Nicholas II (the last Tsar) – the story goes the room Admiral King's to have was the Tsarina's bedroom – an outside staircase leading to her balcony used to be used by Rasputin. The Pres., full generals and admirals and Stettinius all have rooms to themselves and the rest are packed in like sardines. Washing facilities are the minimum but all in all it's very comfortable. The Germans looted all the furniture, pictures etc. so what's been put in is Soviet modern. Hence our palace lacks the atmosphere of the P.M.'s, which was left intact. We overlook the sea and are surrounded by lovely trees of all sorts & varieties collected from all over. Walks are most pleasant but needfully at least half uphill.

I'll let you know more when we meet. Ave went off a couple of days ago to the rendezvous point but he had two days of rest & relaxation, which did him a world of good.

Nothing much at all happened the last month in Moscow. With the New Year Ave decided he'd go out more. I was forever calling up & asking "please can I bring my father" – to dinners, parties etc. Lillian Hellman lived with us and was a very genial asset. I'd never known her before. Ave had slightly. I presume you've got my wire of warning that she was a great friend of Marie's! One evening Ave and I sat up for hours and hours talking about you and he and Marie. He was more or less thinking out loud and needless to say got nowhere. He just can't make himself make a decision while the war's on and life so unsettled. I rather imagine Marie feels the same way too.

Feb. 4

Things got started this afternoon. Sarah's coming over with the P.M. at 5 – to dine with "the children." Anna tells me that Randolph turned up just before the party left Malta & that there was a tense moment all round – whether or not he'd be taken along. He wasn't. Bob Hopkins[1] got here yesterday for lunch, retired straight to bed looking like hell. He's staying put today. The doc says it's over-tiredness. The Pres. arrived in great form & is very pleased with his suite. I dined with him and his entourage last night & then today, just 5 of us. He's really absolutely sweet – very easy to make conversation to – amusing and generally in great form.

Averell went over & saw the P.M. last night late. He's apparently in a discouraged frame of mind. It must be sort of dampening to the spirits of the party – having that accident.[2] At this point everyone is crossing their fingers & hoping for the best.

Ave brought me back a present from Ira (he stopped off in Caserta) – diamond, ruby and sapphire ring. Ira told me about it last time I was in Italy and I'd said "no" very politely. I couldn't accept it & I thought he'd taken it in. Ave didn't see how he could refuse it. Nuts. It's rather embarrassing, don't you think?

Poor Ira is in a very bad mental state. His letters are numerous, lengthy and rather too pathetic (none of this for repetition). He was hoping to be invited to the conference here.

Sarah is about to arrive so I think I'd better go organize tea.

---

1 Robert Hopkins (1921–2006), army photographer who took pictures at Tehran as well as Yalta and other wartime summits.
2 An RAF plane had crashed en route to Yalta killing eleven passengers and crew, including War and Foreign Office staff.

Feb. 7

I'm out in the garden – in the sunshine – sitting on a fountain. It's the only non-windy spot available, uncomfortable but the sun is too good a treat to miss. Walking means the shade. Ave & Ed are over with the Soviets and this afternoon I guess they'll meet again with the big boys.

Yesterday Sarah, Anna, a Secret Service boy and I went to Sebastopol on a trip (6 hours of driving). We got properly lost in a town which we later discovered had been Balaklava, so we were rather pleased to have seen it. (I presume I don't have to check you up on British history!)

Sebastopol is another of these towns with few out of many thousands of buildings still with roofs. Statues had been decapitated – target practice – and there were other signs of wanton destruction by the Germans during their years of occupation.

We sight-saw wildly and had a wonderful lunch on board one of the ships – filet mignon. (I wonder whether when the war's over if food eaten will be a subject for letter writing!)

Rumanian prisoners were cleaning up the rubble, stone by stone in a leisurely fashion. I think Sarah was slightly horrified by their bedraggled state. They certainly weren't the worst I've seen by a long shot. The day was very pleasant. Anna's lots of fun and very easy to get on with.

Later: Sarah came over this afternoon & reported that the C.I.G.S, well equipped with compasses, maps and books went off for the day to Balaklava.

Heard our Admiral Leahy[3] on the subject of France today. My God he hates the French. He has the makings of a prime "hands off for America in Europe," which in my mind isn't far removed from isolationism. It was interesting hearing his views even though I couldn't agree with him less.

A couple of days back an amusing thing happened. Sarah and Anne and I were standing in the entrance room, outside the conference hall, waiting for things to break. They did quickly.

3 Admiral William D. Leahy (1875–1959), chairman of the US Joint Chiefs of Staff.

Vyshinsky and U.J. came out in search of a John. U.J. was shown to one and came out quickly – washroom without toilets. By that time the P.M. was occupying the next nearest John so one of our embassy boys took Stalin way the hell down the hall to the next nearest toilet. In the shuffle, Stalin's N.K.V.D generals got separated. Then there was havoc – everyone running around whispering. I think they thought the Americans had pulled a kidnapping stunt or something. A few minutes later a composed U.J. appeared at the door and order was restored!

Anna Boettiger is swell fun. We (Sarah, she and I) usually spend afternoons together chattering while the big conf. goes on. So far the P.M. and U.J. have come to the President every day, which makes things much easier for him.

The Pres. gave one dinner the first night but that's been the only one so far (females not invited so Sarah joined us for the dinner upstairs).

So far, Ave & I eat all meals with the Pres. & party, which is very genial. It would fascinate you – comparing those meals with Chequers ones. They couldn't be more different. The Pres. is absolutely charming, easy to talk to on any subject. The war is seldom mentioned except its lighter side & the conference discussions get talked about briefly, but in the main it's politics, friends, with everyone swapping amusing stories. One night Marshall & King[4] dined. Marshall told some of the best "this war" stories I've ever heard. He's divine – I know you'd love him.

The President's "party," as it's called, is made up of about 6 hangers-on – who are, like me, here for the joyride: Ed Flynn,[5] a Brooklyn politician who the Senate refused to approve as our minister to Australia, Steve Early's[6] here and being I think very self-important and stuffy. Then there's Pa Watson,[7] a 2 star general and a

4 General George C. Marshall (1880–1959), Chief of Staff of the US Army; Admiral Ernest J. King (1878–1956), Commander-in-Chief of the US Navy.
5 Edward J. Flynn (1891–1953).
6 Stephen Early (1889–1951), White House press secretary.
7 General Edwin Martin Watson (1883–1945), a Roosevelt aide and adviser, who died after a stroke on the way home from Yalta.

couple of admirals and of course Leahy. It's amusing watching them pay court.

The military talks came first & now they've embarked on the political questions. The Pres. is getting a big kick out of presiding over the meetings (he's the youngest you know). As far as I can gather, so far each person has stated his case but the big job of reconciling differences of opinion has yet to start. Harry [Hopkins] arrived not very well and went straight to bed with dia (can't spell it) anyway gyppy tummy and got up two days later for lunch. The doctors ordered him to eat nothing but cereal and the fool had two huge helpings of caviar, cabbage soup with some cream and then his cereal. He really is a fool. That brought his pains back & since then he's eaten in bed, but been at all the meetings.

I saw Peter [Portal] and Pug for a minute after one of the meetings but that's all so far. Ira was quite upset at not being invited here.

Ave's in there pitching, as you can well imagine, and reports so far are very favorable.

I'm running out of gossip.

Best love to you,

Kathy

PS I didn't like the idea of sending you a letter via Lillian (that had to be left open). Sorry you were upset at not getting one. She was a great asset to Spaso House & we all thoroughly enjoyed her stay. Don't you think she's amusing & fun?

Feb. 8

There was great rejoicing last night. They sold U.J. on Dumbarton Oaks. Very good indeed.

At dinner the President was in great form, a mood which must have been dampened by Jimmy Byrnes[8] holding forth and at great length. Lord save me from American politics!

After the Pres. went to bed, Fred came in for a drink (my room seems to be the local bar come late at night). But he didn't have much

8 James F. Byrnes (1882–1972), Democrat politician, served as Secretary of State under Truman.

news of you that was later than the letters. He is so nice. I haven't seen Peter or anyone else at all except to pass pleasantries & it doesn't look as though I will – but I still have fingers crossed.

Enclosed is a set of doilies that Ave picked up in Malta. Hope they look nice. He couldn't get sets with more than 6, but maybe they'll be useful for dinner parties of an intimate nature!

Good bye now. My love to you. Please thank Butch for his letter thanking me for his "trousseau"!

Kathy

PS Romance of the meeting – Joan & Frank McCarthy[9] (Marshall's aide)!

Yalta
February 4, 1945

Dear Mary,

Well I've at last had my wish and met the President. It seems sort of odd it would be in Russia. He arrived last night and Ave and I dined and then again had lunch today. He's absolutely charming, easy to talk to, with a lovely sense of humor. He's in fine form, very happy about accommodations and is all set for the best.

Ave saw the P.M. last night and reports he is all set for the worst. But maybe that mood will change. Anna is great fun. Harry is sick in bed, so she and Ave are cooking up all arrangements and things. For instance, today the conferences are being held here – with a dinner. Sarah is coming over with the P.M. & staying for dinner – a "children's" party.

To start at the beginning. We trained down here, despairing ever being able to get flying weather – a long affair, 3 days and nights. Most of the time spent standing in bombed-out stations. Frances Balfour came down with us and flew out with Averell to Malta – a quick way home for her.

9 Frank McCarthy (1912–86), in later life a distinguished Hollywood film producer. Joan Bright Astley wrote in her memoirs, 'With Frank McCarthy I was on terms of mutual liking and friendship. He had a husky voice, blue eyes and a lot of southern charm.'

The 3 days passed pleasurably, 3 compartments for the 8 of us. We had to take our own food as Soviet trains do not have diners, but our cook did well by us – Turkey, cold ham and loaves of bread and we had hot tea or water out of the samovar at the end of the car. Ave was well escorted by all of his boys – three compartments full! A female porter made beds and every hour or so walked down the passage clearing up the dirt – a wonderful procedure – she'd spray water through her teeth onto the carpet to dampen it and then sweep. Made an intriguing sound. I got bitten as usual by bugs, but no one else did, one eye closed up and it itched like mad. After that I bombed everything thoroughly with DDT.

We saw enough war damage to last me a lifetime. My God this country has a job on its hands – just cleaning up.

The Ukrainian peasants seemed far more prosperous than those around Moscow. Their cottages are painted, have thatched roofs and are quite picturesque – not too dirty. Some stations had vendors, at one we bought 4 fresh eggs (cheap for $4) and made a nice punch – canned milk, bourbon and butter. The train at last dumped us in Simferopol in mid-afternoon. The delegation of Soviets wanted us to spend the night as the mountain pass was too "dangerous" for night driving. Ave was adamant so off we went in a snowstorm and winding roads, but good drivers (one car got stuck once) and arrived in Yalta in about three and a half hours.

Averell left after two days to fly to Italy and then Malta and Eddie and I stayed on. It was absolutely heaven just relaxing. Unfortunately, it rained most all the time but we walked for exercise and just got wet. One afternoon I went and called on the sister of Anton Chekhov. She was a grand old lady of 83 – thrilled to meet some Americans and spent her time asking us questions about America. Her brother spent the last four years of his life down here. It's supposed to be a good T.B. climate.

At Chequers the P.M. holds forth and everyone else listens, but here there's just general conversation and as far as I'm concerned no sweating or wondering "what the hell should I talk about next."

The most fun night was when Marshall and King dined instead of the usual political hangers-on. Marshall told some of the most fascinating stories about the war. As you may gather I've taken a great shine to Marshall, he's full of fun with great dignity. My spies report that at military meetings he stands head and shoulders above everyone else – with Peter Portal (British Marshal of the R.A.F.) second. I guess the comparison isn't really quite fair as the head of the Soviet military delegation is General Antonov – deputy chief of staff – but it's nice to know just the same.

Feb. 9

Ave said he'd never seen Stalin in such great form. He really was terrific. He enjoyed himself, was a splendid host and his three main speeches were swell, something more than the usual banalities. In the Soviet fashion, he sat in the middle of a long table with the president on his right and the P.M. on his left, Molotov and Eden and Stettinius opposite. At times, Stalin just sat back and smiled like a benign old man, something I'd never thought possible. Anyway, I was much impressed. He toasted Churchill as the great war leader who'd taken command when England was without fighting allies. His tribute to the President is harder to explain. Stalin talked about America miles from the war and her leader who prepared her for that war. Stalin kept leaping to his feet and once called himself a "garrulous old man." He talked about allies in war and allies in peace and that allies only deceived each other if they thought they could get away with it. Deceiving was impossible among equals etc.

Molotov was toastmaster and quite amusing at times. The funniest thing of all was when Stalin started teasing Gusev – Soviet ambass. to Gt. Britain – and ended up saying "he is a gloomy man, but sometimes gloomy men are more able than likable ones." Gromyko[10] toasted Ave and Ave answered with a tribute to Vyshinsky and Maisky – "the men he worked with in Moscow." Can't remember that either Eden or Ed said anything of great import. Beria was there and I was most interested meeting and seeing him. Apart from being the head of the N.K.V.D., a role which makes him the most feared man,

10 Andrei Gromyko (1909–89), at this time Soviet ambassador to the United States.

he is on the Defense Committee. Archie toasted him in the former capacity as the man who looks after our "bodies." Archie always seems to get an obscene touch in his toasts. After it Churchill got up and walked over to him and instead of clinking glasses, shook his fingers at Archie and said "be careful, be careful." In other words shut up. He doesn't like Archie. Beria made no toast. He is little and fat with thick lenses which give him a sinister look – but quite genial.

Having females at a party must have made a big problem for the protocol department. We were all wondering where Anna and Sarah would sit. Both were on Stalin's side of the table – down the end – with me opposite Sarah. Stalin toasted the "ladies" and then came round and clinked glasses with each of us – a very nice gesture. Averell informed me en route over to the party that the price of my meal ticket would be a toast in Russian. Neither Anna or Sarah got up, so along about the third meat course, Ave leaned over and told me to get up. Chip Bohlen – the President's interpreter – had told me what to say – or rather how to say what I wanted to say – and General Antonov,[11] on my other side, offered his suggestions. Gee I was scared.[12]

No one got anywhere near drunk and all in all it went off very well. One nice touch – Stalin's palace belonged to Prince Yousupov – one of the men who killed Rasputin. It's interesting too when you think that all the Big Three meetings were held in a Tsar's palace.

Feb. 10

Last night I read a Feb. 6 *Herald Tribune*. We get papers every 2 days but that is the quickest yet.

The conference is now beginning to break up. The chiefs of staff leave today. All are going home very happy. By tonight only the political people will remain and it looks as though all round it's been a good conference – a hellova long one too. Nerves have not become frayed, which is amazing.

---

11 Alexei Antonov (1896–1962), deputy chief of the Soviet General Staff.
12 Kathy proposed a toast for 'those who had worked so hard in the Crimea for our comfort, and having seen the destruction wrought by the Germans here [I] had fully realized what had been accomplished'.

Stettinius and staff of 7 are coming to Moscow and Ed Flynn will remain with us a few weeks. The Lord deliver us! However, he's not as bad as he sounds. He's old and rather sweet and doesn't get in anyone's way – at least hasn't while here. Perhaps his common sense, something which he has a lot of, may keep him out of trouble in Moscow. His quest, described at its worst, is to make the Russians pray!

If you've gotten through this far I take my hat off. I wrote it mostly for my amusement futurely.

I love your black necklace.

Kathy

PS Be very careful what you show other than the family.

Moscow
February 13, 1945

Dear Pam,

Returned here to find a wire from Mary that little André Poniatowski had been killed in action Jan. 23.[13] Though it's an awful thing to say, I'm rather happy for him. He'd never have found happiness in the world postwar.

As you must have gathered, the conference was a terrific success. I think it surpassed everyone's hopes and expectations – even those who to date have had but swell dealings with our friends. You can imagine how elated Ave is, though Lord knows what trouble his new job as Polish gov't conciliator will bring. You saw I expect that the United Nations conference will be held at end of April. Present plan is for W.A.H. [Averell] to attend – so that's something to look forward to.

Suddenly remembered that I'm home and can type and save your eyesight.

Don't believe I wrote you about you U.J.'s banquet – Sarah and Anna and I were all in on it – so as to make it a "family party" as the President put it. Each delegation was invited to bring 10 people, my going (also Ed Flynn) meant that the Chiefs of Staff were left out. When I heard about that, I was horribly embarrassed and told Anna for God's

13 Marie-André Poniatowski (1921–45) was killed fighting in the Netherlands.

sake to change (subsequently discovered Ave had done the same thing) the list and leave me off. Odd though it may seem, more bad feeling and upset pride is caused by people left out of social gatherings than official ones. Lord knows I didn't want to be the cause of any.

Anyway I went and on the way Ave said I'd damned well have to make a speech in Russian – one in English would have been hard enough to do – in Russian made it that much more scary, but I suppose it was a good idea. Neither Anna nor Sarah spoke, not realizing what the custom in Russia is (no one is ever called on). When the "ladies" were toasted Stalin came round and clinked our glasses, which was a nice gesture I thought. He was in top form – a charming, gracious, almost benign host, I thought, something I'd never thought he could be. His toasts were sincere and most interesting – more than the usual banalities. He insulted no one (remember the Tehran dinner!) but kidded Gusev for being such a gloomy man. Ed Flynn kept the statistics for the evening – 30 guests, 25 courses and 45 toasts. As Ed doesn't drink he failed to keep track of the wines. No one was drunk and a pleasant time was had by all.

Must go now – *Swan Lake* etc.

Kathy

Moscow
February 16, 1945

Dear Mary,

It seems odd now to be back – reading all the news about the Crimean Conf. I'm beginning to wonder was I really there?

The President was made to leave Livadia, drive to Sebastopol, spend the night on one of our ships and then drive another long way to his final exit point. We went along too. That night Anna and I had to go to a concert given by a Red Fleet chorus and dance between acts. I was too tired to enjoy it.

To see that everything was properly laid on at the airfield Ave and I were off at 6:30. We passed so many completely flattened towns & villages that I've become immune to them.

The airport was a hubbub of excitement – guards of honor & a band that could play three pieces – our and the Soviet National

Anthems & the third a march. It played the latter for ½ hour straight – only adding to the noise of warming-up engines. One amusing incident: the President's fighter escort started off escorting the wrong plane!

We flew back with Ed Stettinius & co. (numbering 7). Terry Tyson[14] was one of the party. He's very nice & a hellova hard worker – sort of secretary, aide & doc. The shortest flight I've ever known. I went to sleep 10 minutes after we took off, in a beautiful Secretary of State bunk with box springs, and awakened 3 or 4 hours later only with difficulty (to another band playing the same 3 tunes).

They all stayed at Spaso. Everything had been beautifully laid on. An embassy really rallies itself when a Secretary of State is being housed! Unfortunately, the hot water boiler exploded first night, but that was hardly our fault. Second night here we were entertained by Molotov at the ballet – *Swan Lake*. Afterwards we went trooping backstage & met the ballerinas. Quite a disillusionment – lots of hickeys & bad complexions!

Now we're quieted down. We're entertaining tonight – the French and so I must get dressed.

Good bye now.

Love Kathy

14 Dr Terence Lloyd Tyson (1907–75), Stettinius's medical officer.

CHAPTER 24

'OUR GALLANT ALLIES ARE BEING MOST BASTARD-LIKE'

As Kathy herself noted, the post-Yalta honeymoon didn't last long. Back in Moscow, Ave and Archie spent weeks wrangling with Molotov about the interpretation of the Yalta agreement on Poland. The issue was whether the existing, pro-Soviet Polish administration – which ruled the country courtesy of the Red Army's occupation of Poland – was to be reorganised or replaced. Since reorganisation would favour the incumbents that was what Molotov strove for, while Harriman and Clark Kerr wanted a government containing more pro-Western politicians. The dispute prompted acrimonious correspondence between Churchill, Roosevelt and Stalin and remained unresolved for several months.

Bob Meiklejohn's comment in his diary was that 'one cannot help but feel that being an ally of these bastards is only one step better than being their enemy'.

Moscow
February 27, 1945

Dear Mouche,

At the moment we have no escaped prisoners with us, but for a while they were coming in at the rate of several a day – each with a fascinating story – parts gruesome but always interesting. Escaped officers were put up at the army house and we turned our billiard room into a dormitory for enlisted men.

Ed Flynn is still with us and thoroughly enjoying himself – sightseeing and talking to various religious personalities including the man we call Nar Com Bog (short for People's Commissar for God). He gets on well with the Russians and I guess he's doing a lot of good. He's certainly a nice addition to our household – very sweet, no bother and full of fun and interesting stories about backstage American politics. We're now trying to get him to convert Bob. When Flynn went visiting to the ballet school I went along too, having never seen it before and was fascinated. We spent two mornings and watched the top class of 17- and 18-year-old girls and the bottom classes – one girls and another boys. The little kids had been trained for only four months and were amazingly good – the girls that is – the boys were about as awkward as you'd imagine and equally self-conscious. One little girl was beautifully dressed in a little chiffon skirt and pink sweater and the rest in white cotton sleeveless dresses. You see this country isn't much different from any other! The older girls, strangely enough, had the same teacher as the little ones and she was as rough on them as stories tell. She yelled and screamed and ranted even in front of us, made one girl cry, and never complimented them when they did better. With the youngsters she was quieter, but very firm about pulling their legs and arms into the right position. It was all very interesting. Ballerinas seldom send their kids to ballet schools as they say it's too damned hard on them. However, there are compensations – better food and other privileges plus a very good education in all regular subjects.

Last Saturday was Red Army Day with a big celebration in the evening – something which I was dreading – but it turned out very pleasantly, no drunkenness at all. The invariable concert was shorter than usual and not so noisy. The one trouble was that Averell sat next to Madame Molotov and made me do his interpreting – very exhausting. I have a hard enough time putting my own ideas in Russian – someone else's are just that much harder!

Concert over we were ushered into our usual room and to our equally usual table – same people – Molotov and wife, Mikoyan, Budenny (Marshal with magnificent whiskers and an eye for the girls) and a charming general I'd never met before who has succeeded Voroshilov. After we'd had a few drinks, Moly suggested that the Polish ambass. (the one to the government we don't recognize) be invited, with Ave's and Archie's permission. He arrived and seemed a rather frightened mousy little man. Everything was going along very nicely, when suddenly somebody remembered that the French are now a big nation – so General Catroux[1] (newly arrived) was included. He seemed confused but nice. His toasts were splutteringly effusive and not worth much. Much to my amazement I found I enjoyed myself. Perhaps it's because I'm beginning to know these particular individuals. One amusing thing happened – Averell was talking to Madame Molotov and me to Molotov at different ends of the table – at the same time about the same thing – Madame Moly's coming to San Francisco[2] – that it would be a good idea. While I was well on my way on the subject in my bestest Russian, Averell got his interpreter to tell Molotov his ideas on the subject. So it all looked as though it was nicely cooked up.

Couple of nights ago was the opening of Lillian Hellman's *Watch on the Rhine*, called here "The Farrilly Family Loses its Peace of Mind." Actually, by our standards it was god awful, but the Russian audience ate it up and at the end there wasn't a dry eye in the house – vice-commissars and all were snivelling away. I was quite amazed. It was interesting to see how blatant and how completely lacking in subtleties they made it – had to make it, to get Lillian's ideas across. At the end we had a little chat with the cast and they each and every one wanted to know how they'd [diverged] from the original characters. Averell's very good at getting out of those kind of questions. I hate even trying.

Yesterday we went to section number one of Tolstoy's funeral.[3] It's sad that he had to die. He was so nice and so friendly. His ashes were in a marble urn at the top of a pyramid of mostly paper and wax flowers. A steady line of people walked by and had for several hours before we arrived. We stood for about half an hour with the main mourners and then left. There was an orchestra playing good music and occasionally a singer would do a number, one of which was Lucienne Boyer's "J'attendrai" (sung to Russian words).

---

1 Georges Catroux (1877–1969), whom Kathy had met in London.
2 For the founding conference of the United Nations.
3 Alexei Tolstoy died on 23 February 1945.

My typing is particularly bad, but I have two infected fingers tied up in black salve, in an attempt to get them well. It's about my 99th attempt. I've been trying since Xmas. Averell has some kind of fungus infection which he can't get rid of, a friend (nice clean one) has ringworm of all horrible things and lots of people are going around with odd-colored dyes on their faces – all trying to get rid of some nasty skin disease. Moscow certainly has its unpleasant aspects!

We have at long last almost finished getting our worst moth-eaten furniture re-covered. I guess the house looks pretty terrible and dreary, but it's so much better than when we arrived.

My love to everyone,

Kathleen

Moscow
March 8, 1945

Dear Mary,

The war is going wonderfully well again now, what with the offensive on the Western Front. Gosh it's exciting. But the news is slightly dampened here by our gallant allies who at the moment are being most bastard-like. Averell is very busy – what with Poland, P.O.W.s and I guess the Balkans. The house is full of running feet, voices, and phones ringing all night long – up until dawn.

Ed Flynn is back from his Leningrad trip and he's due to leave day after tomorrow. It's sad he's leaving as he's so nice and it's much pleasanter having at least one disinterested guest in the house. Disinterested is the wrong word – but someone who doesn't do Russian work. He's delightful, not at all like I thought a party boss would be.

The housing situation gets worse and worse. Soon we'll have not even an empty day bed in the house.

We gave a party, about 60 people, for Flynn, last night, for him to return hospitality to the Russians and foreigners who'd entertained him. His list was padded nicely with genial people and the result was quite a success. Cocktails eight-thirty, then movie, buffet supper and dancing to the gramophone. With each new party we pick up a few more genial Russians. Now we have quite a collection. Newest member to our group is the actor who plays the part of a Chicago businessman in a current play. He arrived late last night, during the movie, and when I spotted him he was standing alone most unhappily. He told me he didn't know a single soul, either Russian or foreigner, but I soon fixed that up and he was a great addition.

Mrs Litvinov is getting very pally with me. She's sort of a bitch but rather an amusing one and certainly worth cultivating.

At the moment I'm involved in learning something about Russian history, which has always been a complete blank.

Each time I go away, I get one of my jobs taken away from me. The Yalta trip cost my psychological warfare directives (something I don't mind dispensing with one bit). It all means I have less hours that I have to spend in the office.

[Kathleen]

Moscow
March 22, 1945

Dear Mary,

Averell just got a cable from Marie saying that she'd seen Lillian Hellman in N.Y.C. Have you met her yet? She's great fun – though terribly opinionated – both on things she's an authority on and those she knows nothing at all about. If you've read Bill White's blast against the Russians, Lillian would be able to give you the other extreme of the picture!

I went away last weekend to the country. My that sounds civilized! It was great fun. The dacha belongs to a British colonel and a married couple. Due to the snow we had to walk 4 kilometers. For some odd reason the colonel thought skiing would be impossible, so we floundered in knee-deep [snow], with knapsacks, that made us sink that much deeper. We spent most of our time either cooking meals or sawing wood to keep the fires going. We slept in sleeping bags and generally speaking got 24 hours of health. It was quite fun. A nice Frenchman came along instead of Averell. I call him nice as he is not one of those who keep making references to France being treated badly by the Big Three. The French seem to think that overnight they have become a big power and they resent the Stalin, Churchill, Roosevelt friendship that leaves them unrepresented. What's more they seem to want to rub it in on every possible occasion.

We were all very much amused yesterday to receive the contents of the current *Time* on the Polish issue, which takes occasion to call Averell "vacuous." Bob, who takes the direct brunt of Averell's working hours, was exceedingly annoyed.

We can do very little business with the Russians over the telephone. If you write a letter that always leaves the obvious opening to the Russian – just not answer it. Hence I seem to spend a lot of time making appointments, seeing the wrong person. My job is essentially boring anyway – as it is stooging for Joe Phillips, who instead of giving me a whole section of the magazine to run, gives me bits and pieces to do, which he hands me at random.

I've got an Australian friend who broke his leg badly a while back, so I've been going to the hospital every other day to visit him. He's in a room with seven others, all army – kids – who have been badly wounded. Some have been in the hospital over a year and are almost completely well. They cook in the room, dance, sing and play games. If he tries to sleep during the day, the kid next to his bed wakes him up, saying, if he sleeps during the day he won't be able to sleep at night. At this stage he longs for a little privacy, or at least to be left alone, but being a special person (foreigner) the Russian patients figure they aren't doing their stuff unless they are entertaining him. So it is rather a vicious circle. I took him *Esquire* the other day and he has been doling out pin-up girls ever since to the boys who are ready to go back to the front.

Yesterday I went to a mannequin show of children's, men's and some women's clothes. The models tend to follow the average lines of the Russian women, which is short and bumpy. When a model comes in the jury, in the form of people belonging to the commissariat, judge it and either pass on it or reject it as a model to be put into mass production. Anything that takes too much material gets thrown out. Madame Molotov, who was one of the main judges, was particularly strict about saving material.

Spring hit us yesterday so the streets are rushing rivers and damned dangerous. No one has fallen down a main as yet, but that among other things might well happen.

I won 283 roubles at bridge last night, which in value is about $20 – stakes were low so it's quite a feat, particularly as my playmates were far superior bridgers.

We have 13 guests at the moment – a slight exaggeration as that includes Averell and me. Even so, it's a lot of people – one more than we have beds. One is Dick Rossbach[4] – very nice guy and a proper extreme from 10 days of boring hell we went thru with the three publishers who were here peddling their "freedom of the press" wares. Rossbach got "liberated" by the Russians a while back in Poland and the Russians let him run around Poland and organize our P.O.W.s. Our gallant allies wouldn't let General Deane's people out of the backyard. Anyway, on his own initiative Rossbach did a lot of good. He has a wonderful sense of humor.

Three nurses from Poltava are with us – none of Hollywood variety – but nice, also a couple called Davies. He is a new 2nd secretary and she is swell.

Beneš is here, plus Masaryk,[5] who has added considerably to my store of dirty stories. They all sound rather fatalistic, can't say as I envy them.

Lord knows if we'll make it in time for the San Fran. conference. I hope so. Ave needs some mental fresh air and sunshine.

Bye-bye, the pouch is about to close.

Love,

Kathleen

Moscow
March 26, 1945

Dear Pam,

Ira was due to come here on a quick business trip, but while our people were struggling here to get him entrance permits etc., we

---

4 Captain Richard M. Rossbach (1915–87), American POW who ended up on the run in Poland and was liberated there by the Soviets.

5 Edvard Beneš (1884–1948), president of Czechoslovakia; Jan Masaryk (1886–1948), Czechoslovak foreign minister.

heard from him that he couldn't come. A change of job, which I gather is a Washington one – a nice high-sounding title which I suppose is a technical promotion – which from all he's ever said he'll hate worse than ever (unless he's recently changed his mind). Such is life. At least it's nice for his wife.

Just noticed I made a rhyme!

As you've probably gathered the honeymoon after Yalta was short lived – shorter in fact than even the more pessimistic hoped. Lord knows I fell for the Yalta atmosphere of good fellowship, brothers in arms etc. hook, line and sinker. Anyway, Averell is very busy getting nowhere on Poland. Lord knows how long it will take at the present rate!

To change the subject slightly, I went to a mannequin show the other day – clothes designed by people from all over the USSR – men, women and children. The members of the Light Industry Commissariat that deal with clothes were there in full force to choose which models would be put into mass production. It was all very interesting and the first signs of something being done on proverbial "communistic" lines that I've seen.

A model would appear, the panel would judge, make comments and then vote by voice or hands. If anyone chose to disagree with the majority decision he (or she) would get up and make a little speech and there'd be a recasting of votes. Clothes that took too much material were given the axe, also any nice model that happened to be done in a color the panel disliked (stupid I thought).

The mannequins strictly followed average Soviet lines in women – short and square and ample extra fat. For that figure some of the models were quite pretty. But the men's clothes were god awful. Short jackets that hit halfway down the fanny, big shoulders and tightened waists.

Mar. 27

Perhaps this is a bad moment to write a letter. Unless I have something cheery to say I usually stay clear of a typewriter. Tonight Masaryk came to dine – just he, Ave and me and for the last few hours I've been listening to them take the world apart to such an extent that there now seems little left of it! (I've been kicked out of the room now.) Anyway, they discussed the future prospects of common garden decency and freedom – the kind of things we're fighting for without ever thinking much about them – or how hard it will be to keep them once the war is won. Tonight, listening to them made me depressed because I wonder how many of your and my generation realize how tough it will be. This country is certainly the best place to find out! Tonight, the four big high walls loomed awfully high – living here you're always conscious of them, but life is sufficiently pleasant so that they don't seem too damned menacing.

We've gotten into the terrible habit of late, of staying up every night 'til two or three. If I go out, I come home at a respectable hour and find a group chinning and join in. We never get anywhere and it's a bad habit.

My love,

Kath

PS Tell P.P. [Peter Portal] that I will answer his letter one of these days, but as he wanted a correspondence course in brotherly love, now ain't quite the time to give it effectively!

Moscow
late March / early April 1945

Dear Pam,

Today we went to the Tretyakovskaya gallery. It will be opened officially in May, but we spent a couple of very enjoyable hours looking at some of the pictures. The light was poor but it was all very interesting. Particularly the icon art, which has its own individuality and charm. The others – from the 18th century on up – followed the main trends of western art, some Goya like, others strongly Flemish etc.

The current tableaux – Tehran conf. variety – as you can probably imagine are god awful! Ave enjoyed it thoroughly and it was a pleasant change & relaxation. He's busy, as you know, with Polish things, prisoners of war etc. but seems well enough. We've been entertaining wildly & he goes out more, which is all to the good.

My love to you,

Kathy

CHAPTER 25

'MET A VERY FINE OLD LADY AT LUNCH – MADAME KOLLONTAI – A REVOLUTIONIST FROM WAY BACK'

Clementine Churchill's April 1945 trip to the Soviet Union was a huge success. Met by the Soviet elite and greeted by cheering crowds, she was even granted a private audience with Stalin, to whom she gave a fountain pen that her husband hoped would be used to sign many great agreements between Britain and the USSR.

Clemmie saw a lot of Kathy and Ave while she was in Moscow. The visit was going swimmingly, but then news of President Roosevelt's death reached the Soviet capital on 13 April. 'I know that you will feel this very much,' wrote Mrs Churchill to Kathy. 'I send you my love & sympathy. It is a challenging blow & I can't quite take it in & wish I was at home.' While Kathy retrospectively noted signs of Roosevelt's ill health at Yalta, she had betrayed no hint of it in her letters from Crimea. But perhaps she had written them with an eye to secrecy, or to censorship.

On 17 April Ave left Moscow for Washington to consult with the new president, Harry S. Truman, and then attend the foundation meeting of the United Nations in San Francisco. Kathy went with him. On the way back, towards the end of May, they stopped off in London and Paris. For the final leg of the journey, from Paris to Moscow, they were joined by Harry Hopkins and his wife Louie. Hopkins had been Roosevelt's most trusted adviser and was held in high esteem by the Soviets. Truman sent him to Moscow to troubleshoot the dispute about the formation of a new Polish government.

Hopkins's mission was successful and in June the British and Americans recognised the legitimacy of a newly formed Polish administration that included the pro-Western Stanisław Mikołajczyk (whom Kathy had known in London) as deputy premier.

Not long after the trip, in September 1945, *Harper's Bazaar* published an article by Louie Hopkins about her experiences in Moscow. At the Soviet dictator's request, Louie had met Stalin personally when her husband went to see him in the Kremlin. She recalled of the dinner with Stalin that Kathy's toast was to the women of Russia on the home front. She gave the toast in Russian 'and it went over very big. Everyone applauded her attempt to speak the language, and there was a lot of laughing over her accent.' The Hopkinses stayed in Spaso House which, noted Louie, Kathy ran 'with great skill and efficiency. She's a wonderful hostess for her father; she's completely natural and has perfect understanding of protocol.'

After the dinner with Stalin, the group watched some Soviet newsreels, including one about Moscow's May Day Parade, which was led by General Antonov, now the Chief of the Soviet General Staff. When Ave commented on Antonov's well-trained horse it sparked a conversation with Stalin about Ave's interest in horses. Shortly thereafter the Harrimans received two gift-horses from Stalin. Kathy's mount – 'Boston' – was a veteran of the Battle of Stalingrad. According to Kathy, the Harrimans wanted to give the horses back when they left Moscow for good, but the Soviets insisted on shipping them to the United States, accompanied by a couple of grooms. As Kathy related to Pam in a letter dated May 1946, the two guys had the time of their life and were reluctant to go home. Amazingly, Kathy met one of them, Captain Boblev, when she visited the USSR in 1974, by which time he was a professor at the Moscow Veterinary Academy.

Moscow
April 9, 1945

Dear Mary,

I'm mad as a wet hen about my Yalta letters to you and Ave and I have been trying to figure out what the hell I wrote about that was worth censoring – certainly nothing to do with security. Anyway, it's a damned bore. Please save the remains – I've promised Averell I'll rewrite it from here (for future use – color to go with that book he eventually expects to write) but somehow I don't imagine I'll get round to it.

Mrs Churchill left for Leningrad last night, having been here a week. She is wearing a Red Cross uniform – navy in daytime and grey at night.[1] They both make her look every bit as smart as ever. She is certainly a great credit to Britain and doing a really swell job. Lord knows how she will be able to bear up under the unceasing pressure of sightseeing, lunches, teas, banquets, ballets and operas. We have been to most of them and goodness knows I get sick to death of making an effort hour after hour.

Last Tuesday Molotov gave a luncheon for her and for some reason Averell and I were invited. It was particularly long and filled with very dreary flattery speeches about the Red Cross etc. That day Moly was stuttering particularly badly and had a hell of a time getting through his various toasts. Mme Moly was shaking like mad – perhaps nervousness – but I wouldn't think so, anyway between them they were quite a pair. The one asset of the lunch was that it was a sober affair. I sat on the other side of Molotov and he kept filling my vodka glass with white wine and never once suggested that I need indulge in vodka. The pièce de résistance was when I got up and made a speech in Russian, which Averell translated into English.

Another afternoon Averell and I went to a tea party. Mme Moly was officiating. The affair started at 5:30 and I was especially rung up and told not to wear an evening dress. The tea party started with cocktails followed by a concert – string quartet, operatic number – and afterwards tea and piles of cookies and cakes. All the prominent women of the Soviet Union were present – big and bumpy and I guess very intelligent. At such times I'm sore that I can't speak better Russian.

Another morning for some odd reason I was hauled in on an excursion to a candy factory. Mme Molotov had invited me the night before. Perhaps her hubby had told her to be nice to the 'Garriman'

---

1 Mrs Churchill's visit was in her capacity as president of the British Red Cross, which raised a lot of money for Russia during the war.

woman to offset his being bloody to Averell. I wouldn't know, but recently I've been getting great attention. I only wish she wouldn't try to hold hands. Over here it is a sign of friendship, not homosexuality, but I still don't like it.

Now Tito is in our midst. There's a big reception for him tonight. It's the Dutch national day today too – we're off there any minute now. Last night was opening night of Lillian's *Little Foxes*, a really swell job they did too, though the leading lady obviously copied every action of Bette Davis' movie performance. We sat in the director's box, which involved making polite conversation in between the acts and afterwards the cast was brought upstairs and we all drank sweet wine and said sweet nothings for what seemed to me hours. Both the leading lady and the woman who played Birdie were stinking drunk, which amazed me slightly – that they were that way right after the play – maybe one reason for their success.

There was a premiere of a ballet Saturday night – a thing called *Raymonda*[2] – nice as Russian ballets go, but discouraging because it's just the same old thing all over again. We were all hoping that a new production might show a change towards something new. The costumes stank, but the dancing was lovely – the ballet part that is. One amusing thing, in one huge court scene there were two different sets of Polish dances, done by different groups. The Lublin Poles and the London Poles I figured! We sat in the box that usually houses the Japs! None of them were present that night! Speaking about Japs, all the tame Russians we see were thrilled about the announcement that their government won't renew the Russo-Jap pact when it comes up next year.[3] An interesting extreme I got from the boys in the hospital ward I visit: they thought it was terrible (they're very young Red Army officers) and couldn't understand why it had been done etc. etc. and very depressed at the prospect of another war.

---

2 Ballet set during the medieval Crusades.
3 The 1941 Soviet–Japanese Neutrality Pact, which the Soviets renounced as part of their preparations for an attack on Japanese forces in Manchuria in August 1945.

Next Day

Lunch today at the Swedes (boring but they'll have good food). This evening we were to dine at Catroux (French ambass.) but that's off now and instead we go to a command performance of *Ivan Susanin*[4] – a five-act opera that makes [Wagner's] *Parsifal* seem light and airy. It's in honor of Tito. The high spot is when some Poles get brought in in chains. Reputedly, it's Stalin's favorite!

The reception for Tito was as crowded as church on Easter Sunday (in Moscow, not N.Y.). There were marshals galore plus all sorts of people who I've never before seen in a foreign embassy. Tito was in great form – looking even handsomer than when I met him in Italy – brown and gay instead of brown and worried.

Met a very fine old lady at lunch at the Swedes – Madame Kollontai.[5] She's a revolutionist from way back – most famous in America for her glass of water theory (that Russian women should take to sexual intercourse as they do drinking a glass of water). She's seventy plus now – had numerous husbands, the last one acquired when she was mid forties, he early twenties. When she tired of him, she had him sent to Siberia, or so the story goes. She's been Minister to Sweden for years and is back here for consultation. She's semi-paralyzed but carries it well. Averell called on her last week and yesterday she invited me to call Saturday.[6] I'm sure I'll enjoy myself thoroughly. To my knowledge she's the one official Russian who entertains in her own apartment. When Averell paid her his call he remarked that it was the first time he'd been in a Russian home and she said that yes she understood – but that she knew he was coming to see her – not to inspect her living quarters. Though she started out as a revolutionist, now she's sort of risen above it and strangely

4 Mikhail Glinka's opera *A Life for the Tsar* (1836), known as *Ivan Susanin* during the Soviet era.

5 Alexandra Kollontai (1872–1952), leading Bolshevik feminist and Soviet diplomat.

6 Kathy's plan to meet Kollontai on the Saturday was disrupted by a memorial service for Roosevelt. She did meet with her on Monday 16 April, but she left for the US the next day and the encounter is not mentioned in any of her subsequent letters.

enough has been able to survive. In conversation she invariably seems to refer to the Soviets in the third person – instead of "we."

This letter leaves at the same time as John Melby – a long-time Spaso-ite. If he comes to New York he'll probably look you up. Tonight we're throwing him a farewell party (Averell and I will arrive late for there's another do for Tito).

Goodbye now,
Kathy

Moscow
April 12, 1945

Dear Pam,

Thanks for the mail via Clementine. You would all have been proud to see her here in Moscow. She took the town & the people by storm.

Ave and I met her at the airport & [in uniform] she looked young and every bit as snappy as she used to in her civilian clothes. She's staying at one of the government villas. We lunched there – just informally – the following day & she told us about the "splendid" arrangements you'd made for the summer. After that lunch we were at formal lunches, teas, dinners (I was invited one day to visit a factory with her), sometimes 2 a day – after the ballet and opera – all in her honor. The pace set for her was terrific but she was bearing up well on Sunday when she had a family lunch with us here before leaving for Leningrad.

Now we seem to be repeating the process with Tito. The worst was a 4½ hours opera two nights ago. We were hauled into the "royal box" with the prodigal son. Ave couldn't quite figure out whether having Americans present was to build Tito up or flatter us. It certainly didn't succeed in doing the latter, if that was the intent, because it only meant we had to stay for the whole bloody performance!

Tito is radiant – as handsome as ever, if not more so. He's lost the tired & worried wrinkles he wore last summer in Italy. Catroux, who I've grown to like says that Tito reminds him of Mussolini in *The Great Dictator*! I protest!

This letter was started what now seems like ages ago – the day the President died. I remember a couple of weeks ago John Melby (the flowers to Lillian man) and I sat up chatting one night very, very late. We were slowly taking the world apart & finally we reached what we decided was the rock-bottom end – with a Truman president. That thought sent us to bed. I know Averell always entertained the belief that R. wouldn't last out the term. Seeing him at Yalta for the first time was a great shock. But somehow I never quite believed that the statesman who made our wheels move could die. Jesus it was a shock. It still is hard to believe – even now after two days. Can you picture a forthcoming meeting of the Big Three? That name no longer seems to have much meaning. Ed Flynn, if he's still around, can indoctrinate you about Truman. He knows him well. The best that can be said is that he's "safe." What a time to have a leader replaced by a safe man!

We were in the midst of the farewell party for Melby, an O.W.I. gal phoned about 2 a.m. – she had the presence of mind to pass on the news. We stopped the party with rather feeble excuses & then Ave phoned Molotov. In no time flat word came up from our doorman that M. was here. For all that can be said about M. being an impersonal, cold man, that night he showed good instincts. Ave said he was much upset – shocked, as I guess everyone was.

This afternoon we held a memorial service and all the top men turned out. Moly was rather sweet. He sat next to me during the service, understanding nothing, very solemnly picking at the black borders of the program card to see if it would come off.

Red flags with black borders hang from all houses today thruout Moscow – something I'd have not guessed would happen. Now what I wonder. We were to leave for home on Monday, but that's been delayed.

Tonight we had a family movie – *Casablanca* – we haven't seen it for a year & it still is a nice way to take your mind off things!

Your wire about meeting Rossbach and Flynn arrived today. You see we do have some nice visitors.

[Kathleen]

En route to Washington, DC
April 18, 1945

Dear Pam,

We left at dawn – 9 of us in Becky – all set to make a 40 hour trip home. Everything went fine 'til the Azores – 8 hours we were held up. Now we are halfway to Newfoundland. Becky has been juiced up. Nice crew, nice fellow travelers. In fact, all's simply perfect. I need a trip home. Lord knows what our plans for return route will be. With luck 'twill take you all in.

My love to you,
Kathleen

Moscow
May 29, 1945

Dear Mary,

I'm glad our Paris wires got through alright. Jesus it was fun seeing Shirley. He was in great form. Our first evening he, Ave and a Moscow French gal (Moscow friend that is) and I went out on the town – dined and then went to Ciro's. Later we discovered that it was about the only nightclub open that evening due to strikes.

He looks very well – brown – & incidentally he's not bald!!! (That's just in case you're worried.) To me he looks no older – he says he's matured no end due to his experiences. That may very well be true.

After our evening on the town, we agreed to meet in our very Ritzy hotel sitting room for breakfast. After breakfast Shirley went off to organize transportation back to his unit and I went to see Aunt Frances (she's in deepest mourning). Then he and I got collected by Butch (Eisenhower's naval aide) to pick up the general to go to lunch. Eisenhower was in town for his third visit and very much in hiding. Apparently, if recognized he gets mobbed. He was staying at a little hotel, using the back staircase and door. Unlike most generals, when he wants to go unnoticed he uses borrowed cars, has no MP guards, motorcycle escorts etc.!!! Lunch was at Spaatz's in St. Germain. We got horribly lost, but Shirley got us found. Lunch was very genial but would have been more so but for the presence of two congressmen.

I enjoyed it anyway. Food finished, conferences started, so Louie (Hopkins), Shirley and I went back to Paris.

Later

Shirley and I had [dinner] with the Poniatowskis, alone with Frances first, then Constance & later André came. Constance works at a Canadian club & takes soldiers sightseeing in Notre Dame. Frances said she didn't really know what Constance was doing – which though probably ain't true, shows that she's trying to untie Constance. She hopes that all three of them will go to America as soon as André gets demobilized.

London was the same as ever, except that taxis are nonexistent. Since VE Day the drivers have given up. Our one night in town we dined at No. 10, subject of conversation entirely devoted (not quite) to the elections – very interesting. Sarah came in after dinner & at midnight I met Al Newman & Joe Evans and had a fine time catching up. Joe came over from Paris to see me and flew with us. He's as nice as ever. Saw Pam – she said thank you and Bobby so much for the present for Winston. Saw my "fiancé" – now 1st Lord of the Admiralty[7] – God help us! He was most genial. In fact, come to think of it, in 18 hours I did one hellova lot. I escaped seeing *Frankenstein*[8] and that pleased me no end.

I'll start another letter tomorrow when I get my typewriter returned and tell you all the rest of our story – getting lost over Germany (really lost) and suddenly finding ourselves over the ghost city of Berlin. It was eerie to a degree. Since in Moscow I've been trailing around with Louie – hospitals and what have you. Yesterday was routine – today fascinating. We found ourselves in an experimental hospital – plastic surgery, bone work, and repairs of men who'd gotten castrated. None made dinner table conversation – Louie and I discovered when we returned! I will probably have nightmares for weeks. Our poor little Russian interpreter sort of collapsed towards the end.

My love to you,
Kathleen

---

7 Brendan Bracken served as First Lord of the Admiralty for a few weeks in mid-1945.

8 Presumably the 1944 American film, *House of Frankenstein*.

Moscow
May 31, 1945

Dear Mary [copied to Pam],

I remember the first time we flew over the desert – saw the Mareth and El Alamein lines. I thought it was exciting, but after that time I never really bothered to look much. Now I'm wondering if I'll ever just sit and read flying over Germany. The effects of the tactical bombing all the way through were about the most striking – not even one-lane road bridges had escaped. As we crossed into Luxembourg we saw fertile crops in between terrible destruction. No farmers in their fields, no livestock, no transport, not even horse-drawn. The great autobahns were empty of convoys. The impression was a country left bare of its people.

Spaatz had laid out a course for us – deviating slightly from a straight course to take in some of the main strategically bombed towns. There was an overcast so we had to fly under it at from 1,500 to two thousand feet (that's low enough to see dogs, chickens and mud puddles). There was no one to get into radio communication with, none of the crew had ever flown over Germany, we'd been given the wrong wind directions so that the net result was that we got ourselves properly lost (we didn't realize that for quite a while). Permission to fly over Berlin had not been granted by the Russians. In fact, since the armistice signing not one plane was allowed near Berlin. We crossed the Rhine at Coblentz. Magdeburg we know we saw, the other towns we don't as we weren't where we thought we were, but in general the pattern was the same – centers of the towns were intact, not badly bombed at all, but the finger-like suburbs with their factories and marshalling yards were battered beyond use. We saw no signs of work reconstruction. West of Berlin there were amazingly few signs of destruction in the countryside – I guess because we overran the country so fast towards the end.

The pay-off came when a couple of huge ruined palaces came into view and then suddenly stretching out before us was a huge city it took minutes to fly over. Stalingrad is a dead town, but Berlin is just unbelievable – mile after mile of grey skeleton walls, that made me think of an old ragged but fine lace table cloth – fragile, full of holes and with jagged edges. Those sections of the city were beautiful. Others, destroyed by fire were black. Some whole areas were flat – like a beach. Apparently the Russians have set the German inhabitants to work clearing up the streets. The main ones seem cleared.

One huge fire was raging, with no effort to put it out. There wasn't much traffic, but people were out in the streets. Churches, hospitals – nothing was spared. Even now writing about it, the sight seems incredible, as though dreamed. It was a great treat seeing it.

From Berlin on out to Poland signs of battle were many – whole towns burned out or blasted – effects of our bombing, whole fields torn up by artillery, forests too. A sharp contrast to the areas we fought thru. Crops looked poor, we still saw no people working. Finally we arrived at the Vistula – the airfield we wanted on the other side – a German concrete one, so all was well. We landed, took on a Russian navigator and radio operator and received the astounding news that it was snowing in Moscow. For a while Poland wasn't much different from eastern Germany – except that tank traps and slit trenches were being filled in. The big change came when we crossed over into White Russia – poor soil, sparsely settled, grey, barren and dreary. I went to sleep. An hour out of Moscow things became more interesting. First there was not one sign of reconstruction, then piles of planks were visible, stacked on the outskirts of burned-out villages. A little further on (nearer Moscow) rebuilding had started. Finally we hit new villages, at least villages with some new or repaired houses. Reconstruction well underway.

Then came Moscow with its thin layer of snow. The whole trip had taken 9 hours.

Moscow
June 4, 1945

Dear Pam,

The 1st three days here Louie & I did some concentrated sightseeing – a sizeable mileage on foot. All except a huge Red Army hospital I'd seen before. It was extremely interesting & we saw what we were most interested in – plastic surgery. Actually, it's the 1st place I've been to where things weren't laid on. The hospital was huge –

3,000+ beds. The plastic surgery cases I'd seen in England schooled me for what I should expect. This was far more horrible – treatment more cruel. The way their top doctors use patients for experimentation was slightly terrifying, but the morale of the patients was terrific, surpassed anything I've seen anywhere, either England or home. One Professor told me "You have the techniques & equipment, but we also have ideas."

L & I got in on the Stalin dinner, which was a real treat. On one side of me was a 40ish man – fat, pig-eyed with a baby face & peach fuzz. I don't think he ever needed to shave anywhere. Conversation was hopeless. When I was having trouble manipulating my Russian lobster with a knife & fork, he grunted "use your fingers" & laughed at my difficulties with the cutlery. The suckling pig course was positively revolting. He'd cut a slice, masticate it for a while & then spit out the remains in neat mounds on the side of the plate. On my left, I had more success – a 4 star general – N.K.V.D. – but a nice man, spoke a little French.

[Kathleen]

Moscow
June 4, 1945

Dear Mary,

Molotov had a huge sort of victory reception – a pleasant, sober affair, with the invariable concert – food & dancing afterwards. My feet suffered most – having gotten well stepped on by 2 Soviet generals.

The following night Stalin gave a dinner – to which Louie and I were invited "if we wanted to come." Probably the Soviets hoped we'd not, as women haven't ever been included in Kremlin dinners before. However, as you can imagine we weren't that tactful. Madame Maisky was turned on to represent Soviet womanhood.

Unlike at the Yalta dinners, Stalin made no formal toasts – merely interjected asides to Molotov's – all amusing. Ave, who sat opposite him, said he was in an unusually good humor, but by comparison to Yalta I thought him very quiet.

The most interesting thing of all really was seeing, for me the first time, all the more sinister members of the government. We arrived and shortly after Stalin came in accompanied by the members of the Defense Council, mostly all O.G.P.U.[9] or N.K.V.D. They were a frightening bunch. The worst, Malenkov, was dressed in light grey – sort of a civilian Soviet suit with buttons all the way up the front – big, fat and puggy – pig eyes, never smiling. At dinner I sat next to a four-star N.K.V.D. general – head of internal security – charming, spoke a little French and made great effort in conversation. On the other side was a fat under-cover man – young (meaning fortyish), with peach-blossom skin and baby fuzz. He'd never shaved. Conversation with him was impossible – anything I initiated he'd [respond] with a curt "yes" or "no." If neither were appropriate, he'd just grunt or not even volunteer that.

Though wine bottles were in front of each person, the vodka soon disappeared. Chip and Averell figured that was due to the presence of ladies – no one was going to be given a chance to get drunk.

There were 40 guests, seated at one long table that took up the long length of the Catherine the Great ballroom. The Russians were divided into very distinct types – the educated, fine-looking variety – usually with tiny beards (all in uniform) & the big fat sinister type – with pig eyes and pince-nez. They were in the vast majority. The terrifying thing is visualizing them as ever cooperating with foreigners.

After dinner we adjourned next door & had coffee at little tables. Then came movies – 3 newsreels – May Day Parade – the capture of Vienna and Berlin.

Averell commented to Stalin about the horse the Chief of Staff rode. It was a beautifully trained animal – as Antonov was obviously no horseman. Stalin expressed interest in Ave's interest in horses and ended up saying he'd give him a couple. Today a general called officially. When he made the appointment through Russ, he refused to say what was the reason. A half hour later, Ave came upstairs with a document, beautifully covered with red leather – the pictures and pedigrees of two horses. One of which Ave had admired in the movie (English breed) and the other a Don basin horse – for me apparently,

9 Russian acronym for the Soviet secret police.

the first named Fact, the second Boston! Now we've really got to scurry around and find a dacha with stable to put them in.

Moscow
June 8, 1945

Dear Mary,

The Hopkins left early yesterday morning – Harry none the worse for wear, which was a great relief. I think Louie enjoyed herself and made a big hit with all the Soviets. One afternoon Mrs Molotov gave a tea party – us and the wives of all the Vice-Commissars of Foreign Affairs. Mrs Litvinov behaved abominably and embarrassed Louie and me no end. She lambasted everything brought up – whether American or British or Russian. Towards the end Mrs Moly even got exasperated. Minus Mrs Lit it would have been a very pleasant function, but as it was we squirmed a good deal. A rather terrifying thought: she gave the impression of literally being slightly mad – a change that's taken place in the last few months. One thing, I'll be surprised if she's ever again produced for such a function.

The British at last have a new general – one I knew last year in Italy, who's very nice. We went to a cocktail party for him night before last and had dinner last night. Tonight Madame Catroux[10] is giving a dance – a farewell party to the last of the Normandy squadron. A nice gesture – the Soviets are giving all the boys the Yaks they fought in. Despite that, they're a very browned-off lot. The same I gather is true of our Poltava group. The Soviets certainly don't seem to be able to sell themselves to the men who have to do a job of work with them, which is really too bad.

Speaking of Madame Catroux, a set-to with her was narrowly avoided. When I got back, it never occurred to me to call on her immediately. I was traipsing around town with Louie and anyway didn't have time. She, Mme C, went to Archie (Dean of the diplomatic corps) and asked why she hadn't yet been approached by me. Did I presume to think that she should make the first advances etc. A couple of days ago I went scurrying over, all dressed in my Sunday

10 Marguerita Catroux (née Jacob, 1881–1959).

best (she was likewise). Six different servants ushered me up the stairs and into the correct room. But once there it was very genial. She's a battleaxe at heart, a great organizer, but really fun (if you don't see too much of her). She's leaving soon though, she hopes for good, as she can't stand it. As you probably know there are thousands of Frenchmen either in Poland or Russia, some even in Moscow in hospitals and she's been allowed by the Soviets to see only a very few of the less sick ones. Lacking patience, she's ranting, which you can't blame her for. But then what else can be expected. I told her that Louie and I had been to a big Red Army hospital, that brought on her rage. Why had we been allowed to see hospitals when she wasn't? The answer was obvious (no sick Americans in it). Having been here this long, I'm beginning to take more and more for granted – forgetting my original period of education learning how things work in this town.

To change the subject – this afternoon Averell and I went riding. The arrangements were most formal, and we had not the slightest idea what was in store for us. At 2:30 sharp a general (one we knew), his female aide and a senior cavalry officer turned up and we set off and landed up at a military riding academy about 10 minutes from here. As we walked into the riding rink, I suddenly had a horrid thought that maybe they might expect me to ride side-saddle, luckily not. Averell's animal is bay, mine chestnut and widish between the knees. First time I mounted I almost got kicked. I got very confused when the Russian groom wanted me to ride with the curb reins in one hand, the snaffle in the other. My animal had a trot that damned near threw me over its head at each step – it was plenty hefty, but I finally got used to that.

The Russians were charmed by Averell, who schooled his horse and caught on to the signals he should use very quickly. He got it to do all the things a circus pony does, as well as figure eights, including kneel down. I was most surprised when I saw that happen. He got a great kick out of it, so maybe he'll go often. My horse has just returned from the front. I imagine Averell would have considerable success with it. I tried no tricky business!

[Kathleen]

Moscow
mid-June 1945

Dear Mary,

It makes me feel quite ill & weak every time I think what you must have been going through these past few days.[11] Your first cable came yesterday evening followed this morning by the slightly more encouraging one. Last night Ave & I figured out that perhaps he could get Shirley transferred here. Once in bed, between nightmares & thoughts, I got some even more fantastic schemes. Now I'm going to see what Russ Deane has to say about getting someone "unfrozen" from a job.

In Paris we should have followed thru with the scheme to get Shirley to Moscow as Harry's Doc. At the time Shirley figured it might do more harm than good – besides giving him a feeling of guilt.

The main thing is not to bitch up anything Shirley may be doing.

This comes with all our love and thoughts.

Kathy

Moscow
June 18, 1945

Dear Mary,

We went riding again today, first time in about 5 days. The Poles are taking up a great deal of Averell's time. I just fooled around and enjoyed myself and did a moderate amount of schooling, which annoyed Averell no end. His idea of fun riding is getting into a big sweat over whether or not the figure 8 comes out right.

We had Morawski (P.M.) and Bierut[12] (President of Warsaw gov't.) to lunch the other day. Just us and an interpreter. It was the first time I'd met either. I remember the P.M. talking about the Fox, the Snake and the Skunk when referring to Morawski, Bierut and Zimerski. At lunch it was easy to figure that Morawski was the fox, but Bierut doesn't seem to fit either name. He's the small-town politician type. Puts his case forward well, answers questions in a direct manner, but lies like hell. To

---

11 Mary's husand Shirley had been notified that he was being posted to the Far East.

12 Bolesław Bierut (1892–1956), Polish communist.

hear both of them talk, Poland sounded like a happy country – no reign of terror. Morawski I took a distinct dislike to. He gave Averell the kind of stock answers to questions that a school kid over here is made to learn by heart. I figured he must be singularly stupid to think he could get away with using them on Averell. The following day we had Gholovski and Kutrzeba to lunch. The former is a professor, the head of the Polish Academy of Science, the latter the head of the Socialist Party prewar. Both looked in their 70s – very old, very tired and very eager to answer any questions Averell asked, but, as old men do, their eagerness strayed into garrulousness. What they said I guess I can't write. The conversation filled me partly with pity but mostly with horror. Horror for the future of Poland – that we must sit by and watch what goes on, being able to give only moral support and such meaningless things as sympathy and understanding. Poland's young strong men have been killed by the Germans. What remains is what spent the war outside, either in London or Moscow and men like the two who came to lunch. Accentuating the patheticness of the situation, the little professor, whose false teeth clicked continually, had to keep jumping up and going to the can. His friend explained he has an inflamed bladder – the result of his session in a German concentration camp. All the time the two old men talked, I kept thinking of Bierut–Morawski, who with their toughness and stubbornness could run circles around [their] sincerity and pleading eagerness. Professors can't stand up very well in politics when dealing with well-trained politicians.

Moscow is preparing like mad for a Victory Parade on Sunday – which only a very few thousand reportedly will be allowed to see. Saturday we entertain 150 scientists.

[Kathleen]

Moscow
June 18, 1945

Dear Pam,

It seems ages and ages since I last saw you. Once in Moscow the outside world quickly becomes remote.

Ave is up to the gills with Poles at the moment. Soon I guess he'll be thinking in Polish – dreaming too! The last couple of days in two batches we've had the Warsaw Poles and the Poles from inside Poland to lunch. I was allowed in. Being my first introduction to anything of its kind, it hit doubly hard.

First day we had the Warsaw President and Premier. Both in their early 40s.

Next day we had in a Professor and the head of the Socialist Party (prewar). To look at they almost made you weep. Both very old. The Socialist was the greater realist – "we realize that compromise is necessary." But thinking back on the two Poles I'd seen the day before, I wondered how those two stolid men could or would budge an inch towards compromising.

Now the 16 Poles are on trial.[13] Tomorrow I think I'll go. Today *Pravda* devoted 2½ of its four pages to the listing of the Red Army's accusations. For good or bad, those men fought [for] their country – while others sat in Moscow or London – against the Germans. The aftermath of war is certainly confusing. Men who fought [are] now considered traitors.

Moscow is preparing for a Victory Parade on Sunday. At night – starting one a.m. – we can hear the [tanks] and artillery rumble down the huge boulevard a block away, making enough noise to wake you, if you're lucky enough to be already asleep.

Archie and I are competing on corn growing. Averell stands by the sidelines, never working in the garden and says we ought to plant more! After 10 days of warm weather, it's now autumn-like. I'm scared that everything will die.

As far as my job goes I'm not working very hard – mornings only – a new O.W.I. man has taken over a big slice of my work – something that bothers me not one bit.

Incidentally if you have a new picture of you and baby Winston, please let me have it. The two I have are way out of date.

I can't think of any news or gossip, but I've got till tomorrow to finish this.

[Kathleen]

---

13 Leaders of the Polish nationalist resistance, accused of terrorism by the Soviets.

Moscow
June 26, 1945

Dear Mouche,

The sun is out – for the 1st time in 2 weeks – & using the 4th of July party as an excuse, I'm sitting out in it instead of working. There's practically nothing for me to do anyway.

On Saturday we had a reception for scientists – ours, the British and Russians (there's a big jubilee at the moment).[14] I was expecting 120 & 170 turned up. More Russians came than were invited & we were eaten out of house and home.

As all scientists look alike I was scared stiff I'd figure wrong and start talking Russian to an American. By looking at men's shoes before starting a conversation, mistakes were avoided. We showed them *Mickey Mouse* & *Fighting Lady*.[15] One woman, an academician (highest rank given scientists) slightly floored me. I went up & said how nice it was to see her again (one of my stock Russian phrases) and she answered "have I ever met you before?"

We had 3 of the handsomest men in Russia that night – all with either full beards or goatees & of course over 65. They were charming. I came out of the evening pro-scientist. Interestingly enough, our agriculturalists say that Russia's way ahead of us in experimental work. Thanks to the collective & state farms they can carry out experimental work on a very large scale, which of course we can't.

The night before our scientists' party Averell threw one for the Poles. Last night the Polish ambassador, who we as yet don't recognize, gave a reception & we saw the Poles all over again. I consider it a major feat that I know them now by name (mostly all unpronounceable). Besides all the Poles, the Czech government was on hand. Fierlinger (ex-ambass. in Moscow & present prime minister) was his old greasy self and his French wife has turned into much the gracious lady.

---

14 The 250th anniversary of the Soviet Academy of Sciences.
15 *The Fighting Lady* (1944) was a documentary film aboard an American aircraft carrier during the Pacific War with Japan.

On Sunday we stood for 2½ hours in the pouring rain & watched the Victory Parade. We almost escaped having to, as we arrived and found we were expected to stand right next to the Japs. Ave was furious and said he was leaving. After much scurrying we were placed elsewhere (Archie came with us). The schedule was a 2½ hour military parade then 2½ hours of civilians. The latter was called off, probably because the doctors felt that Uncle Joe had had enough of a wetting. I was very glad, but it was sad for the poor civilians, who had been standing in line for 5 hours – waiting for their turn to parade thru Red Square.

No one saw the parade except those in Red Square (about 15,000 of the elite – government people & the wives of senior officers who paraded). All the streets were closed off, people not allowed to look out of windows along the routes the paraders formed on. Very strange. After months of practice and preparation only a few favored ones were allowed to watch & this in the land of the proletariat.

One distinction Ave shared honors with Jap ambass. They were the only ones who decided, rain or no rain, they'd wear top hats!

Zhukov took the salute mounted on a white charger. The soldiers cheered him – their voices echoing back and forth in a way that made shivers run down my back. At the same time gun salutes went off. Everyone was beautifully trained – the whole thing most effective. Rokossovsky – the other mounted marshal almost came to grief. His horse wasn't the best trained. The Leningrad Front representatives led the parade off, with soldiers, airmen and tankists from all the other fronts following & finally men carrying captured German banners. These were flung at Zhukov's feet – a swell idea. After that we watched 1½ hours' worth of motorized infantry, cavalry, tanks, guns etc. etc. etc. I got colder & colder. My back was aching & I was very happy when we heard the second & longer half of the parade was called off. Having seen one parade once, I hope I'll never have to again!

My love to you,
Kathleen

Moscow
July 9, 1945

Dear Mary,

I wired you to see Bob Lovett[16] – he knows the War Dep't routine & should be a help.

Averell and I were talking tonight about it & he suddenly made me realize that now Ike is out as an aider – Shirley not being in his theater. Nuts. I'd already mentally composed a letter for Ave to take to [him].

Unfortunately, talking to people on the spot, in Washington, who are actually doing the job is what best clicks. Bob Lovett, as a friend, should know best where to start.

Life here has been one ghastly mess arranging for a 4th of July party – 10 days before, I stopped work at the office and did nothing else.[17] I had to do all the damned invitations – about 650 of them. As far as food arrangements [went] everything fell through at the last minute. Then a horrid organization called "Intourist," after saying they would provide us with the necessary plates, glasses, platters, announced they'd give us nothing. Cooks that we'd hired from another Soviet organization never turned up. In fact nothing went according to plan & all had to be done by us in the end.

The army gave us back half of the ballroom which they used for offices and that we turned into a fairly respectable dining room. We ended up having to drive 250 kilometers to buy the necessary glassware. The truck turned over on the way home, breaking little glass – but that, thank God, I didn't know until the truck limped into our backyard the morning of the party.

It all ended happily – big success – I have no idea how many guests there were. Someone stopped counting after 500. We didn't run out of food or liquor, the orchestra decided to turn up, the weather was fine so we used the balcony to sit on. A vast number of Soviets turned

16 Robert A. Lovett (1895–1986), Assistant Secretary of War for Air, who seems to have been an admirer of Kathy's.

17 Kathy's provisions request to the Soviets included 60 turkeys, 50 kilos of sturgeon, 25 kilos of caviar, 400 cucumbers and 500 fresh eggs.

up, including the Molotovs who heretofore never have gone to National Holiday receptions.

I wore a Slavonic costume – given to me that day by a Folk Dancing group. It was very attractive, though the boots hurt my feet & I soon removed them. There were few drunks and at about 3 a.m. I figured I'd stop the orchestra. I was too dead to go on. (Averell double-crossed me and made them play two more tunes.) Now that it's over hope I'll never have to put on another ever again. Averell's entire entertainment allowance for the year will just about cover the liquor bill!

Beside the party we had a boat ride for clerks and enlisted men and their guests. It was apparently great fun. Yesterday I spent most of the day counting glasses, knives and forks and spoons and plates etc. The army is about to open a new house for 65 enlisted men and I'd borrowed everything they had, down to electric bulbs and lugged it to and fro myself with one officer. None was broken, with the exception of 5 glasses, which got tossed out on our cement garden walk by some extra-exuberant Americans.

T.V. Soong[18] is here. Ave's seen a lot of him. He's much younger than I expected, rather quiet. (I've met him at our party & one Molotov gave the evening before.) Chiang Kai-shek's eldest son apparently came to our party too.

Today V.O.K.S., the organization that deals with cultural relations, had a lunch day. Started at 2 p.m. & we figured with luck we'd get out shortly after 4. Four came & sure enough we'd eaten our way through umpteen courses of food and drink to dozens of stupid meaningless toasts. I thought things were on schedule, we moved to the drawing room for coffee and cakes and candy and fruit and there was the same jazz orchestra we'd had two nights before. About 30 grown men and women started to dance around a huge room. It was quite revolting. Almost before it was decent, Averell and I left, a movie was coming up and I suppose more dancing after that. The guest of honor was the president of the Society of American–Russian Friendship. I wonder if anyone enjoyed it.

18 T.V. Soong (1894–1971), China's foreign minister.

July 11th

This ends hurriedly, I'm off to Stockholm and Ave leaves a few hours later – so Moscow'll be deserted. At the moment I couldn't feel less like travelling. Up-chucked for six hours yesterday due to the curse. However I'll probably live!

Love,
Kathy

CHAPTER 26

'SWEDEN'S DEFINITELY SECOND-RATE'

Kathy didn't have a lot of time for neutral states like Sweden, and she had several run-ins with that country's diplomats. Her trip to Sweden began with a train journey to Leningrad on 12 July, where she stayed for a couple of days before travelling to Helsinki. From there she sailed to Turku and then to Stockholm, arriving on the 18th.

Meanwhile, Ave was in Berlin, attending the Potsdam summit of Churchill, Stalin and Truman. Upon being congratulated by Harriman for the Red Army's capture of Berlin, Stalin replied that Tsar Alexander I had got as far as Paris when he defeated Napoleon.

Halfway through the Potsdam conference Churchill returned home to receive the result of the recently held British General Election, which Stalin was not alone in expecting him to win by a good majority. Somewhat surprisingly, Clement Attlee's Labour Party won with a parliamentary landslide and Churchill didn't return to Potsdam. Attlee replaced him as head of the British delegation, while Churchill's foreign secretary, Anthony Eden, was replaced by Ernest Bevin, the trade union leader and Minister of Labour in the wartime coalition government.

In early August, Ave turned up in Stockholm and he and Kathy flew back to Moscow together.

Grand Hotel, Stockholm
July 19, 1945

Dear Mary,

Moscow seems very far away at this point – quite a happy thought! Averell I guess is in Potsdam but I hope he'll come this way from Berlin and pick us up – I've had enough of Russian and Finnish trains to last me a lifetime!

Eve Smith, Canadian, and Pat Davis[1] are with me and so far it's been lots of fun. Leningrad was even lovelier than I dared hope. The architecture in the center of town – up and down the Neva – is very attractive and very much the same – yellow painted plaster covering bricks with white Greek columns. Most of its buildings are like Moscow's few best. The damage done by artillery is rapidly being patched up, with lots of plaster and more paint and the windows being glassed in. Compared to Moscow it is a deserted city. The parks are only pleasantly filled and you can walk down the streets without needing to push or be pushed. Small canals with bridges run in and out cutting up the islands and the whole city was quite charming. The outskirts are modern, huge apartment houses etc. but the center has been left alone by the Soviets. We stayed at the Astoria hotel – a great luxurious and modern place compared to either the National or Metropole, clean and uncomfortable. I was given a 4 room suite and we all had to eat there – no foreigners allowed in the main dining room. "Intourist" turned themselves inside out and we had cars for sightseeing and were able to see mostly only what we wished to. One afternoon we went to Pushkin (Tsarskoe Selo) where Catherine the Great had a huge palace and where Nicholas II (the last Tsar) had a smaller one. Prewar the Catherine Palace was a museum, but the Germans looted, burned and destroyed most of it. Enough remains so that we got a good idea of how elaborate it was. On the way out there (30 miles out of Leningrad) we saw small groups of rather healthy-looking Germans working – guarded by women.

---

1 Eve Smith was married to Canadian diplomat Arnold C. Smith (1915–94); Pat Davis was the wife of US diplomat Richard H. Davis (1913–72).

The Hermitage, where prewar the famous Rembrandts were hung, is in the midst of wholesale restoration. Due to damage none of the pictures are yet hung so we weren't allowed in it. The parts I enjoyed best were the sections of the city built by Peter the Great. His own tiny log cabin has been carefully saved – his granddaughter Elizabeth built a strong brick house around and over it.

The Church in the Peter and Paul Fortress filled me with a deep loathing. Outside it's lovely – inside it's ornate – badly copied Italian and Byzantine mixed, but interesting because it's Leningrad's first church. The Tsars are all buried there and along their tombs are huge poster boards, white with slogans by Stalin written in red on top. Exhibitions and rolls of honor are posted on them. One slogan told the Russian people they could read about and revere Peter the Great because "he did many good things for Russia."

Catherine the Great still isn't in the good graces of the Soviet historians. Her palace at Tsarskoe Selo for instance was repainted in the colors of her mother-in-law. (Apparently, each Tsar painted his palace a particular color, some chose blue, others greyish purple or green and of course yellow.)

Though all other visitors to Leningrad seem to say that the people there dress better than Muscovites, I saw little difference. One evening I went to the operetta theater and saw the most pathetically awful first act of a musical I've yet to see in Russia. The singers were old, bad singers, costumes terrible. Even the Moscow vaudeville, which is considered terrible, was better. One other evening there we saw a Tchaikovsky opera at the Marinsky theater, the famous Leningrad one. I enjoyed it immensely. The theater is lovely, not as big as Moscow's Bolshoi theater, where the ballet is held, but less ornate and heavy. Its huge central chandelier was lovely. Unfortunately, no ballet was on.

[Kathleen]

Grand Hotel, Stockholm
July 25, 1945

Dear Mary,

Rumor has it that Averell may blow in here today from Potsdam. I hope that means we will get a lift back to Moscow.

Sweden was not at all like I expected. It's definitely second-rate. The city is utilitarian and hideous, with the exception of a small "old" section. The apt. houses flank hilltops, thereby ruining the scenery – huge matchbox affairs they are, modern and very ugly. The Swedes themselves seem very second-rate, stuffy, formal with a "we're holier than thou" attitude, thanks to their not getting into the war. I disapprove of people who spend a week in the country & figure they're authorities – but all the Americans I've talked to about it seem to agree. I've been out a couple of times with Swedes – once to a huge country show place, about 60 miles from town. One night I was exceedingly annoyed playing bridge (a boring State Dpt. party) with 2 Americans and one important Foreign Office man. The Swede cheated like mad, and we weren't playing for love.

Their "skol" system of drinking is divine, it's so pompous. At dinners and lunches conversation is spoiled by routine toastings between the host and guests and between guests and guests, all according to schedule. The rules are [so] numerous I have not had time to learn them all by a long shot. But when a man asks you to drink with him, you nod without a smile, raise your glass to the top of your chest, look him in the eye, nod, drink and nod again and lower your glass. This happens umpteen times. At restaurants I get the giggles watching the other diners.

Aaron Kesters is military attaché here (he was the first commander of Poltava) and has been absolutely sweet to us. We have been out with him twice, once a swimming party out of town, dinner and more swimming, which was great fun. Our first few days here were very hot, so we did a lot of swimming.

I've been shopping for everyone in Moscow as per usual, and gotten not much for myself. Everything in the way of clothes is rationed. I go to a store, ask to see unrationed clothes and they sell me rationed things minus coupons. Some country!! All clothes and drinks are made from wood, cars and other forms of transport are run on that. Our hotel has hot water but that's the exception to the rule apparently. The State Dep't people are pretty awful but, aside from the military, some of the other people attached to subsidiary organizations are quite genial for an evening. So all in all I'm thoroughly enjoying myself.

The Swedes treat their women worse than animals, but go in for much hat-taking-off & hand kissing. There's no ladies first here. Men push women off the trolleys so they can get a seat! It's all rather incongruous. Morals are non-existent when it comes to sex and our American boys have a hard time not getting raped.

Food is good, but unexciting and eating in Swedish homes you get delicious French wines and of course lots of schnapps. Women are expected to drink port too at the end of the meal. Your host or hostess must be toasted at the end of a meal and in port only. Then everyone rises and shakes hands.

August 7th

I'm back in Moscow now, can't remember what I have written but the main news is yours, today the wire arrived and I'm so excited I don't know where I'm at.

Must end suddenly – goodbye.

Kathy

Will write later about Berlin, etc.

Moscow
August 8, 1945

Dear Mary and Shirley,

Yesterday was a big day for great news. First the atomic bomb story, followed a few hours later by your cable. I was in such good spirits that I said "okay" when Averell suggested 'twould be nice if I went to the Egyptians for cocktails (he couldn't make it).

I can't wait to hear the particulars about Shirley's job. I got very scared sitting in Sweden, hearing no news as July came to an end.

My two weeks' vacation got stretched considerably thanks to Potsdam (Babelsberg as Ave calls it) and Averell's stay in Stockholm got considerably cut, thanks to T.V. Soong arriving here.

The big hero of the [Potsdam] meeting I gather was Bevin. He stood up to our friends at every turn and cracked down hard when 'twas needed. Unlike all others he didn't go thru a teething process.

Averell reported that the [General] Election really did come as a big surprise to the British politicians. In Stockholm we got English papers three or four days late. They certainly showed what a nasty mudslinging election it was.

Incidentally, when you plan your second honeymoon, you can leave Sweden out! The people and the country are completely devoid of charm. Formal to a degree I never thought possible. I'm glad to have been there. After being initially entertained by some of the local Stockholm gentry, I hated the place – but as I changed and started going out with Americans I liked it better. Some of our legation people are quite nice – others god-awful! I saw a lot of both groups.

In Helsinki I stayed with Max Hamilton, who was minister when we first arrived here. His wife is a Bookmanite and extremely nervous. Poor Max, though I'm sure he once hated me, treated me like a long-lost friend.

Leningrad I've written you about, it's a really beautiful city – lived up to all my hopes and expectations.

Finnish trains are hell, wood driven, slow and dirty. We took seven days to go to Stockholm and returned in 7 hours! Coming back we flew nonstop and were supposed to circle a certain field at Leningrad, and by using colored flares, the Leningradites were scheduled to tell us whether weather conditions were good at Moscow. We circled all the fields in Leningrad area, saw no flares, but got some ack-ack as an alternative.

I got me a new boyfriend in Stockholm. He kept our sitting room filled with flowers, being the six dozen roses a time type, and was very useful.

I'm sending you a Swedish souvenir with perfume to go with it.

My love to you,

Kathleen

PS later: Ave's just returned with the news that Russia is at war with Japan! I wonder how many people will attribute it to the atomic bomb. I'm going off on the town to see the reaction. There will be no joy unless I'm very much mistaken.

Moscow
August 8, 1945

Dear Mouche,

I'm writing under the light of a street lamp at the front door of the Foreign Office, so perhaps this won't be readable.

Tonight the Soviets declared war on Japan and I am about to go out on the town and see what the reactions are here. So far the atomic bomb hasn't been played out very big. Apparently the Japanese ambassador has said that the Soviet declaration on top of the atomic bomb means the end. I wonder if it is true. Among other things it means the end of my session here is in sight! What next?

Your compatriot Mr Bevin was apparently terrific at Potsdam. Averell came out of it sort of a wreck. I'm glad I wasn't there. Sweden was interesting, but necessarily I had to spend several boring evenings and luncheons being entertained by American officials and Swedes. The rest of it was fun though and the whole trip was worth the two days in Leningrad. I loved that town.

I have to go now.

Best love,

Kathy

Moscow
August 13, 1945

Dear Pam,

I was delighted when Ave's wire came thru that he was England-bound. After Potsdam, he certainly needed it. It's all rather sad, isn't it? We've had one short chat about plans – but with things moving so fast these days, there's really no point in making 'em.

Ike's here now with General Davis[2] & your beau General Clay,[3] who I think is terribly nice. They want me to go back with them on Wednesday for a short visit, which I may do. It seems stupid not to see all one can and it might be fun.

---

2 Benjamin O. Davis Snr (1877–1970), the US Army's first African-American general.
3 Lucius D. Clay (1898–1978), Eisenhower's deputy in the US occupation zone in Germany.

My exciting best news is that Shirley's gotten a job with some malaria research outfit – that came before the atomic bomb or the Russian declaration of war – and was very comforting. Sitting here so far away and not being able to do anything about it at all was very worrying.

Yesterday I went to the most grueling experience of my life I think. A physical culture parade. It lasted 5 hours. Ave, Ike and Russ Deane reviewed it from the top of Lenin's tomb with U.J. and all the state bigwigs. That's the first time any foreigners have ever been invited to do that. The parade was something unbelievable. It went off without a hitch and Stalin told Ave that some 100,000 people were involved. Each of the republics put on a show – exercises, dances, acrobatics etc. It was spectacular but rather terrifying.

Stockholm is a much-overrated place (to change the subject). As a town it's hideous. The Swedes I met were stuffy to a degree. But the food was plentiful and the shops filled with everything imaginable. Things like clothes were definitely second-rate but fine for Russians & servants. There was kitchen-ware galore – aluminum – flat irons etc. At last I have Spaso House properly outfitted.

We swam a lot, went sailing. I developed a very useful beau, who kept the sitting room well stocked with flowers and all in all I had a lot of fun.

I got back here and found that three wives had arrived in my absence. They came a-calling at tea time, all dressed up to kill. God that kind of thing is silly – between Americans.

We went riding the other day & my animal has been really worked on and does all sorts of fun tricks. I thoroughly enjoyed.

This letter is disjointed mostly as I'm trying to organize a party tomorrow night and I don't have the vaguest idea whether it's for 100 or 200 people (not that that's unusual).

My love to you.

Kathy

CHAPTER 27

'I CAN'T THINK OF ANY MAN I'VE YET MET THAT'S AS GREAT AS EISENHOWER, PLUS HE'S SO DAMN SWELL'

If anyone was Kathy's war hero, it was Eisenhower. Ike's visit to Moscow in August 1945 was the highlight of her final summer in the Soviet capital. Stalin shared her admiration, telling Averell, 'General Eisenhower is a very great man, not only because of his military accomplishments but because of his human, friendly, kind and frank nature. He is not a *grubyi* like most military.'[1]

The Far Eastern war ended with Japan's surrender on 14 August 1945 and Ave was keen to resign his ambassadorship and get out of Moscow as soon as possible. He suggested to Truman's foreign minister Jimmy Byrnes that they meet in London before the first session of the newly created Council of Foreign Ministers (CFM), which had been tasked with negotiating the terms of the peace treaties with Germany and other defeated states. Byrnes fobbed Harriman off, telling him to come to London around 20 September, by which time the conference would be in full swing.

Accompanied by Kathy, Ave travelled to London as requested, but they spent a few days with Ike in Cannes on the way. By the time he met Byrnes the CFM was in the throes of failure, the sticking point being British and American refusal to recognise and establish diplomatic relations with pro-Soviet governments in Bulgaria and Romania in advance of elections in the two countries. In retaliation,

1 The Russian word "*grubyi*" means rough, rude, coarse, crude.

Stalin ordered Molotov to raise procedural issues designed to torpedo the conference which, after a month of discussions, terminated with nothing agreed.

The conference's abject failure gave Byrnes the excuse he needed to insist that Harriman go back to Moscow and sort this mess out with the Soviets. He and Kathy departed London on 4 October, arriving in Moscow on the 9th, after a journey that took them through Frankfurt, Berlin, Vienna and Budapest.

Moscow
August 14, 1945

Dear Mary,

These last few days have been very hectic, ever since the return from Stockholm – the war ending, T.V. Soong here, to say nothing of our guests. It's such fun having nice guests and this bunch certainly are the tops. I can't think of any man I've yet met that's as great as Eisenhower, plus he's so damn swell.

Last Sunday we saw a parade to end all parades. Physical culture with all the trimmings. Averell and the general and Russ stood with U.J. and all the boys on top of Lenin's tomb, something which no foreigner's been asked to do ever. That's quite a tribute to Eisenhower. U.J. entertained them last night and tonight we're giving a reception – mostly all military. I'm wondering if it's our last reception.

I'm in a wonderful mood today. I woke up this morning minus an earache, something I've had for days and days. Penicillin did the trick.

Today we had a lunch to end all lunch parties. Eisenhower was out visiting collective farms with Zhukov and wasn't expected back till after lunch. Just as we were to go into lunch, Eisenhower with Zhukov and plenty of others turned up, hot, dirty and tired and very hungry. They had to be divided into 2 bunches for eating purposes and for conversation. Our own luncheon just got started when Soong called up and Averell dashed over to see him. Just about then the cook sent up a hurry call – she'd run out of vanilla for the ice cream for tonight, would I provide immediately. Fun, fun.

Hurriedly,
Kathy

Moscow
August 19, 1945

Dear Mary,

It's a rainy Sunday, so for the first time since we got back there's nothing urgent to do. Five of us are playing bridge – my rubber out. There was to have been an air show. The way I look at it, standing and looking up into the sky is just that much worse than standing and looking out over the ground. I hate parades.

The past week has been very exciting but I was sorry not to have been home for V.J. Day. Averell brought in the Jap surrender announcement towards the end of our Eisenhower reception, around 1 a.m., and after that we had a very hard time getting rid of some of our drunken Soviet guests. I took a great shine to Marshal Zhukov that evening. He's very genial and fun and apparently easy to work with. Once during the evening he called Eisenhower "Ike," a great departure for a Soviet!

Things were happening so fast I didn't leave with Eisenhower for a few days in Berlin and Frankfurt, and seeing them all off at 7 a.m. in the morning after the party I was terribly glad that I too wasn't boarding a plane with a few hectic hours in Leningrad in the offing.

Driving back to Spaso, Averell and I decided we'd throw an all-American party the same evening. Servants were swell about doing it – two parties two nights in a row means a lot of work. The head cook had been hoarding food for just such an unexpected party so we had dinner enough for our 200 Americans. We drank, we danced, we ate and we danced some more. 12 congressmen blew into town and to the party – a terrible bunch but I'll tell more about that later. Finally our party moved over to the enlisted men's house and I continued on until way after dawn. (I'm being called back to play bridge – that was a very quick rubber.)

Later

Yesterday morning Averell almost hopefully stuck his head in the door while I was trying to confront my breakfast egg and asked if I had gyppy tummy. Fortunately for me I couldn't oblige with a "yes." The day before we took one of the worst beatings yet – all the worse for all the previous V.J. Day celebrations.

We'd gone to Smolensk and Ave had dedicated a hospital. We went through the hospital, made speeches, listened to more, got clapped and cheered and in true Russian fashion we clapped and cheered back. We went to a luncheon banquet – more toasts, singing and I had to dance around a large table to an accordion. The local bigwigs were genial but dancing was not one of their strong points. After being full of food we toured the town. It's as desolate and destroyed as when I was there 18 months ago.

Our host was the head of the *oblast*, small, fat, young and full of fun. He and I had a long chat about American freedom to criticize. He was well informed though we agreed on little. He said he had been told that the individual American felt he knew how to run the country better than the President (any President) and was slightly nonplussed when I said that was true! Towards the end of our banquet Eddie Gilmore A.P. correspondent passed Averell a note saying it took Napoleon months to conquer Smolensk, the Germans 3 weeks and Averell 4 hours!

Finally we were restored on our plane (a Soviet one) along with 5 huge bunches of flowers I'd collected at various stages. The whole day was rather like banging your head against the wall and calling it pleasure. Once returned to Moscow we set out to dinner at the organization that deals with Cultural Relations – in honor of Mr Carter[2] of Russian War Relief. We arrived late but in the middle of Mr Carter's speech. In all it lasted some 32 minutes. Even the Russians found it embarrassing. He dragged in all the freedoms and other unmentionable subjects. I'm still shuddering from the experience of listening. The usual dinner speech here is 3 minutes. On one side I had Litvinov, his comment was "it's more comfortable not to listen." On the other side I had a Vice-Commissar of Foreign Trade. I asked if he was bored and he answered "probably not as bored as you, because I can't understand a word of English."

"Dinner" ended long after midnight and we headed home. The one comforting thing of the evening – about 8 of the 11 members of

---

2 Edward C. Carter (1878–1954), chair of the Russian War Relief Fund.

our Wickersham Committee of Congressmen[3] were there and they behaved very well.

The night before I'd gone to a concert with them. They'd been told that the Russians take their concerts seriously, but even so they acted like 5-year-olds in church. One even started to pull the hair of the woman in front of him – trying to be kittenish I suppose. They lambasted Russia in the presence of English-speaking Russians. I came home a wreck! One little Jew from Philly came here expecting the millennium. He hit rock bottom the first night – reason: his cold water tap wouldn't work.

This group is the 1st of four arriving within a month. God help us! I'm off to bed.

Goodnight,

Kathy

Moscow
September 7, 1945

Dear Pam,

Your wire arrived last night and I couldn't be more amazed to hear that Quent's in town. Hope you'll still be around when we arrive. Expect us anytime after the 18th. Ave has to be there on the 20th. We're going to take about a week's trip through Germany and I guess Austria, which ought to be fun.

Can't wait to see you. It will be for several days – instead of the few hurried hours we've had the last few times.

Life here is ordered mostly by a steady stream of guests, mostly congressmen. It's a good thing every time another comes and takes even a short look-see – even though from the entertaining point of view it's a bore, to say the least. Winter's almost hit us – the trees are turning & I think a few weeks away will be mighty fine.

My love to you,

Kathy

---

3 A Congressional commission that examined the implementation of laws on the prohibition of alcohol.

Moscow
September 8, 1945

Dear Mouche,

There isn't an awful lot of news. Averell is working a lot less hard, which means we ride more often and even play bezique in the afternoon. In a few days we are leaving for about a week's visit with Eisenhower, which I expect will include a bit of travelling around Germany and Austria. It will be interesting but I expect gloomy. Cannes too – with swimming and sunning.

We are having a deluge of congressmen – 4 separate committees or subcommittees. They are all very demanding, very badly behaved and I find coping an awful bore, but the more people who come here the better it is, particularly our government folk. One man, after he had been thru THE show factory here in Moscow asked his Soviet interpreter, "How can the workers stand it?"

We seem to have had a lot of very long Soviet dinners lately. As winter approaches, the diplomatic corps is entertaining more. The former I put up with, particularly as I figure the end is in sight, but receptions of the foreign colony [are too much], and now I rebel. I got 'flu about 10 days ago and am still using it as an excuse for going to [few] evening parties etc.

One Saturday we had a four-hour lunch given by the Soviet Red Cross for Mr Carter. It was a beautiful day and everyone was very restless, except Mr Carter who made about 7 long speeches. I sat between two non-English-speaking Russians, which made conversation extra difficult; me and one of the men settled that. We had our own little private ant race thruout the meal. Ants were plentiful – they kept dropping off the floral decorations, so time passed faster than it might have. However, even childish games become boring after 4 hours.

The ballet has re-opened and so have most of the theaters. Then too, Averell has started playing bridge, so we're always busy.

It will be fun getting to London. I imagine we'll be there about a week.

Changing the subject slightly, I discovered from Eddie Page that his wife thought that he was in love with me. That explains a lot, but rather horrifies when I think back over our little lunch that you helped with.

Love,
Kathleen

Claridge's Hotel, London
September 20, 1945

Dear Mouche,

London is as much fun as ever. The other evening Quent, Jack Kelly and I went to dine at our favorite pub and it was as though we'd never been away 2 years. Lots of our friends, like Ismay and Portal are out of town on long holidays, but there are still plenty around. Last night I got in after dining with Sidney Bernstein (he used to work in the film section of the M.O.I.) and Alan Morehead[4] – to find Averell and Brendan Bracken chatting. Brendan's hair is almost white, which makes it more wig-like than ever. He is contesting a by-election in November in a Conservative stronghold and he says if he doesn't get elected he guesses he never will!

We're going out to spend the night at the Beaver's on Friday. He is rampant on the subject of his Empire policy, and to read his papers you'd not know there was a Foreign Ministers' conference on. For news purposes *The Times* and the *Daily Herald* are the only ones worth reading. Quite a change.

Shopping is worse than ever – long queues. Taxis very hard to get – but on the whole people are not complaining.

We had 4 wonderful days staying with Ike in Cannes. I sunned like mad and swam and slept and played bridge for exercise and thoroughly enjoyed every minute of it. We were in a lovely villa and took a boat ride to Cannes and I can't say as I remembered it!

[Kathleen]

---

4 Alan Moorehead (1910–83), Australian war correspondent who worked for the *Daily Express*.

Claridge's Hotel, London
September 24, 1945

Dear Marie,

London is full of friends – mostly Americans – from all over the world, so the longer the conference lasts the better I like it. I haven't discussed plans with Averell recently but the way they last were – a couple of days ago – we return to Moscow for a couple of months and then clear out for good. I still hope we'll make it by Xmas.

England these days is terribly dreary. It takes hours standing in queues for food & then you are not sure of getting enough. Everyone is grumbling as there's not much hope of things improving this winter. It all adds up to an unhappy atmosphere for those home-coming.

<u>Later</u>

We're still here. The conference continues. Everyone's now beginning to look slightly harassed. Already the talks have lasted days longer than scheduled. Averell doesn't sound too discouraged. Though these days his one and only interest in life is to get out of Moscow for good & ever. He's wonderfully well. We had four days in Ike's villa at Cap d'Antibes which was absolute heaven, beautiful sunshine, swimming and good company. Eisenhower and Clark were there for two days & we always had a bridge 4-some. Russ Deane was with us, but didn't come on here. He scurried back to Moscow to get his mission closed up. I see by the London papers Mrs FDR is coming to Russia – no idea of date given. The Lord deliver us!

My love to you,
Kathy

Claridge's Hotel, London
September 27, 1945

Dear Mouche,

This is the first time I've been in London for any length of time since Russia. Our original few days have stretched into a good [deal] longer – and I'm enjoying every minute of it, seeing all my old friends, press and otherwise, who are in town for the conference.

Oct. 2

Somewhere in my mess of letters and notes is a letter started to you – can't find it, maybe I will!

The conf. continues, ended 4 a.m. this morning and back again at eleven. Maybe we're leaving tomorrow, I've given up wondering. Future plans haven't completely jelled yet, but the general idea is we go back to Moscow to clean up and out. The earliest we'll get home will be early Nov. and the latest the end of December.

[Kathleen]

Moscow
October 12, 1945

Dear Mouche,

We got back three days ago after a wonderful trip. In fact the whole last month has been about the most fun I've had in a long time. (Not that I don't usually enjoy myself wherever I am.) After we left London we flew to Gen. Ike's headquarters in Frankfurt, due to bad weather we couldn't go direct to Vienna, so stopped at Berlin, [a] town I figured I never was going to see, so that was a special treat. I drove around town and saw all the damage etc. The people looked well dressed by our Moscow standards but seem alien and listless. To live in, for the occupation troops, it must be very dreary. One night General Clay got in three singers (they got no pay for performing, just a meal afterwards). The pianist, a very good one at that, looked as though he'd take great pleasure in bouncing us all off! It must be hard, living amongst silently hostile people.

Finally the weather cleared and we went off to Vienna. That city was far more destroyed than I imagined – due mostly to fighting. It too is dreary, rather empty, at least the streets are. We were thoroughly organized every minute of our stay with lunches, dinners and a cocktail party with the local Russians, French and British. Kay Summersby, Eisenhower's aide, came along with us, which made it doubly nice for me. One pleasant surprise: we got to Budapest. That day Kay and I reneged on the luncheon and did some extra sightseeing and shopping. We bought a lot of loot and spent next to no money as the dollar exchange rate was very much in our favor.

The town must have been really lovely before the war. It still has great atmosphere, more so than Vienna. All the palaces were demolished in the fighting, which is sad. They are huge and even the ruins quite lovely. Apparently during the battle the Germans and Soviets made use of the bomb craters for graves. They haven't yet been dug up so sections of the city are rather unpleasant. But for most part it was alive with men and women working to clear up the rubble. There was loads of horse-driven transport, some trams and the civilians looked quite well dressed.

We hit the town the day after a local Budapest election, which showed the most conservative party getting a sizeable majority over the communists (Soviet controlled). Result: everyone was jubilant. There were parades and several demonstrations. We were taken around town by a Hungarian now in the U.S. army. Time and again he was stopped by friends in the streets and told "we've won our elections, now you must help us in the rest of the country." Obviously, in the rural sections, the Soviets are even more unpopular – due to their looting. All of which I found very interesting. It was interesting too that they were allowed to hold a relatively free election.

All too soon we flew back to Vienna. It was the first time I'd stayed in an area controlled by General Clark. The way guests are treated is strikingly different from an Eisenhower area. We had a motorcycle escort plus a jeep full of M.P.s wherever we went. With Eisenhower everything is simple and unpretentious. Interestingly enough I was glad to note that the Austrians weren't by any manner of means scared off the roads into ditches by our cavalcade – only the Russians went obediently to the side!

Kay leaves tomorrow on Grandpappy,[5] which is sad, she's great fun to have around.[6] Then I suppose I'll have to settle down to work. My week of vacationing makes any work seem a bore. Most all the O.W.I. projects have been stalemated by the Soviets – an indirect result of the London Conference, so for the next while everything will be hard to get thru. However, it's not the first time we've been thru a downgrade in our relations.

---

5 The name of Averell's ambassadorial plane – the successor to 'Becky'.

6 Summersby had flown with the Harrimans back to Moscow, and spent three days in the Soviet capital.

My love to you and thanks for all your letters.
Kathleen

Moscow
late October / early November 1945

Dear Marie,

This letter goes out on the same plane as the last of the people who were in Moscow when we first arrived. The plane leaves in a few hours and we've just finished celebrating. It seems hard to believe that we've outlasted an entire embassy & Military Mission.

Life here is much the same as ever. The Red Army is practicing like mad for a parade upcoming on October Revolution Day [November 7]. I only hope it won't be too long. I hate standing!

Now that the Military Mission have moved their offices from our ballroom, we've set up badminton [and] there's no end to our riding.

Did Averell tell you his scheme to come home the other way 'round via Tokyo? It's nice thinking about that happening.

My love to you,
Kath

Moscow
December 11, 1945

Dear Marie and Mary,

This comes mostly to thank you both for your birthday cables. It's sad about our not making home by Xmas. We've all had our fingers crossed for weeks, but now it looks like us and a lot of other people will be here come the 25th.

We're putting up eight of the conferrers[7] and I think feeding the stenographic pool, who will work in the ballroom (now badminton court, all nicely marked out with white painted lines!).

Someone took the trouble to add up the weight of the food I have ordered for Spaso during the conference. It comes to over a ton![8] And that doesn't count an all-American Xmas party on Xmas eve.

---

7 Participants in a conference of the American, British and Soviet Foreign Ministers, held in Moscow, 16–26 December 1945.
8 Including 100 kilos of bread.

Averell threw a lovely birthday party for me – which consisted of three cocktail parties first and then dinner, dancing etc. here. A pleasant time was had by all.

Last weekend I went to the country – to a British dacha. It was more work than I've done in a long time, but healthy and fun. A Russian gal (wife of the A.P. correspondent) and I shared cooking responsibilities. The three men chopped and carted wood, tried to keep the stoves going, but we never did lose a thick coat of ice on the inside of all the windows, including the kitchen. That gives you a slight idea how cold it was.

First evening I went skiing in the dark thru the forest. It was really lovely – new snow on the pines and silver birches. It's nice to find something beautiful in the otherwise very dreary Moscow flat landscape. While skiing we suddenly decided we were rather stupid – the forest is reportedly full of hooligans (bandits) and scurried home! Our latest and rather sordid pastime is collecting and swapping the latest hooliganism stories. They're certainly not very pleasant.

[Kathleen]

CHAPTER 28

'OUR BIGGEST NEWS IS OUR OWL – ALOISE – SOUNDS FEROCIOUS BUT QUITE BEAUTIFUL & FULL OF CHARM'

Averell and Kathleen's last task in Moscow was supporting a conference of the American, British and Soviet foreign ministers (16–26 December). It was October 1943 all over again, but with Kathy fully in charge of Spaso (boarding) House.

The conference was a cut-down version of the Council of Foreign Ministers, the Soviets having insisted on the exclusion of representatives from China and France, countries that Stalin did not consider truly Great Powers. Kathy's scepticism notwithstanding, the conference successfully broke the logjams that had developed during the CFM's London discussions. Not until 1947 did the so-called cold war begin in earnest.

When the conference ended, Ave and Kathy had one last excursion – to Bucharest, Paris and London. Then on 24 January 1946 they finally embarked on a homeward-bound journey, which took them first to New Delhi, where they stayed with the British viceroy Lord Wavell. They then flew over the Himalayas to China, where they met up with General Marshall, Chiang Kai-shek and T.V. Soong. Next came Korea and Japan, where they saw the aftermath of the massive American bombing campaign as well as glimpses of Mount Fuji. They crossed the Pacific to San Francisco via Guam and Honolulu, and having clocked more than a hundred hours of flying time, arrived in Washington, DC, on 14 February.

In April 1946 Ave returned to London as US ambassador to Britain, but Kathy didn't join him. She was back working for *Newsweek* and stayed put in New York. Just before he left for London, Averell wrote to Kathy that while he 'felt very sad' at leaving her behind, he was 'thrilled' at what she had done – 'and very proud'.

Moscow
December 21, 1945

Dear Mary & Shirley,

The conference is in full swing. They meet at 4 p.m. & usually we dine at 7:30 – so that shows you how short the sessions are. Pretty much everyone is scared that tempers will be lost – as in London – but so far so good. The atmosphere, if describable, is grim. Rather different from the [October] '43 Moscow conference when Hull & Eden were here – & we still passed out blank checks.

The bunch we have staying in the house are swell – Conant[1] (atomic bomb), Carter (State Dept, Far East), Cohen (lawyer), Doc Matthews (used to be in London, he's in the European Dept), Chip, the Secretary's colonel aide (who's sort of a poop & sings Irish songs) and Byrnes. Conant is full of fascinating tales of the atom. He's completely charming. There have been no special shows at the ballet – like at previous conferences. Yesterday Molotov gave a cocktail affair, which lasted only about 1½ hours.

Our biggest news is our owl – which Ave's chauffeur brought in the other night. It's a baby (we think) & we call it Aloise (Bob named it that). It clicks its beak – sounds ferocious but it's quite beautiful & full of charm. It sleeps in Bob's slipper all day & flies around his room at night.

[December 23]

It's now the day before Xmas eve. Yesterday I wrapped 8½ cases of liquor – no production line this year for the operation – last year Lillian Hellman tied the bows, but then we had 250 Americans in Moscow.

---

1 James B. Conant (1893–1978), a chemist, president of Harvard University and Truman adviser on the atomic bomb.

The conference progresses & as time goes on I get to like our houseguests better than ever. No one has lost his sense of humor yet. There's not much I can write about it (the Conf.). If I weren't so damned used to "Russia" as a subject of conversation, I'd feel the world were coming to an end – the peace at any rate. Thank goodness none of the delegation are starry eyed.

We gave a lunch today – for the bigwigs. It started exactly 1½ hours late – so the kitchen was in a dither as they invariably are when we entertain Molotov.

<u>Next day</u>

Stalin gives a dinner tonight so that means Averell won't be here for our Xmas party. Last night Moly entertained Byrnes & Bevin at the ballet – the new one – *Cinderella.* They got a terrific hand from the audience. I sat next to Bevin & found him absolutely sweet – something I had not anticipated.[2] He wore a lady tag on his lapel, which someone told me was a teamster's badge (seriously) – so I asked him & he said no – that it was given to him for luck by a lady friend the night he got bombed out and he's worn it off & on ever since. That's nice I think.

After the ballet I had to go to the French embassy – a dance. They had a mixture of French and Russian champagne – result disastrous – particularly as I ended up at another party about 2 a.m., where whiskey was being drunk.

Dec. 26

Xmas eve Uncle Joe gave a banquet for the delegations, but they (the Americans) turned up here around midnight & the Secretary was swell about meeting all our people here, which gave them a kick. The party ended at 4:30 & all but about killed me. Yesterday, the afternoon conference ended at midnight, which meant we served drinks soon after. I don't know how our servants survive. I've just come back now from walking my feet off at an art gallery – with Doc. Conant. Last night at 10:30 I took him on a tour of the subways. He figured he ought to see them!

Love,
Kathy

---

2 Kathy forgot that she had met Bevin in London.

Moscow
December 26, 1945

Dear Mouche,

If the conference doesn't end tonight I think the servants will die of exhaustion. They have been wonderful – serving meals at all hours for all the delegation and staff. Last night began at midnight, our Xmas eve party the night before didn't end until 4:30 and when I arose at noon the house was completely back in order. The cook, I hear, had a minor heart attack this morning!

At present the schedule is for the conference to end tonight, with our folks airborne at 8 a.m. However, at this time last night I also figured they'd be off today – so there is no telling. Such is life. I can assure you the results of this meeting are not the ushering in of a new era of sweetness and light – not that that was anticipated. I'm glad all our big shots got here and saw this country. They are a swell group.

The nicest thing that has happened to us is the new member of Spaso House in the form of an owl called Aloise. It's small, chirps, but does not hoot. I know not whether it's male or female, young or old. It is very sweet and has just come to pay me a visit. It lives next door in Bob's room.

There's still enough chance Ave gets to Tokyo for me to want to stay on here and get in on that trip. In a day or two we are going to Rumania.

I'm off to bed now.

Love,
Kathy

London
early January 1946

Dear Mary & Shirley,

It was a very great and pleasant surprise finding ourselves in London rather than Moscow-bound from Bucharest. We got grounded in Paris for the night and left early next morning. Ave spoke to Aunt Frances on the phone and got not much out of her. London is as swell as ever. I've been busy seeing friends and more friends. We probably have tomorrow or the next day before a few hectic days in

Moscow packing up and then we start on our trip. At the moment I can think of little else.

Bucharest was fascinating. We arrived New Year's Eve – first had a delicious dinner at one General Schuyler's house & left it for a Russian "reception," which turned out to be a seated banquet. All the Rumanian government were there – Groza[3] looking every bit like a pug-ugly Irish Catholic policeman or gangster. Tatarescu[4] (Foreign Minister) is shifty eyed and bloated like a slug. Vyshinsky & Susiakov[5] presided over many long loud toasts to the glorification of Soviet Russia. The orchestra tried to keep up with the pace. Once when Molotov was toasted they sprang up with the Star-Spangled Banner – which gave the situation its only feeling of comedy.

After that party I went on to a Rumanian private party given by <u>the</u> big industrialist. There the women were as beautiful as I've ever seen – extravagantly dressed. The whole atmosphere was too sophisticated for words – quite a contrast to the party we'd just left.

While Averell and Archie worked, I shopped – got a $30 fur coat & some perfectly lovely underwear which I trust will arrive safely in the U.S.A. before long. It had to be made. The exchange rate is fantastic – a million lei being about $30 odd. My largest handbag was only just big enough for money. For some reason they don't print very large bills. We ate quantities of pate de foie gras, which was delicious. Went nightclubbing and dancing. When we finally got to bed it was only to be awakened by street shootings.

Bucharest is modern & never felt the war 'til the Red Army hit it. You've got a combination of extreme wealth and poverty. Loads of beggars. My phone rang all day – people trying to sell emeralds, chinchilla, oriental cups etc.

The nicest people we met were the King and Queen but neither has a drop of Rumanian blood – so perhaps that's the reason. We went once to a formal lunch in town & then later went to their country palace in the mountains for a very pleasant 24 hours visit.

---

3 Petru Groza (1884–1958), Rumanian prime minister.
4 Gheorghe Tătărescu (1886–1957).
5 Ivan Susiakov (1903–62), Soviet tank general.

Vyshinsky, much to our hostess's delight, didn't spend the night! In the afternoon the King took Averell, Archie and me out for a ride in his jeep. We went mountain climbing, forded one river & had loads of fun – all done at 90 miles an hour.

He's an excellent driver so not even Averell felt like backseat driving. The skiing country looked very tempting but unfortunately there wasn't time to try. It all made me very homesick for Sun Valley. Incidentally, I saw in the Paris *Stars and Stripes* that Sun Valley opens July 15th. The plans for redoing the place over sound very extravagant. What other news?

I could go on about Rumania for ages but it can wait to tell. It's a wonderful feeling knowing I'll be home for good soon.

The Labour gov't has done damned nothing improving things here. There are <u>no</u> signs of rebuilding London and a lot of grousing results, which is well called for I should think. However, I find the luxury of hairdressers, manicures, face cleaning & friends galore very intoxicating. Went to one cocktail party given by the Byrnes & have never seen so many cackling old women – Mrs Vandenberg, Mrs Connolly etc. – God they're quite a bunch!

I'm off now to lunch.

Best love,

Kathleen

PART THREE
KATHLEEN HARRIMAN'S MOSCOW MEMOIR

CHAPTER 29

'DO THE CROWS STILL ROOST IN THE SPASOPESKOVSKAYA TREES?'

In October 1946, shortly after she returned to the United States from the USSR, Kathy gave a talk to a Bennington College dinner in New York City. Her assigned topic was Soviet education but she took the opportunity to reflect more generally on her experiences in Russia.

Kathy prepared for the talk by writing some notes and then composed a text for delivery at the dinner. In her notes she wrote, 'If I fail to portray Russia as a nation of blackguards I get damned as a would-be commie. Other times, if I don't create the image of a noble experiment, I find myself called a Russia baiter.' According to the finished text of her talk, Kathy told her audience, 'I find that people think about Russia in extremes and react with extremes and if your ideas don't happen to coincide, you get a nasty name thrown into your face – or at least I seem to.' The biggest mistake people make when visiting Russia, she said,

> is to get all hot and bothered about things a Russian takes for granted. The complete absence of free-speech, free-thought and free-movement doesn't bother a Russian, because he's never known it. He takes his lot for granted. I've heard Russians complain about their luck, but never seriously contest their inability to choose their fate. When I got over trying to judge Russians by American standards, I became a great deal happier

and living in, and running, an embassy residence became a great deal easier.[1]

Kathy's balanced presentation reflected lingering hopes that the Soviet–Western alliance could yet develop into a peacetime collaboration. But the fraternal atmosphere of the war years was rapidly dissipating. By 1947–8 the Grand Alliance that had defeated Hitler had collapsed and been replaced by a Soviet–Western cold war that by the mid-1950s had reached bitter depths. Asked by a reporter in 1955 what she now thought about the Soviet Union, Kathy replied that 'the most wonderful thing about Russia is leaving it'.

Apart from the Bennington talk, Kathy's only extended reflection on her time in Russia was the following short memoir, which was prompted by a request for anecdotes about life in Spaso House from Rebecca Matlock (1928–2019), whose husband Jack was appointed US ambassador to the Soviet Union in 1987.[2] Rebecca knew Spaso from Jack's previous postings to Moscow, and when they met Kathy's first question to her was 'Do the grey crows still roost at Spaso House?'

Rebecca subsequently wrote a book that drew on the memories and experiences of Kathy and other Americans who had lived at Spaso House.

> On October 18, 1943, Averell and I flew into Moscow with Secretary of State Hull for the Foreign Ministers' Conference. Mercifully Spaso, though incredibly dank and dark, had hot water – a luxury I soon learned to savor. (Two years later, the boiler exploded the day before Secretary Stettinius flew up from the Yalta conference with us.)
>
> General Eisenhower, Harry Hopkins, General Eaker, General "Wild Bill" Donovan, General "Pat" Hurley, James Conant, Mark Ethridge,

1 The text of Kathleen Harriman's Bennington dinner lecture may be found among her private papers in the Library of Congress.

2 Kathy's only publication about her time in Moscow was a March 1946 article on "Opera in Russia Today" in *Opera News*.

Lillian Hellman and Ed Flynn were among our many guests. Others included the first U.S. prisoners of war; nurses from our shuttle-bombing air force base at Poltava. The "regulars" at Spaso during our two and a half years included George Kennan, Chip Bohlen, Max Hamilton, Eddie Page, John Melby, "Doc" Michaels, the delightful Agriculture Attaché, and Bob Meiklejohn, Averell's secretary.

Food and its procurement was a never-ending worry and time-consuming affair. Invariably, at the end of the month we'd be short. Slabs of spam, very attractively arranged around a scalloped mound of mashed potatoes, and ringed by hospital-green canned peas, would bring howls of displeasure from all boarders, Averell included. As the conflict over the future of Poland became acute, without advance notice all our Soviet employees lost their ration cards – adding to our tight food budget. In the bowels of Spaso's basement, cabbage was pickled by the barrel for all Americans. We laundered their clothes and linens too. Often on winter nights, I was to discover, the more lowly help refused to leave. Spaso was a maze of privileges, from who slept closest to the hot-water pipes to who got the leftovers from the pantry, from our table, and, literally, from our plates.

Gin and his brother Tung presided over all these activities, quite aside from seeing to our well-being. The chef was an elderly Rumanian lady given to hysterics when she didn't get her way, but a marvel on festive occasions. Easter was her favorite, and her painted eggs rivaled Fabergé. (Even Averell was deprived of his Sunday soft-boiled egg as Easter approached.)

Getting "things" fixed was the subject of lengthy dealings with "Burobin." Most all of Spaso's windows that faced south and east had been shattered in the bombing of Moscow early on in the war. It took until the summer of 1944 to have the beaver-board replaced by glass, and the sun could at last filter in.

Adelina, a quiet, efficient, very religious Volga German looked after me. What a marvel she was at sewing! Once she even washed a tweed suit of Averell's in my basin, using a precious cake of Ivory soap. The suit came out unshrunk, looking like Anderson Sheppard new. When a particularly fine, dry snow started falling, we, at her instigation, laid the living room curtains on the lawn for four hours. They came out clean, and for weeks (until the next snowfall), I viewed the sooty oblongs on the lawn with dismay.

Wednesday (?) afternoons, we provided a "Hollywood" movie for the "Dips." As our military mission grew, I asked General Deane if our projector could please be repaired "by an American" as it seldom did not break down during a showing. The army sergeant given the task reported back that the machine was a marvel of improvisation. Wire, string, even three of my bobby pins held it together. He threw up his hands. After *Phantom Murder at the Opera* (*Marx Brothers at the Opera*?), nobody walked under the huge chandelier in the reception room. A "sweeper" called Stefan, a tiny gnome of a man, twice a year would climb into the chandelier to clean it. Late one evening Adelina was waiting outside my door, long past her hours on duty. She warned me that Stefan was under my bed. He'd had a knife fight with another member of the staff and refused to come out until I could escort him to safety. Thank God for Adelina, I thought, as we coaxed him out.

You asked about pets. Bob Meiklejohn nursed a baby barn owl, christened Aloise, back to health and kept it loose in his bedroom that also served as Spaso's main communication center.

For sports, there was "bottle" pool in the library after dinner for the regulars. I organized badminton in the ballroom (too large to heat) until the military mission took the room over for offices and "war games." In summer we played on the front lawn. Averell, Bob Meiklejohn, Eddie Page and I skied on Lenin Hills on Sundays, with Averell's four N.K.V.D. "angels," as we called them, in tow. On V.J. Day, Averell decided a party for all Americans was in order. But where to get the necessary liquor? Gin smiled and said to me, "OK, I have something to show you. Please follow." He led me into my bedroom. Behind the ample, shabby huge curtains he rummaged and pulled out bottles of champagne (one of French vintage – a gift from General Donovan months before). In the upper reaches of my closets (I had few clothes) came more bottles. "I saved for a victory party," Gin grinned. What safer place in all Spaso!

I went to Moscow from London, where I was a *Newsweek* correspondent, on three days' notice. Tommy (Llewellyn) Thompson sent me a message from Moscow, where he was holding the fort: "bring clothes hangers and a Bondar." Clothes hangers in wartime London were hard but not impossible. But what in the world was a Bondar? I ended up borrowing his. Bondar was the American author of the best Russian grammar. Though my Russian teacher spoke only French, she could read Bondar and so we proceeded from Bondar to French to Russian and back again and over again, month after month.

Aside from working with V.O.K.S. for the O.W.I. and getting out a daily *New York Times* summary that lesser embassies lived by for their war news, I laid the groundwork for the publication of *Amerika*, a glossy magazine.

I still think I ran a reasonably successful boarding house under unusual conditions. We were a congenial, but definitely not convivial group. Cocktails (vodka) and tiny canapés of caviar or spam mixed with pickle before dinner if you chose, a variety of conversations at dinner. Afterwards, work for Averell and the regulars drafting telegrams – or visits to the Kremlin or F.O. and then the drafting of telegrams until the early a.m.s. Averell and I often played bezique awaiting the expected phone call from the Soviets. We kept a running score on a slip of paper in the box that held the two markers and the 6 packs of cards used in bezique. Early in '44 I was some 100,000 points in the red. As tensions increased, I almost got even, but it had nothing to do with my ability versus that of Averell, a very accomplished bezique player, as Churchill has attested.

Soon after we arrived in Moscow, Ivy Litvinov (wife of Maxim the former Soviet ambassador to Washington) said to me at an F.O. function "I hear you and your father enjoy bridge. Isn't it too bad we can't play with you." My education on life in Moscow had begun. (I was 25 years old at the time.)

Eventually, Eddie Page and I shared a Buick, bought from the departed John Melby. I used it during the day, he at night. Anti-freeze was precious, and the ambassador felt I could not "borrow" from the Embassy's meagre supply. No problem, I thought. Vodka has a low freezing point. Idiot that I was I gave Mashkov, Averell's chauffeur, two bottles to put in the Buick. Result: Mashkov drank the vodka and siphoned anti-freeze from the ambassadorial vehicle. I gaily went off skiing with my Russian friends, and guess who got stuck!

At a Kremlin banquet honoring Harry Hopkins (his wife Louise and I were invited "if we chose to accept"), Molotov's wife sent a bottle of vodka across the table to add to the already ample array of wine bottles at my place. She met my eye, and we drank a silent toast. The bottle she sent me contained Narzan water.[3] Friendship of the first order!

3 Mineral (spring) water from the Caucasus.

PLATES

1. The Harriman family at Sun Valley, Idaho, c.1936/7. Reproduced with kind permission of the Harriman family.
2. Kathy en route to London, May 1941. Associated Press / Alamy.
3. Mary Harriman. Reproduced with kind permission of the Harriman family.
4. Pamela Churchill, 1941. © The Estate of Nancy Sandys Walker / Mary Evans.
5. Kathy with Averell and Brendan Bracken, October 1941. Associated Press / Alamy.
6. Winston, Clementine and Mary Churchill. Associated Press / Alamy.
7. Kathy's Pearl Harbor-day letter, 7/8 December 1941.
8. Agniya Maisky unveils a plaque to Lenin, March 1942. Associated Press / Alamy.
9. Eleanor Roosevelt and Margaret Biddle at the American Red Cross Club, London, October 1942. Associated Press / Alamy.
10. American women war correspondents, 1943. Reproduced with kind permission of the Harriman family.
11. Eisenstein's drawing of Kathleen Harriman. Reproduced with the permission of the Russian State Archive of Literature and Art.
12. Kathy, Averell and Molotov at a reception in Moscow. Reproduced with kind permission of the Harriman family.

13. Kathy at the Katyn massacre site, January 1944. Reproduced with the permission of the Russian State Archive. Photo provided by Paula Chan.
14. Polina Zhemchuzhina. Heritage Image Partnership Ltd / Alamy.
15. Maxim and Ivy Litvinov. Pictorial Press Ltd / Alamy.
16. Kathy at the Poltava air base. Reproduced with kind permission of the Harriman family.
17. Kathy and Ira Eaker. Reproduced with kind permission of the Harriman family.
18. Sarah, Anna and Kathy at Yalta. Reproduced with kind permission of the Harriman family.
19. The family of Elsie Marshall ('Mouche'). Reproduced with kind permission of the Marshall family.
20. Alexandra Kollontai. Sueddeutsche Zeitung Photo / Alamy.
21. Averell and Kathy land in Washington, DC, 14 February 1946. Associated Press / Alamy.
22. Boston, Stalin's gift-horse. Reproduced with kind permission of the Harriman family.
23. Kathy, Stanley Mortimer and Elsie Marshall ('Mouche'), 11 October 1947. Reproduced with kind permission of the Harriman family.
24. Spaso House, Moscow. Sovfoto / UIG / Bridgeman Images

SOURCES AND ACKNOWLEDGEMENTS

The primary source for this book is Kathleen Harriman's private papers, which contain the bulk of her wartime letters. I had the privilege of access to Kathy's papers many years before they were transferred to their current home in the Manuscript Division of the Library of Congress (LoC). For that advance access I have to thank Kathy's eldest son, David Mortimer, and his wife Shelley Wanger, who welcomed me into their home for days on end, enabling me to copy virtually all of Kathy's archive. They have been tireless in their encouragement of my research and without their support the book would never have been produced. David and Shelley have also, together with Kathy's niece Kitty, provided the family photographs reproduced in the book. I am also extremely grateful to Bob Marshall for sharing his memories, knowledge and photos of his Aunt Elsie - AKA 'Mouche'.

The foreign travel involved in producing this book would not have been possible without the generous financial support of the School of History and the College of Arts, Celtic Studies and Social Sciences at University College Cork.

My research on Kathy's letters started in the LoC a quarter of a century ago. In 2025 I returned to the library to check out its holdings of Kathy's papers to make sure I hadn't missed anything. As in 2001, the Manuscript Division Staff couldn't have been more helpful. I would also like to commend the friendliness and efficiency of

Information and Reference Specialist Rebecca Rose, who prior to my visit had supplied hundreds of scanned images from Kathy's collection.

The LoC also contains the papers of Averell Harriman and Pamela Harriman, in which may be found, respectively, Kathy's letters to her stepmother Marie Whitney and those she sent Pam from Moscow. Among Pamela's papers are also a number of letters she wrote to Averell and Kathy in Moscow.

The papers of Averell's biographer Rudy Abramson are also in the LoC. These contain his interviews with Kathy and her sister Mary (Kitty's mother).

The papers of Elie Abel, who co-wrote Averell's memoir *Special Envoy to Churchill and Stalin*, may be found in several different locations. The collection I consulted is the one in Columbia University's Rare Book and Manuscript Library, which contains transcripts of the interviews that Abel conducted with Averell. From the collection at the Hoover Institution Sarah Patton kindly sent me a copy of Abel's correspondence with Kathy regarding the excerpts from her letters that were used in *Special Envoy*.

The Churchill Archives at Cambridge University have been enormously helpful in providing Kathy-related documents from among Clementine Churchill's papers.

Other archival sources consulted include the Lillian Hellman Papers at the University of Texas and the Truman Presidential Library's oral history interview with John Melby, while a Russian historian friend, Vladimir Nevezhin, provided copies of documents from Russia's foreign policy archives.

Another important primary source was Kathy's testimony to Congress about the Katyn killings of Polish POWs: *Hearings before the Select Committee to Conduct an Investigation of the Facts, Evidence and Circumstances of the Katyn Forest Massacre*, part 7 (June 1952), US Government Printing Office, Washington, 1952.

I was fortunate to be the recipient of several astute and expert reports from Yale University Press's anonymous readers of my book proposal and of the draft manuscript. These were full of useful criticisms, corrections and suggestions. Be it on my own head that I did not act on all their points. I have benefited greatly, too, from the comments of Boston University Professor David Mayers – a renowned scholar of US foreign policy and World War II diplomacy – who read the penultimate draft of the book.

Frank Costigliola has been highly supportive of the project and his own writings on the personal politics of the Soviet–Western Grand Alliance have been inspirational. A particular thanks to him for providing a copy of Rudy Abramson's interviews with Kathy.

Marie Brenner was the first person to explore Kathy's wartime correspondence in any depth. Her 2011 *Vanity Fair* article shifted and broadened my view of Kathy and her letters, as did Catherine Grace Katz's 2020 book *The Daughters of Yalta*. Giles Milton's *The Stalin Affair* also made extensive use of Kathy's private papers and drew my attention to some interesting notes she wrote about a weekend spent with the Churchills at Chequers in June 1941. Many thanks to Giles for sending me a copy of those notes and some other documents, too.

Sergei Eisenstein's vision of Kathleen as a 'dollar princess' is an angle I might have missed without the benefit of Maya Garcia's fascinating research on cinema shows at Spaso House, which she generously shared with me.

Paula Chan guided my request for Russian archival permission to reproduce a picture of Kathy at the Katyn massacre site in January 1944, and then provided a copy of the actual photograph.

The first talk I gave about Kathy was in 2014 at Columbia University's Harriman Institute. In 2015, the Institute's magazine published an article by me about Kathy's letters.

This is my third book with Yale (London) and I have become accustomed to the highest professional standards. Once again I was not disappointed, so big thanks to my editor Joanna Godfrey and her Yale colleagues. As ever, many thanks to my agent, Andrew Lownie, for negotiating the contract.

Last, but by no means least, I wish to thank my life partner and personal editor, Celia Weston, who, as ever, has contributed more than anyone to the successful realisation and writing of this book.

FURTHER READING

This section lists the books, memoirs and diaries that I found most useful and illuminating in editing Kathy's letters and reconstructing the narrative arc of her wartime experiences. But it would be remiss of me not to say that my constant companions on this journey of discovery have been Rudy Abramson's biography of Averell Harriman and Ave's own memoir, *Special Envoy to Churchill and Stalin*.

• • •

Abramson, Rudy, *Spanning the Century: The Life of W. Averell Harriman*, William Morrow, New York, 1992.

Astley, Joan Bright, *The Inner Circle: A View of War at the Top*, Monthly Review Press, New York, 1971.

Birse, Arthur H., *Memoirs of an Interpreter*, Michael Joseph, London, 1967.

Brenner, Marie, 'To War in Silk Stockings', *Vanity Fair*, November 2011, pp. 208–20.

Catroux, Georges, *J'ai vu tomber le Rideau de Fer: Moscou, 1945–1948*, Hachette, Paris, 1952.

Chamberlin, G.A., *Kathleen: The War Years*, Crown Eagle, n.p., 2014.

Chan, Paula, 'Refractions of Katyn: Photography and Witnessing in Soviet Investigations of Mass Atrocities', *Slavic Review*, 83/2 (Summer 2024), pp. 211–31.

Channon, Henry, *Henry 'Chips' Channon: The Diaries, 1938–1943*, ed. Simon Heffer, Penguin, London, 2024.

Churchill, Sarah, *A Thread in the Tapestry*, Andre Deutsch, London, 1967.

Colville, John, *The Fringes of Power: Downing Street Diaries, 1939–1955*, Hodder & Stoughton, London, 1985.

Cooper, Duff, *The Duff Cooper Diaries, 1915–1951*, ed. John Julius Norwich, Weidenfeld & Nicolson, London, 2022.

Costigliola, Frank, 'Archibald Clark Kerr, Averell Harriman, and the Fate of the Wartime Alliance', *Journal of Transatlantic Studies*, 9/2 (June 2011), pp. 83–97.

— 'Pamela Churchill, Wartime London, and the Making of the Special Relationship', *Diplomatic History*, 36/4 (September 2012), pp. 753–62.

Cucuz, Diana, *Winning Women's Hearts and Minds: Selling Cold War Culture in the US and the USSR*, University of Toronto Press, Toronto, 2023.
David-Fox, Michael, *Crucibles of Power: Smolensk under Stalinist and Nazi Rule*, Harvard University Press, Cambridge, MA, 2025.
Deane, John, *The Strange Alliance: The Story of Our Wartime Efforts at Co-operation with Russia*, Viking Press, New York, 1947.
Edy, Carolyn M., *The Woman War Correspondent, the U.S. Military, and the Press, 1846–1947*, Lexington Books, Lanham, 2016.
Folly, Martin, 'W. Averell Harriman 1946' in Simon Rofe and Alison Holmes (eds), *The US Embassy in London 1938–2008: 70 Years in Grosvenor Square*, Palgrave Macmillan, Basingstoke, 2012, pp. 1–17.
Harriman, W. Averell, and Elie Abel, *Special Envoy to Churchill and Stalin, 1941–1946*, Hutchinson, London, 1976.
Hellman, Lillian, *An Unfinished Woman*, Little Brown, Boston, 1969.
Ismay, Hastings Lionel, *The Memoirs of Lord Ismay*, Heinemann, London, 1960.
Katz, Catherine Grace, *The Daughters of Yalta*, HarperCollins, New York, 2020.
Kennan, George F., *Memoirs, 1925–1950*, Atlantic–Little Brown, New York, 1967.
Kirk, Lydia Chapin, *Distinguished Service: Lydia Chapin Kirk, Partner in Diplomacy, 1896–1984*, ed. Roger Kirk, Syracuse University Press, New York, 2007.
Kleiman, Naum, *Eisenstein on Paper: Graphic Works by the Master of Film*, Thames & Hudson, London, 2017.
Knight, Claire, 'Mrs Churchill Goes to Russia: The Wartime Gift Exchange between Britain and the Soviet Union' in Anthony Cross (ed.), *A People Passing Rude: British Responses to Russian Culture*, Open Book Publishers, Cambridge, 2015, pp. 253–67.
Lawrence, Bill, *Six Presidents, Too Many Wars*, Saturday Review Press, New York, 1972.
Lipien, Ted, 'Voice of America Freelancer Who Promoted Stalin's Propaganda Lie on Katyn Massacre', Cold War Radio Museum, 25 April 2024, https://www.coldwarradiomuseum.com/voice-of-america-freelancer-who-promoted-stalins-propaganda-lie-on-katyn-massacre/.
Matlock, Rebecca, *At Spaso House*, AuthorHouse, Bloomington, 2020.
Mayers, David, *FDR's Ambassadors and the Diplomacy of Crisis*, Cambridge University Press, Cambridge, 2013.
Milton, Giles, *The Stalin Affair: The Impossible Alliance That Won the War*, John Murray, London, 2024.
Newman, Robert P., *The Cold War Romance of Lillian Hellman and John Melby*, University of North Carolina Press, Chapel Hill, 1989.
Pechatnov, Vladimir O., 'Averell Harriman's Mission to Moscow', *Harriman Review*, 14/3–4 (June 2003), pp. 1–47.
Purnell, Sonia, *First Lady: The Life and Wars of Clementine Churchill*, Aurum Press, London, 2015.
— *Kingmaker: Pamela Churchill Harriman's Astonishing Life of Seduction, Intrigue and Power*, Virago, London, 2024.
Reynolds, Quentin, *By Quentin Reynolds – An Autobiography*, McGraw-Hill, New York, 1963.
Roberts, Geoffrey, '"Do the Crows Still Roost in the Spasopeskovskaya Trees?": The Wartime Correspondence of Kathleen Harriman', *Harriman Magazine*, 2/2 (Winter 2015), pp. 12–23.

Schlogel, Karl, *The Scent of Empires: Chanel No. 5 and Red Moscow*, Polity, London, 2021.

Sherwood, Robert E., *The White House Papers of Harry L. Hopkins, 1939–1945: An Intimate History*, 2 vols, Eyre & Spottiswoode, London, 1948–9.

Smith, Sally Bedell, *Reflected Glory: The Life of Pamela Harriman*, Simon & Schuster, 1996.

Soames, Mary, *Mary Churchill's War: The Wartime Diaries of Churchill's Youngest Daughter*, ed. Emma Soames, John Murray, London, 2021.

Sorel, Nancy Caldwell, *The Women Who Wrote the War: The Riveting Saga of World War II's Daredevil Women Correspondents*, Arcadia Publishing, New York, 1999.

Warnecke, Grace Kennan, *Daughter of the Cold War*, University of Pittsburgh Press, Pittsburgh, 2018.

Winant, John Gilbert, *A Letter from Grosvenor Square: An Account of a Stewardship*, Eschenburg Press, n.p., 2017.

Zilanov, Vyacheslav, *Stalinskie Rybnye Narkomy: Polina Zhemchuzhina*, Aleksandr Ishkov, Rodina, Moscow, 2025.

INDEX

Footnotes are indicated by *n*; plate numbers are indicated by *p*. The following abbreviations are used: AH (Averell Harriman) and KH (Kathleen Harriman).